EXPERIMENTAL CINEMA IN THE DIGITAL AGE

EXPERIMENTAL CINEMA IN THE DIGITAL AGE

MALCOLM LE GRICE

First published in 2001 by the
British Film Institute
21 Stephen Street, London W1T 1LN

The British Film Institute promotes greater understanding of,
and access to, film and moving image culture in the UK.

Cover design:Paul Wright/Cube

Set in Minion by Fakenham Photosetting, Norfolk

Printed in England by Cromwell Press, Wiltshire, UK

British Library Cataloguing-in-Publication Data
A catalogue record for this book is available from the British Library
ISBN 0–85170–872–2 (pbk)
ISBN 0–85170–873–0 (hbk)

Contents

Preface: The Colour of Time

Have we already forgotten? Why we got into this in the first place? How it was that the moving lights, the washes of colour, first brought us to this world and thanked us, with their generous presentation of themselves, for being there with them? Has the memory faded so radically of those first inklings of beauty, scattering in all its ungraspable ephemerality across our skins as much as our eyes, beams traversing and dragging into motion muscle and bowel, as music drags us into the dance? From a politics of renunciation through an aesthetic of minimalism to a phenomenology of ecstasy, Le Grice's films return us to a primal encounter with the physical power of our first perceptions.

There's a phrase in P. Adams Sitney's debate with Le Grice that's an apposite place to start: 'All artists are also critics,' he says. 'A powerful artist will also turn out to be a volcano of strong opinions about his tradition and his contemporaries.' Of no one is this more true than of Malcolm Le Grice. The media in which he has worked for thirty-five years now have been marginalised for all but the last ten, at which point the previous twenty-five were maddeningly – for those of us of the older generation – erased. But there is this to say of the 'old British artists': that without them there would be no yBa. Moreover, there's this: Le Grice is one of the most significant artists to have worked in the UK in the last half-century, and among the finest to have worked in the moving image media. His embrace of the digital media – since the 1970s! – only calls us to recognise the continuing importance of his work.

Le Grice's *Abstract Film and Beyond* remains a key text for contemporary film-makers, and many of his essays still circulate from hand to hand out of those lost ephemeral magazines of the film underground. Their urgency and intelligence survives the apparent loss of a culture which supported them. We hear in contemporary art discourses the constant cry that the medium doesn't matter: Le Grice is here to remind us that the matter is the medium, and that art is material work in a material world. With remarkable consistency, he has argued for three decades, in print, in public debate and as one of the UK's most influential teachers, that the physical dimensions of the artwork, art's matter, matters profoundly. This is not a fading modernism but a vital discipline for makers, one which, once forgotten, produces the thin post-physics of a metaphysical art in which even the materiality of the concept has been evaded. To have recognised the political as well as aesthetic importance of this danger in contemporary art and media arts and to have pointed to it in the face of fashion is the mark of a singular intelligence.

Film and video, as Le Grice has practised them, are strangely ill-suited to the task he sets for them. Though the electronic media at least can function 'as live', Le Grice's usage involves recording, a way of establishing something that, if never permanent, is at least lasting. Yet what forms the core of Le Grice's practice is exactly what is not lasting, what evades the record, what is never established. We sometimes feel that, because the image moves, because the film travels and the tape heads transport video, that the moving image is precisely fit for the ephemeral marbling of water, sunlight through leaves, dissipating curls of smoke. We grew up with the fascinating dust motes caught in the projector's beam and never lost that awareness that there is no permanence to film. And yet Benjamin was wrong: there is no serial production. Not only is every print of every film unique, as Paolo Cherchi Usai argues from the archivist's perspective, but there is no projection of that print that is not unique, just as, Rick Altman recalls for us, the sound of the record we play is always full of the acoustic signature of the environment we play it in. *Forbidden Planet*, somewhere around 1960 or 1963, at the Saturday afternoon kids' matinee at the Starlight Picturedrome is unrepeatable.

Yet Benjamin was also right. Film, once exposed, takes on a certain relation with time that involves what is repeatable. The material circumstance is not – Le Grice's experiments with refilming demonstrate this unforgiving truth with utmost clarity. But there is that which endures from screening to screening, that sense which apparatus and audience conspire to reproduce, of expectation rewarded, event restored to itself. But since we know that perception will become expectation, and that that unique moment of apprehension will become an experience to be recommended or undergone a second or a third time, albeit differently, that first time is deprived of its uniqueness. It is as if it were no longer true, as it is for every virgin, that no one has ever felt this way before, and so we cannot feel that way either.

Yet it is just this 'never before', this 'never to be repeated', this moment fluttering at the brink of non-existence, that constitutes the goal of a lifetime's efforts and the impossible outcome of the artist's demand that it be film – and cognate media – that be its vehicle. The simultaneous proximity of moving image and ephemeral perception is the basis of that tension which Le Grice's film-work has given us.

It is in this light, accompanied by the chatter of the optical printer and rendered sculptural by the smoke caught in the beam, that we must read these writings as thinking conducted by other means. These writings are the voice, transcribed, of a historical as much as a biographical journey. Most of all, they are the traces of a mode of thinking whose ordinary practice has been practical. Film, video and the digital image are media, as are the spoken and the written word, and like them and like all media they are not condemned to essentialism. Mediation is the nature of our conversation as species, and though we mostly spend our time communicating – our passions, our ideas, our needs – we must also give a certain respect to the sheer fact of mediation, the obdurate materiality of our message-making. And if, as is the case with the audiovisual media, these mediations characterise a new mode of thinking and a new mode of becoming thought, then we are wise to slow down and consider what it is that they perform as they intervene to create the times and places of our commerce. What we will find there is more than an anti-metaphysics.

Stripped to nudity, film's body does not become less but more fascinating, a punctuated, gap-riddled torso which in its own way perceives us more intensely than we perceive it. Light is delayed in film, light that for seventy years has been more acutely observed by film stock than by human eyes. Already in the 1930s we hear complaints that Eastman Super-X penetrated mists and revealed distant landscapes invisible to the human sensorium. What then of our remote sensing by satellite, those false-colour images in which cunning and kindly machines render as red, green and blue the invisible spectra of radar, infrared, ultra-violet and the rest of the electromagnetic spectrum? Those instruments that, in Auden's poem, agreed that the day of the pet's death was dark and cold, are also perceivers, and their perception enlarges ours. In such a way, too, Cézanne's apples not only tell us of Cézanne's eye, but instruct us in the apple's arts of seeing, its sense of its skin as a light-sensitive emulsion over its sweetening pulp and ripening seed. And in the same way the treated images of apples in Le Grice's more recent work begin the slow instruction that we need to understand if we are to inhabit, as we must, an entirely mediated world. Their moment on the screen, electronically transformed, enlarges on the alien quality of organic perception removed from the tyranny of the eyes.

So the film work and the theoretical writings come together in a realisation dated 1972, 'an affirmation of the projection event as the primary reality' (real time/space). In Le Grice's writings, there is always the feeling that the lines of argument have been extended in response to and in fellowship with interlocutors like Sitney or Brakhage or, a constant presence, Gidal. But that nonetheless, in these dialogues and through the articles that trace, from the late 1960s through the period of Film as Film into the 1980s, an articulation of minimalism with the politics of 1968 and the Arts Lab movement, there sounds a constant, urgent demand for a purity of film form. That purity no longer belongs to the world of the film text itself, the presence of the film to the projector, but the event of film in the audience's engagement with the image stream. It is this moment that extracts film from its particularity as apparatus, frees it from the ogre of its determination by the cyclopean gaze of the camera and its reduplication in the cinema. The multiple eyes of the audience defuse and disseminate the monocular vision of the dominant cinema. But more than this, the liveness of the moment captures Le Grice's imagination, as if the theorisations are always an afterthought, a justification of what is always, was always, primarily an aesthetic decision.

It is this concern for the present as the moment in which art actually becomes that seems to have inspired his first approximations of a theory of computerised film-making. While others enthused over the textual results, or merely gasped at the technology, Le Grice acknowledged very early on what has become a truism of digital arts: that what counts is not the end result but the programme. Few if any significant works of digital media art have been made using off-the-shelf software. The artist has to become his own engineer if the artwork is to be more than the record of an event always already over, always already consigned to the past. If audiences are to share in the joy of creativity, and to learn their liberation by means of it, then they must share the creative moment as the artist experiences it: as a living moment of transition from the present into the unknown future. Thus in the essay 'Computer Film as Film Art' he already places the computer as an instrument, almost like a musical instrument, which serves its purpose only when it is played. The playing of the computer film, controlled by software but also always open to manipulation and rewriting, is never settled. Openness to the present as its own unfolding is central to Le Grice's move from photomechanical to electronic media.

The languages of cyberspace have emphasised the geographical metaphor that governs its discourse of frontiers and voyages. Le Grice's thinking makes these spaces not geographic but geotemporal. As the event of the screening expresses itself as unique, it also points to other screenings, other unique events in space and time, specified by the size of the image, the angle of the keystone, the grain and texture of the event as well as the autonomy of the audience's reactions. What links these events is not the author, nor the audience, but the film. And yet the film, selflessly, is also changing, becoming, in each unique event. It is an agent, and evolves as such, rather than a kind of bullet that retains its own integrity at the expense of that of its target, delivering its impetus to a presumed passively receptive mass.

Of course no medium operates like this, but too many media artefacts are designed as if they did, as if, in the manner of Hitchcock's boasts about controlling the audience, TV, cinema and advertising could command our attention and our constructions of meaning. By granting the film-work its autonomy, the arrogance of authorship as well as the political domination enshrined in this attitude are not just denied. In their place, a more fluid and more autonomous art is given space to evolve. In handing over these aspects of authorship to the apparatus and the event, Le Grice abnegates the thesis that film is exclusively the product of conscious or even unconscious technique. While automatic writing might claim to reveal contents of the personal psyche, passing decisions on imaging technologies cannot. Dragging the film strip by hand through an optical printer, the technique employed for *Berlin Horse*, does not tell us about the artist's inner being. Scripting algorithms that will run an image through permutations that the artist has not foreseen does not give us a short cut to the unconscious mind of a human individual. Instead, these techniques are of a kind: they work towards an aleatoric art which drives towards the dialogue of human and machine that lies at the heart of contemporary society. In an industrial or an information economy, the freedom of the worker depends on the freedom of the machine. If we enslave one, we enslave the other. Just as green politics has unmasked the drastic impacts of environmental exploitation, the new aesthetic towards which Le Grice has been working for so many years reveals the full horror of human, and specifically capitalist, tyranny over technology.

While Marx observed that relations between people appeared to them in the fantastic guise of relations between things, and Debord noted that the relations now appeared in the form of relations between images, Le Grice notes a further change: that relations that in an older order appeared as temporal now appear to us as spatial. From the apparently unassailable logic of global capitalism to the evacuation of history from popular culture, the post-modern is spatialised. By emphasising the event as the intersection of humans and their machines in unique and unrepeatable conjunctures, Le Grice opens us up once more to time, to history and to the utopian moment of hope for a different future, one in which neither chronology nor geography rule, but in which space/time becomes the live air in which we take our being.

And it is this that inspires his deep understanding of the nature of digital film. Linearity produced the conditions for narrative as a linear unfolding of time. But as he observed in 'Kismet, Protagony and the Zap Splat Factor', this is not the limit of film's aspiration. Already in Vertov he catches the sense of time as an organisation of events, a matrix in which various times can be accessed and manipulated. This is the function of the editing suite, of course, where all the moments of a film are available synchronously. What digital media permit is the entry into the edit suite. The structural-materialist aesthetic already constructed conceptual technologies, mathematical maps that controlled the production of the edit in the same way that the twelve tone row's inversions and reversals control and constrain the production of a temporal experience from the material – sonorous or visual – that lie to hand. In digital film, Le Grice discovers ways in which time can be spatialised.

Narrative offers only tyranny to the spectator. The linear plot, the sequential ordering, the patterning of causes and effects, determine how an audience is to respond, and infects even the composition of individual shots, so that we are guided by framing, focus and composition towards perceiving that, and only that, which is of primary importance to narration: a gesture, a prop. But rather in the manner of Schönberg's democratisation of the scale, so that no one note could determine the completion of the melody, so the escape from narrative's linearity and consequent control over perception must also imply liberation from the ostensible content of images. The spectator is no longer constrained to see only what has been placed there for seeing. Instead, the eye wanders over the screen as it wonders over the all-over canvases of Pollock or Newman, freed of the obligation to obey the constructions of perspective or storytelling.

At this point editing too loses its *raison d'être* as the principal tool through which, perversely, time is made to disappear in the dominant cinema. When we praise a long film that goes by quickly, or when we complain that an artist's video drags, we are celebrating the theft of time through the techniques of continuity cutting, and berating the artist who invites us to experience time. But something else happens to editing in the post-minimalist development of structural-materialist ethics, something that gives it a new purpose in life, no longer strapped to the ticking clocks of narrative. The edit, the cut and the process of cutting, the manipulation of times from a pool of possible moments, reveals itself as the art of film itself. Time becomes a sort of spatial matrix, a multi-dimensional grid through which we navigate, an architecture whose rooms we choose to enter or pass by. The film becomes a map, a periplum, a vision of a circumnavigation, describing a moment or an era as if it were some Captain Cook of Einsteinian space/time, a chrononaut, a horologator.

And it is to be emphasised that in Le Grice's world, it is exactly the film that lies at the centre of this process, constituted as an event in its unique position between makers and perceivers, constructed and constituted by their actions, rather than constitutive of them. Many art school students and their teachers still resist desperately the by now unremarkable view that the author is dead, that the medium speaks, writes and depicts rather than the expressive force of the artist's ego. For Le Grice, one feels, this is not a disappointment but a liberation. More specifically, it is a socialisation of the mode of production. Dominant cinema operates a bogus collegiality, organising its crews into hierarchies in the interests of commercial success, and suborning the technology to do the will of its masters. The artist's cinema, however, strikes a genuine, and genuinely innovative, partnership between the artist and the tools. No longer constrained by the dominance of authorship, film-maker and film apparatus can enter into dialogue, produce a democratic microsystem inside the belly of the beast. That fragile flame of liberty, dependent on a new alliance with technology, opens the door whose existence was first sniffed out by those touchstones of Le Grice's writings, Vertov, Fischinger, Eggeling, Léger and the Futurists. Mechanical perception – how our devices see, experience and mediate the world – is an autonomous entity in Le Grice's work, written and screened. It is not there to serve purposes of mastery over space through representation or mastery of time through narration, but to enquire into the potentialities of space and time for new navigations and new explorations.

This collection is effectively the intellectual autobiography of an artist. In a certain way, read in this direction, it is a literary work itself, challenging and reconfiguring what it might mean to be an 'author' in an intellectual tradition for which authorship is not a category. The anthology necessarily dispenses with some of its history: pages set on electric typewriters and pasted up on boards, typo on typo from late night layout sessions in smoky studios, but still the smell of an era drifts back, the madeleines of the materialist film movement. The first three sections bring together important documents of a film practice too long left in the long grass, disowned by both the art and film establishments. There are still vital lessons to learn from the optimistic foundation of the London Film-makers' Co-op and the Arts Lab, quite as important as their significance for a historical understanding of the avant-garde cinema (as indeed the roots of video and digital culture) in the UK and internationally.

Le Grice's opinions on other film-makers have always been prized by connoisseurs: they speak of the existence of a tradition whose engagement has been with the stuff of film, light, movement, space and time, a history that does not need the heavy rotation of the secondhand notion that the avant-garde is merely anti-dominant, a position that leaves vanguard art effectively dependent for its significance on what it opposes. This is rarely the case with Le Grice, whose generous and timely accounts open the conceptual working spaces of his predecessors and contemporaries for new generations of audiences and makers. Consider, for example, his accounts of Sharits, and especially his understanding of the extraordinary work which Sharits made from his film *Ray Gun Virus* by encasing the still frames in plexiglass. What is this if not a realisation of the temporal grid? Isn't this an exact metaphor for the limitations of linearity, and an expression of a then utopian desire to transgress its borders, to define a cinema that would be navigable as a map is navigable?

The debates section you might expect to find dated. The flames of war have by and large gone out, sager counsels prevailing, and the occasional vituperation, you presume, will do no one any good. On the contrary: there is still a freshness, robustness, anger in these exchanges that once again urges, from a different rhetorical perspective, the importance of the art of film, and the importance of going beyond it.

The three theoretical sections hold their own not least as the journal of a quest. Here a little-recognised facet of Le Grice's work comes to the surface, and at the risk of a phoney connoisseurship, I would like to emphasise it here. English painting has spent a large part of the century in pursuit of a certain quality, a subset perhaps of the 'painterliness' associated with the New York avant-gardes of the 1950s. Artists like Patrick Heron and Howard Hodgson are celebrated for their performance as colourists. Other artists, excluded from pantheon through institutional racism – Balraj Khanna and Aubrey Williams in particular – demonstrate the power of colour as a mode of work in Britain during the period. Le Grice's work, I would like to argue, outdoes certainly the claims of painting to undertake serious work in colour in the last quarter of the twentieth century. From his use of filters in the hand-remade Debrie optical printer at the Film-makers' Co-op to the most recent work in digital formats, Le Grice has shifted our perception from what colour is to what colour does, just as it has shifted the ground from pigment to chrominance and luminance, the parameters encoded in electronic transmission and storage of colour data. Not merely because he deals not with reflected light but with the light source itself, but because of his understanding of colour's ability to work on our senses as what Laura U. Marks calls 'haptic' cinema, a sensory experience that translates light into touch, the lick of light across the colour field, across the eyes, across the skin. Though perhaps less rigorously intellectual than some of his contemporaries – Gidal or Snow – Le Grice brings to cinema and perhaps even more to digital media a much needed sense of the embodied nature of vision, the sensory, sensual, sensuous fabric of the spectrum in motion through time.

The painterly colourists deprive their work of movement. Their art is exclusively spatial, and as such against time, becoming, change and history. Alongside the ill-understood themes of de-materialisation that have accompanied the rise of the cultures of the Post, there has been a shift towards space as the ground for a post-historical, post-urbane culture. While the pursuit of this theme in works seeking to illuminate the nature of postmodernity has been understandable and often illuminating, the shift cannot be understood as a programme for either political or aesthetic work. Le Grice's theoretical and practical concern with time as a raw material for art is an important corrective to both the spatialisation of art and the mistaken idea that space is the place where an ethics, blending political and aesthetic concerns, can be conducted. With a full understanding of the spatial underpinning, his writings bite on temporality in a way that is if anything more relevant in the cybermedia than the photomechanical. As the metaphor of cyberspace overdetermines our de-historicised and merely virtual political notion of the digital media, to speak up on behalf of time as an occupation, an environment, a medium is of vital importance.

Nowhere is this more apparent than in the field of what was called, for a spell in the 1990s, interactive art. As many commentators have pointed out, art has always been interactive. What alters is the degree of manipulation of the physical manifestation of the work which is open to the viewer. I can ponder and reflect upon the *Mona Lisa*, but I cannot rearrange her or the rocks among which she sits. I can however change the route I take through a hypertext novel or the dimensions and colours, even the frame-rate, of a downloaded QuickTime movie. The digital is by nature manipulable, unfinished. While artists will continue to pursue the possibilities for maintaining the integrity of their works in these changed conditions, we have spent less time considering what new roles are demanded of audiences. In Le Grice's more recent writings, there emerges a clear sense that what the artist relinquishes by way of responsibility for the final form of the work does not evaporate into thin air. On the contrary: the audience member, the inter-actor, must now take on the responsibility that was once that of the artist. Irresponsible viewing is still an option, an option moreover still very much favoured by mainstream media, where the broadcaster retains the maximum power over the image and invites us to take as little responsibility for it as possible, whether in on-line commercial sites or in the entertainment cinema. But the idea Le Grice plants is that responsibility is no longer optional: we take responsibility for art, or there is no art at all.

This is the meaning of the event, as I understand it, in Le Grice's essays. This is the moment in which we confront the film, either as another strip of time to be filled with another commodity, or as the unique moment of the present in which, if ever, we make history. The past is already determined, which is why the recorded media have been so challenged to create the conditions for historical intervention. The future is unknown and to a large extent determined by the conditions of the past: the large-scale structures of the global economy, the small-scale structures of personal biography. The present alone is open. This is why the movement from performance-oriented work to digital is so logical. The aspiration is towards drama, not spectacle, and towards a drama which spills over from the work (and the working) of art into the live, historical time of the screening event.

In a characteristically elegant fashion, I believe that Le Grice's passion for colour is the thread that pulls together the aspects of his work that I have emphasised here: the spatialisation of time, the responsibility of the audience to the unique event of film, the dialogue with the machine and the insistence on the historical nature of film. We cannot be sure that a given wavelength of light is experienced in the same way even physiologically by different people, let alone that it has a certain meaning that is shared between us. Colour exists then as difference, as a continuous field of intensities operating on our senses in ways that are to some degree incommunicable. By making his medium the temporal diffusion, evolution, transition of colour and from colour to colour, Le Grice suggests that there is no determined present, but that time too is a field of intensities, a vibration threaded through with overtones. The specificities of each and every screening – the ambient light, the reflectivity of the screen or its luminance, lines of sight, proximities – alert him to the truth that there can be no control over colour, and that its immediacy, its sensuous reach, depends for its operation on the autonomy of the moment in which it is perceived. It is not the artist alone then who must talk with the apparatus: the audience too must undertake a unique rapprochement with the technologies of viewing, at the same time that they embrace the solidity of the photon streams that bathe not only eyes but skin and bodies too. The post-modern enters the present as the sublime moment in which all history is annulled, an eternity stripped of duration, rendered as pure extension, as absolute space. Le Grice, however, seizes on a modernist tradition of abstraction and wrests from it an understanding of the present as the open gate through which the future perpetually arrives, as the evolving times of colour, the evolving colour of time. It is beauty he strives for, not sublimity; the ephemeral, not the monumental. There is no sense of awe here, but only of the urgency of the arriving moment, and the constant possibility of its arriving otherwise.

In classical modernism's greatest aesthetician, Theodor Adorno, this moment of arrival was the moment of the most intense negation. Art's task was to refuse the present, to cry out its antagonism to the delirium and destruction of daily life and its economic and political underpinnings. Since then, however, it has become apparent that the dominant culture itself is negative. Adorno loathed the positivity of the world he inhabited. Today we need no longer fear that, for the dominant culture, from Baudrillard to neo-metal, performs its own rituals of self-abasement and negation in heavy rotation. The task confronting the contemporary artist is no longer refusal of the present but affirmation of the future. This is not to commend naive utopianism, but to say that defeatism is no longer the prerogative of the avant-garde. It has become the dominant thesis of a global culture that revels in its own superficiality. The response need not be a (in any case impossible) return to depth models of realism or romanticism. Rather, as Le Grice's practice and critical writing proposes, it is to grasp the necessity of making, because in making we seize responsibility for our own futures. Just as, in beauty and its ephemeral caress, we scent the possibility of lives less ugly, beyond modernity and its post-modern ghost.

Sean Cubitt
Professor of Screen and Media Studies
University of Waikato, New Zealand

Note on Editing and Sources

All the articles and essays included in this collection are exactly as they were published but with any newly discovered typographic or grammatical errors corrected. The exception to this is 'Towards Temporal Economy' published in *Screen* in January 1980. This article when first offered to *Screen* was almost one-third longer than it eventually appeared. The editing process was fraught and I believe a version prior to the final galley proofs I corrected was mistakenly used by the printer. The effect was not major but one or two sections from the published version read awkwardly and have always irritated me. Though I have some contemporary working notes I have not been able to find the original version nor the later galleys. Consequently, for my own sake and that of the reader, I have been through the piece and changed some wording slightly and clarified one or two paragraphs. I am sure I have not added any ideas that were not in the original published version. I have resisted the temptation to modify any of the concepts even where I would not now agree with them or would have expressed the ideas differently.

I History

'Thoughts on Recent 'Underground' Film', *Afterimage* no 4, Autumn 1972, pp. 78–95.

'Presenting Avant-garde Film in London', *Film/Video Extra* no. 3, December 1974, p. 4.

'The History We Need' in *Film as Film*, Hayward Gallery Exhibition Catalogue, June 1979, pp. 113–17. Reprinted in *British Avant-Garde Film*, ed. Michael O'Pray (Luton: Arts Council/ University of Luton Press, 1996).

II On Other Artists

[On Leger and Vertov and the Flicker Film], *Abstract Film and Beyond* (London: Studio Vista, 1977), pp. 36–40, 54–60, 107–7; 'On the Flicker: Tony Conrad', *Structural Film Anthology*, ed. Peter Gidal (London: BFI, 1978), pp. 135–136.

'Kurt Kren', *Studio International*, November/December 1975, pp. 183–8. Reprinted in *Structural Film Anthology*, pp. 56–63.

'Some Introductory Thoughts on Gidal's Films and Theory', originally published in a BFI dossier, November 1979. Reprinted in *Millennium Film Journal* no. 13, Fall 1983, pp. 19–30.

'Takahiko Iimura – Getting the Measure of Time', published in *Takahiko Iimura at the Lux*, catalogue for exhibition, Lux Cinema, London, September 1998.

III Debates

'Stan Brakhage and Malcolm Le Grice Debate', *Criss-Cross Art Communications* no. 6, 1978; reprinted in *Cinema News* 78, 3/4, 1978, pp. 3–4 and 18–26. Full transcription of public debate between Brakhage and Le Grice, Boulder Colorado, December 1977

'Letters from Gidal and Le Grice', *Millennium Film Journal* vol. 1 no. 2, Spring/Summer 1978, pp. 50–7.

'Narrative Illusion vs. Structural Realism' – Malcolm Le Grice and P. Adams Sitney, *Millennium Film Journal* nos 16/17/18, Fall/Winter 1986/7, pp. 309–27. Full transcript of a public debate between Le Grice and Sitney, 19 December 1977.

IV General Theory

'Real TIME/SPACE', *Art and Artists*, December 1972, pp. 39–43.

'Material, Materiality, Materialism', *Cinema News* nos 78–82, 1978, pp. 15–18 (based on paper delivered in Buffalo, May 1976).

'Problematizing the Spectator Placement in Film', *Undercut* no. 1, March 1981, pp. 13–18 and in *Cinema and Language*, American Film Institute Monograph Series vol. 1, 1983 ('Cinema and Language' conference papers, Milwaukee, March 1979), pp. 50–62.

'Towards Temporal Economy', *Screen* vol. 20 nos 3/4 , January 1980, pp. 58–79.

'Cinemology', *Undercut* no. 5, July 1982, pp. 27–9.

V Digital Theory

'Outline for a Theory of the Development of Television, *Cinemantics* no. 1, January 1970, pp. 1–2.

'Computer Film as Film Art', in John Halas (ed.), *Computer Animation* (London and New York: Focal Press, 1974), pp. 161–8.

'The Implication of Digital Systems for Experimental Film Theory', (Dijon: PRISM [Pub. Pole de Recherche sur les Médias], 1994), pp. 389–400.

'Kismet, Protagony and the Zap Splat Factor', *CAD Forum* no. 4, 1993 (conference papers, Zagreb, Croatia, 1993), pp. 243–7 and *Millennium Film Journal* no. 28, 1995, pp. 6–12. 'Algunos conceptos teoricos para un cine interactive' published in *Arte en la era electronica* (Barcelona: ACC L'Angelot and Goethe Institute, 1997), pp. 46–52.

'The Chronos Project', *Media Scape* (Zagreb) no. 3, June 1995, pp. 28–33 and *Vertigo* no. 5, Autumn/Winter 1995, pp. 21–5.

'Colour Abstraction – Painting – Film – Digital Media'/'L'Abstraction chromatique: Peinture – Film – Vidéo – Image numérique', *La poesie de la couleur* (Paris: Auditorium du Louvre/Institut de l'Image, 1995), pp. 14–26.

'Mapping in Multi-Space – From Expanded Cinema to Virtuality', *White Cube/Black Box* (Vienna: E. A. Generali, 1996), pp. 261–80.

'A Non-Linear Tradition – Experimental Film and Digital Cinema'/'Eine Non-Lineare Tradition – Experimentalfilm und Digitales Kino', *Katalog 43. Internationale Kurzfilmtage Oberhausen* (exhibition catalogue, Kurzfilm Festival, 1997), pp. 145–150.

'Art in the Land of Hydra-Media'/'Kunst im Reich der Hydra-Medien', *Film & Computer – Digital Media Visions* (Frankfurt: Deutsches Filmmuseum, 1998), pp. 116–27.

'Digital Cinema and Experimental Film – Continuities and Discontinuities', *Bild – Medium – Kunst*, ed. Yvonne Spielmann and Gundolf Winter (Munich: Wilhelm Fink Verlag, 1999), pp. 207–18.

Introduction

After studying painting for seven years, in 1965 I started to experiment with other media. I made some little 8mm experiments, including the still life film *China Tea*, then started to montage found footage sequences gleaned from the rubbish bins in Soho which led to my first 16mm film *Castle 1* in 1966. A chance meeting with David Curtis led to this and my other early film work being shown at the first Arts Laboratory in Drury Lane, where he programmed the cinema. Soon afterwards I did some work with portable video studio equipment at Goldsmith's College which led to a number of video installation works in an exhibition in 1968 'Drama in a Wide Media Environment', an extended performance and improvisation show which included Mike Dunford also at the Arts Lab. I was an early member of the Computer Art Society (membership number 008) which then included John Lansdown and Gustav Metzger and I produced a work for actors entitled *Typo Drama*, presented at 'Event One' at the Royal College of Art in 1969, where performance text and instructions were generated by a programme I devised in collaboration with Alan Sutcliffe. This involvement with computers led me to make my first computer film in the same year, *Your Lips*, using the only film-plotter in the UK at that time at the atomic energy establishment at Harwell. I made some primitive electronic sound-to-light conversion devices as part of one or two music performances with AMM, with Keith Rowe and John Tilbury, and also for those performances Cornelius Cardew, at a very short-lived gallery in Kingley Street. Though I have continued to experiment in a range of media and particularly with computers, my main work has focused around film and since the mid-1980s, video.

I began to write short theoretical pieces originally as programme notes for screenings and drifted almost by default into publishing articles and reviews from the early 1970s. This included a regular contribution on film and video to *Studio International* running to over thirty monthly columns from 1977, and a number of short pieces or reviews for *Time Out*, none of which are included in this book as the line needed to be drawn somewhere. My writing falls into three or four categories, broadly reflected in the structure of this book – the history of avant-garde or experimental film – reviews and essays on other film artists – general theory of cinema and experimental film – theoretical speculation on computer art and digital media.

At a recent symposium in Siegen, Jon Jhost describe himself as an auto-didact. Some of my essays begin with a similar apologia. I am an artist rather than a scholar.

My education as an artist was thorough and quite formal. What education I have outside art stems initially from the Penguin Classics, black, oil-stained copies of Dostoevsky, Flaubert, Tolstoy or Zola, first read when I ran the garage of the Grand Hotel in Torquay during the summer vacation as an art student in Plymouth. At the Slade, for my sins, I randomly but avidly read: philosophy – Plato, Machiavelli, Nietzsche, Descartes, Sartre; psychology – Freud and Piaget; kept up an interest in genetics; dabbled in the mathematics of topology. I was fascinated by information theory, J. S. Pierce, and the concepts of electronic coding, was influenced by Chomsky on the politics of language, read *Das Kapital* right through at least once and some modern political history including A. J. P. Taylor and Schirer. As the debates in film theory became dominated by semiology, modern French philosophy and psychoanalysis in the 1970s, I did my duty reading Metz, Lacan *et al*. This involvement in theoretical discourses has run parallel to that of film practice itself and has been pursued as a film-maker/theorist rather than as a critic – the theoretical ideas have been imported where they have stimulated practice but I have always been wary of expecting any direct link – the theory does not explain the films nor the films demonstrate the theory.

Another general caution for the reader should be the polemical aspect of some of the writing. Making experimental, independent, avant-garde films in the UK in the 1960s was outside both the cinema and art establishments. Promoting and publicising the work was a struggle and often involved distinguishing the work strongly from commercial cinema and the art gallery mafia while paradoxically stressing its credentials for inclusion. There also developed a fierce debate between the experimental film practitioners and the new generation of film theorists dominating the British Film Institute and *Screen* magazine. This was a problem not only for those from the London Film-makers' Co-operative axis but also for those attached to groups like the Berwick Street Collective or Cinema Action. Despite *Screen*'s contemporary (French) theory, it largely ignored contemporary radical practice in favour of the established cinema of Hitchcock or Ford. The third main polemic was between the British or more generally European experimental film-makers and the dominance of work from the US. Even those British critics sympathetic to the avant-garde paid more attention to American work than that being made in the UK. Whatever their justification for this critical bias, film-makers who could also get into print, mainly myself and Peter Gidal, found it necessary to counter it. As always, a polemic skews what might be a more 'relaxed' view. I might be interpreted, from my writing, as having been utterly hostile to film-makers like Stan Brakhage, Hollis Frampton, Paul Sharits or Michael Snow. Nothing could be further from the truth – an early viewing of *The Art of Vision* by Brakhage for example was immensely influential on my theory and practice as was Frampton's *Zorns Lemma* and Snow's *Wavelength*. At the same time, the battle to have European work – Kurt Kren,

Annabel Nicolson, Lis Rhodes, Gill Eatherley, the Heins, Peter Gidal etc. – discussed at an equal level with their American counterparts was a major issue during the period.

I History

My main work on the history of experimental film in general is contained in *Abstract Film and Beyond*. Some items from that book are included in the section On Other Artists and there is a historical perspective in some of the theoretical articles. The articles selected here are not a description of historical events but instead reflect on a cultural context in which the avant-garde or experimental film developed in the UK and more generally in Europe.

'Thoughts on Recent "Underground" Film' was published in *Afterimage*, edited by Peter Sainsbury and Simon Field, the only journal in the UK which took experimental, independent and political film seriously until the launch of *Undercut* in 1981. This article represents my first attempt to classify contemporary work linking the formal developments in the UK with those from the US. It is significant that at that point the term 'Underground Film' was still the most common designation. The films were still in a sense 'underground' – out of sight and unrecognised by the mainstream. There was no public funding for production nor for the distribution or presentation of the work. Without the London Film-makers' Co-operative it is possible that the experimental cinema in the UK would not have survived this period. The article also proposes a strategy of taking experimental film into the art galleries in order to provide a context for multi-projection and performance work, and by implication, to relate to an audience more attuned to the visual references of formal and abstract work. Though commonplace now, this was by no means generally understood when the article was published in 1972.

'Presenting Avant-Garde Film in London' is a very short piece from 1974 in the critical news sheet *Film Video Extra*, initiated and edited by Keith Griffiths and published by Greater London Arts (GLA). At the time, I was a member of the GLA film funding committee as well as a member of the British Film Institute Production Board and was heavily involved in the political issues of experimental film funding. The article reflects how it was necessary to address a relatively wide range of people interested in the broader independent film at the same time attempting to shame organisations like the Tate and the Institute of Contemporary Arts into taking a greater role in film and video. It is at best curious that a quarter of a century on, the adverse comparison made between the Tate and the Museum of Modern Art in New York remains as true as it did then. While contemporary film and video artists frequently win the Turner Prize, the history of this aspect of art remains completely marginalised in the national collection and exhibition.

'The History We Need' was written for the Hayward Gallery version of the exhibition 'Film as Film' (1979) initiated in Cologne by Birgit Hein and Wulf Herzo-ganrath in 1977, with the title 'Film als Film (1910 bis heute)' and curated in London by David Curtis and Richard Francis. The article continues to reflect a crisis in the institutional context for film. By making the history 'hypothetical', the article attempts to open up the understanding of what might constitute the historical context for the work beyond the existing institutions. In retrospect, I think the experimental film work which came out of the London Film-makers' Co-operative axis was the most radical anti-commodity art work of the period. It rejected the mass-cultural aspects of commercial cinema and TV but equally rejected the commodification represented by the art institution and the link between art dealers and public collections.

II On Other Artists

Much of my writing on other film and video artists has been in short reviews for *Time Out* or in the monthly column for *Studio International* from 1977 to 1982, where I wrote about artists like Richard Serra, John Baldesari or Gilbert and George as well as avant-garde film-makers. The selection made here is of articles or extracts where the discussion of the work has more critical depth and concerns more general, theoretical ideas. Extracts from *Abstract Film and Beyond* on Dziga Vertov, Fernand Léger and, via 'The Flicker Film', Peter Kubelka, Tony Conrad, Takahiko Iimura, and Birgit and Wilhelm Hein, have all been selected for their reflection on issues of montage, representation, abstraction and perceptual structuring.

'Kurt Kren' was initially published in the Film Issue of *Studio International* in 1975 together with extensive illustrations from the work. Austrian Kren was one of the first truly experimental film-makers to emerge in post-war Europe. His fellow Austrian, Peter Kubelka, had developed an international reputation as a leading figure in the New American Cinema through the presentation of his work and ideas in New York while Kren remained little known. At the time my article was published I, and many other European film artists, acknowledged both a debt to the work of Kren and a sense of his significance which went beyond awareness of his work. This article gave me the opportunity to represent my appreciation of his work, help to offer it a wider international stage and take on the challenge for myself of the extreme dichotomy between the formal and psychological aspects of his films. Kurt Kren died in 1998 but thankfully had experienced a period in which his work had become widely celebrated internationally and recognised in the US and his own country.

'Some Introductory Thoughts on Gidal's Films and Theory' was first published in a British Film Institute monograph in 1979 but received wider distribution through the *Millennium Film Journal* in 1983. My own work and that of Gidal have been frequently cited together. There is probably a greater justification for this link at the level of theory than there is in any specific aspects of the film work. As a theorist, Gidal offers a far more secure scholarship and breadth of contemporary reference than I have ever pretended, but I find more points of agreement in the concepts than I find disagreements. The term 'Structural/Materialist Film' originates with Gidal and his theoretical writing on this subject remains the main reference point for that continuing debate.

'Takahiko Iimura – Getting the Measure of Time' was written for a monograph published by the Lux to accompany a retrospective of Iimura's work in 1998. His films and videos have, like Conrad or Gidal, consistently represented an extreme reference point. More than any other film-maker, Iimura produces works which are propositions rather than expressions. He brings us as audience in as subjects in our own perceptual experiments – almost an art-science. I have always found the austerity of his articulation of time perceptual systems challenging and revealing. It is we – the spectators – who are the subject of the films.

III Debates

This section contains three debates, two of which were live events where I disputed ideas in public with Stan Brakhage then later with P. Adams Sitney. The other was a debate initiated by the *Millennium Film Journal* aimed as clarifying the theoretical stance adopted by myself and Peter Gidal.

'Stan Brakhage and Malcolm Le Grice Debate' was published in *Cinema News* in 1978 as a transcript of a public debate between Brakhage and myself in Boulder, Colorado, in December 1977. This public debate, which played to a full house in a large cinema, was set up to pit two opposing views of cinema against each other. For my part it represented both a consequence of the polemic against the undervaluing of European work and some fundamental differences in the ideology of individualism against a more 'collective' cultural model expressed chiefly in *Abstract Film and Beyond*. Brakhage understood and objected to this cultural model, and his own inclusion in it, as the description of a machine in which art works were determined – an undervaluing of the individual and the idiosyncratic. As in all debates of this kind, they stress the differences rather than the agreements – they are set up for a firework display. However, as with the Sitney debate which follows, these are arguments between artists and critics who are basically on the same side in a greater commitment to experimental and independent cinema.

'Letters, Peter Gidal and Malcolm Le Grice', published in the *Millennium Film Journal* in 1978 responds to questions posed by the editors in developing a dialogue relating to European and American experimental film. I have included the questions and also Gidal's reply.

'Narrative Illusion vs. Structural Realism' was a public debate with P. Adams Sitney, set up by Howard Guttenplan at the Millennium Film Workshop in New York on 19 December 1977. I am sure that in retrospect both Sitney and myself ought to have taken a bit more care of the title for the debate as this does not reflect either the content or the real opposition of our respective positions. It is possibly not clear from the transcript that the discussion took place in very good humour with Sitney on his best witty form. Pictures published with the Millennium transcript show a bottle of Fundador brandy mischievously placed between me and Sitney by Jonas Mekas which the pair of us consumed completely during the hour or two of the debate without apparent effect. Though it is not directly part of this debate, the role of the Millennium, and particularly Howard Guttenplan, in providing a consistent showcase for film, discussion, and, through the journal, publication for thirty-odd years deserves comment. Not only has the Millennium offered the most powerful international context for screening work over this period, more than any other show-case in the US, it has properly represented European and other non-American work in its programme since its inception. This breadth has been reflected in the journal which, as a consequence, now provides the most comprehensive and thorough historical reference for critical publication around the independent, experimental film movement.

IV General Theory

There are two distinct aspects to my theoretical writing. The first deals with general concepts of cinema and media and the second, more recent, with two particular exceptions, deals with the impact of computers or the digital on film and video practice. It is interesting that all the my earliest publications were either in fringe, specialist 'underground' film magazines like *Cinemantics* or art publications like *Art and Artists* or *Studio International*. It was not until 1983 that a general film journal, *Screen*, was prepared to acknowledge experimental cinema.

'Real TIME/SPACE' was published in *Art and Artists* in 1972 with illustrations mainly from a red and green spectacles, 3D shadow performance work. It primarily related to a period of my film work which brought the focus very strongly onto the 'reality' of the spectator's encounter with the work at the moment of projection. It coincided with performance shadow works like 'Horror Film 1' and 'Horror Film 2' and with projections like 'Pre-production' and 'Principles of Cinematography' which included live readings of texts about cinema materials and history. Though, as would be expected, I would revise my ideas in retrospect, this article remains relevant for me in the way in which it distinguishes the relationship between different forms of temporal experience – screening time, filming time and the illusory time, normally that of the narrative.

'Material, Materiality, Materialism', slightly developed and revised for publication in *Cinema News* in 1978, is a paper based on one presented at a symposium in Buffalo in May 1976. This in turn was based on a paper first presented in a debate at the London Film-makers' Co-operative earlier that year where Peter Gidal and Peter Wollen also made presentations. In part, this paper can be understood in the context of a dispute with Wollen on his interpretation as idealist of the 'minimalist' aspect of the non-narrative work championed by myself and Gidal. I counteracted this by arguing that minimalist work was also semiotic and referential. Though not explicit in the paper, I presented a phenomenological approach to the film experience as a partial alternative to semiology as a way of making the idea of direct, present experience compatible with materialist interpretation. This paper was also the first publication where I outlined a concept that film art practice could be concerned with problematics (implicitly opposing the assumption that art is locked into a retrospective expressive function or into a critical theory-led process of deconstruction). The theoretical ideas in this paper were being developed alongside the reinvestigation of the retrospective through refilming minimal events from the screen particularly in *White Field Duration* and *After Leonardo* leading to *After Lumière – L'arroseur arrosé* and *After Manet – le déjeuner sur l'herbe* which reintroduced actions in front of the camera.

'Problematising the Spectator's Placement in Film' was initially published in the first issue of the London Film-makers' Co-operative magazine *Undercut* in 1981. It had been written as my contribution to the 1979 Milwaukee conference 'Cinema and Language' and was later published with the other papers from that conference in 1983. It represented the theoretical counterpart to the film *Emily – Third Party Speculation* which was also shown at the Milwaukee conference. The essay attempted to examine the relationship between the various forms and stages of spectator identification with represented character, camera and author and to explore these transitions of identification as they are inscribed within film language and conventions.

'Towards Temporal Economy' was written after 'Problematising the Spectator's Placement in Film' but was published earlier in *Screen* in 1980. It was an ambitious attempt to synthesise a range of concepts and ideas at the same time promoting the debate about experimental film practice among the – largely hostile – critical academics then in the ascendancy within the British Film Institute and *Screen*. I and others felt a considerable frustration that the BFI in general was led by film appreciation and criticism rather than by the active and more risky involvement with the development of new film-making culture. Inclusion of this article in *Screen* was more a result of pressure than any desire on the part of the *Screen* board and the editing was more difficult than with any other piece of writing I have done. The original article before editing was substantially longer and allowed for a more thorough development of certain of the arguments. Difficulties in editing led to some inadequacies in the final version which went to print. There were no fundamental inaccuracies in that version but certain cuts had left concepts less well articulated than they might have been. I have made some modifications to the text published here in the spirit of making the ideas clearer. Any scholar concerned with absolute accuracy of the published material will either need to refer to the original in *Screen* or acknowledge revisions I have made for the present publication. I believe none of the revisions, which are relatively minor and only add a little more elegance to the expression, alter the initial ideas.

The essay, when first published, was being developed as a theoretical parallel to the film *Finnegans Chin – Temporal Economy* and was partly initiated by my reading (creative reading and probably misreading) of Stephen Heath's ideas about 'a political economy of film meaning-production and use' expressed in his article 'Repetition Time'. It sparked the notion that some links may be made between the (material, financial) economy of constructing a film sequence and the psychological economy through which a spectator would construct the experience – an exploration of the effect of this difference of investment. My essay, attempted to retain a theoretical argument which defined, not an essence of cinema but an intrinsic arena for its *effective* discourse based on its materials, technology and special terms of expression – broadly, but not wholly – a continuation of concepts from modernism. As a result, the relationship between form and content ('content' normally understood as the represented narrative) is replaced by that of the intersection of a discourse of the cinematic – what is evidently containable in the visual and auditory experience of the film – with other non-cinematic (non-visible) discourses always contained, by definition, through the speculative construction of the audience at the 'edges' of the visible. In other words what seems to be content (the narrative or whatever) is never part of the evidential – ultra-specific – inscription. The essay teases its way through this partly formed notion in relationship to various aspects of the cinematic discourse – the camera, the editing, the screening and the processes of spectator identification. I believe the essay still contains many challenging notions about cinema. The greatest challenge to these come from the partial incorporation of cinematic devices and expectations within the new electronic, digital media.

'Cinemology'. This rather bland diagram, published in *Undercut* in 1982, follows up the concept of the practice of cinema – its sequential processes from Precedence through Production and Presentation to Subsequence (its effect on the world through its presentation) – as an arena for intersecting discourses. The processes are read from left to right and the intersections with their consequence in the process are read from top to bottom.

V Digital Theory

My interest in what has come to be known as digital media originates with my desire as an artist to explore novel technologies, the concepts initially of information theory and a less hierarchic concept of society. Through membership of the Computer Arts Society I made two art works with computers in 1969, a primitive computer-generated drama text and an equally primitive abstract film sequence. The technology was so difficult to access and time-consuming to use at that time that I put that direction aside until the emergence of the Sinclair Spectrum and then the Atari in the early 1980s. The very cheap Atari having a fast processor, good visual routines and built-in MIDI (Musical Instrument Digital Interface) allowed me to write my own visual- and audio-generating programmes from which I made a number of works, three of which were transferred to video and included in *Sketches for a Sensual Philosophy* which I made for Channel Four. While developing another TV commission 'Chronos Fragmented' I devised a different form of programming aimed at modelling memory in the selection and editing of video sequences. Most of my attempts to develop some theoretical understanding of digital media are contained in articles published since 1990 and draw on the understandings I developed in working with computers at a level which required an understanding of the hardware function and programming and linked this to earlier cinematic theory. There is some repetition of the concepts in the recent articles as they develop and are modified, but I have selected the articles which consider these issues in a variety of different contexts. The exceptions to this later theory are two articles written in the 1970s, one of which was wildly speculative and the other, which linked the history of abstract film to computer animation.

'Outline for a Theory of the Development of Television' dating from 1970 was my first published article. It is clumsy and badly written and a précis of an even more badly written long essay thankfully only circulated to a very limited number of people. However, even if the writing was dreadful, the ideas were both interesting and surprisingly prophetic. It would be an exaggeration to claim that the article predicted the modern understanding of the internet. But it did propose the concept of using TV as a user-demand access system for a range of information and the fusion of computers, broadcasting and communications. It also understood the problems of achieving this within the constraints of limited transmission capacity (bandwidth). It is of historical interest even if the ideas have shifted from crazily radical to commonplace. This first issue of *Cinemantics* also contained articles by Simon Hartog and Umberto Eco but only survived for one other publication.

My short chapter contained in *Computer Animation*, edited by John Halas, was an attempt to shift the understanding of computers in film beyond the level of being merely a convenient technology for producing commercial animation. It drew on my practical experience of making a computer film but also on close contact with Stan Vanderbeek who I helped rework and colour one of his computer-generated sequences and through John Whitney Jnr for whom I organised a European tour of the Whitney computer films. At the same time I wrote the chapter on computer film for the German book *Film im Underground* by Birgit Hein.

'The Implication of Digital Systems for Experimental Film Theory' began as a conference paper for Im Off Der Geschichte held in Vienna in October 1990 and was later published in *Interfaces – Image – Texte – Language* by PRISM. This began my attempt to define the characteristics of the computer as if it were an art medium. In the essays and articles that follow in this section, particularly 'Kismet Protagony and the Zap Splat Factor', 'A Non-Linear Tradition', 'Art in the Land of Hydra Media' and 'Digital Cinema and Experimental Film', the concept of intrinsic characteristics for digital media is gradually redefined and reworked. At the same time the essays trace my growing awareness of the difficulties of applying modernist principles to electronic media and communications technologies. These articles and 'Mapping in Multispace' also repeat and refine the theme that the history of experimental and expanded cinema represents a precursor to the artistic concepts most appropriate to the technology of digital media. 'The Chronos Project' and 'Colour Abstraction – Painting – Film – Digital Media' are part of this developing argument and awareness but had quite specific contexts. 'The Chronos Project' was written as a theoretical paper directly related to the screening of my video work 'Chronos Fragmented' initially at a media festival in Zagreb in 1995 and 'Colour Abstraction – Painting – Film – Digital Media' was written for the catalogue of an exhibition celebrating the Centenary of Cinema at the Louvre, Paris, including my multi-projection works *Threshold* and *Berlin Horse*. 'Art in the Land of Hydra-media' was also written for a publication accompanying an exhibition including my digital work at the Deutsches Filmmuseum, Frankfurt, but in a context dominated by digital 'special effects' explaining the short tirade against computerised dinosaurs. 'Mapping in Multispace' was commissioned for the catalogue of an exhibition in Vienna which featured work by Valie Export but also gave me the opportunity to explore the relationship between expanded cinema and the development of computers and the internet.

I

HISTORY

I

Thoughts on Recent 'Underground' Film [1972]

For at least two years I have felt ready to make some theoretical statements about film language in relation to the 'Underground' film. A problem which has held me up is the discrepancy I feel between the actual experience I get from film-making and viewing – the erraticness, impulsiveness and irrationality – and the linear logic that emerges from writing about it. The clarity of a verbal statement creates a misleading feeling of having understood or stabilised a set of experiences or phenomena, and one is tempted to let it substitute for the less conveniently comprehended physicality of image–experience. Another aspect of the problem is the awareness that writing is a medium in itself, with its own potential and reality, the constructs of which are often more illuminating about the forms of awareness they are capable of creating than about their apparent, specific content. It is probable that the main function of writing is, for me, the clarification of my own mind; so I present what I have to say with some diffidence and ask readers to pay more attention to their experience of the films than to my verbal constructs.

Many of the notions here have been clarified in recent conversations with film-makers Birgit and Wilhelm Hein and Peter Gidal, painter Mike Thorpe and sculptor Roelof Louw; there is no consensus of viewpoint, though they may recognise some influence on what I say. Another factor shaping this piece has been the recent Hamburg Filmschau, a major section of which, organised by Klaus Feddermann, was given over to a review of what P. Adams Sitney has called 'structural film'.[1] This gave me the chance to see most of the recent 'formal' films I had not seen and to see the whole development in a very concentrated way.

Structural Film

Sitney's use of the term 'structural', to cover what he makes it cover, is totally misleading and does not help the perception or understanding of any of the films which he puts into the category. Who does he include? Snow, Frampton, Jacobs, Sharits, Noren, Wieland, Kubelka, Conrad, Landow and even some of Brakhage, Baillie and Anger. If he knew the European scene well enough (which he ought to, but does not) he would now doubtless include Kren, the Heins, early Nekes, Schoenherr, Gidal, Crosswaite, Nicolson, Hammond, Drummond, Siep, Raban, Leggett and myself; he would also probably include the Americans, Gottheim and Gerson, and the Canadian, Rimmer.

Is there anything which these film-makers do have in common with each other? If there is, it is certainly not a simple thing; a film by Sharits and one by Frampton are different enough to keep a critic busy for a few weeks without including others. The most I think it is possible to say on a broad, general level is that there has been a new formal tendency among film-makers who have a base in the 'underground'. (We must realise that the underground is now an established tradition and culture of a kind, even if we exclude the 1920s 'pre-history' people like Fischinger etc. Many of the first generation of underground film-makers are well into middle age.)

I shall make an approach which does not set up strict categories, but indicates a range of specific areas of concern. Many of the film-makers in the above list have done work which is a composite of the directions I shall outline, and it must be recognised that my own work has conditioned my analysis and the emphasis which I give to various aspects.

1. *Concerns which derive from the camera: its limitations and extensive capacities as a time-based photographic recording apparatus.*
   Limitations: frame limits, lens limits (focus, field, aperture, zoom), shutter.
   Extensions: time lapse, ultra high speed, camera movements (panning, tracking etc.).

   Concern in this area inevitably involves a complex interrelationship between the thing filmed and the system, procedure or limits through which the filming/observation takes place, demonstrating and exploring the way in which the construction of reality from perception is inextricably related to the method by which observation takes place. The most spectacular evidence of this is in the films where the procedure transforms perception in a radical way. Mike Snow's ↔ displays how perception at a physical level can contradict information which is directly available. We know that the screen is the standard format yet my experience of the film is as if it were panoramic, and the various stages in the transformation of perception are rich and complex. Matteijn Siep's *Double Shutter* shows how specific methods of cinematic sampling from the environment drastically alter the physical perception of the time and space; William Raban's *River Yar*, a combination of twenty-four frame, real-time sampling and strict time lapse over two three-week periods, day and night, with a static camera, compresses the information into a completely cinematic experience with a curious relationship with the original situation through the inclusion of 'real-time' filming. But many of the less perceptually spectacular 'observational' films of Larry Gottheim (*Fog Line, Barn Rushes*), Andrew Noren (*The Wind Variations*), Peter Gidal (*Bedroom, Hall*), Roger Hammond (*Knee High*) and John Du Cane (*Lenseless*) allow very subtle comprehension of the nature of cinematic observation/

reality and its relationship to one's assumed day-to-day use/perception of similar visual phenomena, in a much cooler way.

2. *Concerns which derive from the editing process and its abstraction into conceptual, concrete relationships of elements.*

An awareness of these possibilities in film began in the earliest avant-garde period (Vertov, Léger) but because of economic and political problems never developed significantly at the time. This is perhaps the only area of the new formalist tendency where the term 'structural' might have a useful application, in so far as many of the films have some defined, time-based structure or pattern: the use of a fixed 'score' of relationships in some kind of mathematical pattern (Peter Kubelka's *Adebar Schwechater, Arnulf Rainer*, and Werner Nekes's *Gurtrug No. 1*) and, in my view, more sophisticated procedural, programmed and systematic approaches which can include the use of computers; Kurt Kren's *TV* and *Trees*, my own *Reign of the Vampire*, recent Stuart Pound (*Clock Time*) and David Crosswaite (*Film No. 1*) and John Whitney's *Matrix*. Other major possibilities created by the abstraction of editing are the more obvious semantic aspects (linked to the whole montage theory but with more self-conscious 'linguistic-mannerist' possibilities than foreseen by Eisenstein) and the concern with perceptual thresholds. I shall deal with these two possibilities separately.

3. *Concerns which derive from the mechanism of the eye and particularities of perception.*

As a consequence of single-frame editing and the minimalisation of semantic (image) content there emerged the beginning of a completely filmic abstraction (as opposed to a quasi-painterly abstraction) giving rise to Kubelka's *Arnulf Rainer* and Conrad's *Flicker*. Subsequently a number of films have explored the flicker, in colour (Sharits) and black and white (the Heins), as a form in its own right. Perhaps the most interesting aspect of the flicker is the way in which 'content' is directly related to the 'behaviour' of the film's observer. Conrad in particular has neutralised the film-maker's construct (the internal complexity of the film) towards a situation where the audience can treat their perception as 'content'.

4. *Concerns which derive from printing, processing, refilming and recopying procedures; exploration of transformations possible in selective copying and modification of the material.*

Work in this area indicates the way in which each stage in the cinematic process is a reality in its own right, and the way in which the film is, at each stage, 'raw material' for new transformation, the transformation becoming an overtly integral part of the meaning and implication of the work. Ken Jacob's *Tom, Tom, The Piper's Son* is a most perfect demonstration of the subtle changes of meaning brought about by selective scrutiny of a small piece of very old silent film.

Many of my own films work largely in this area: *Yes No Maybe Maybe Not, Berlin Horse, 1919, Threshold*; Pat O'Neill's *Runs Good* and recent films. Film printer based work also contributes to the emergence of programmed, systematic structure (see 2 above): Pound and Crosswaite. These developments are strong in London because of the film printing machinery at the Film-makers' Co-operative.

5. *Concerns which derive from the physical nature of film; awareness of the reality of the material itself and its possible transformation into experience and language; celluloid, scratches, sprockets, frame lines, dirt, grain.*

In some respects this development is parallel to a development in twentieth-century art, particularly painting, where the physical properties of the material become the basis of the language, counteracting, contexting or denying the associative and illusory nature of the image. Although recent and more extreme concern with these factors in film are prefigured by direct scratching and collage onto film by Len Lye, Breer and Brakhage, the philosophic and aesthetic movement in film towards this twentieth-century 'existentialism' is late emerging, and slow to evolve, like all the 'plastic' and abstract notions of the medium. This possibility was first exploited in a deliberate and conscious way in Landow's *Film in which there appear Sprocket Holes, Edge Lettering, Dust Particles etc.* (projected as a loop 1965, complete film 1966), my own *Little Dog for Roger* (projected as loops on two screens 1967, complete two-screen film 1968) and Birgit and Wilhelm Hein's *Rob Film* (1968). More recently, Fred Drummond's *Green Cut Gate*, Annabel Nicolson's *Slides*, Peter Gidal's *8mm Film Notes*, Paul Sharits's *Inferential Current* have all worked with reference to the physical aspects of the film strip itself. This concern has been linked in all the films mentioned to other physically present components, namely the projection apparatus and the projection situation.

6. *Concerns which derive from the properties of the projection apparatus and the fundamental components of sequential image projection; lamp, lens, gate (frame), shutter, claw and the screen.*

It is interesting to note the complexity of interpretation open to what seems a very minimal form, the flicker. Two possible modes have been touched on: the minimal structure or time pattern (Kubelka) and the perceptual threshold exploration (Conrad and the Heins). There can also be reference to the intermittent nature of projection necessary to construct an illusion of smooth movement and to the basic elements – light and darkness – in time. But concerns in this area are not limited to the flicker form. Film-slip in the projector (continuous motion through the gate rather than intermittent phasing of shutter and claw) is a feature of both *Little Dog for Roger* and *Rob Film* and, more recently, of *Tom, Tom, the Piper's Son* and *Inferential Current*. But in all these cases it is dealt with by

printing the effect onto the film or refilming from the screen. There is a significant difference of meaning, implication and attitude in deliberate reference to a
property as opposed to actual manipulation of that property. In the area of direct
concern with the physical nature of projection as content and experience (rather
than through reference) I know only of my own work with live shadows: *Love
Story 1* and *3*, and *Horror Film 1* and *2*, which deal with projection direction, the
light beam and its current interruption and modulation, manipulation of focus,
screen scale and format. But recent work by David Dye, using an 8mm projector as an analogue for the camera, in most instances where the work can only
possibly be completed by the hand manipulation of the projector, draws attention to the projection situation itself and to the complexity of its relationship with
the camera event which preceded it.

Tony Hill has done some interesting work projecting onto the floor directly
where the audience stands, either from below or from above, but though this
requires a new concept of the relationship between the screen and the audience,
it does not seem to me to make direct reference to the projection situation as
such, or as 'content'.

7. *Concern with duration as a concrete dimension.*

The presentation of film takes place within a finite time; this is as real as the
actual spatial dimensions of a piece of sculpture. But film language has evolved
in such a way as to subsume the real time of the film under the illusory time of
the narrative – compression of events, flashback and jump-cut. Likewise, the
notion of rhythm as a concern with time pattern has occupied many editors, but
rhythmic perception only relates to relatively closely spaced events in time and,
as rhythm, does not extend to larger time units. Exactly what our perception of
duration entails is difficult to say, but it seems to require unbroken continuity
before an event can incorporate an experience of its duration as a factor of awareness. Some film-makers have begun to pay attention to the problem of the real
time of their films and to draw the attention of the audience to it either as an
equivalent for the actual duration of the shooting, by deliberate unbroken continuity at the camera end and elimination of editing: Warhol's *Harlot, Couch, Sleep*
etc., my own *Blind White Duration*, or in specific relationship to time manipulation, Snow's *Side Seat Paintings Slides Sound Film, One Second in Montreal,*
Raban's time-lapse films, or as a concrete dimension with no reference to another
time/space, my own *Love Story 2, Blue Field Duration*, to some extent Sharits's
N:O:T:H:I:N:G and *S:TREAM:S:S:SECTION:S:ECTION:S:S:ECTIONED*, and
though constructed from an abstracted sequence of 'shot' film, Leggett's *Shep-
herds Bush*.

8. *Concern with the semantics of image and with the construction of meaning through
'language' systems.*

Two problems may arise from a statement like this: one is the assumption that there is no alternative to the use of 'language' systems for conveying meaning, and the other is that there is at least nothing exceptional, or new, about constructing meaning out of 'language', this being what every author or film-maker does all the time. Taking the points in turn, I consider that there are situations in all plastic arts where the notion of communication through 'language' is not appropriate. The more the form and means move through abstraction towards direct physicality the less any communication or effect is dependent on a system of symbols and the more it is subject to differentiation and organisation as sensory 'raw material' by the observer. As for the second problem, I make a distinction between that function of 'language' where it becomes structured as an unselfconscious expression of experience or emotion, where it works as a seemingly passive and neutral element in the organisation and communication of experience, and its function as a tool for the 'creation' of meaning. This second function requires the conception of 'language' as non-neutral, flexible and manipulative in its own right and postulates the dependence of new constructions of thought on new developments of 'language'. Here there are all kinds of problems of the stability of meaning in 'language' systems, the degree to which one person's range of associations and constructs of meaning from the same set of symbols in the same context do or do not coincide, what in a visual situation constitutes the extent of a symbol and what the background, and what happens when two or more distinct 'language' systems interact and so on. While film-makers have made innovations in 'language' from time to time, very few have been primarily concerned with 'language' as content. Much of the work of Hollis Frampton is concerned with semantics, particularly *Nostalgia* and *Poetic Justice* in which a story is told through the sequential presentation of sheets of paper with the film script written on them. Two recent Landow films, *Remedial Reading Comprehension* and *Institutional Quality* are perhaps the most thorough examples of this type of semantic questioning, but unlike Frampton's films do not have a didactic or 'essayist' quality. Peter Gidal's latest film, *Upside Down Feature*, explores the problem of simultaneous function in two distinct language forms, which draws attention to the fallacy of assuming that communication occurs during the process of sympathetic involvement common to the technique of the commercial movie. It does this by keeping before the viewer what is being communicated and how; rarely, if ever, allowing him a 'standard' representation or reference to reality.

As we approach semantic complexity, the use of referential images to allow the construction of meaning within the film to have some analogous or metaphorical relationship with events in the world outside the film, then my very loose categorisation becomes too simplistic. I do not think that any of the films I have used as relatively pure examples of functioning in narrow areas of concern are in any way 'explained' by a definition of their means. There is also the problem of 'image' and the nuance in the 'means' and quality of the work. Without resorting to any 'mystical' notion about art and the artist's process, it seems clear to me that more factors of control take place in the construction of a work than are available to analysis, and these stem from a multitude of forces within the artist which are a result of his lifestyle, priorities and experience, and enter the work through his impulsive response. The work of Kurt Kren is an ideal example of what I mean. His film *TV* conforms to a system of repeats of five short sequences, but a description of the system ignores the particular content of the 'shots', minute factors about camera positions, distribution of tonal masses within the frames, the rhythmic relations in the movement, the location and why Kren was there filming. All enter the implication and reality of the work, in a way which analysis is incapable of dealing with. I have tried to find some fairly clear areas of concern in method, language and technique, sticking to what is internal to the films as more or less hermetic works. I now want to ask questions of two kinds – the first about 'reasons', motivation and philosophy, the second about pragmatics, context and social function.

Philosophy and Content

The relation between philosophy and aesthetic means is clearly not arbitrary. All the film-makers I am discussing display a self-conscious awareness of the interrelation of means and meaning and to a large extent demand that the 'actuality' of their means, processes and material become a significant part of their 'content' or make it possible to 'see' the dichotomy between 'content' and language/technique through deliberate indication of means; there is certainly a strong tendency to counter any notion of the 'neutrality' of means. Through the film-makers discussed here it is possible to approach a precise consideration of the way, and the extent to which, the transient events recorded are always and inevitably particular samples from an infinity of possibilities. The 'before-camera-reality' as it is available to us through its physical/chemical recording and projection is given a more 'credible' reality because it defines more clearly its actual relationship to the original situation and never becomes a confused 'substitute' for it. Where then does this leave the notion of 'content'?

Since, it is usually assumed, William S. Porter's *Great Train Robbery* (1903), the mainstream of cinema has been concerned with developing techniques designed to create the greatest possible audience involvement in a portrayal of 'reality'. The aim is 'transparency' of means and technique so as not to disrupt the continuity of involvement by any obtrusion of the 'actuality' of film, its means of production, finances, the nature of the shooting situation, processing, printing, editing, distribution, promotion, presentation, projection, social function and implication. This conditions the behaviour and role of the audience which is largely passive in response to large-scale structures of experience. The capacity of photography and sound recording to present a great deal of information to the two prime senses allows the basic 'building blocks' of these structures to stand as convincing substitutes for reality, invoking involvement through recognition and stimulation of common fantasy tensions growing out of the prevailing environmental and social conditions. Criticism of this situation normally comes (from the more politically conscious) in the form of condemnation of the 'content': the portrayed situation, the pattern of consequence and the development of action and motivation in the characters. But rarely does criticism question the roles and behaviour available to the audience. What I find strange, having the 'displacement' of viewpoint possible from a deep involvement in the problems of actuality/reality in the cinema, is that the extraordinary compressed continuity, the extreme contrivance of situations and their portrayed developments in the narrative film, and much of the documentary film, are both presented and received as credible representations of reality. Mainstream film language conventions have sophisticated techniques for creating highly contrived structures of relationship, at the same time building up and maintaining a cultural habit of perception so that it is now difficult for most people to be aware of the extreme divorce between the actuality of the film and the reality it purports to portray. The film fantasy (now mainly through television) has become a regular element of daily routine. The so-called 'realist' innovations of Italian neo-realism and cinéma vérité are little more than minor re-directions of emphasis, but in any case their incorporation into mainstream film, by giving more credibility to the associative, simulative end of the process, only makes films like *M.A.S.H.* and *The French Connection* more dangerously confusing and effective.

The motives behind the neo-realist and cinéma vérité movements are in my view similar to those of present film-makers concerned with the actuality of film as material and process. They all stem from a dissatisfaction about the way in which film relates, through its current language, to reality. They all seem to me to seek an existentialist position and an alternative to the cathartic fantasy, as the basic form of communication with the audience. I see a parallel between many of the new developments in formal film and the developments in painting from Courbet, Corot and Millet through the directions of Impressionism, gradually de-structuring portrayal through Cubism to a growing concern with material and process of painting as content. Some fairly convincing correspondences can be found: the perceptual distortions of the visual (photographic) reality in Snow's ↔ are similar to the perceptual distortions encountered by Cézanne through deliberate perceptual organisation, and Siep's *Double Shutter* continues the parallel to a cubistic space and image by swinging the camera and fragmenting the sampling with a secondary rotating shutter, both film developments building on the liberation of camera movement brought about by

Brakhage in the development of an 'impressionistic' style. If this approach is followed up it leads me to the view that the language and formal developments of film in relation to their philosophical and social bases are retarded in comparison with the other plastic arts. (The causes of this retardation can be convincingly explained in terms of the social function which has evolved for commercial cinema and television.) But this movement in film is not as directly linear as that in painting because it is taking place in a compressed, simultaneous way, separate from the historical conditions appropriate to certain of the tendencies. While much of the intention is related to current philosophical/aesthetic impulses, the language, forms and conventions do not provide the necessary sophistication because of this retarded evolution. The whole process is confused by a (seemingly) necessary dialectic with the current forms and social function of commercial cinema and its inherited language.

Function and Context

All this leads to a consideration which tends to be ignored in thinking about the meaning and implication of works of art and communication. Methods of consideration are, broadly, in terms of 'internal' meaning (largely what I have been doing), considering the form, the language and the direct or implied content and extending to questions of social function as a method of assessing value and meaning. What tends not to be considered is *context* as a direct aspect of meaning and implication. In the most simple terms, one makes a film and this produces a misleadingly credible object which one assumes to have a stable set of internal structures, relationships, content etc. What it is difficult to realise is that in almost every sense, having produced a film (or any other 'object of art') what has been produced is a set of potentials which require a finite and particular situation of presentation, containing an element of human consciousness and response before that potential begins to be realised. This situation and the consciousness and effects which it initiates are an integral and probably the only reality of the work. In other words, a film in a can on a shelf is a reality, but one which can only be defined in terms of its present condition of effective relationship with consciousness/experience/environment. It is a very different reality to the 'same' film when it is being run through a projector, lit by a lamp, focused onto a screen and viewed by an audience, and the 'same' film is a very different reality depending on the particular situation and method by which it is being presented to the audience. In fact it seems to me more reasonable to develop the attitude that it is not even the 'same' film when the relation of the film's potential to the particular manifestation is different. The point I am concerned to make to film-makers is that their films are neither more nor less than their actual interaction with the world, the effective consciousness which they initiate and its ramifications in the world.

The context and particularities of the presentation become a significant and integral part of the passage of the work into effective consciousness. In addition to this, the prevailing context feeds back to the notions of 'internal' structuring in the film. The actions involved in film-making are conditioned by conscious or subconscious, habitual awareness of the context in which the film is likely to be seen.

My own understanding of the development of 'underground' cinema is that, in its early stages, it knew a lot more about what it did not want than what it did. It reacted strongly against the restrictions of film form and language, against industrial means of production and distribution, and questioned the cinema format. All its development has really taken place in the last twenty-five years and in two areas the underground has made considerable innovation: the first is in methods of film-making, bringing about the 'one-man' film, allowing its construction the integrity and continuity available to music, sculpture, painting and poetry, almost entirely the product of the 'underground' direction. This development continues, gradually bringing more and more aspects of the film-making process under the plastic control of the individual film-maker, extending into processing and printing. The second is in form and language. More possibilities of content, kinds of continuity or connectivity and formal ideas have emerged from the 'underground' than from any other period of film history. But although the co-operative mode of distribution has been an attempt to create a new way of getting films to their audience, and although it is important in avoiding selective and 'hard sell' promotion, it has not created a significant new relationship between the film-maker and his audience and has become a stagnant compromise. Some of the reasons for this follow:

1. The main outlet for distribution from the co-ops has been university film societies and has become confused with an existing situation for viewing minority cultural or historical films. This has been successful enough to inhibit the search for a new structure, and in any case seems to have reached some of the 'right' audience – the students.

2. Film-makers have encountered enough difficulty producing films with insufficient resources and very little time or energy has been available to deal with the problem of distribution. Although in Britain the distribution from the co-op (which has never been enormous) is growing very steadily, in other places the peak may have been passed and film-makers may again begin to see distribution as a problem. I hope that modishness, which creates a false and short-lived peak of interest, may not be a feature of the English situation, but I do not think that the essential problems here are very different from those in America, Canada, Germany and Holland, the main centres of co-operative experiments.

3. There is an inherent weakness in the non-selective concept which allows unformed and mediocre films to be available for distribution, so that bookers may not persist beyond their first booking.

4. There is an inherent weakness in non-promotion which eliminates persuasion and taste-forming which are open to competitors.
5. There are inefficiencies stemming from the low-level finances of non-profit organisations.
6. A problem which has always existed but which has become more acute with new formal developments is the difficulty and hostility which audiences have when confronted with new forms, concepts, content and language.

Because I see non-selectivity as a weakness in the present situation of confusion between co-operative distribution and commercial or rational distribution does not mean that I oppose non-selectivity. I am committed to open access, and I still get more out of seeing a bad 'independent' film than out of most products of the industry. My conclusion is rather that the motives that encourage people to use film as a way of ordering and articulating their thoughts with some possibility that the product becomes a communication with other people are sound, but it is the format and context for the distribution/presentation which are unsatisfactory. Non-promotion by co-operatives, likewise, seems to be basically sound, as it tends to decrease the alienation of the film-maker from the presentation of his work and the audience from the film by its presentation as a commodity. Many of the inherent inefficiencies are defensible as they stem from a rejection of hierarchic organisational structures. But films need to be seen by people and are not made just to lie on shelves. There are always paradoxes when idealist motivation is related to an unsatisfactory pragmatic situation. Context and presentation should also be considered in terms of the way in which film showings come about and the kind of physical and social context in which they take place:

1. The film-makers' cinema: a cinema within an arts lab or film co-op set-up, specially constructed and in a particular social ethos with the advantage of being closely related to the day-to-day influence of film-makers themselves. There have been very few of these, short-lived and mostly constructed under difficult financial conditions, there being no public funds available for such developments. None of these cinemas has been physically flexible enough to allow great expansion of the form and structure of projection, although they have all been more convenient than regular cinemas for experimental projection (a problem of direct concern to me and to a lot of other film-makers currently working here). Invariably in regular cinemas, where there is good equipment like arc projectors, good sound and comfortable conditions, there is an inflexible projection booth and restrictive projectionists; where conditions are flexible and people helpful, the projectors are falling apart, there is no screen and there is more stray light coming in the windows than from the projector lamp. All this leads to the inhibition of

experimental presentation and encourages the production of films to fit prevailing projection facilities.

2. Public cinemas: some attempts have been made to make regular screenings in public cinemas: the Electric Cinema in Amsterdam, the Progressive Art Productions Cinema in Munich, for a while the Sudcoop at a Stuttgart cinema, a similar set-up in Hamburg and the longest surviving, X-Screen in Cologne. Audiences have rarely been very large and have probably been comparable to the kind of audience gradually built up around the two London Arts Labs and later the Prince of Wales Co-op Cinema. Most of the people running these attempts to put 'underground' cinema into the same context as commercial cinema without compromise have said that they would prefer to construct their own special cinemas.

3. State-financed cinemas: the national and regional film theatres. Recently here, as in America, France, Belgium, Germany, Denmark and Sweden, there has been growing official recognition of the 'underground' as a significant development in film culture. The problems of relating to 'official' organisations for screenings or film-making finance could use up a lot of paper, and I am not the only one who has some paranoia about castration by inclusion. It puts the films into the existing context for 'cultural' cinema and this is bound to feed back into the film-making if the context is a regular one. The NFT has a fairly clear function as a film museum, reviewing the past. With the growth of independent film production outside the commercial circuit facilities and outside the perceptual habits of the audience, the film museum has expanded its role to the presentation of current work. But in doing so it has tried (in line with international film archive policy) to maintain the same financial arrangement of non-payment for programmes in an area where requirements are quite different. Methods of presentation are confused, providing an unsatisfactory context for the work; it looks like history at its first screening. If the NFT is to continue its presentation of current work it needs to:

a) reassess the financial structure instead of merely finding loopholes for making half-payments; b) adjust the method of presentation to give more significance to current work; c) allow for a period of development of understanding and education of an audience whose awareness of the language is largely elementary; d) construct a special cinema for 16mm experimental projection (witness the recent fiasco in presenting double projection and stereo sound in the new NFT 2, when no one in the organisation took any notice of clearly stated needs).

If film-makers accept an easy compromise it will soften their work and feed back into future film-making.

4. Film festivals: a significant and increasing proportion of the screenings my films get take place in film festivals or one-off special group reviews. I have little doubt that many films have been made with a half-conscious eye on their future impact

at a festival; context becomes 'real', conditioning the films internally and externally. By not being aware of this it is impossible to perceive the actuality of one's
own films. I think the festival format will become increasingly a way in which
'underground' films are seen, a presentation method in its own right, not to be
confused with prior functions as a market for the industry's product, or as a competitive area in which new 'talent' is incorporated into the industry.

5. Art galleries: two possible developments:

    a) the sale of film prints to collectors has been talked of for a long time and
has been used by Brakhage, Connor and probably others, but has not made an
impact as a context. However, I would still expect an increase in the number of
public and private collections of 'underground'/independent films connected
with collections of painting and sculpture. I have misgivings about the art-world-
cultural context but I find some attraction in the development of a situation
where a film can be seen in a relaxed atmosphere of choice; b) Exploration of
presentation and projection formats. The attraction of this lies not only in reconsideration of technical potentials but also in the possibility of setting up different
kinds of relationship with the audience. I have felt dissatisfied right from the
beginning of my film work with the impersonal nature of film projection, the
restriction of the audience to a static and passive role and with the aggression
this arouses when the work makes the condition of the audience clear to it (unlike
the commercial cinema where the technique is designed to work through this passivity so that its real implications are never experienced as an intended part of
the work). A number of film-makers prefer to work in an open hall rather than
in a cinema, presenting their films in personal contact with the audience (e.g.
Annabel Nicolson and Barbara Schwartz); Tony Hill, David Dye and I have made
things which are impossible to relate physically to the cinema format; many others
have expressed the wish to do so if an alternative context could be developed.
Paul Sharits has presented at least one special-purpose, static film installation in
an art gallery both to explore the physical possibilities and to create choice for
the film viewer. At an earlier date the multi-projection work of Vanderbeek and
the Vortex Concerts (Belson and the Whitneys) and some incorporation of film
into happenings showed the need for and possibilities of extension beyond the
cinema format, but have failed to establish a stable alternative context. More
energy output is needed to set the situation up than for the making of films, and
it is always easier to use existing channels than to open new ones.

The main points I want to make are directed mainly at film-makers. The 'underground' film has been concerned with change and the establishment of new and
alternative forms for all aspects of the medium, and because some things have been
achieved, and have begun to be recognised, it is tempting to accept the situation

and get on with the work of making films without the disruption of dealing with the general issues. I see this as dangerous; it could lead to soft compromise (as with Nekes and others in the German situation who have been partially incorporated into the commercial cinema context).

I think film-makers should pay more attention to the 'reality' of their work in terms of its passage through the world. Where it is screened, how often, who watches it, how do they relate to it and what kind of function does it have in their lives, how is it screened, what are the picture and sound qualities, what is the social ethos in which it works? Are you satisfied with the context? Is it what you want? If not, is there any direction indicated in the film which would give a lead to establishing a better context? The most important point which, I think, becomes more evident with the new formal developments, is the inevitable fusion in meaning and implication of content, form, material, method and also context. Film-makers must recognise that the reality of their work is not different from the 'reality' it achieves in its passage through the world.

Note

1. See P. Adams Sitney (ed.), *'Film Culture': An Anthology* (London: Secker and Warburg, 1971).

2

Presenting Avant-Garde Film in London [1974]

The term 'avant garde' film can be taken to mean a number of different things. For the regular 'Classic' or 'Academy' film-goers it would probably mean Straub or Godard. In this case, the main distributor is the Other Cinema. Also seeing the avant-garde in relationship to the more conventional commercial cinema, the most regular and consistent programme has been run by Derek Hill, with his New Cinema Club venture which ran for about four years before closing in 1973. Hill then took over the programming of the ICA cinema, where he continues to present a basically similar spectrum of work. Newly arrived on the scene is the Gate Cinema – the cinema which used to be the Notting Hill Classic. This is being run by David and Barbara Stone, film-makers from New York, and by Alan Power, who is backing the venture financially. Their main programme is similarly chosen from the avant-garde of the commercial cinema, showing films like *Fear Eats the Soul* by Fassbinder. However, films of this kind, and those presented by Derek Hill and the Other Cinema, represent only the most 'conventional end' of the avant-garde film. Beneath, beyond or ahead of this 'conventional end' is a region of film use or experiment which could broadly be divided into two. On one side, direct action political film seen in its most developed terms in the work of Cinema Action, and on the other, the uncompromising treatment of film as an independent medium of art, mostly centring in Britain around the London Film-makers' Co-operative.

For the film-maker concerned with film as an 'art' medium, the problem of presentation is crucial. Though some of the film-makers have recently been able to raise grants, mostly they continue to finance their own work – making films cheaply and covering the costs by screening rentals. The main 'outlet' for this work is through the distribution services of the Co-op, mostly to film societies in universities and polytechnics. In London, the Royal College of Art film society have increasingly shown programmes of this kind, advertising them in *Time Out*, and welcoming audiences from outside the college. As well as its main public programme, the Gate Cinema also runs a late-night film club, starting at 11.15 on Mondays and Tuesdays, where it has begun to show 'genuine' avant-garde film. Maintaining this programme will depend on the size of audiences. This could be difficult with the shows ending well after London Transport is already a'bed, though the organisers at the Gate are considering running a get-you-home bus with a circuit round North London. The Electric Cinema has run occasional films from this area of cinema, but they are far from regular. A number of other organisations like Cinema at the Hut, the Bush Theatre, and the Pied Bull have started up, only to run for a while and fold.

The only organisation which has maintained a virtually unbroken programme in this field is the Co-op itself. Since 1971, organised first by Peter Gidal, and since April this year by Annabel Nicolson, the cinema has always just remained solvent, paying film-makers and overheads. It plays on Wednesday evenings to an average audience of about forty, but this increases to seventy or a hundred on odd occasions. Unlike its 'sister' organisation in New York, the Millennium Film Workshop, which runs a similar programme subsidised by the New York State Council for the Arts, allowing increased payments to the film-makers, the Co-op has had to be completely self-sufficient.

In the last few years, many of the film-makers working in this area have wanted to show work in the context of the art gallery, either to relate to audiences informed about the plastic arts rather than the cinema, or simply for the kind of spaces needed for multi-projection and performance work – a direction many young British film-makers have followed. In the last few years, when the British avant-garde film has generally become very strong, at least two major institutions, the Tate and ICA, should be censured for not having made any real contribution to its presentation. In fact, it is curious that while many of the London film-makers have shown frequently in public galleries in Holland and Germany, except for two shows in the summer of 1973, and a week of David Hall this year, the Tate has done almost nothing. This should be compared to the excellent film programme of the New York Museum of Modern Art. The ICA did provide the venue for the Expanded Cinema section of the 1973 Festival, but through its cinema programme it has made no real effort to present the latest in film art, and when Tony Hill presented a multi-projection installation to a very good audience in the summer, he had to pay for the use of the space. Though the Garage and the Art Meeting Place may begin to provide a possible alternative, since the closure of Gallery House, no independent gallery has had the space or inclination to continue the interest which Sigi Kraus and Rossetta Brooks had in showing film and video. This lack makes the failure of the Tate and the ICA all the more damaging.

3

The History We Need [1979]

The underlying thesis of a historical construction not only affects the ordering of facts but also the articulation of what constitutes the facts themselves. In addition a historical formulation has a different function for the involved practitioner in a field than for the less involved 'general public'. For that nebulous 'general public' (in whose name so many decisions are made) a historical exhibition like 'Film as Film', as well as drawing attention to a particular field of past activity, also validates those current practices which derive from them – providing them with historical credentials. In effect, while a current practice is evidently determined by its historical relationship, definition of a structure for this causality is a constructive production very much parallel to the practice itself. It is only when the historical enterprise becomes an aspect of defining and analysing the determinants of current practice that it begins to have a real function for the involved practitioner. Unfortunately, the basic level of public awareness in the area covered by 'Film as Film' is such that the didactic intention has played the major part in defining the direction of the exhibition. That this may be seen as inevitable does not remove the need for a critique and this article affords me the luxury of making one from the standpoint of the involved practitioner. Bearing in mind that the 'we' of the title may be no more than a conceit which disguises an 'I', it symbolises an attempt to be more than idiosyncratic. The 'we' addressed is broadly the involved practitioner, film-maker or theorist so committed as to be illiberal about films or their presentation. 'The History We Need' implies a recognition that a neutral and inclusive history is broadly impossible and that the historical enterprise should be aimed at aiding the development of contemporary practice. While clearly given a didactic framework, the involved practitioner will polemicise inclusions or exclusions, recognising how this serves promotion and suppression. On the other hand, even outside the polemical motive, selection and suppression is inevitable, implying no question of falsification but one of evaluation and priorities.

One of the problems with the current exhibition is the difficulty of defining its underlying thesis. This difficulty has increased with the expansion of the exhibition through a committee structure for the London presentation. In its original form, being largely conceived by Birgit Hein and Wulf Herzoganrath and aimed at a particular situation in Germany, some of its underlying principles were more readily discerned. Even then, expediences, like limited availability and the presentability of works in the art gallery affected the selection, tending to obscure some principles. Other inclusions, particularly the extent of attention to the American West Coast abstract films, signalled unresolved and, in the context of the exhibition, seemingly unproblematic contradictions.

Before attempting to unravel some of the fundamental assumptions which underlie 'Film as Film', I should point out that the critique is simultaneously a self-critique. This exhibition was initiated as one stage in a series of publications and exhibitions which have developed and refined the concepts it embodies. My own writing, in particular *Abstract Film and Beyond*, has formed a part of that development. Its historical view is very similar to that which underlies 'Film as Film'. My own book is based on many of the same fundamental assumptions, makes the same suppressions for similar reasons and fails to resolve similar contradictions.

Two fundamentals for the cultural enterprise represented by this exhibition can be defined by tracing a negative and positive expression. Negatively, it is contained in the rejection of what constitutes the mainstream of commercial narrative cinema. Positively it is the progressive exploration of the potentialities of the medium in-its-own-terms. The consistency of the positive expression with the basis of modernism is evident – 'painting as painting', 'sculpture as sculpture', 'art for art' – a general set of notions designating special and particular qualities to the medium in question. Thus the consistent tendency in this framework to talk of 'film', the material, rather than 'cinema', which has come to mean the form of the dominant commercial film institution. The negative and positive expressions are in a sense axes which have simultaneously motivated the actual practice. In general it would be tempting to argue that the negative expression has been primarily a feature of theoretical pronouncements and critical writing supporting the practice, which, on the other hand, has attempted to seek a non-narrative rather than anti-narrative cinematic form. But already some caution must be introduced on the degree to which negation functions as a constructive principle within art work. More at issue is the problem of defining what is being rejected in the general opposition to narrative cinema.

At first look the cinema, born only a few years ago, may seem to be Futurist already, lacking a past and free from traditions. Actually, by appearing in the guise of a theatre without words, it has inherited all the most traditional sweepings of the literary theatre. Consequently, everything we have said and done about the stage applies to cinema. Our action is legitimate and necessary in so far as the cinema up to now has been and tends to remain profoundly passéist. . . .

– Futurist manifesto (1916)

Filmdrama is the opium of the masses.
– Dziga Vertov (1920)

All current cinema is romantic, literary, historical, expressionist, etc.
– Fernand Léger (1926)

Narrative is an illusionistic procedure, manipulatory, mystificatory, repressive.
– Peter Gidal (1971)

These few quotations briefly illustrate what has been a continuing, consistent and explicit rejection of the dominant narrative cinema. On the one hand, this rejection is of the commercial cinema institution with its constriction of independent experiment and radical concept by the strangle-hold high finance has on production, publicity and the presentation system – a deep cultural control. On the other hand, and unclearly differentiated from it, it is the rejection of the forms and devices of narrative – identification with characters, story structure extending to a more general rejection of work whose images are broadly 'expressionist' or 'symbolic'. That the dominant cinema has grown up on the basis of the forms of identificatory narrative indicates a correspondence between them and the social effects desired (consciously or otherwise) by that sector of society controlling its finance.

Within the history represented by 'Film as Film' and *Abstract Film and Beyond*, the most obvious first level of exclusion is based on the rejection of works made within the dominant cinema framework. It has been seen as confusing to discuss work like *The Cabinet of Doctor Caligari* or Gance's *Napoléon* for example even though aspects of certain films from this context might relate to the motives of 'Film as Film'. But much more problematic has been the definition of the borderline of exclusion of films within the experimental area whose makers also reject the commercial cinema institution. (Some film-makers who are otherwise considered as central to the history even have works excluded if in some way they suggest a return to 'narrativity'.) For example, while Man Ray's first two films, *Retour à la raison* and *Emak Bakia* are both clearly 'in', I have not been alone in the impulse to reject his subsequent films as a retrogression. Man Ray's case illustrates this borderline which represents the basis of the major and most contentious exclusion made by this version of experimental film history. Though some of these works are included in the film programme of the London show, whose selection has been on more liberal and inclusive lines, the surrealist, mythic and broadly symbolist work from the Buñuel–Dali collaborations on *Un Chien andalou* and *L'Age d'or*, Dulac's *Le Coquille et le Clergyman/The Seashell and the Clergyman*, through much of the mainstream of the American underground film, like Maya Deren, Ron Rice, Jack Smith, Gregory Markopoulos, Kenneth Anger and so on has been placed outside this historical concept. Most of the work in this direction rejects the dominant cinema institution but for the concept of this history does not sufficiently reject its forms. While in my book I explained this exclusion primarily on the basis of scope, it now demands fuller consideration, resting on the need for a better articulation of the distinctions within the broad category of 'narrativity'.

If this history is seen as the history of a certain contemporary practice, loosely designated the 'formal' or 'structural' film (in other words assuming the validity of a certain state of current work and tracing its precursors, the history of its ideas), then the loosely defined surrealist, symbolist axis is difficult to integrate. But its over-simplified exclusion on the basis of narrativity masks many issues within the work which is included. As well as the issues of spectator 'identification' to which I shall return, the broadly symbolic work initiates consideration of the mechanisms of psychological association as it functions in the representational image. A very large proportion of so-called 'formal' and 'structural' film makes use of representational imagery. The psychological signification in these films needs attention and in this respect the critical tradition which has emerged along the symbolist axis is a necessary reference. Invariably, the issue of signification within the image of much 'formal' work is masked by attention to the formal manoeuvres. Whether reference to the surrealist, symbolist tradition would function to refine further exclusions, rather than include films from this axis, is not to be pre-judged, but if there is a distinction in kind to be made between the image signification in the 'formal' film and the surrealist/symbolist work then it needs clarification.

Image signification is not a problem confined to films which make use of representational imagery. Even in extreme non-representational art, the production of the image and its subsequent 'received' meaning is affected by the mechanisms of psychological association. The image, however abstract, is read associatively and signifies, produces and takes on meaning. Furthermore, and most important in 'formal' cinema, it must be understood that association and signification are not processes of meaning confined to the constituent images, representational or abstract, but belong also to the formal manoeuvres themselves.

What is designated form or structure in film is primarily related to the pattern of its temporal construction. Each work is a particular instance of temporal pattern, having likenesses to, and differences from, other instances of form. It, like the image, is subject to the mechanisms of association and, by its instances of difference, signifies. Rejection of symbolist/surrealist practice does not eliminate the issues of signification from 'formal' cinema but may encourage a false assumption in the practice that it does.

Through attention to the temporal manoeuvres (form) in cinema we may clarify some of the issues in the rejection of narrative. Rejection of the commercial cinema institution as repressive through vicarious satisfaction has carried over to a general rejection of the narrative forms through which it functions. In the film culture represented by 'Film as Film' the rejection of narrative structure might be simply interpreted as the basis of a search for 'new' form, but I think it is more properly understood as primarily motivated by rejection of the social function associated with it. A number of recent works by film-makers who clearly come out of the culture represented by 'Film as Film', have to one degree or another worked in areas which have related to the mechanisms associated with narrative. That *Rameau's Nephew* by Michael Snow, or my own *Blackbird Descending (Tense Alignment)*, for example, might be seen as some 'return to narrative' is, in general, false. At the same time these films and works by Hammond like *Some Friends* or Gidal's *Condition of Illusion* tend to problematise, rather than simply oppose, some of the mechanisms to be found in narrative film. Work in this direction demands a more refined definition of narrative because implicit is the question 'are all aspects of narrative irrevocably embroiled with the repressive social function it has come to serve?' This development in the practice has been accompanied by an emerging theoretical concern focusing on the psychological formations in the activity of the film's spectator rather than on the intentions or psychology of the maker. This is particularly true of the film-makers like Hammond, Gidal, Dunford and myself who, more or less from the outset of our film work, have couched the issues of structure primarily in terms of the spectator's act of structuring. Recent theoretical work from another direction, stemming mainly from Christian Metz's 'Imaginary Signifier' article, indicates that some awareness of this problem exists outside the limits of 'structural/materialist' film theory. This theoretical direction focuses on fundamental psychological strategies involved in the process of identification. Many questions are raised by this radical change of focus from the issues of film structure embedded in the concerns of film-making to that of film viewing. For example, if, by implication, certain processes of structuring meaning or unconscious reaction are either fundamental or very deeply embedded by the culture in the psyche, how can the posture of diametric opposition dialecticise these processes? A continued discussion of these particular problems is outside the scope of this article, but it indicates some possibility of distinguishing between the processes of identification with portrayed characters, identification with the film's viewpoint on the scene via the camera on the one hand, and the consequential structures of narrative on the other.

In the simplest sense, narrative is the story, it is the story told in the act of narration. A narrative represents a temporal chain of occurrences, a thread of causality. The narrative is not the events themselves, but a representation of events. It is a method of representing consequential temporality by way of a temporal presentation – the narration. A sophisticated narration may present the narrative in a sequence which does not represent the events in a simple sequential correspondence (making use of conventions like flashback for instance), but whatever the complexity, one temporality is used to represent another. A narrative may represent a series of events which have taken place (in the world) or it may represent, from fragments of the possible, events which never have, nor will, take place – a fiction. The former, based on 'fact', is not strictly a fiction, though as a narrative, with its inevitable linear ordering, its selected representation of causality is not simply factual. The narrative form within 'documentary' cinema raises its own particular questions of veracity and the relationship between document and documentary is of particular importance to film, based as it is in the mechanical recording of photography. In a practical sense, the culture represented by this exhibition raises the general question of the relationship of a presentation's sequence to the implications of meaning brought about by that sequence.

Though various experiments have been made in presenting films without sequential projection, it is none the less basic in general to film that, through projection, film controls presentation sequence – one section inevitably precedes another. In the history of the search for non-narrative structure, the notion of simultaneity represents the earliest alternative to developmental narrative. As in aspects of Dziga Vertov's *Man with a Movie Camera*, for example, some of the sequential presentation does not imply that the events depicted took place sequentially as a consequence of each other, they are rather to be read as continuing independently at-the-same-time, related by some thematic similarity. The dissolution of consequential relationship in the narrative sense makes possible various systems of connective relationships between film images or sequences, analogous in a sense to collage as opposed to conventional story montage. These concepts attempt to establish a kind of a-temporality within the temporal presentation of the film. Many of the formal developments which have occurred with this history, including Brakhage's *Dog Star Man* and Kren's development of editing systems on mathematical principles, stem from the concept of a-temporal montage.

Another direction which has initiated alternatives to narrative form comes from stress on the presentation sequence itself, mainly by way of repetition devices. This work, traceable back to Léger's *Ballet mécanique*, subverts temporal representation by containing the consequentiality of image/shot transformations within the film itself. Or, if there are no transformations within the film then the transformations in perception or response in the spectator become central.

An allied direction, but leading to other conceptual problems, is that of extremely minimal change, not necessarily involving repetition. This direction mainly emerges from Andy Warhol's early films, like *Empire* and *Sleep*, drawing attention to the material passage of time in the presentation. Though there are works which follow Warhol which concentrate on duration without use of a camera, when based in photographic representation the material durational aspect becomes linked to those problems surrounding the notion of document.

Within the specific limits of the mechanism, the photograph as a mechanical trace of particular aspects of reality has veracity as a document – evidence within definable limits. With particular conditions of unbroken durational recording, cinephotography carries similar implications and problematics. This has little to do with 'documentary', which by manipulations at the level of sequential reconstruction breaks any possibility of durational veracity. Work which is an extreme of photographic, durational representation in fact subverts temporal representation by a change in terms. This involves the need to distinguish between representation and recording. When the cinephotographic makes its specificity evident within the work the record is no longer read in its secondary sense as narrative representation but as temporal document. It is outside the present scope to pursue the implications of this difference and the conditions necessary within a film's structure to resist the reading of 'record' as 'representation'. My further reference to cinematic representation carries the implication that this terminology is inadequately resolved.

It is evidently possible to pursue a film practice which is not based in photographic 'representation' (recording) but the historical development of the machinery is largely predicated on this function. The photocinematic recording is clearly a primary level of representation in cinema, though through the practice of editing this level of representation is not its primary *narrative* means. Literature shows that a narrative representation is possible without the facsimile representation afforded by cinephotography – words bear no resemblance to those objects to which they refer. As we have seen it is possible for films which are representational at the level of their images to be non-narrative at the level of their temporal structure. Conversely a film which is non-representational at the level of image may be quite justifiably interpreted as narrative at the level of temporal representation if its structure is readable anthropomorphically.

The resistance to anthropomorphism, which may be seen as a more general expression, and includes within it the resistance to narrative, is similarly a problematic enterprise again raising issues of psychological mechanisms of interpretation and the function of resistance to them. Gidal has pronounced the need to resist and frustrate anthropomorphic interpretation in general; considering the fact that his films are representational in the special sense of photographic recording, this can be interpreted as a tactic to dialecticise what would otherwise be assumed as inevitable (that the human spectator integrates all experience in human terms). Clearly the dominant cinema brings up no problem of this kind, it is anthropomorphic with no resistance at any level – its pictorial representation matching the identificatory desire of the spectator within the narrative – there is no conflict of interpretation, no dialecticisation. Whatever the adequacy of theorisation of this issue, in one form or another, the opposition to representation in painting, the resistance in music to classical (and because of the physics of the ear it can be argued, natural) harmony, can be seen as a thread of opposition to anthropomorphic interpretation in modern art.

From the positive axis of the fundamentals underlying 'Film as Film', the exploration of the medium in-its-own-terms, the exhibition demonstrates how the earliest approaches to this concept came through the application of the abstract developments in painting to film. I have argued that this early direction, rather than setting the terms for film as an autonomous art practice, tended to replace the dominance of literature and theatre over cinematic form by that of painting and music. I have further argued that a more appropriate basis can be found in work which relates itself to the photocinematic aspect of the medium rather than its suppression (thus the emphasis given to Léger and Man Ray's first two works and the photographic contribution of Moholy-Nagy). Paradoxically, the concept of appropriateness in film reintroduces issues of representation that in painting it served to resist.

While my general rejection of the abstract film tradition from Fischinger to the American West Coast is primarily based on the dominance of these painterly concepts in film, it does not invalidate the possibility of a cinematic form with no basis in photography. Unless an argument can be made in general against the temporal, aural abstraction – music – then no argument can be made against the possibility of its visual equivalent.

At a more fundamental level, the underlying assumption that a practice would seek autonomy is problematic. This assumption, implicit in 'Film as Film', inevitably draws all those arguments which can be brought against modernism. In a historical sense, there is no doubt that tendencies which were at work in other arts are reflected in the attempts to define an art practice intrinsically cinematic. As in painting this process has concerned itself progressively with an exploration based on the materials and properties which can be defined as 'belonging to the medium'. Unfortunately the rhetoric of this enterprise has tended to reflect an essentialism – pure painting, pure film – to encourage tautologies like painting is painting, film is film and to become attached to phenomenalism in a way which assumes a kind of unmediated direct response leading to expressions like: 'the work is just itself, an object'. However, this is more an issue of faulty theorisation than faulty practice. In effect, the attempt to determine the intrinsics of a medium is always in one sense or another a relativist and historically placed activity. Any assumption that absolute irreducible essences can be uncovered in the enterprise is not borne out by its practice, the very definition of seeming fundamentals is always open to historical redefinition. The possibility that an autonomous film practice can be postulated already rests on certain historical conditions. The technological development of the materials and machinery is a prerequisite, but the form which this technology takes is already enmeshed with historical preconditions of its social function and psychological determinants. It is impossible to separate the materials and the practice to which it is attached. It is in this sense that any engagement with the medium becomes a signifying practice within the historical framework. At the same time, if seen in a relativist sense, aesthetic strategies which suppress, in one form or another, current significations make possible manipulations leading to new meaning (so-called 'work on the signifier').

Instead of treating the attention to the photocinematic basis of film or any other definable aspects of its machinery or materials in the terms of fundamentals or essences of cinema, they should be considered instead as predominant problematics of the medium in its historical placement and signification. The terms in which this issue is theorised is important not only for an understanding of the practice which has taken place, but also as the basis for a critique. The critique affects the developing practice. For example certain concerns on the one hand with the cinematic materials and machinery and with exploration of a variety of non-narrative structures, by becoming critically dissociated from their historical signification, can become simply recuperable formalist exercises. However, a formalist critique of some developments within the 'Film as Film' direction should not be made without consideration of the critical institution within which it is made. It must be in productive rather than destructive terms lest it merely assists the dominance of mainstream cinema by weakening the only real cultural alternative.

Though still fragile and largely unrecognised, the cinematic development represented by 'Film as Film' is a substantial history. It has already begun some definition within its own terms, but the didactic necessity in its presentation inhibits this definition as it is veered towards polemics. This tendency of the committed to polemicise is in its turn counteracted by a tendency of liberal inclusiveness, a classical balancing of viewpoints. The major historical problem for the involved practitioner is the definition of the issues. Without stressing my own formulation of the most demanding current problems, in the course of this brief outline, I have indicated where I think some might be taken up.

So the 'history we need' is more a question of the manner and function of the enterprise than a polemical assertion of its constituents. To function as it should towards the critical development of current practice it needs to begin from a more limited theoretical definition of the problems and be designed as an operation to elucidate them rather than as an exhibition to present a particular construction.

Neither the current institution surrounding cinema nor that related to the presentation of the plastic arts has forms which suit such a concept of presentation.

II

ON OTHER ARTISTS

4

On Léger, Vertov and the Flicker Film [1977]

Léger

Léger's work as a painter needs little introduction. Though broadly attached to the Cubists, his work always contained incongruous, directly drawn figurative elements. His one film, *Ballet mécanique*, seeks a similar juxtaposition. Some sequences are simply live-action shots, others are animated circles and triangles, and yet others come in between, either the animation of figurative elements – like disembodied legs from a stocking advertisement – into abstract relationships, or the transform-ation of normal photography into simple images or shapes. Like Man Ray's first film, there is no single formal direction, but many diverse ideas are tried out. The film is, however, long enough and sufficiently co-ordinated in some formal directions to show that Léger had abandoned any semblance of episodic narrative or symbolic structure in favour of new co-ordinating principles. However many ideas remained undeveloped in *Ballet mécanique*, Léger was trying to establish a formal unity for the work, fully aware that he sought a film structure based on plastic principles.

Two years after completing the film, Léger wrote an article entitled 'A New Real-ism – the Object (its Plastic and Cinematic Graphic Value)' in which he says:

> Every effort in the line of spectacle or moving picture should be concentrated on
> bringing out the values of the object – even at the expense of the subject and every other
> so-called photographic element of interpretation, whatever it may be. All current cinema
> is romantic, literary, historical, expressionist, etc. Let us forget all this and consider if you
> please: a pipe – a chair – a hand – an eye – a typewriter – a hat – a foot, etc.
>
> Let us consider these things for what they can contribute to the screen just as they
> are – in isolation – their value enhanced by every known means …
>
> The technique emphasized is to isolate the object or fragment of an object and to
> present it on the screen in close-ups of the largest possible scale. Enormous
> enlargements of an object or a fragment give it a personality it never had before and in
> this way it can become a vehicle of entirely new lyric and plastic power …
>
> To get the right plastic effect, the usual cinematographic methods must be entirely
> forgotten. The question of light and shade becomes of prime importance. The different
> degrees of mobility must be regulated by the rhythms controlling the different speeds of

projection – 'la minuterie' – the timing of projections must be calculated
mathematically.[1]

Whatever else this shows, it indicates that Léger had some developed ideas of a
general nature about new possibilities for cinematography and how they could be
achieved. In particular it shows a grasp of abstract directions for lighting and rhythm.
As in the first films of Man Ray, *Ballet mécanique* makes use of the abstracting techniques which separate the visual qualities of an object from its specific identity. For
example, there are a number of sequences in the film of various kitchen implements,
chosen for their textural qualities (metallic and partially reflective), and their simple
geometric shapes. These qualities are isolated by the framing and the lighting, while
the short duration of the sequence frustrates any attempt to identify the object. In
the same article, Léger says:

> Take an aluminium saucepan. Let shafts of light play on it from all angles – penetrating
> and transforming it. Present it on the screen in a close-up, it will interest the public for
> a time yet to be determined. The public need never know that this fairy-like effect of
> light in many forms, that so delights it, is nothing but an aluminium saucepan.[2]

Also like Man Ray, Léger develops in his film the idea of linking images on the
basis of visual similarity to the extent that the repetition of triangular forms becomes
a major formal basis within the film. As well as the animation of a triangle, intercut
with a circle, the triangle reappears continuously in the live-action sequence where
mirrors are arranged as a triangular tube in front of the camera lens. This 'kaleido-
scope' technique was first introduced into photography by Alvin Langdon Coburn
in his vortographs of 1917.

As well as linking sequences through similarities in centrally placed geometric
shapes Léger also uses a kinetic linkage based on similarities of movement. Yet in
the kinetic linkage, the elements of movement tend to be confined within the screen,
like the rotation or pumping action of machine parts, the swinging of a glass ball or
a figure on a swing, and never reach the kind of pace which is capable of fully separating experience of movement from other qualities of the object in motion. Rather,
movement is orchestrated as a sculptural, rhythmic quality, its direction is used in
the shot, and also differentiates qualities such as a gentle oscillation and a mechanical pumping, much in common with Ruttmann's sensibility in his *Opus* series.

It is also the first exploration of another form of rhythm – that constructed from
the change of image itself. Lengths of film are used deliberately in a rhythmic beat
structure. Though this structure may relate to movement or rhythm within the
frame, it is essentially of a more basic order, analogous to the relationship of a drum
beat to melody in music. This form of editing was also taken up by Eisenstein, par-

ticularly in *October*, by Gance in *Napoléon* and by Vertov in *Man with a Movie Camera*. As with some of the other works of this period, Léger's film was accompanied by a specially composed music score, in this case by George Antheil, which would have considerably heightened the pace and rhythm of the film.

Possibly as a by-product of the rhythmic editing of sequences, Léger, also for the first time in a film, introduces lengths of film with no image – strips of black film – as elements of the rhythmic and optical interchange, and thereby also prefigures a concern within abstract cinema, which later almost takes on the proportions of a 'genre', the flicker effect.

There are two other firsts which can probably be claimed for *Ballet mécanique*, and which have an important place later. One of these is almost an aside within the film and may have been the result of accident, though some of the implications may well have appealed to Léger when he saw the result. In one sequence a mirrored glass ball is swung backwards and forwards. As well as creating a link with the woman on the swing at the beginning of the film, its circular shape connects it with the circle theme established by the geometric shapes, and its polished surface links it with the dominating metallic quality of many of the objects in the film. But, as the ball swings, the camera and its operator (presumably Dudley Murphy, who is so credited) are mirrored in its surface, creating the first direct reference to the machinery of cinema as part of the content of film. This is a notion which Vertov developed more consistently later, and which anticipates some of the most recent formal notions occupying contemporary film-makers.

The other 'first' is the multiple repetition of a sequence, again prefiguring what is now almost a 'genre' – exploration of the 'loop'. The sequence is of a woman, with a bag on her back, climbing a set of steps, filmed from above. Certainly, the repetition in this sequence is prophetic, for example, of Warhol's multiple repeat paintings. But how does it work in Léger's film? It follows a series of sequences of machines which establish certain machine rhythms. In this context the repetition of the woman's movement on the steps could originally have been thought of as the application of machine 'rotation' to the human movement. This is consistent with Léger's paintings, where his figures have the predominant quality of machine parts. It also confirms other statements in his 1926 article, for example referring to a list of objects:

> In this enumeration I have purposely [sic] included parts of the human body in order to emphasize the fact that in the new realism the human being, the personality, is very interesting only in these fragments and that these fragments should not be considered of any more importance than any of the other objects listed.[3]

In case the reader is disturbed by the 'inhumanity' of this statement, it should be understood in the context of the period in which it was made. To the Futurist, the development of machinery and manufacture was viewed with optimism as the means by which real human progress might be made. Far from seeming inhuman, the machine was seen as a means of salvation and was celebrated in film by, for example, Vertov, and in a poor copy of aspects of *Ballet mécanique* by Eugène Deslaw in his *Marche des machines*. One of the earliest films to consider the effect of the machine on human behaviour in an unfavourable light was *Modern Times* made by Chaplin, ironically the subject, in cubist form, of the animation sequence which begins and ends *Ballet mécanique*. The twentieth century and our manner of life, as many of the artists of this period rightly foresaw, has been and will continue to be, closely linked to the machine and manufacture. What is important, aesthetically, in the machine references of Léger's film, is the way in which they constitute an appropriate parallel for the mechanical aspect of cinematography itself – a central aspect of the film's meaning.

Vertov
'Filmdrama is the opium of the masses'

Many of the artists seeking a new formal basis for cinema expressed a direct opposition to its theatrical and narrative background, but no film-maker of the period understood this problem as clearly as the Russian Dziga Vertov, and few since have expressed this opposition with his fervour and flair. Vertov was no academic theoretician, but in a polemical manner aimed to eliminate the gap between theory and practice. He always demanded to be able to think through the practice of film-making. Before the October Revolution he had studied at the Moscow Psycho-Neurological Institute, a point which has some significance in his statements and later editing style.

Born in 1896, Vertov came of age at the outbreak of the revolution. In Moscow, Mayakovsky, as a Futurist poet, could hardly be avoided, and Vertov, who also for a time wanted to be a poet, adopted much of Mayakovsky's aggressive public style and terse writing. It was Alexandre Lemberg, the son of a cameraman, who introduced Vertov to cinema and his first practical experiments. Within seven months of the Bolshevik revolution, he was, as secretary of the Skobelev committee (the newly formed state film production unit), in at the very beginning of Soviet film production with the release of the first cinema weekly. With a team which included cameramen Giber, Tisse and Ermlov, and the editor Elizabeta Svilova (his future wife), by the summer of 1918 he had become the centre of the operation.

There can be no doubt that Lenin saw this work as being of fundamental importance: in a period when all accounts are of shortage of filmstock and equipment, by 1919, Vertov had not only produced nearly fifty of the weekly newsreels, but also three general compilation films. Before beginning his next major set of newsreels, *Kinopravda* ('film truth') in 1922, he had produced a number of other films. He had been a major figure in establishing and running a film-car on the agit-train of President Kalinin in 1920, which had facilities for shooting, developing, editing and projecting film daily throughout their travels in the Russian provinces.

In Russia, as elsewhere, the dominant mode of cinema was the film drama, having its roots deeply in the forms of literature and theatre. In its earliest days, cinema had been popular in a way very similar to music hall or vaudeville, and the earliest short films were often produced by people who had worked in those fields. At a primitive level they were simple entertainment 'sketches' of a vaudeville kind. Not only was their main audience the urban working class, but for some time their production roots were largely from the same section of society. The rise of the more sophisticated, longer narrative film occurred simultaneously with the invasion of business interests into cinema. In a gradual process cinema established a particular social function and with it forms which engendered a particular kind of psychological reaction from its audience. Though the roots of its content remained in the fantasies and aspirations of the working class, the manipulation and resolution of these fantasies through film came increasingly under the control of the films' financiers. They encouraged films that conditioned the fantasies of the mass audience in ways which would create no threat to the current social order – a function now taken over by television.

It can be argued that any society involves repression, particularly of sexual and aggressive behaviour. The commercial cinema, having taken as its basis of content the fantasies, fears, aspirations and tensions of society, forms around them cinematic conventions intended to create a popular acceptance of the existing social order. Other commentators begin to see this at the relatively simple level of plot, the dramatic resolution of the various subjects in film. There is another level to this issue: not only should we look at the reactionary nature of a film's 'message' – the social meaning implicit in the resolution of its plot – but we should also be concerned with the manner of perception and response which is engendered in the formal construction of a work.

In many respects, the formal construction of illusionist cinema has a more basic effect than the stories themselves. A 'revolutionary' story, which creates an essentially passive response in the audience, may be as reactionary in its social effect as a story which has no revolutionary aspirations. In theatre, this is a problem which Bertolt Brecht was the first to express clearly. In cinema, awareness of the political implications of form is first clearly expressed in the writings of Vertov and the Kino-Eye group. In 1920 Vertov wrote:

1 Filmdrama is the opium of the masses.
2 Down with the immortal kings and queens of the screen! Long live the ordinary people filmed in everyday life and at work!
3 Down with the bourgeois imagination and its fairytales! Long live everyday life!

4 Filmdrama and religion are deadly weapons in the hands of the capitalists. Only through showing our revolutionary daily life do we strike the weapon from the enemy's hand.

5 The modern art-drama is a relic of the old world. It is an attempt to press our revolutionary reality into reactionary forms![4]

In 1924, he shows his awareness of the reactionary effect of conventional narrative cinema and thus the link between politics and the mode of perception engendered in the film audience:

If we want to understand clearly the effect of films on the audience, we have first to agree about two things:
1 What audience?
2 What effect upon the audience are we talking about?
On the movie-house habitué, the ordinary fiction film acts like a cigar or cigarette on a smoker. Intoxicated by the cine-nicotine, the spectator sucks from the screen the substance which soothes his nerves.[5]

And later from the same discussion:

To intoxicate and suggest – the essential method of the fiction film approximates it to a religious influence, and makes it possible after a certain time to keep a man in a permanent state of overexcited unconsciousness … Musical shows, theatrical and cine-theatrical performances and so on above all act upon the subconscious of the spectator or listener, distorting his protesting consciousness in every possible way.[6]

Consciousness or Subconsciousness

We rise against the collusion between the 'director-enchanter' and the public which is submitted to the enchantment.

The conscious alone can fight against magical suggestions of every kind.
The conscious alone can form a man of firm convictions and opinions.
We need a conscious people, not an unconscious mass ready to yield to any suggestion.

There can be little doubt about the vehemence with which Vertov and his famous Kino-Eye group viewed the function of the prevalent culture of cinema and its forms. He was certain that the history of cinema to that date had succumbed to a pervasive reactionary content, and he was also aware that this deeply infected the language, convention and forms of cinema and the habitual responses of its audience. He knew that his task was a practical one – to establish a strong new form – and this meant experiment with the means and functions of cinema. It implied a radical rethinking of all assumptions, an attitude in common with the experimenters active in France, Germany and Italy, but of whom Vertov would have had little knowledge at this time.

Although at the beginning Vertov settled on the alternative of newsreel or documentary, his own development leading to *Man with a Movie Camera*, and a close look at other statements he made, indicates that his approach was not simply one of the 'actuality film' against fictional cinema. The strength of his polemical statements should not be seen to imply a rigid dogmatism in their practical application, since experiment was essential to discovery of new forms. Between 1922 and 1925, while he had control over *Kinopravda*, he also organised the other major newsreel enterprise *Goskinokalendar*, and used *Kinopravda* increasingly for the experimentation of the Kino-Eye group.

As he was violently opposed to the scenario as the basis of film and deeply committed to catching life 'unawares', it is not surprising that his main attention focused on the shooting and editing stages. Kino-Eye had never considered the camera as a substitute for the human eye, but had always affirmed it as a machine in its own terms capable of extending or creating new perception. Vertov stated: '"Kino-Eye" makes use of all the new techniques for high speed representation of movement, micro-cinematography, reversed movement, multiple exposures etc.'; and: '"Kino-Eye" does not regard these as mere tricks or special effects but as a normal technique which should be used as widely as possible.'[7]

Before considering how Vertov's concept of editing constitutes his major formal contribution to film, I would like to illustrate a little further the link Vertov's experimentation in this period has with that of his European contemporaries. He reports the invention of new film genres by the *Kinopravda* group as follows: 'Review films, sketch films, verse films, film poems and preview films made their appearance … Considerable work was done in the utilization of new methods for subtitling, transforming titles into pictorial units equal to the images.'[8] The inclusion in this list of 'verse films' and 'film poems', together with his expressed annoyance after seeing René Clair's *Paris qui dort* that Kino-Eye had not made such a film first, suggests strongly to me that he would have also been greatly impressed by all the work already described, particularly Léger's *Ballet mécanique*.

It is interesting to note that Léger, far from seeing his own 'abstraction' as being in conflict with realism, considered it to be the 'new realism'. In fact, work which affirms the basic material and processes of its own medium has more claim to the term 'realist' than that which denies the medium in favour of simulating life, which deserves the title 'illusionist'. (In many respects this represents a reversal of popular usage.) Vertov's development of a greater fragmentation in temporal continuity certainly did not, for him, contradict the 'realist' nature of his work:

> 'Kino-Eye' employs all the resources of montage describing simultaneously phenomena from opposite poles of the universe, in an order which may be chronological or not at will, violating, if necessary, the conventions and precedents for the construction of a 'kino-object'.

> 'Kino-Eye', flinging itself into the heart of the apparent disorder of life, strives to find in life itself the answers to the questions it asks: to find amongst a mass of possibilities the correct, the necessary fact to solve the theme.
> 'Kino-Eye' is:
> montage – when I set myself a theme (one chosen from thousands)
> montage – when I take care to guard against irrelevancies in developing the theme (to make the only appropriate choice from thousands of observations)
> montage – when I decide upon the order in which the filmed material will be presented (to choose from amongst thousands of possible combinations the one that seems most appropriate, bearing in mind the nature of the filmed material itself or the demands of the chosen theme).[9]

In case Vertov gives the impression that he was only concerned with relationships in the symbolic and semantic sense, and that his idea of theme was literary, the continuation of the quotation shows that there was no such convenient separation of the semantic from the material aspects of his film images.

> The 'Kino-Eye' school demands that the construction of the film should be based on the 'intervals' of movement between different planes, on the correct relationship of these intervals to each other and on the movement of one visual impression to another … To find the best route for the eye of the spectator to penetrate the chaos of the mutual reactions, attractions, repulsions of images on each other: to reduce these innumerable 'intervals' (intervals of movement between one image and another) to one simple equation, to one spectacular formula which presents, in the best possible way, the essential theme of the film. These are tasks which the director must fulfil.[10]

From an understanding of Vertov's process in constructing a film-reality – a 'film-understanding' out of direct articulation of the material – it is possible to see the essential difference between his concept of montage and the other dominant school of Russian montage, that stemming principally from Eisenstein. Although the notion of 'collision' and its parallel in 'dialectical' thought, articulated by Eisenstein, contributes to Vertov's sensibility, and both share a dynamic sense of motion within editing, Eisenstein's essential purpose remained that of using cinema to create an expressive narrative. In this respect, his innovations in editing were only a means towards this end. Viewed in this way, Eisenstein breaks much less with conventional cinema than does Vertov. For Vertov, editing was essentially a process, and as such, a way of structuring the raw materials of film-thought – the collected 'shots' – and thereby structuring experience. The active process of thinking-through-editing is the central process of his film, and, fortunately for us, this did not remain a theoretical idea, but was realised in *Man with a Movie Camera*.

This massive work, whose emergent theme is the interrelatedness of activity, enterprise and movement of the Soviet metropolis, functions through the most intricate weave of thematic connections. The basis of these connections is multi-levelled, but clear. For example, the sequences interplay at the level of surface distribution of light and dark patterning; they interplay at the levels of direction and rate of movement; they establish, in relationship to these other factors, the independent rhythmic beat of the intercutting rate. But in addition to this co-ordination at the visual and kinetic level, thematic relationships are continually established through identification of the material. These themes are maintained in a developing flux, for as well as the general theme, based on the pattern of activity as it increases and subsides throughout a day in the metropolis, other sub-theme relationships are being woven: comparisons of bodily movement in work and recreation, bodily movements with machine movements, machines with radio communication, music and speech with the gramophone, and so on. In order to create this weave, a temporal simultaneity is effected by clusters of short sequences of images intercut in rapid succession. Though a precision in these relationships is sought and achieved in the film's editing, the spectator always participates in synthesising the material for himself. One of the film's many significant aspects is the change in behaviour which is elicited from the spectator. It clearly makes impossible the passive, cathartic, emotionally manipulated mode which is normal in the popular cinema culture. This is achieved by the manner and process of the film's editing, and is further reinforced by the direct reference to the machinery.

This is the first film which clearly defines the camera as a participant in what it sees, and is a forerunner of several recent films which explore self-referential structures. It contains film of the camera itself, of projection machines, the cinema auditorium and public, the cinema screen, the film within the film, and the selection of shots at the editing table. In addition, the film explores various forms of superimposition and split-screen forms, which further assist the complex networks of connections. He frequently uses this to establish idea relationships, as in the superimposition of a singer within a gramophone loudspeaker, but also for various kinds of counter-motion, as in the three-way horizontal division of the screen with tram-cars moving in alternating directions.

Eisenstein's film with most in common in its montage is *October*, completed nine months earlier. While I consider this to be the best example of Eisenstein's editing, and the work most structured towards an active perceptual mode in the spectator, even here he did not really escape a form which was basically manipulative of the audience. In fact, as conditions changed in Russia and the kind of film which was called for was one which could reinforce nationalistic tendencies, Eisenstein's work regressed into a form which was basically little different from that of the capitalist cinema. It was increasingly used to tell historical tales which did nothing to arouse or maintain a revolutionary consciousness in its Russian audience.

Vertov, subsequently accused of being a formalist as Stalinist nationalism gained strength, was never able to develop his fundamental principles further. With the decline of Eisenstein, *Man with a Movie Camera* is the highest point of Soviet cinema. Together with Vertov's theoretical statements, it creates the basis for considering how formal innovation in film and radical politics can be related.

The Flicker Film

The first area of inquiry to look at is the perceptual film. The term normally used for it is the 'flicker film' though it is too specific to define it by a single characteristic rather than its region of function. This area of cinema attempts to examine, or create experience through devices which work on the autonomic nervous system. Where the main characteristic of Op Art in painting is the use of simultaneous contrasts in sufficiently close planar relationship to stimulate an essentially retinal reaction, in film this reaches its purest form in a concentration on the temporal equivalent – rapid sequential contrasts. Duchamp's *Anaemic Cinema*, at least in relationship to the revolving visual discs, directly initiates perceptual cinema. Other work in the abstract field has also tended towards an optical phase, where the kinetic aspects of interior motion are replaced by large-scale change of whole areas of the screen. Editing of live-action sequences in the avant-garde film has increasingly tended towards extremely rapid rates of change. One possible motive for this is an implicit search for a film which can function essentially on the psycho-physical rather than the psycho-interpretative level. Action on the autonomic system seeks to create a nervous response which is largely preconscious, the psychological reactions sought being a direct consequence of physiological function.

Cinema, as a mechanism, is designed to project one separate picture every 1/24th of a second. If the period during which the projection shutter is closed is taken into account, each image occupies the screen for approximately half that time, about 1/50th of a second, while the rate of image change in film is deliberately located just beyond the point where the eye can discern flicker. This factor is economic using the smallest number of separate images necessary to create smooth movement. However, film's 'location' on this optical threshold makes it ideally suitable for examining the threshold itself by exposure to optical events and rates of change which move progressively into the region where flicker is discerned, by increasing the ratio of dark to light frames in increments of 1/24th of a second.

The first film to show this perceptual possibility in an extreme form is Kubelka's *Arnulf Rainer*. However much its retinal bombardment of alternating short black and white sequences may initiate optical effects, like that of colour afterimage, the film is constructed in such a way that no stroboscopic rates are maintained in a sufficiently unbroken sequence to allow it to be described as concerned with the optical factors. The first such film is Tony Conrad's *The Flicker*, made six years later, in 1966, and conceived entirely in terms of retinal response. It explores different stroboscopic systems first, and then systematic interactions between them. The result is a film which enables awareness of changing modes of response to recognisably different strobe conditions – awareness of how the autonomic response begins to shade off into pattern recognition as the black and white units increase in length; how the different systems interact; how the difference in colour afterimage relates to different strobe rates; and possibly becoming aware of other physiological changes as the retinal activity affects the rhythm of other areas of the nervous system.

In the same year, Paul Sharits made *Ray Gun Virus*, a fourteen-minute film with no images, which explores the optical interaction of single-colour frames. In 1966 he also completed two other films which rely heavily on the optical interaction of colour, but both of these, *Word Movie* and *Piece Mandala (End War),* also contain associative material, in the first instance rapidly changing words, in the second single-frame images of himself and a couple. It is only in 1968, with *Ray Gun Virus* and *N:O:T:H:I:N:G;* that the optical experience is uninterrupted by associative or semantic issues which also encroach on his longer optical colour works of 1968, *Razor Blades* and *T,O,U,C,H,I,N,G,*.

In his work as a whole we see a pull in three directions. The first is the obvious factor of colour interactions in time, which affect the retina; the second is a confusing romanticism which results in unintegrated images and inappropriate interpretation of the material aspect of the experience; the third is a systemic intention in the overall form of his films. The interesting interaction is between the first and last. It is in the nature of the autonomic experience that it should be localised in the immediate clusters of perception, counteracting awareness of his overall systemic concept. While in Conrad's *The Flicker* the overall experience is due to awareness of gradually changing modes of perception, with Sharits the structural concepts are conceived in terms of a two-dimensional pattern through which the film traces a particular path. It is perhaps his awareness of the difficulty of perceiving the formal pattern during the projection of his films that has recently led him to explore an alternative presentation of some as a matrix – whole films installed as adjacent strips between plexiglass, where the system becomes immediately apparent. In his optical colour work, even after seeing the system in this static way, I have found it impossible to experience it from the sequential presentation of the films. (end section of The Flicker)

Other film-makers have produced works which directly explore one or another aspect of the perceptual film, mostly involving the extreme of white and black interchange, though some developments have also been made in the area of colour. Since 1966, the perceptual problem in cinema has become a fairly clear area of study. There are two works which have sought to increase the contrast between black and white by using the extremely light-resistant magnetic sound recording stock, out of which holes of a single-frame duration are punched. In America Taka Iimura presented some loop projection experiments using magnetic stock and clear frames in 1969, and my own film *Spot the Microdot* using a similar technique was made independently in 1970.

Birgit and Wilhelm Hein began a number of consistent studies in the perceptual area with *625* (1969), the strobe being achieved by refilming at camera speeds from an imageless television screen. They followed this in the same year by an untitled film (part 3 of *Work in Progress Reel A*), in which a single still image was interchanged with black film spacing, three frames of each at a time, for approximately ten minutes. In this work the Heins uncovered a curious visual phenomenon. Not only can continuous strobe produce colour as afterimage, but it can also create an illusion of motion where none exists. The still picture of two girls seated together, continuously repeated, gradually seem to move, the faces seem to smile and one figure seems to lean closer to the other. The cause of this phenomenon may be similar to the inevitable mental reordering of repeated verbal phrases. The perceptual process seems to demand change even where there is none. In the near scientific way in which they have come increasingly to follow up their experiments, the Heins made *Foto-Film* (1970) which further tested the phenomenon. Like Iimura and myself, using the light-resistant magnetic stock for maximum contrast, they produced a flicker film which could be projected over a large still photograph attached to the screen. The effect of apparent motion remained, even though in this case it could not be explained by possible small movements ('jittering') in the projected picture.

Their most developed work in this field is not stroboscopic. Made in four parts during 1971–2, it is a two screen film titled *Doppelprojection I–IV*. Various rates of rapid fade are explored, with a completely blank screen in two of the parts, and with a simple static camera shot (not a refilmed still) in the other two parts. The optical response to this film is directly related to the two-screen format, where the fading screen shifts the eye continuously backwards and forwards from one to the other, sometimes causing an apparent lateral rotation of the screen surface. Like many works in this area, and particularly in the Heins' perceptual work, the screen itself and its illumination become extremely physical.

As in the Op Art of Victor Vasarelly and Joseph Albers, or the spirals of Duchamp, the illusion factor is significantly different when it is the result of physical experience than when it is the illusionism of spurious pictorial narrative involvement. It is an area in which we may genuinely study ourselves and our reactions.

Notes

1. *Little Review*, Winter 1926; reprinted in Lewis Jacob's introduction to *The Art of the Movies* (New York: Noonday Press, 1960), pp. 96–8.
2. Ibid.
3. Ibid.
4. Translation by Christophe Gierke, *Afterimage* no. 1, April 1970.
5. Luda and Jean Schnitzer and Marcel Martin (eds), *Cinema in Revolution* (New York: Hill and Wang, 1973).
6. Ibid.
7. *Afterimage* no. 1, April 1970.
8. Quoted in Seth Feldman, 'Cinema Weekly and Cinema Truth: Dziga Vertov and the Leninist Proportion', *Sight and Sound*, Winter 1973/4.
9. *Afterimage* no. 1, April 1970.
10. Ibid.

5

Kurt Kren [1975]

The temptation in writing about Kurt Kren is to present him as some kind of father of European avant-garde film. His work is certainly held in very high regard by almost all the film-makers this side of the Atlantic involved in so-called structuralist film. At forty-six years old (born in Vienna on 20 September 1929), beginning his experiments with film on 8mm as early as 1953 and completing his first 16mm film in 1957, he has at least a ten-year start on those like Birgit and Wilhelm Hein, Peter Gidal, Werner Nekes, Peter Weibel, Valie Export or myself who otherwise have been the main generation initiating the 'formal' direction outside the US.

However, to see Kren in this way is somewhat misleading. Though his historical role is of great importance he should in no way be condemned to the history books, as he continues to be a leading figure of the avant-garde. Secondly, none of the innovators who started work later, in the mid-1960s, was a follower of Kren. Most, like myself, had already started in this direction before encountering Kren's films. The lack of information here about the American underground film was matched by a similar lack of exchange within Europe itself. I first saw a Kren film in 1967 or '68, during one of the early presentations of the London Film-makers' Co-operative. It was in a programme dominated by some very poor and obscure films from the US. (The first American works to be distributed here came mostly from Robert Pike's Creative Film Society catalogue, and my reaction was very unfavourable to what I came to realise later were films quite unrepresentative of the New American Cinema.) The Kren film, *10/65 Selbstverstümmelung*, was one of his less evidently formal works, but even so, I recognised a close affinity in filmic concept with the work I was doing. This was borne out by seeing some of his other films soon after, particularly *15/67-TV* which remains for me his most influential film.

In many ways, in post-war Vienna, the art scene revived as an independent force more quickly than it did in most other European centres. It was also less dominated by the powerful new movements originating in the affluence of post-war America. Though the development of the Austrian Direct Art and Material-aktion movements of Brus, Muehl and Nitsch parallels the Happenings movement and has similar roots in abstract expressionism, the Viennese development was an independent growth from the already strong expressionist tradition of Klimt, Schiele or Kokoschka. Film experiment in Vienna also significantly preceded any other similar development in Europe and was likewise completely independent of the American underground cinema. Apart from Kren's early 8mm films, which he does not consider as 'public' work, the first important post-war experimental film from Austria was *Mosaik im Vertrauen*, made jointly in 1955 by Ferry Radax and Peter Kubelka. In 1957 Kubelka made *Adebar*, Kren made *1/57 – Versuch mit syntetischem Ton* and Marc Adrian began work on *Black Movie*. Though Kubelka collaborated with Radax on the one film, these four Viennese film-makers were not a group; they worked separately and had no significant influence on each other. Kren and Kubelka, whose respective films represent the most radical innovation in film thought at that time, demand some comparison. By 1961, both film-makers had produced at least three films, which together with contemporary work by Brakhage (particularly *Sirius Remembered*, 1959) and a little later Warhol (*Sleep*, 1963) brought about the biggest changes in concepts of film form since the early experiments of Man Ray, Léger, Eggeling, Richter *et al*. As such, I see these four film-makers as the main precursors of the current direction of avant-garde cinema.[1] In the case of Kubelka, the three films are *Adebar* (1957), *Schwechater* (1958) and the exceptional, blank screen, alternating black and white *Arnulf Rainer* (1960). For Kren they were *2/60 – 48 Köpfe aus dem Szondi-Test*, *3/60 – Bäume im Herbst* (both 1960) and *4/61 – Mauern-Positiv-Negativ und Weg* (1961). Perhaps Kren's first 16mm film should be included as it certainly breaks significantly new ground, but it is not as clearly successful as the other three.

Though, unlike most other commentators, I have never considered Kubelka's *Unsere Afrikareise* to be more than a well-made but ordinary film, his three earlier films are rightly recognised as major points of reference, and it is a source of consternation and surprise to myself and many of my contemporaries that Kren's work is not similarly recognised by American critics. An atmosphere of recrimination has come to surround the comparison of these two Viennese innovators, and it is difficult to maintain an impartial stance, but my concern is with the contribution they make through their films.

Kubelka's best film remains the imageless, cinema-concrete *Arnulf Rainer*. Considering the time at which it was produced, it makes an extreme and surprising challenge to preconceptions about film content, eliminating both photography and representation. *Adebar* and *Schwechater* are also important and accomplished works, but their concept of abstracting kinetic qualities by high-contrast printing and the use of negative, and counterpointing this with the orchestration of the montage, can be seen to fulfil a graphic function similar to certain abstract avant-garde films of the 1920s (i.e. sequences from Hans Richter's *Film Studie*, 1926). Through the image contrast and the editing rate, the photographic trace is separated from the identity and association of the image. Movement and rhythm are thereby abstracted into the visual-musical play of forms, consistent with the often explicit aims of early abstract films. The development of this graphically abstract aesthetic in film had lagged behind through the lack of experiment between the wars. But by the late 1950s, in comparison with contemporary developments in the other arts, it no longer represented as fundamental an aesthetic challenge as *Arnulf Rainer*, or posed as complex artistic problems as the Kren films of the same period. In fact, a major distinction in Kren's work is the broad rejection of the abstract-graphic solution to the search for new film form. The image never becomes divorced from the thing filmed or the processes of film. His work maintains a constant, tense dialectic between conception and structuring on the one hand and experience in the subjective, existentialist sense on the other.

With thirty-one 16mm works to date Kren's historical role in Europe is comparable to that of Brakhage in America, as is the way in which they each historically represent some aspect of the transition from the existential to the structural within their work. Though Kren's work chiefly initiates and contributes to the formal/structural axis, and my own bias will tend to stress that contribution, it is very complex at the imagist/associative level. The fullest examination of Kren as an artist needs to ask questions about the psychological basis of his imagery, through which biographical details would inevitably become significant. Though his films are in no way 'diarist' or directly autobiographical, not even to the degree in which Brakhage's are, he has always maintained an extreme existentialist stance which integrates all levels of his work with his life experience. I do not feel well qualified to deal with this aspect in the detail of psychological interpretation, but I cannot avoid some speculation or at least some general consideration of the work's functioning on this level.

As a Jewish child in Vienna, Kren grew up with the spreading anti-Semitism of the emerging Third Reich and was sent to spend all the war years hidden in relative safety in Holland. He rejoined his family in Austria in 1947, but seems never to have been able to recover a satisfactory emotional contact with them. He became a cashier in the Austrian National Bank, continuing to work there until 1968. Since his first 16mm film, *1/57 – Versuch mit syntetischem Ton* (all his film titles are methodically prefixed by the number of the work in complete chronology, followed by the year of realisation, thus *1/57* denotes film no. 1, 1957), there have been three distinct phases in his work. The first extends from 1957 to 1962 during which he completed five films; the second from 1964 to 1967 when he made eight (*6/64* to *13/67*), all based around the work of other artists, particularly the actions of Otto Muehl and Günter Brus, though *11/65* is based on an Op Art picture by Helga Philip; and the third is from 1967 to the present, continuing individual film work (*14/67* to *31/75*). But it has extended to include the production of drawings, collages, prints and in particular, five limited-edition boxes, each containing an 8mm copy of one of his films, facsimiles of the preparatory diagrams, documentation and photographs, sold in the same way as prints. In the last phase there have been further collaborations with Muehl – but in the more clearly defined role of cameraman or participant in Muehl's work – and with Brus, where Brus has been simply a participant in a Kren film.

In many ways the work divides more simply in two, the wholly individual films and the two years of deep involvement with Muehl and Brus. The notoriety of the Muehl actions, and the overwhelming content in the films which are based on them, perhaps explains some of the lack of understanding of Kren's work in America. Even among English film-makers there is a tendency to dismiss this period as irrelevant to Kren's main contribution. This is short-sighted, since the films stand as satisfactory works and certainly have an important bearing on his work as a whole. Though out of chronological order, I shall consider Kren's involvement with the Direct Art, Material-aktion movement first.

It is evident from Kren's films of the Muehl actions and from statements made by Brus that some of the initial impetus for the movement was an extension of the expressionist, action-painting concept into performance and away from a static end-product. Brus, for example, took the psychological analogy between the therapeutic action of dripping paint and shitting, to the logical conclusion of shitting 'on-stage'. As the painterly component of the actions gave way increasingly to the bodily function component, issues of inhibition and common morality grew unavoidable. The work became concerned with presenting the less acceptable (if ordinary) bodily functions, and with extending awareness of the range of sexuality, violence, sadism and masochism. In the repressive public atmosphere in which performances took place, there was a constant danger of criminal prosecution, and the work consequently developed a strong political and didactic character. In the historical sense, this direction is consistent with an existential concern with the basic materiality of human experience, and with the aims of psychoanalysis through bringing to 'public' consciousness, sub- or un-conscious tendencies and connections. It is also consistent with de Sade through the amoral exploration of human capability, wherever that project might lead.

Considering the particular historical and geographical situation of Vienna after the war, it is not surprising that the Austrian psyche was much preoccupied with accommodating the shared responsibility for the atrocities of the Nazi era. It is quite wrong to see Brus, Muehl or Nitsch as simply expressing this guilt or as therapeutically catharsising it. However, in addition to the relatively less contentious material-body-psychology element, the growing engagement with violence, sexual sadism and sexual masochism confronts some of the major emotional responses to the war. Kren's involvement with this direction of 'enquiry' is not arbitrary or peripheral, as can be seen in what I consider to be his best film of the period, *10/65-67 – Selbstverstümmelung* (Self-Mutilation),[2] which is based on a Brus action. As in all Kren's work, though not immediately evident in this film, it has a strong underlying system for the montage. Even on the surface, there is a quite clear formal play between the white identity of the cinema screen and the white face covered in dough and pigment filmed against a white floor. But the expressionist symbolism of the action and objects is unavoidable. Surgical knives, scissors and pins pull and distort the dough-flesh of the face, and drawn gashes are confused with the holes of mouth and eyes. The cruelties of Dachau and the torture of the medical experiments of Dr Sigmund Rascher are unavoidably implicit in the images of this film.

With Kren a Jewish child in Holland, it is absurd to consider him sharing public responsibility for these events. At the same time, the mechanisms of accommodation are complex. Supported by the evidence of two of his later films, *20/68 – Schatzi* and *24/70 – Western*, which have clear references to images of war atrocity, Kren's attitudes and responses are, like Goya's, ambivalent. There is no simple condemnation but a seeming search for identification with both victim and protagonist – in the Brus film, characterised by the symbol of self-violence. The ambivalence is indicated in a different way in *Schatzi* and *Western*. *Schatzi* is based on what is presumably a concentration camp photograph of a uniformed officer (nationality undefined) surveying a heap of bodies, and *Western* on the anti-Vietnam poster *and Babies*. In both these films, the closest Kren comes to a simple political content and direct reference to this underlying element of his imagery, the recognition of the image is withheld. In the earlier film this is done by the superimposition of negative and positive, making an almost undifferentiated grey surface, and in *Western* by an exploration of the poster in such extreme close-up that it is again the surface rather than the 'message' which forms the dominant experience. The ambivalence – first choosing the material for its connotations, then denying simple interpretation by withholding early or, at any stage, certain recognition – is evident through the irony of a 'formalist' presentation of emotionally loaded images. At the same time, the irony is not a satire: it is a device for confronting the viewer with a complex response even where simple condemnation would otherwise suggest itself as a self-evident reaction.

Another aspect of Kren's later work which extends his involvement in the direction he shared with the Direct Art movement can be seen in two other films, one of which, at least, displays a similar psychological ambivalence. They are both concerned with the existential question of bodily function. The first of these, *16/67 – 20 September*, is a relatively simple didactic work using rapid interchanging montage to establish an experiential link between the acts of pissing and drinking, and shitting and eating. But the more recent *26/71 – Balzac und das Auge Gottes* (Balzac and the Eye of God) cannot be so simply explained by its evident content. This is simple enough, confronting the spectator with the facts of sexual response to strangulation. In turn, both a man and a woman hang themselves. The man has an erection and ejaculates (a normal response in hanging and the basis for a not uncommon but risky sexual deviation) into the woman's mouth. After a conventional fuck while still hanging, he comes down. She is then strung up and fucked from behind, after which she proceeds to shit copiously into the eye of God in one corner, while the caption 'Aber Otto' ('but Otto', a cryptic reference to Muehl) appears in the other. The whole film is over in thirty seconds and is hand-drawn animation, originally made directly, frame by frame on 35mm (reduced to 16mm for the projection version). As one would expect from the technique used, the film has the visual comedy of a Popeye cartoon, counteracting the psychological weight of the imagery. This film illustrates Kren's extreme self-irony and the ambivalent attachment–detachment of his accommodation structure. In the Muehl/Brus axis of his work, this element of content is more accessible. But in a way more difficult to define, such ambivalence imparts a charge, through a knife-edge of rejection, to the imagery in all his work.

The psychological approach is inevitable for many of Kren's films, but almost all his work raises philosophical questions about the relationship between experience and structure. Almost all his films, including those in the middle period, have used systems to govern either the editing or shooting. In most cases this has taken the form of preparatory diagrams and graphs drawn with mathematical precision, indicating the various correlations of shots and their durations. Whatever the general implications of using mathematical systems for ordering experience, considering how, with constant projection speed, the single-frame unit of cinematography provides a simple link between duration and number, in film, system becomes particularly apt. In this attempt to order experience through film, Kren has made this number/duration correlation basic, discovering for it a variety of functions and potentialities. The germ for most of these functions can be traced to his first four films, but because the development is not tidy and some films characterise a direction well, while other films take more than one direction, I will not consider the work chronologically.

In classical montage, shots follow each other in a combination intended either to maintain the illusory flow of action, or as in the Eisenstein sense, to maximise the dramatic, expressive collision between them. From his first 16mm film, Kren has counteracted both the narrative and expressive concepts of montage through mathematically organised montage configurations. Consequently, many of his films make use of a limited number of repeated shots in various combinations and lengths. Though some of his films, like *3/60 – Bäume im Herbst*, employ system at the shooting stage. In these the connection between shots should not be considered as montage in any sense, a problem to which I shall return when considering the structuralist question.

I will again begin with some of the middle period films, for while I find the Muehl action films, like *6/64 – Papa und Mama*, *7/64 – Leda und der Schwan* or *9/64 – O Tannenbaum*, quite satisfactory works as a whole, I find their use of system the least aesthetically challenging. In spite of the strong content, it is in these films that the montage is most abstract, in a sense, with the greatest divorce between image and system. As in most of his work, these films are constructed from shots fragmented into very short lengths, rarely longer than one second, and frequently as short as a few frames. In the Muehl action films, the result of this fragmentation is to minimise recognition of the objects in favour of increasing attention to their abstract qualities of colour, texture and movement. The systems explore an intricate network of links based on these abstract qualities. In addition, the rhythm of the montage itself in these films tends to work as a 'musical' composition, the system giving an overall co-ordinating shape. Although the rhythm of movements within the shots in these films may combine with the rhythm of the montage, because Kren more typically uses fairly static images and camera, the montage rhythm is frequently a dominant feature of his work. Kren has developed a considerable control of visual rhythm in this musical sense, the concepts being comparable with the note-row techniques of Schoenberg rather than with more classical compositional ideas. As with Kubelka's *Adebar* and *Schwechater*, this visual abstraction of the shots and musical concept of montage is consistent with the aims of the early avant-garde abstract films, though in Kren this never becomes a graphic light-play, and always maintains some link with associative identity, particularly in these films with tactile, body associations.

Even though initiated within a similar compositional concept of system, certain of his works lead in another direction. In *20/60 – 48 Köpfe aus dem Szondi Test* and *11/65 – Bild Helga Philip*, for example, the element of perceptual enquiry becomes dominant. Watching the films provides the basis of information about optical and cinematic functioning, which becomes the films' chief content. Especially in *48 – Köpfe aus dem Szondi Test*, where a set of still photographs of faces (the contents of a box originally intended for an obscure psychological test) are sequentially permutated using different rates of image change, the system provides the visual changes in information but does not constitute a unifying composition in the classical sense. This shift in attitude, where the film becomes, as it were, perceptual raw material, makes way for a reflexive engagement by the viewer, where his own, rather than the film-maker's, perception and reaction become the primary content.

Kren's use of system provides an opportunity to look for some clearer edge to the loose terminology of structural film. In my view, there are very few cases where any useful relationship can be drawn between the so-called structuralist films and the broad field of structuralism in general. System and structure should not be used synonymously. Almost all Kren's films are systemic, but only a certain group raise structuralist questions. (Though in the loose concept of structuralist film which persists, all his work would be classed as structural.)

Broadly, I see structuralism as a result of the dialectical problem of the concept of order (ordering) in relationship to experience. In this respect, far from being in conflict with existentialism, it can be thought of as a development from it, making extreme subjectivity compatible with order by removing from the notion of structure either an *a priori* or authoritarian implication (the main bases of existential rejection of order). Order is no longer seen as a fixed, immutable condition of the world, but the consequence of changing and developing acts of ordering. While there is a recognition that no fixed structure for experience exists, there is also a recognition that there can be no neutral state of unconditioned experience. The development of experience depends on developments of structuring. I see the movement from Cézanne to analytical Cubism as the historical basis of visual structural art. Structuralism in art would seem to imply a broadly representational, or more accurately, homological, condition. This 'homology' is defined by Lévi-Strauss as an analogy of functions rather than of substance. In *The Structuralist Activity*,[3] Roland Barthes talks of a process whereby the structuralist decomposes the real and then recomposes it. The reconstructed 'object', which I take to imply mainly the structuralist art object, is described as a simulacrum of the 'natural object' and is seen as 'intellect added to object'. He stresses that 'between the two objects, or two tenses, of structuralist activity, there occurs *something new* …' (Barthes's italics). Structuralist art can be thought of as the material formation of experience through the explicit incursion into the thing (event) observed by the mode of observation. In this sense, structuralist art does not *express* experience derived from the world: it *forms* experience in the trace of a dialectic between perceiver and perceived. It is perhaps this concentration on structure as process or activity which most recommends the project to the time-based film medium at the present time. However inadequate it might be later, I would like for now to confine the use of the term structuralism in film to situations where the space/time relations of a filmed situation are reformed or transformed through a definable structuring strategy into a new 'experiential' (as opposed to didactically conceptual) homology. In this notion of structuralism, while the shape or wholist element of Snow's films, most evidenced in *Wavelength*, would not constitute a structuralist problem, the transformation (or fusion) of time/space in the experience of his ↔ and *Central Region* would. In both cases, the space/time experience can be thought of as a homology brought about by the consistent application of a camera strategy.

Kren's first structuralist film then is *3/60 – Bäume im Herbst* (*Trees in Autumn*, incidentally the first film in general I would call structuralist). Its structuralism is a result of the application of system, not to subsequent montage of material already filmed with an unconstrained subjectivity, but to the act and event of filming itself. This limitation, by narrowing the space and time range of the shot material, gives rise to a greater integrity in the film as homologue. In *Bäume im Herbst* the new space/time fusion of the experience of branches shot against the sky *is* the plasticity of the shooting system become the relations of the objects – shots, and their space/time

observational relations are inseparable. Structural process becomes object. This prefigures Snow's ↔ and echoes the plasticity of time/space relations in a Giacometti
painting. Though similar conditions occur in a number of Kren films, particularly
the window sections in *5/62 – Fenstergucker, Abfall etc.* and *17/62 – Grün-Rot*, it is
most perfectly illustrated in *28/73 – Zeitaufnahme(n)*, a film which has a striking
relationship to a Giacometti portrait (I would cite Giacometti as the clearest
example of a contemporary structuralist painter).

Kren's preparatory drawings for the shooting of this 'portrait head' film show how
he sees filmic space as a result of the interaction between various focal lengths of
lens, the minimally changing camera position and the rates of change of both. Sections of the film have successions of single-frame shots made with small changes of
viewpoint, and other sections superimpose viewpoints on each other. In the film,
the transparent, vibrating head defines its space/time image as a function of the filming procedure. As in *Bäume im Herbst*, it is the nature of the relations established
between the separate 'shots' (significantly different in kind to montage relations
through editing) which determine it as a structural homologue. In a sense, what is
represented in these films is neither the trees nor the head (as Strauss's 'substance'),
but instead, the space/time relations of the film viewing and shooting process (as
'functions'). Objects are seen as an amalgam with their space and especially with
their time as the process of their accessibility through acts of perception. So again,
what is 'represented' in the films is not a tree or a head but a filmic act of perception. It is also not represented in the sense that the film becomes a description,
expression or even model for the generalised act of perception existing prior to the
'representation'. The films are acts of perception taking place under particular constraints of procedure and medium – acts of film-perception. The result of this
activity is a genuinely new 'object' (the film being Barthes's second tense of structuralist activity) wherein certain 'postulates' of time/space procedure have been
added to the 'natural object' (Barthes's first tense of structuralist activity).

That film structuralism, structuralism in literature or anthropology, differ, relates
to the specificity of the medium. In the same way in which a Truffaut or Godard
film, illusionistically portraying an existentialist hero, is because of its interior filmic
relations not an existentialist film, so a structuralist film is not defined simply by the
structuralist attitude of its maker. There must be an integrity between the capacities
and material properties of the medium and the structural procedures adopted. That
these procedures are not confined to the application of numerical system, but can
be achieved through other strategies, is evident through films like *Bedroom* by Gidal
or Snow's *Central Region*. However, I have drawn the structural definition in this
instance in a very narrow way, including the provision that the work should have an
homologous relationship with a particular observational situation, so that the two
tenses of structuralist activity may be appreciated within the film.

Some of the difficulties of maintaining this narrow definition in the light of some recent conceptual and reflexive works are also raised in Kren's *15/67 – TV*. Although the filming situation is narrow in this film, being confined to five short sequences all filmed from within a dockside café, the work does not aim to be a homologue of the space/time relations intrinsic to the situation and procedure of the filming itself. The filmed sequences are largely separated from their representational function, to become the subject of subsequent systematisation where their relationships within the film presentation are much more significant than the procedural relationship with their origin. The broad effect and historical significance of this film lies in shifting the emphasis of structural activity away from the film-maker's ordering of his filmic subject to that of the spectator's structuring of the filmic presentation. The film's viewer must engage in a speculative, reflexive structuring of the film as it proceeds. There are of course a number of other undeniable levels of content in the work. These include the subjective choice of situation and image by the film-maker, his attitude to the act of filming, and the similarly subjective choice of mathematical system and its application in the film. But by far the most significant level of content in *TV* is the viewer's awareness of his own behaviour in structuring the experience of the film itself. This is not simply an attempt to elucidate the film-maker's hidden system, but an experience of the various phases, stages and strategies which are encountered in the act of attempting to structure the events of the film.

The five sequences (each appears twenty-one times in all) are sufficiently similar to each other to ensure that the initial problem faced is the discrimination of the shots themselves. All the shots, which are about one and a half seconds long, are separated from each other by periods when the screen is black. Again the viewer begins to discriminate the differences in black duration, becoming aware that there is a consistent pattern and that this forms a system of punctuation, first separating the shots, then longer gaps between the 'sentences' (groups of five shots), then even longer gaps marking the ends of the 'paragraphs' (which vary in length). At a certain stage of discrimination and recognition of the shots and their pattern of combination, the viewer begins to speculate, attempting to predict the development; and this prediction is subsequently confirmed or denied by the film. Though the system is basically logical, it is not ultimately consistent as a permutation or symmetrical structure. In some more recent films like Bill Brand's *Moment* and even Hollis Frampton's *Zorns Lemma*, a similar concept has tended to become a more mechanistic puzzle, encouraging the viewer to identify content with a specific solution to the 'scrambler'. The inconsistency in Kren's system eliminates any simple goal for the viewer's reflexive, structural activity. In *TV*, the viewer is drawn into a mode of behaviour by the systemic aspect of the film, but not permitted to identify 'content' with a systemic abstract of the work. The content, which continues to develop after repeated viewings and even when fully aware of the system, lies in the experience of the stages of a structural activity from perceptual discrimination, to awareness of a rhythm of repetition, to the conscious use of memory and prediction in conceptual patterning.

In the same way in which I would quote *Bäume im Herbst* as the first structural film, I would quote *TV* as the first thoroughly realised work of reflexive cinema transferring the primary arena for structuralist activity to the viewing of the film itself.

Notes

1. See Malcolm Le Grice, *Abstract Film and Beyond* (London: Studio Vista, 1976).
2. Kren has recently released another Brus 'action' film, *Silberaktion Brus* (Silver Action), completed at the same time. At the present both films are confusingly numbered *10/65*, though they are quite separate works.
3. From *Essais Critiques* (1964). Translation by Richard Howard in *Partisan Review*, Winter 1967.

6

Some Introductory Thoughts on Gidal's Films and Theory [1979]

Like a large proportion of experimental film-makers, Peter Gidal came to film from the background of modern painting and is of the generation which was influenced by, but sought ways out of, abstract expressionism. Also, like a number of film-makers, he played a little jazz. Though he had no serious ambitions in this direction, at some time more critical attention might well be given to the significant influence which the ethics and aesthetics of jazz improvisation have had in the attention to process in art.

His first film *Room 1967*, which I knew as *Room (Double Take)*, was followed in the next two years by half a dozen films produced simultaneously with a number of written works published as articles in *Cinemantics* (1970); five essays on films by Snow, Dwoskin, Iimura, Warhol and myself in *Ark* (also in 1970) and a book on Warhol (1971). This pattern of film production and publication of critical/theoretical writing continues.

I first encountered his work through a screening of *Room 1967* at the Arts Laboratory, Drury Lane in 1968. Though I was critical of the film's dénouement – the image of a reclining man, 'stoned' and smoking from a hubble-bubble – I was particularly impressed by the slow camera movement over the unspectacular surfaces and objects of a room and even more so by the extreme device of an absolute repeat of the whole film. At that period in London, with so little work in experimental and independent film, it was particularly important to discover another film-maker whose sensibility was sufficiently close to my own to help reinforce the more radical (and consequently least acceptable) aspects of my own work. At that time, except for some art students making tentative experiments with film, Gidal, and when I saw their work in 1969, Birgit and Wilhelm Hein, were the only film-makers whose work I felt close to aesthetically (and ideologically).

Since then, my work and Gidal's has frequently been bracketed together, most recently under the term structural/materialist (a Gidal formulation) – the bracketing being applied equally to the films and theoretical writing. This double harness has caused us both some problems, obscuring the differences between our work; none the less, with the level that the public critical debate has reached, I would rather have my position confused with his than with any other film-maker. Which is to say, as the lines are drawn to date, in spite of our differences, there are considerable areas of agreement between us. In the strict sense, we have never developed a joint position nor presented any co-operative manifesto, but we have had many long conversations over the last decade which have influenced the development of our positions considerably.

It would be impossible to trace the path of those discussions, the effects of which have become incorporated in our work, but it is partly to develop some of the thoughts which have passed between us recently that I am writing this introduction. As Gidal pointed out when he asked me if I would do it, I have never written on his work at any length (nor he on mine for that matter) – though we have been publicists for each other. I could not let this preamble pass without pointing out that if the fact of film-makers writing on each others' films seems a little incestuous – before cries of nepotism – if some of the critics in this country had spent a little more time on the current British film culture we could have spent more of our time on film and theory and less on publicity, reviewing and polemics.

Our most general area of collaboration, which I will not dwell on, has concerned the development of the working context for experimental film. We have both been deeply committed to establishing conditions for production, presentation and distribution of independent film in a pattern radically different from that of the dominant film industry. Gidal, like myself and a number of other avant-garde filmmakers, has put a considerable amount of time into these issues through entirely practical and frequently mundane tasks mainly within the London Film-makers' Cooperative, but also within the Independent Film-makers' Association and on committees in the British Film Institute.

Our most general area of agreement has been a deep hostility to the way in which international capitalist corporations have controlled the development of film culture and the effect this has had on the predominant assumptions about film structure. This hostility has been expressed variously as an opposition to narrative, illusionism, identification, catharsis and so on. As the dialogue between Gidal and myself has become more sophisticated, some of the approaches to these oppositions have differed in detail, but the underlying resistance to compromise with the forms and mechanisms of dominant cinema remains common. If my own recent films have related themselves overtly to the problems of narration, identification and cinematic illusion, it is because I have encountered them (perhaps in error) as a consequence of the direction of my work.

Gidal has maintained a more distinctly oppositional stance, certainly at the level of theory, frequently expressed in the prefix 'anti-' (anti-narrative, anti-illusion), and while his films would seem to maintain this opposition into their construction, they are more problematic in this territory than the diametric rhetoric would suggest. On the other hand, his major theoretical work, the 'Theory and Definition of Structural/Materialist Film' and its extensive footnotes, traces many of the difficulties and complexities this oppositional enterprise encounters.[1]

To deal with Gidal, it is necessary to consider both his work as a film-maker and a theorist. He has referred to Althusser to support the independence of the two practices and he has further pointed out how historically there have regularly been discrepancies between artists' work and their theorisations and rationalisations. Whatever the independence, one from the other (and it is clear that they are distinguishable discourses), in Gidal's case they should be related to each other. Not only does the theory seem to address some of the films' problems quite accurately, but he has particularly encouraged through the form of presentation of his work, that the achievement of the films, as it were, be tested against those aims defined in the theory.

If we were concerned with a general review of Gidal's work, then like with any other artist, his early films would be seen to contain many of the initial issues which become more clearly reworked later. However, without dismissing his earlier work, it is possible to encounter the most pertinent problems which he raises through reference to a few more recent films and his major theoretical text 'Theory and Definition of Structural/Materialist Film' (*Studio International*, November 1975). Any one of *Bedroom* (1971), *Room Film 1973*, *Film Print* (1974), *Condition of Illusion* (1975), *Fourth Wall* (1978), or *Silent Partner* (1977), can be studied and related to his major theoretical article, and while they are all different works in detail, their concerns are remarkably consistent.

In my book *Abstract Film and Beyond*, I said of Gidal and *Room Film 1973*:

> Gidal's major contribution comes in his concentration on issues of structuring directly related to the act of perceiving through the camera and the projection of the film. His work in this area represents a complex dialectic between subjective existential response on the one hand and a reflexive structural concept on the other. His work is procedural in the sense of establishing specific limitations to his action, like length of film in the camera, the space in which he will work (repeatedly a single room), and the objects which will occupy the space.
>
> His work does not deny his own response to light, surface or the identity of the object, but it contexts this subjectivity within the recognisable limits of the process. In fact his handling of the camera, framing, focus and zoom are clearly apparent, indicating his moment-to-moment response to the visual field. However, he is not aiming to reconstruct his own motives for the viewer, but to alert them to their reflexive attention in relationship to the 'events' which occur before them on the screen. Such systematic devices which Gidal has used, as in *Room Film 1973* where 100-foot continuous takes are broken down into equal five-second units and each one shown twice, maintaining their original

sequence, are concerned with acts of perception, and its various stages of recognition and conception. In it the perceptual stages are deliberately prolonged – an indistinct region of light on the screen will become more definitely a surface, though not clearly the surface of an object. Then it may take on an edge, but the scale has to be guessed at, being gradually confirmed, denied or neither by the film's subsequent progress. Then it may, or may not become recognisable as a book, or a shelf, only for the camera to move on to another region – every stage being drawn out by the nearly indecipherable double view of each segment. Experiences which in our everyday perception are over in an unconscious flash, in Gidal's films become extended processes for conscious attention and structuring.

In discussion with Gidal on the above passage (some of which took place before publication), his main objections revolved around the implications of personal subjectivity, both of the film-maker and spectator. Two or three small changes which I made to the text before publication in response to this objection involved some change of emphasis in this respect. For example, 'His work does not deny his own response to light, surface, or the identity of the object, but it contexts this subjectivity within the recognisable limits of the process', in my original manuscript read: 'His work does not deny *subjectivity or his own particular response* to light, surface or the identity of the object, but it contexts this subjectivity within the recognisable limits of *his* process.' (Italics show the deleted or changed words.) Gidal would have had it read: 'His work does not deny his response to light, surface or object, but it contexts this within the recognisable limits of the process,' and I suspect that even in the form which he would have liked, the implication of the personal subjectivity of the film-maker was still too strong. To understand why Gidal resisted this implication and why I both understood his resistance but determined to maintain it within a modified tone it is necessary to look at the historical context out of which this concern for the 'enunciating source' derives.

As an industrial, corporate system of production, dominant cinema runs directly counter to the radical individual subjective integrity (in its sense of integrated rather than simplistically honest) which underlies the major art movements of the century – Impressionism, Cubism, Surrealism and abstraction in painting; existentialism in literature; serialism, music-concrete and improvisational jazz in music. In conventional cinema, individual responsibility for a work is made impossible by the scale of the corporate production whose modes of finance, systems of production and distribution are determined to serve the social purposes of the corporate producer (private or state). In this context the auteur theory was a desperate critical invention to seek out a form of cinematic integrity which could relate film to the critical modes of the other, individually produced, art forms. This theory, applied to commercial cinema, only served to obscure the lack of radical integrity permissable within cinema. On the other hand, a more pragmatic response to a related motivation (largely made possible by the spread of 16mm facilities during World War II) was the eventual emergence of a cinematic form which could be based on individual production. Though the roots for this form exist in a limited prehistory in the 35mm era, and though the European contribution to this post-war culture (particularly in Austria) is continually played down, its emergence was largely in the US. That this was so can be directly related to the decimation of European economies by the war while the American economy flourished in the role of major producer of the goods needed in Europe for the conduct of the war and subsequent rebuilding. Whatever the economic causes, the concept of personal cinema is now directly bound up with the concept of 'New American Cinema' most adequately characterised by the critical writing of P. Adams Sitney. Simplistically the options of cinematic enunciation might be characterised as, on one hand, the falsely 'neutral', 'omniscient' enunciation of dominant cinema (which poses personality through names of directors, producers and stars, but which is 'falsely' neutral not because of their lack of 'personal' integrity but because its enunciation is that of the hidden cultural ideology expressed through the agents of the corporate production) and, on the other, the personal enunciation of the individual film artist. The first option is relatively easy to reject theoretically even if its effects on film practice and structure are difficult to eradicate. However, the problems implicit in the second option and particularly the forms which this has taken on through the New American Cinema practice are more difficult to articulate.

Before these problems can be engaged it must be pointed out that through the development of a history of 'personal film art' – an actual body of practice which looks and functions differently from the commercial cinema – it is now possible to transpose critical problems from the other fields of modern art to film. And conversely any problems which occur through the concept of individual subjective enunciation in personal cinema apply equally to any other art practice. What must be further pointed out is that this historical body of film work and its equivalents in the other arts form the concrete basis of discourse within which we produce film works. Our options (and the critical interpretation of our choices/creations) are determined by this film historical discourse.

Gidal's theory, if less demonstrably his film work, is the best focus we have for the consequence of a refusal of both options of enunciation. Here we begin to encounter some confusion which the rhetoric, or polemics of negation brings about. It serves Gidal's purpose (and is in many cases correct) to stress the latent narrativity and identificatoryness which continues to reside in the cinema whose history is posed as the alternative to dominant cinema. In other words while he shows up the limits of radicality of New American Cinema in its assumed non-narrativeness by highlighting its recuperations – that remains the cinema whose history forms the major constraint for Gidal's filmic articulation. This is not to say that Brecht in particular does not constitute a major influence for Gidal's practice or that Godard was not a significant point of reference, but the actual filmic articulation which emerges from Warhol or Brakhage is already more Brechtian, even if unrecognised as such, than the expressly Brechtian aim of Godard or Straub-Huillet becomes when translated to film. In effect, though expressed differently, Gidal's critique of this latent narrativity in NAC (NAC is not confined as a body of work to the US, but is also produced in England, Germany etc.) is similar to my own: through the rejection of depicted stories, acted out between the characters, the 'person' of personal cinema has become the first-person singular, as it is in the, by now, classic existentialist novel. But, while no characters or narrative action may be depicted, if the co-ordinating factor of a film's structure is the subjectivity of the film-maker, even without overt diarist or autobiographical intention, the film veers towards the narrative interpretation where the film-maker (unseen) replaces the chief protagonist of a more conventional narrative film. The American critical tendency, by stressing the film-maker as text, through a continuation of the mythology of romantic individualism (fundamental to the American hero) has helped to reinforce this 'veering' even where (in another critical framework) other, radical aspects may have been definable within works. We have then a radical change of form in the rejection of 'omniscient' enunciation towards the subjective and existential enunciation of personal cinema but a reversion to narrative, identification through the route of film-maker as individual, heroic central text of the work. This veering is not simply an issue in the interpretation of a particular film, but through subsequent production, the 'interpretation' becomes inscribed in the forms and devices of work which follow, unless it is dislodged. A hand-held camera, for example, comes to be interpreted as representing the film-maker's subjective vision and as the culture develops, this inscription of meaning for hand-held camera movement becomes predetermined – becomes part of 'the language' – and refined in subsequent films within those terms.

Gidal not only vehemently rejects narrative as it is understood in conventional cinema, he rejects a broad 'narrativity' as it comes to reappear in 'experimental' film variously through: the replacement of story diegesis by coherent (mechanistic) 'structure'; the illusion of documentary transparency (particularly under the guise of representing the process of a film's making); and most centrally, through any form of anthropomorphic, individualist identification with the film-maker.

This fundamental opposition to identification with the film-maker raises difficulties in general concerning the non-identification of self, either of the film-maker/self or the spectator/self. In footnote 12 to 'Theory and Definition …', Gidal says: 'This psychological centring of the self must be nullified in order to be able to set up a concept of dialectically posited distanciated self.' It has particular difficulties in the location of 'responsibility' for the source of enunciation. This in turn reflects a general political difficulty as the location of an extreme individual integrity of formu-lation frequently represents the only form of opposition to the enculturated ideology, at the very least in our culture, individual integrity seems invariably to be the initi-ating source of such opposition. In this sense, Gidal's sought-for 'anonymity' for the film-maker should clearly not be interpreted as a revision from individual responsi-bility to the loss of self in the 'corporate'. What is deducible from the theory is a general 'aim', involving transformation in the assumption of psycho-social relations with film as an agency in this transformation. In this project, 'Theory and Definition of Structural/Materialist Film' functions as a lure (or goad) and it is in this func-tioning that its discourse intersects with that of film-making (its intersection with film criticism might be different). That Gidal posits a desire for a relatively defined form of anonymity (footnote 2 cautions '… but a superficial anonymity brought into false existence through such things as "coldness" – heavy atmospheric intervention – functions precisely as the opposite of its supposed intention') does not, of itself, assist directly in discovering the form which such a desired quality would need to take up in a film. That Gidal recognises this difficulty of transposition from theory to practice is indicated through the following sentences of the same footnote:

> Anonymity must in fact be created through transformation dialectically posited into the filmic event itself. That is, anonymity must be the result, at a specific instance; it too must be produced rather than illustrated or obliquely 'given' in a poetical sense.

This footnote is used to clarify the following notion in the text: 'The content thus serves as a function upon which, time and time again, the film-maker works to bring forth the filmic event.' This theoretical notion applied to painting might be illus-trated by the way in which Jasper Johns works on and into the image/form of a target to the point that an 'event' of painting is brought forth or traced in the resultant object. The process of *Room Film 1973* may be interpreted in a similar way where certain choices as to the filming space, the lighting, the length and type of film material to be used might be seen as analogous to the target, and where the film-maker's looking-at/working-on through the manipulations of the camera and subsequent working-on through the structuring of the material – in this film the five-second repeating segmentation and a sequence of optically stretched image – brings forth what is specific to that filmic event.

This concept suggests that the anonymity of the film-maker is achieved primarily through establishing the autonomy of the produced work – albeit a work which does not efface the traces of its worked-on-ness and is a work of process. Wherever Gidal's theory moves away from negation (the definition of what should be opposed) and ventures to indicate that which might be affirmed he tends towards what might be described as belonging to filmic presence – 'materialist flatness, grain, light movement ...' (or the presence of time's passage, 'duration', which is too complex an issue to be dealt with here).

Gidal proposes this 'materialist flatness, grain, light movement' as a dialectic polarity with the 'supposed real reality that is represented'. There is certainly an echo in this concept of the quite fundamental historical step in modern painting and sculpture whereby the pictorial illusion was counteracted through attention to physical properties of the medium itself. In the history of avant-garde film, the opposition to narrative, illusion and identificatory content has largely been through an attempt to determine works outwards from the materials and mechanisms special to the medium. Though this development has taken place much later in film than in the other arts (which I have described in terms of general historical retardation in *Abstract Film and Beyond*), as an aesthetic fact it is less of a problem than its adequate theorisation. Gidal and I have frequently been criticised in our attempts to relate the attention to film's material substances and processes to 'materialism'. For example, Peter Wollen saw it as seeking an ontology based on an essence of cinema, taken up again by Anne Cottringer in her criticism of 'Theory and Definition ...' and extended to a critique, via Derrida, of the concept of presence (as physical presence) which she understands as fundamental to Gidal's formulation.[2] She quotes Derrida:

> To question the secondary and provisional character of the sign, to oppose it to a 'primordial' difference, would thus have the following consequences:
>
> 1. Difference can no longer be understood according to the concept of 'sign' which had been taken to mean the representation of a presence and has been constituted in a system (of thought or language) determined on the basis of and in view of presence.
> 2. In this way we question the authority of presence or its simple symmetrical contrary, absence or lack.

What must be pointed out, with reference to Gidal's theory and more evidently his films, is that the notion of filmic (physical) presence is seen by him as dialectical. While his argument seems at times to move towards the unproblematic physical 'reality' of the filmic materials as 'present', at least as the pole of a dialectic which counteracts the apparent (illusory) presence of the filmed objects, he has clearly opposed the kind of seeming complete autonomy of the physical film object which abstraction might be thought to offer. Like Cottringer, I have had problems with Gidal's tendency to use the term 'dialectic' where it might be interpreted as 'diametric' and it was partly in response to this concept of presence in his theory (and as a critique of Metz where similar confusions occur) that I wrote (in a paper prepared for the March 1979 Milwaukee Conference on Film Language):

In a film which, for example, draws attention to the screen surface, the projector beam, the intermittent mechanism or whatever 'material' aspect might be chosen, is it correct to assume that the signifier is present? At the moment that the signifier functions as a signifier, whatever the medium, it becomes transparent. Attention to the signifier in its material sense (as the signifying substance) does not escape the process of standing for that which it is not. It is incapable of standing for itself in any more than a representation of some *aspect* of its properties. Films which may be described as working on the signifier counteract transparency more by making aspects of the signifying *process* evident (tracing the path of shifts and transformations between signifying substance and signification) than by asserting the unproblematic presence of the signifier ... The signifier is neither unproblematically present as substance, nor absent as signification.

Though Gidal may talk of 'materialist flatness, grain, light movement', in a film like *Room 1967* a grasp or utilisation of their 'presence' is just as problematic for the spectator as a grasp of the photocinematically represented objects which they seem to become – dissolve in and out of.

It would be right to be critical if either the theory or the films advocated that an oscillation between the unproblematic illusion of the presence of objects and the unquestionable reality of the presence of the filmic materials constituted a dialectic. We must beware that attention to certain problems in the theory does not obscure that the films are made in relationship to the options in a certain film history. When Gidal, like any other film-maker, makes choices in the production of a work he does so within the constraints of that historical discourse and the strategies which he can adopt as a film-maker are highly determined by what has already been filmically articulated. The choice, for example, to hand-hold the camera rather than place it on a tripod will tend to orientate the resulting images towards certain meanings – these meanings will derive from previous work by the film-maker and other film-makers within the culture. They are not escapable, they can only be transformed in the practice through detailed shifts demanding other interpretations.

It is tempting to say that Gidal has developed a language or vocabulary of camera movement. This would be misleading but would hint at the sophistication of his sensibility (worked for over a large number of films) to the nuances of interpretation and meaning which have formed themselves around certain manoeuvres and devices. If, for example, a camera moves in a particular way close to a body or object as in Takahiko Iimura's *Ai* (*Love*) of 1966 this enables certain implications of tactility to be inscribed into the filmic, visual aesthetic – the camera becomes not just hand-held but is in a sense 'hand/touch'-held. Or Warhol's sudden zoom into Marie Menken in *Chelsea Girls*, followed immediately by a slow drift away from the detail it so eagerly seemed to seek out, inscribes the complexity of a desire to see more closely followed by an almost immediate disenchantment either with what is revealed or with the motive which led to the earlier impulse – or at least, if the meaning is to be considered at all in such a verbal equivalent it might be expressed in this way (though any real grasp of its meaning can only become available through familiarity with the filmic, camera movement discourse in its own terms).

Gidal's camera movements, particularly in *Bedroom, Room Film 1973, Condition of Illusion*, and *Fourth Wall*, however much he would want it otherwise (or however much he would like it played down critically) are at one level predicated on the sensual lure and the visual pleasure which he derives from the objects looked at (already an aware sublimation of a sexual object onto another object even before the film is shot). The camera slowly moves over the beautifully patterned bedspread (or rug, which Gidal chooses because he already finds it visually pleasurable), and even where it encounters objects with no intrinsic implications of beauty, their separation (framing) from their visual and more important, utility, contexts transforms them into 'to-be-looked-at-objects'. This is one level of the inscription of desire in the objects, their images and in the camera's movements. But, at the same time as Gidal is lured by the objects he sees, by the images they form in the viewfinder, by the movement of the image in the frame, he also resists this lure – refuses to give greater attention to an object which for some reason appeals more, perhaps refusing to indicate a response (the slight refusal may even be inscribed in a momentary hesitation on, then acceleration from, the object), or moves away purposefully, or lets the camera seemingly drift down and away. Both the lure and his resistance are inscribed minutely in the camera movement and thereby recorded as a trace in the photosensitivity of the film. This set of moment-to-moment decisions and the sensibilities on which they are based are made even more complex by a learned prediction about their likely effect (their probable transformation or reordering) when they are projected and confronted by a spectator. In this consideration for the image, as it is to be in its utilisation by the spectator, might be found some of the reasons for the various resistances inscribed with the visual lure, into the image. 'Why', Gidal might be asking of himself through the movement of the camera 'should the spectator of this film be un-resisting subject to the exercise of my visual pleasures and sublimations?' He is not only resisting his own lure (resisting in a way which transforms rather than negates or ignores) but he also inscribes the possibility of resistance of the spectator. In this way, in a sense, as film-maker, he becomes the spectator's representative – linking his attractions, attachments and resistances to theirs.

This inscription, not only of Gidal's resistance to (distanciation from) the lure of the sensual, sublimated visual object but also of the spectator's possibility of similar resistance is not just a parallel resistance to the sensual object(s) photographed in the image, it is an attempted inscription of the spectator's possibility of resistance to the identification with the pleasure of the film-maker in that object or even an identification with the film-maker's act of resistance. In Gidal's films, the first level of resistance, that of the film-maker to the lure of the object, is chiefly inscribed through the action of the camera in its 'looking-at' the space – variously through: motion; distance; focal length's effect on perspective; zoom or focus. The second level, the attempt to distanciate the spectator from identification with the enunciator, is chiefly inscribed through devices like: repetition; graining out or darkening out of the image in printing; or disruptions in the flow of images and motion. It is particularly in the devices of the second level of distanciation – the effects on the screen of 'material flatness, grain, light movement' – where Gidal, in an attempt to produce a condition for the spectator of response to the film, rather than identification with the film-maker, that he has recourse to those features 'intrinsic' to film. In his attempt to reduce ('eliminate' his rhetoric would tend to demand) identification with the film-maker, he attempts to stress the film act itself. The film work presented as a film *work* is an attempt to permit the spectator to utilise, appropriate, transform the film unencumbered by the ego of the film-maker – its terms are public rather than private – a public discourse. However, the terms of this discourse, the attempted definition of properties as if intrinsic to the film (even if open to criticism as a tendency towards 'an ontology based on an essence of cinema'), are a condition of a particular stage within the history of a cinema transformation – again, not primarily in the arena of theory, but in the films themselves.

Two uncertainties must be expressed at this point. The first asks: Is Gidal's attempt to produce an autonomy for the film work to be interpreted entirely within the concept of effacement of the film-maker as personal ego-centre of the film's construct, or does it seek a more absolute autonomy as object and experience from all other objects and experience – is it to some extent predicated on a definably modernist artistic endeavour of direct phenomenalistic response to the art object?

The second asks, as an extension of the first: If the attempt to produce a degree of autonomy for the film work through its operation in the discourse of film as film is to be considered as historically dialectic, either in the film-making or film-viewing discourse, does this not both undermine its autonomy as object (even process-object) and tend to reinstate as problematic the ego of the film-maker as enunciator, as producer within the dialectic?

My inclination of course is to assume that the second question is more appropriate to Gidal's work, but the doubt adds weight to Cottringer's critique of Gidal's concept of presence as metaphysical. Even momentarily, a belief that 'at least' in the physical presence of the film object countering the illusion of presence of the depicted objects, but at the same time substituting for the sense of loss in their disappearance from the screen, would tend to locate the film in a secure ideal position outside of history and outside the materialist contingencies of production.

My own, and I suspect Gidal's, unwillingness to abandon the theoretical issues concerning filmic materiality and, more important, the film constructions to which they relate stems from the current condition of cinema. These constructions represent the only counteraction to transparent belief in the presence of the depicted scene in terms other than literary devices being transposed to film. For example, attempted verbal deconstruction of the image in Godard's *Letter to Jane*, apart from its own ideological entrapment of simply replacing one secure but dubious reading for another, fails to engage the photocinematic image on the level of the photocinematic. The literary/verbal cinematic component itself being *unproblematised* as authoritative enunciation, as signification, as recording, as auditory 'substance' – in other words, if unproblematic in its terms as a *cinematic* component – is capable of making little more than a gestural problematisation of the cinematic component of image. A verbal reinterpretation of an image is only a partial aid to the transformation of the image *as image* (though a thorough critique of image signification of course has a function in the developing discourse of cinema).

Gidal's adherence to a concept of 'the cinematic', rather than being interpreted as purist, or idealist should be seen as a recognition that the primary arena in which the condition of filmic discourse must be changed is that of the cinematic image itself. He is concerned with the transformation in the meaning of the cinematic image through the transformation of the image not through the surface of its interpretation. The area of meaning of the image on which Gidal primarily works concerns the function of that image in the support and structure of the ego. His films are a dialectical enterprise, resisting, counteracting and transforming the cinematic image (a flow of image in duration) and transforming simultaneously the functioning of that image in the structure of the ego. The work, as I have shown is made doubly complex in this respect through Gidal's representation to himself, in the production of the work, of the condition of the relationship between the spectator's ego and his own as film-maker. In this way, not only is the source of enunciation made an issue in the work, but so are its structures of coherence and most importantly, the status of the film-maker's discourse in relationship to that of the film's spectator.

That Gidal establishes devices for a distanciation of the spectator from the work, veering towards an aesthetic autonomy for the work and its durational period of encounter, does not eliminate that the work traces the film-maker's transformational processes. The film-making discourse is unavoidably privileged in status (in power and effect within the cinematic discourse as a whole) over the film-viewing discourse. However much the spectator is placed by the work in a position of appropriation rather than consumption, the terms of this encounter are inevitably the traces of another (more economically privileged) encounter, that of the film-maker's discourse.

While the predominant conditions of the current critical discourse tend to produce forms which personalise and subjectivise enunciation (or worse, revert to the false neutrality of unspecifiable enunciation of commercial cinema), I should beware of stressing the conservative aspect of Gidal's work against its more radical aspiration (albeit so often formulated as a negation almost to the extent of classic nihilism). But it can only lead to a confusion if the aspirational rhetoric – anti-narrative, anti-illusion, anti-identification, anti-anthropomorphism, or, the '... psychological centring of the self ... nullified ... to set up' the 'dialectically posited distanciated self' – was thought to be simply accomplished by the films. These theoretical aspirations are components in a complex definition of aim which guides aspects (and only aspects) of Gidal's film-making, wherein they become transformed to more detailed, particular effects. In many respects though, the films are about that which they oppose – illusion, psychological centering and even narrative. But they are also about that opposition, its difficulties and obstacles in the culture, embodied in both film-maker and spectator, and they are in filmic terms about the definition and transformation of those difficulties to new forms, states and definitions of the problem.

References

1. 'Theory and Definition of Structural/Materialist Film' in *Structural Film Anthology* (London: BFI, 1976).

2. Peter Wollen, 'The Two Avant-Gardes', *Studio International*, November/December 1975. At the time of preparing this collection I am unable to retrieve the publication details of Cottringer's article.

7

Takahiko Iimura – Getting the Measure of Time [1998]

Though I shall concentrate on Taka Iimura's consistent exploration of time and space perception through film, there is also a range of work from the political – *Film Strips II*, the erotic – *Ai (Love)*, the poetic – *Ma:Space/Time in the Garden of Ryoan-ji* and the downright comic – *AIUEONN*.

From the early 1960s, though Japanese, Iimura was well known as one of the first generation of the New York underground – for many years, Japanese experimental film was Takahiko Iimura. Identified with Fluxus, the formal aspect of his work which appealed to the European structuralists was already there in one of the first of his films I encountered, Ai made in 1962, with music by Yoko Ono. This film, which abstracted the patterns of light and dark movement on the screen, was created mainly from extreme close-ups of a man and woman in the act of making love. It was erotic, but not through a simple depiction of sex. Its eroticism worked through rhythm and proximity – a metaphor for tactility – as if the camera were a hand passing over a body. The film, rather than the content, is erotic – for much of the film it is impossible to be sure whether the image we see is that of the woman or the man. The surface of the bodies we assume we see in the images becomes fused with the surface of the screen and film-material surfaces. We are constantly made aware that we – the viewers – are superimposing the recognition and identification onto what is merely a pattern of light and dark – a condition in truth of all cinematic images – all images. But additionally in *Ai* we become strongly aware of the separation between the physical and the semiotic – the perception and the recognition. We understand from this work how in creating meaning, at even the most basic level – in the process of recognising a lip, a breast, a wisp of hair – there is a more primitive stage of pre-differentiated sensation. The film, through its form, becomes an arena where we relive that visual learning process, the transitions from raw perception of light and dark, its structuring into coherent pattern, to the projection onto the pattern of a set of associations which make these abstract images stand for a body or a face. This is sexuality embedded deeply in the perceptual and semiotic process.

Of course, I am sure Iimura did not begin this film from theory. Like most art works, it was born out of a complex interrelationship between instinct, response to other works of art, chance, sensibility, provocation and a range of motives and emotions. The experience of *Ai* remains strongly in my memory (certainly now transformed as I have not seen the film for maybe thirty years), but its initial appeal was the evident distance created between its expressive content and the materiality of the image. It was this quality, and a similarity I saw with film ideas being explored in London, which led me to take a serious interest in Taka's work.

In 1970, I had made a film *Spot the Microdot*, where, according to some simple arithmetic patterns or progression of frames, I punched holes directly into the magnetic coated 16mm film used for laying soundtrack. I used the magnetic film because, in projection, it let absolutely no light through, then, with the hole, it let all the projector light hit the screen and thence the retina with the maximum possible contrast. Though containing other features, my film was in part a simple experiment in perception, not unlike some Op Art of the period. It was an experiment into our optical mechanism – persistence of vision, afterimage, colour sensation produced without colour – but extending this concern into the perception of time's passage. When Taka encountered my film he told me of his own experiments made the previous year also using magnetic film for the way in which it produced an extreme optical contrast, in his case, cut in 'full-frame' numerical pattern with sequences of clear leader. As with Peter Kubelka's *Arnulf Rainer* (1960) and Tony Conrad's *Flicker* (1966), I was interested by this use of film to isolate the material of film, the process of cinematography and material perception of the work. I saw Iimura's work becoming overtly and truly experimental by exploring a deliberately restrained range of cinematic experience. In concentrating on this set of problems, often wrongly seen as 'minimalist', Iimura went much, much further than any other film artist in exploring a kind of art-science. Though Taka continues to develop a range of approaches to film, video and now digital work, this concern with the experience of time, its measured passage and the analogy between time and space, has been the main recurring theme at the centre of his work. Of course there are always layers of meaning and interpretation beyond the overt expression – this is true even in the most pared down of Iimura's films – but we can trace his central concern most clearly in a number of films and installations starting in 1968 and going through to the very precise time interval films of the 1980s. It is seen very clearly in the seminal installations like *Timing 1,2,3* from 1972 and films like *Repeated/Reversed Time* (1980) but it is also there in the video work like *Moon Timed* (1971) and in the poetic exploration of the garden at Ryoan-ji made in 1989.

In the installations, *Loop Seen as a Line* and *Timing 1,2,3*, we see Iimura's first attempts to draw a precise connection between the experience of the passage of time and the definition of a space. In these works – and there were many versions and variations – the essential structure is the projection of film loops which include measured intervals – black and clear sections or marks on the film. These films are seen projected onto a screen but also seen traversing space and time as the loop is passed physically across the projection space between projector and screen.

These installations were genuine experiments, not expressions in the traditional artistic sense. Iimura designed and set up the experiment – a restricted set of 'known' inputs consisting of the film/time intervals and spatial distances, held in a concept of the way in which they would interact. Both we as the spectators and Iimura, the film-maker, were in the same position – we were the subjects of this experiment – and the content was not the film as such, but the way in which our experience became constructed and transformed by this experiment. At the first level there was nothing mysterious at all. Iimura did all he could to stress the mundane, matter-of-factness of the installation – it was all very physical and material. However, what was surprising was the way in which, in experiencing these events on the screen, we began to link them with the sense of space defined by the passage of the film across the room. Not only did we have the experience, we also saw how we were having it, and most importantly, we saw how the experience became transformed during the period of looking. We were forming a perceptual, then conceptual, fusion between our experience of temporal interval and the space we, and the film projection, occupied. At a more complicated level, we saw also how an initial experience of the mundane, crude material of the projection and space could become refined and transformed. We saw how something we thought we knew became unknowable and transformed into a refined inner experience based on our transforming perceptions. The mystery was in us not the film.

In the installations, the spatial element, out of which we created the time/space fusions in our experience were linked directly to the physicality of the space. In the very austere film works of measured interval, *Models Reel 1 and 2*, *Plus and Minus*, *1 to 60 Seconds* through to *Repeated/Reversed Time* (made between 1972 and 1980), the spatial analogy with time is not achieved by establishing an actual physical space. In any case, the relationship between a temporal interval in film and the length of film on which it is carried was always arbitrary not absolute (8mm, 16mm, 35mm, fast or slow projection would change this relationship), and disappears all together in a digital system where the intervals have no material carrier.

In the films, Iimura and we (the spectators) rely on other factors for the construction of our experience. These works, which are a variety of experiments with interval using different lengths of alternating black or white film sequences, to numbers on the film, are exasperatingly simple in construction. And we should not underestimate this exasperation. There are no comforting characters with whom to identify, no sexual encounters to intrigue and excite, no demons to scare us and no Tarantino blood splatter to fuel our psychoses – Iimura's films are more disturbing than this. They are empty and through them we confront absence. We are thrown back onto ourselves and our own experience of the empty time or space. However, the object of Iimura's work is not this confrontation itself. They are not Dadaist nor are they Minimalist for the sake of the minimal. They are, as with the installations, constructed as experiments in which we see ourselves, perceptions and conceptions, as subject. The works have content, they create experience which then becomes meaning – but the content and meaning is located clearly in us not in the films. As with all Iimura's work the initial simplicity is deceptive. At one level we always begin with something which we seem to know completely – there is no mystery – we know the numerical system of the film – we have already been told the end of the story before we start.

Then the film starts. I see intervals of dark and light screen – I perceive the sensation-shock at the retina. At certain frequencies of change I can experience a rhythm (a Gestalt of time). My bodily sense of rhythm 'predicts' the next shock. But at other, longer, intervals I cannot 'feel' the distance between the intervals. I know it is longer but how much longer? I start to make my own rhythm, I start counting in one-second intervals – but is it a second I am counting? How do I know, do I check my watch? – I physically feel my pulse with a finger – try to hear my heartbeat. I am making a measure for myself by which to grasp the intervals and trying to predict the next change. This interior dialogue continues and I begin to see some consistencies in how I structure the time and where I have difficulties. I have moved from the perceptual to the conceptual and now, using memory, am layering recollected experience of one set of intervals on experience of another.

What I thought I knew – a bland description of the abstract system – I am now aware is quite different from my experience. My knowledge is shifting from the identification with the abstract description to an experiential knowledge of my body and mind – its structuring of the experience of time and interval. In more complex works, like *Repeated/Reversed Time*, not only do I experience the different levels of time perception, but by implanting a concept that one duration is to be added-to or subtracted-from another, I am forced to conceptualise a reversing duration, a negative time. I now discover an interplay between a preconception and its ability to make one experience stand for another – as experience not symbol. In all of this, the exasperation with absence is one (necessary) component of the subjective measure of time's passage and the desire for the next moment of sensation is also a desire to fill the absence. Expectation of the sensation is a basic temporal and cinematic response of apprehension (a-pre-hension), suspense is a fundamental consequence of this interplay between absence, sensation, desire and prediction.

Unlike the installations, the physicality of the projection space in these films is not established as an analogue for the temporal experience. As there is no 'represented' space within the picture any fusion between space and time in these works must be conceptual and imaginary. Is this where we find the Japanese concept of Ma?

The conceptual fusion between space and time explored by Iimura is deep in Japanese culture. We can understand better the implications of this fusion if we consider these austere, time-interval films alongside Iimura's film *Ma Space/Time in the Garden of Ryoan-ji*, or perhaps even better by looking at the garden itself, which was first laid out about 500 years ago.

This archetypal Japanese garden – fifteen quite small rocks set in carefully raked gravel, all within a walled rectangular space smaller than a tennis court (as I recall about half the size) – is not to be walked in but sat in and contemplated from a slightly raised wooden terrace on one of its long sides. While at one level, the rocks might be taken to represent islands in a sea or mountains in a plain – perhaps a three-dimensional picture of a larger landscape – the predominant experience is not of romantic projection but of abstract interval. This is based on 'grasping' the spaces between and becoming aware of the differences in size and shape of the rocks which form the points of reference. We are continuously re-appreciating (trying to find a logic for?) the concept of space fused in our experience of a tranquil time of contemplation (I sat there on a warm, quiet, early autumn day). The parallel between the spatial aesthetic of Ryoan-ji – a small number of simple elements widely separated by unfilled space – and the time-interval films of Iimura is easily drawn. This parallel is reinforced by the treatment of the garden in his film which uses slow horizontal tracking shots and zooms (viewed from beside not tracking three-dimensionally between the rocks) as an analogue for time in the spatial experience. This notion of temporal interval as an equivalent for spatial interval is continued in the montage through intercutting poems by Isozaki between the filmed sequences.

In watching the time-interval films, I am reinforced in my suspicion that our conceptual processes for determining interval whether temporal or spatial are similar and difficult to disentangle. Certainly the two forms of experience can be used metaphorically for each other but I am truly not sure of the entire similarity nor how the relationship should be debated. Neither a metaphysical argument about space and time nor the abstract debate around Einstein's space/time continuum would solve this problem. Iimura's films are not a debate in this sense, nor do they lead us to conclusions. They lead us out of (apparent) knowledge through experiment into the uncertainty of our human experience and perhaps to an awareness of its specificity.

It is this grounding in human experience related to concept and to concept as experience which makes Takahiko Iimura's work crucial and a reference point in art. His is an art-science or an art-philosophy which enhances our experience, humanity and understanding.

III

DEBATES

8

Stan Brakhage and Malcolm Le Grice Debate [1978]

In December of 1977 Malcolm Le Grice and Stan Brakhage met in Boulder to publicly debate the issue 'Structural versus Personal Film-Making'. The event was organised by Virgil Grillo and Don Yannacito of the Rocky Mountain Film Center. Both film-makers showed a selection of films prior to the debate. What follows is the entire transcription of the evening's activity.

Introductory Remarks

STAN BRAKHAGE: I'm very happy to begin with this film. It sort of fell out that we begin with this film, *Valentin de las Sierras* of Bruce Baillie's because it so exemplifies some of the things I particularly want to speak for this evening. First of all, that it doesn't look at all like an avant-garde, experimental, or even art movie. Even in the specialised sense of art movies that those desperately courageous people are trying to take away from the pornographers and the documentarists of painters' painting. But it does speak, to me at least, from the beginning in the language of film without feeling the need to speak for itself as film, if you know what I mean – and that it exists very simply on many different levels of meaning. That is, it can be followed through by its shifting changes of colours as a melody – that is colours recur and return in a pattern that is very akin to being melodic. Though it doesn't at all do so in a way that would be any imitation of music. That is, it does so in a kind of searching, struggling, moving, shifting, changing formal way. Along the line of the different shapes that this colour inhabits throughout the film. Those are created not by some obviously superimposed colour, but just very much as he was able to lift that light and those colours thereby off the creatures and the plants, the animals, vegetables and minerals that he's photographing and that it suggests so many things about this village he was living in. I just think of one shot for example: where you have the horse's mane on one side of the image and you have rope on the other, a twist of that. You have an extremely out-of-focus bar of the same colouration as the wheat in the field coming in the near foreground of that image and all of these things, though they have different rhythms within that shot, are in a relationship to each other – by composition, and then as the mind is moved one step further by their actual physical relationship to each other. And so goes this weave of Bruce Baillie's throughout the entire film. I think the bluntest example of his reaching into anything experimental or left field in order to bring out a quality that he had seen and wishes to have the film contain is the superimposition of the ancient statue over the little girl's face – and almost by its being there it demonstrates the subtlety of the rest of the film in leaving the viewer free and in being, in the first place, a film which simply presents, through the concern of the film-maker, the artistry of itself as a final film.

You know what bothers me so much and what's caused me to speak out finally against 'structuralism' as an aesthetic and against many films that don't come under that banner, is what I would call a self-consciousness as I encountered it in a person and an extremely public self-consciousness. It started really in the history of film at the very beginning, because we have a medium that nobody understands what its life is to be. But when it comes to the point that whole films are made primarily about their own coming into existence and being existing and that's the primary level in which the film is speaking – that seems to me as boring almost immediately as those people who are always speaking about their own coming into existence and being existing. And in addition to that – I mean what is so remarkable about Baillie's film is that it can, indeed, be seen in that fashion. I think all of you who experienced it as more than just another documentary – if you can rerun those images in your mind, you can perhaps sense what can easily be proven maybe some other time. This whole film can be run absolutely out of focus and it will hold up out of focus as a purely moving visual. Just the rhythms of these shapes and the shifting tones and colours of them and their movements in relationship to each other will hold up as an absolutely abstract experience and in fact, indeed, just a set-up where people were requested to look at the projector beam going overhead and watch the rhythms of the shifting changes of these tones and the shape of that beam would also have an integral aesthetic experience. That is, one with integrity. So that that possibility exists also within this film without that becoming the primary or indeed the only focus of the film. It can, as well as carrying that, it can also carry symbol in a very subtle and charming way. The children passing through that deck of cards and that they do just naturally seem to, or he did certainly, just naturally catch that pause and that special attention that they give to the sun and to that spot of colour of the sun not only just as symbol but as that possibility and that part of the frame has been retained there for that full blossoming of that circle of red – along the line of the introduction of what looked to me like poinsettias and what begins as a red spot, several images back. So that, again, even symbolism and myth to this extent – he suggests it, and a variety of consciousness of something of these people's lives – and an integrity to film as film as film can exist consonant and not be separated from each other. So it seems to me a film with many arms, many strings that can be played upon, that reaches out to a world in a way which films that concentrate upon film-making do not seem to me to do. I guess that's about all I have to say as an opening statement.

MALCOLM LE GRICE: I think that one of the problems that I feel about the way that this discussion is set up is that it seems as if my function is in some way to defend 'structuralism' – and really I don't think that I feel I should be here to do that. Neither do I think I should be here to attack what Stan calls personal cinema. My interest in this discussion between myself and Stan and hopefully between other people in the audience is to see if we can come to some further clarification about what the categories of activity are. Now I have on a couple of occasions publicly, also, attacked the use of the term 'structuralism' for the kind of work that is going on. It is not a term which I've ever been happy with. Where Sitney first used it, it seemed to me it was very confusing and very loosely used. I never saw the relationship between what Sitney calls 'structuralism' and those things which seem to have gone in the name of 'structuralism' in other fields. The things that came out of Lévi-Strauss, and people like Roland Barthes and so on. I always found it extremely difficult to make some link between that work and work in cinema. And so when I tried to analyse what went on in the period which I think starts in about 1966 when there is clearly some shift in the underlying concept of cinematic practice, I tended first of all to just say it was a broad formal development. A broad concern with form and then in one article in '72 and also in my book I tried to give a broad kind of – not exactly categorisation, but a set of what seemed to me to be the various concerns of that development, not as categories of work, but as a series of definable concerns within the work, which any one work may have more than one of. So it wasn't so much categories as what you might call a set of parameters of concern and interest. On top of which I've also considered a number of the more mechanistic interpretations of the formal development in cinema to be a misunderstanding of the potentialities of concerning oneself with the cinematic language at the same time as one is functioning with the language. And one of the main areas which I've tended to oppose quite strongly is the area which has, in a sense, replaced either narrative or, as it were, the existential, personal, co-ordinator, behind the camera and behind the editing, by the use of some kind of mechanistic system. I think a large part of what I see going on with art schools, under the sort of guise of 'structuralism', is for me a very easy route towards a structural concept, which is the use of some sort of definable mechanistic system, either by which to shoot a film – like taking a number of frames as a basis for a system, or by, after shooting, editing a film. And this broad direction, which I think is the thing most identified with 'structuralism', is I'm sure equally uninteresting to me as it is to Stan. I don't want to speak for Stan. We should almost get him back here now to start the discussion on that.

The other thing is: the question of form. There is a lot of confusion, again, about form. One has to go back to Sitney for this. Form as some kind of unification of the whole. I'm not really happy with that concept either. What I have been proposing almost as an alternative to talking about structure in film – one of the reasons for opposing the notion of structure is its tendency to move towards a kind of a static, skeletal concept – the concept of a skeleton, both form and system tending to function as a skeleton within the film around which content is sort of attached. The concept which I've tended to move towards is one of process and procedure which seems to recommend itself because of the dynamic implications of that – and allowing the concept of, if we want to go back to structure, to be seen as one which permits a dynamic shift during its construction. Which leads to another kind of split in the concept of process, which I feel that I need to make theoretically, and that is the concept of process as the processes of the film-making strategy. That is process from the point of view of film-making. But then there's the whole set of questions which I think are extremely significant and that's the processes of film viewing – the processes by which a film image is read, a film structure is read. I am talking about the audience's viewing of the film, but in a sense, the film-maker is also audience. It seems to me there are two sets of interconnected questions of process which emerge. The processes by which a film is constructed – and process can lead to questions of strategy and various kinds of predetermined devices, and so on and so forth – and the processes of viewing, which means that we have to consider and investigate the structures by which human beings develop their concepts of meaning, develop their concepts of reality, and so forth. I think that I could go on a lot longer with this because each of these questions leads to another question. Just from the point of view of the timing of the whole thing I think that we can take this up further in the second part of the evening.

STAN: I'd like to ask a question. … This is really a farce when you consider that I really wanted to just discuss these matters with Malcolm in my living room. And that is what I said to Don on the phone. I said, 'Gee, I really would like to debate him about that.' I didn't realise the danger about getting into language. I should have said, 'talk to him', or something. Don got all excited, and arranged this debate. But this is not my living room. But my question is, I've noted that you are now skittering out from under the term 'structuralism'.

That's the way it sounded to me. As particularly in New York, when I got up and spoke strongly against the aesthetic of 'structuralism' after biting my tongue for ten years. Suddenly, Annette Michelson, the world famous representative of it among critics in the United States, gets up and in a very haughty manner, proceeded to tell me that it is all over ... even went so far as to suggest that because I come from the sticks or something of that sort – I'm not quoting her, but that was the inference – I didn't realise that this movement was all over. I said 'Annette', and I am going to pose the same thing to you, 'why is it that now that some of us have begun to speak out strongly against it, do you now say it is over or that you are not a representative of it?', because *you* are also world famous as a representative of structuralism. Now you may wish to eschew it or rename it and certainly I have never been happy with any of the names that independent film has had. Independent is the only one that's barely tolerable and I have to share that with every independent documentary film-maker and all those television ad makers and so on all over this country, but I felt no affinity with 'experimental', which was hatched by someone showing contempt for both science and art – to say we weren't making anything, we were just experimenting. 'Underground', I never related to, I live above ground. 'Closet drama', I never related to. 'Psycho drama' certainly sounded offensive to me. But all these terms do have currency in the society and you either are some kind of representative of it, of this drift of persuasion of movie-making that is primarily concerned with the actual structure of the film – you can call it a skeleton or whatever you like – or you are not. Now which are you?

MALCOLM: Well, I'm not really willing to be forced into doing something other than what I've done publicly and in all my writing all the way along. And that is to try to define what we mean. I've got a long history of not wanting, like you, to be put into that kind of category unless we know what that category means. And it seems to me that there are a lot of things which go on inside that area which is being called 'structuralism' which I would want to dissociate myself from. One of those things is that whole development of system art. System in the sense of some kind of editing system, some kind of mechanical system for the shooting of a work. But then it goes into more complex things. For example, with Michael Snow's *Back and Forth* or *Central Region [La Région Centrale]* – I wouldn't exactly describe that as a system film. I would say that was a film which develops itself out of defining some kind of camera strategy. Some kind of strategy or limitation for the camera operation, which isn't exactly a system in as far as the construction of the whole isn't determined by a system. And in fact, while Snow wanted in *Central Region* to program the whole operation of the camera, he didn't do that. His operation of the camera was often quite subjectively, perhaps randomly, determined. But it seems to me that I'm wanting to clarify what it is that we are talking about here. I didn't want to be forced into being a simple defender of something which I am not.

STAN: I didn't mean to imply that at all. Twice in your book, you suggest, and I can paraphrase the second time, if you will forgive me. It's near the end. You suggest that the only way to avoid the habits of previous forms is to determine a form before you begin the work and then you are not too clear about sticking with it, but I assume you at least feel there should be a high degree of formalism before you begin to create something, in order to avoid previous forms. Now that's a tactic that actually is very prominent in this century. I've only to think of Arnold Schoenberg and his Twelve Tone System which was specifically devised in order to avoid previous harmonies of music. Do you still feel that way about it?

MALCOLM: Yes—

STAN: Good. Because I'm dead set against it. Now we have a clear definition to work on. But maybe – I don't mean to interrupt you. Do you want to say something about the film?

MALCOLM: Yes, maybe it's a good time to look at a film. But yes, the point I was trying to make in the book is that like you said with someone like Schoenberg there are a number of cases where – I'm not sure that I extend this in a total sense – but I think there are a lot of cases where it's certainly been necessary to do work directly on the structure of the language before new perception takes place. I mean in my own experiences as an artist one of the most surprising things to me, as a painter, was that I was seeing through the means which I had to record what I was seeing [Malcolm's microphone goes out] Do you mind? Can we take this up later?

[Malcolm shows his films, *Academic Still Life: Cézanne* and *Time and Motion Study*. Earlier he had shown *After Lumière*. He elected not to speak again until the debate itself.]

STAN: The films I've chosen to represent personal films, for this evening, begin with *Choreography for a Camera* by Maya Deren and that will be a good comparison maybe, in a way, with – because it is a time and motion and space study – so it would make some good comparison with Malcolm's time and motion study. But the impulse for Maya Deren to make this film was that she had devoted much of her life to the dance and had been very actively involved as a dancer, modern dancer. And she had reached that age where not having achieved any purchase on the public scene or any fulfilment in herself as a dancer she had come to a time where it was – she was facing that tragedy of all dancers except those few great, brave ones who are beginning to choreograph the dance of maturity and the dance of old age. But for Maya, who was always struggling and somewhat resistant to this sense of herself as growing older, it was an enormous crisis for her. And film – she was also breaking up with her husband with whom she had made the first two films – and so finally she was with the camera in hand. And as I found out recently, with the help of her ex-husband's new wife, beginning – who was a photographer – beginning to see whether all of this impulse that was being stifled as a dancer could find some, could translate itself for her, most personally into the possibilities of film. And certainly she thought quite formally about this film and certainly there was preplanning. That there had to be a great deal of preplanning. But all along the – in order to effect the shifts of scene that you will see in this film – but all along the way of this it was subject to and constantly disrupted by what was before the eye when the actual moment of shooting occurred and more importantly to me by this crisis that had entered her life. And similarly to some extent – I've chosen carefully that none of these films represents any kind of a school. They are as different a kind of making as you could ever find but they share this: that always the impulse to create rises through either overwhelmingly joyful or as we usually use the word, extremely disturbing crises in the life of the maker. To such an extent that, in fact, the maker has to, as everyone in their lives do, to very often fall back entirely upon the resources of the self. And then what becomes interesting to me at that moment is that therein do they find a universality, that is, a possibility for expression that will meet something in all other people. You see, to me, it's as simple a matter as that the one thing I've ever been sure of on this earth is that there are no two people alike at all. In fact, it's maybe better expressed in the mystery of really looking at snowflakes. There are no two that are at all alike. And in a way, that might be said to be the only thing that we really share. That each person is unique and lonely and then working out of that uniqueness and that loneliness or insides of the self comes something along the line of feeling, shaping form that does seem to be meaningful to others who are also equally alone and unique. Each of these represents certainly utterly different examples.

Number two, *Cosmic Ray*, by Bruce Conner, is a taking of that vast outpouring of material wherein we are all supposed to be joining in the tribal dance under the false, as always false, assumption in the tribe as well as the local movie theatre or as well as through the viewing of television. But that false assumption that we do absolutely share certain symbols and certain archetypes in a communicable way. And there that word again has been denigrated not from the full sense of communication as kinesthetologist, Ray L. Birdwhistle, might define it which would include not just the talking we say or just the gestures but also everything, the slightest shifts of wrinkles in the face, the effluvium, all that considerable industries are seeking to obliterate by spray-gun technique under the armpits and so on, that we sniff each other and that we sense each other in a variety of ways that totality of which constitutes a sense of communion which is a little better than 'communication' as it's been so destroyed in our time. But he works just with these symbols, and takes them quite personally and desperately so, again because the whole social possibilities for Bruce Conner were collapsing at the time in his life that he was making this. As an artist he had become very famous as a sculptor and found himself actually coming into a contract, a short contract, with galleries in New York, and was totally having a nervous breakdown under the expectations that he should, yes, live in that area and that he should attend so and so many cocktail parties per year and live up to and fulfil that contract in order to be an 'American Artist'. He was not going to be able to renew that contract. And it is in that kind of sense of crisis, social crisis, that *Cosmic Ray* is made.

Three is *Arabesque for Kenneth Anger*. That's really a case of one, not film-maker, but one friend who happens to be a film-maker, Marie Menken, reaching out to another who happens to be one also, Kenneth Anger, across film so it's kind of a wondrously, desperately written letter – sort of her trying to tell him from a totally alien world of her background and being a woman all the way across to his world which is absolutely different from hers which is something of what they might share of the arabesque in this crazy mosque that they travelled through so differently.

Four, *Our Lady of the Sphere*, is really an extraordinarily and obviously hermetic work but the process wherein Larry Jordan made this film again is one where he, being drawn for reasons he could not understand to a whole area of nineteenth-century engravings and having those before him on the table, felt moved to begin to cut them out and then to let them tell him where to move them. He was in one sense like all – every time a person gets extremely personal and might be regarded as tremendously self-involved, if that's truly personal, but as distinct from what I would call introspection – then there seems to be an area that's reached in the creative process for most makers where mysterious persuasions as I call them now as distinct from forces as young people do, but mysterious forces or persuasions seem to act through persons as if it came from elsewhere, not having at all to do with society but from something mysterious that we can't quite tab. Some people thought for a while they had it tabbed with the term, 'subconscious', but that doesn't seem to hold up even across this century as quite explaining the mysterious persuasions that come to bear on someone lending his or her most personal experiences and habits to the unknown and yet, again, through this process, his roots can be traced. It doesn't just exist on any flat level, but that also of all of fairytales, all of anybody's experience of fairytale or the cultures or traditions of that come through this personality.

And then, five is *Hymn to Her*, which is a film which I was given to make to my great delight because there had just been a couple of years, or a year before, an interview with Hollis Frampton which was printed in *Artforum* magazine and during this interview, at some point, Hollis had assumed that I had portrayed Jane accurately and she suddenly jumped up and said, 'No, he's never taken a picture of the real me!' Well, it was a shocking and electrifying moment and Hollis, in great embarrassment, said, 'Well, Jane, you're obviously one of the more photographed woman in the twentieth century, what are you talking about?' She said, 'Well, these are all roles in a way that I play.' That was a very desperate consideration for me. I felt it as an enormous failing. Not that I could then go out and commission myself to do something, but that it worked inside me. Not that she blamed me in any way, I mean, it was all very light between us in a way, but I felt desperately sorry that somehow there was not, in all that photography, an image she could identify with. Then there came, it just fell out one afternoon, where this need in me, quite kin to Maya Deren's crisis as a dancer giving up dance, a way to lend myself again to film even more personally. I mean I got outrageously personal in taking pictures of Jane … sort of poaching on some of her greatest privacies and out came this film which, much to my delight, she did feel gave an image of her. So, for me, that was really the birth of the possibility of portraiture which, again, did not come from looking at someone else, from reaching this way out, but from reaching this way in. It absolutely, certainly did not come from trying to see what film might be, that it might be, that it might be. Okay, let's look at them.

[Stan's films are shown]

The Debate

MALCOLM: The question of the role of the individual and the personal. You know, I find myself in no way opposed to the idea of the individual and I think that the point which I want to make is not so much to do with the question of the immediate practice of film-making and where the, as it were, the underlying source of the energy lies, but to do with the larger-scale praxis and the conceptual context in which we work. In other words, it's more a question, really, to begin with, of the analysis of the condition under which we work and what I am suggesting is the notion of film as a kind of cultural discourse: that film is, in a sense, an intervening mechanism which already exists both in the machinery sense, I mean in the more obvious sense of the apparatus, and in the sense of cultural historical state of affairs. I mean, there is, as it were, a history of cinema and the history of cinema at any one point in time provides the context of the usage of the film medium. What I'm saying is that all of us, as artists, are, in a sense, constrained by the apparatus and the historical condition of the medium which we're operating in … and I'm suggesting that the individual's relationship to that is one of a dialect between the individual and the culture through the engagement with that mediating field; the mediating field being the area of discourse that's conditioned by the physical properties of the medium and its apparatus *and* the historical constraints which are built into the language and that the individual has to, in a sense, work on and through that mediating field. Now, that's a concept really of our relationship to the medium.

STAN: Well, I see one problem with this immediately for me, Malcolm, which is that, first of all, how do you envision the Lumière Brothers constrained or Méliès constrained? Do you see them constrained by the other art forms or by the developmental history of seeing as it can be seen through the history of painting, let's say. Or, I'd like to know what you mean by *constrained*, because I don't quite feel constrained by things that are given. In other words, I feel constrained at times by lack of place or recognition within the society, or something of that sort, which sometimes gives me very much less money, therefore less film to work with than I might otherwise have … very much less time to work with film, which is the real cut. But, I don't feel constrained by what is given which is where I begin to work, when I begin to work with something I don't sense that a sense of constraint is there, and maybe that's a difference between you and me: that you may feel constrained at the point you begin to work via historical context and therefore would feel a strong need to take some arms against it, or to make answer to it or something of that sort in a straightforward dialectic. I don't feel that because at the moment that it's clear to me that I have a necessity to work and I have a given possibility for a given set of machineries and film to work with, then I start working. That's the whole world and I tend to work that way also, I mean, as in editing at some point I say, 'well, that is the world, the possible world out of which the film can come', and then I'm not constrained from that point on. Whatever is going to be made is going to come out of this pool of film. I don't tend, for instance, as some film-makers do, to go out and shoot more material. So, maybe if you can define 'constrained', where the constrained …

MALCOLM: Okay, well I see three things coming in on this, certainly three points that I'd like to make. One is my seeing the economic constraint as being one of the real factors of the apparatus which I think exists within our cultural situation. It's one of the real constraining factors in the sense that society functions in relationship to the priorities determined by that society's economic order, and so, one of its methods of infringement on you is the constraint which comes from the economic structure. I would say that that's one of the elements of the constraint within the mediating field. The second thing, just to take up Méliès and Lum—

STAN: Do you feel that constraint once you begin working?

MALCOLM: Yes, I think that I'm aware in the construction of the work of the economic substructure for the work. I would say that within the construction of the time and space within the film there is some kind of inscription. Exactly how, well I can suggest some roots to its inscription. I would say that there is an inscription of the factor of that constraint within the work. I mean, in the sense of the kind of limit of time and space which I'm tending to deal with. For example, one's capacity to occupy time and space and have power over time and spatial factors is directly related to one's economic substructure. They form the economic base from which one works. It's fairly obvious if you examine our work against a high-budget Hollywood movie, for example, that there's an inscription in our work of its, as it were, roughly of its cost. Your films and my films describe to some extent their cost. They have an inscription of this, and in the same way a high-budget Hollywood movie also inscribes its cost and the kind of real priority it implies for the social condition in which it exists is part of the inscription of the work. Do you see what I mean?

STAN: Yes, but I don't myself see where that is so … I've seen films made by Hollywood that they say … I remember the first such shocking example is the filming of *The Old Man and the Sea*, which I was told cost eight million dollars and at the time it was absolutely inconceivable that it ever could have. It was essentially Spencer Tracy in a rowboat from almost beginning to end and, I mean, it was just inconceivable to me that that could have cost eight million dollars and still is to me even by today's price, whereas, on the other hand, I have seen independent films that were very approximate … dramas, for instance, to Hollywood movies that cost very very little money, so I don't buy that. But I want to say something about 'constraint'. I was sitting here feeling constrained because I felt, I always feel, a little embarrassed in front of an audience to chew tobacco. So to end this constraint I put some snuff in my mouth, which will very shortly force me into what I was fearing, that I then have to pull out my travelling spitoon and then proceed to spit into it, okay? This is very much how I make a film. And also, then I have to go out on the road, and usually it is to explain to audiences, as I often do with this action, that, no, I am not drinking, that you are being taken in by symbolism, rather than watching my movements if you're thinking I'm drinking because this is so much a symbol of alcohol, but really if you watch the motions it's inconceivable that I have enough suction to be drinking. That's what I'm doing, and that, I would say, is a very good metaphor for the essential extent of what my lecturing consists of. So those are good little ... all of which I didn't introduce just to be cutesy, but to *permit* myself to chew my snuff in public without creating confusion.

MALCOLM: The analogy is that you're chewing your snuff in your films I think—

STAN: No. [inaudible]

MALCOLM: Am I misreading the symbol?

STAN: Yes ... I might say in a typical intellectual's way ... I might fancy Annette Michelson as saying something similar. No, on the contrary, what I'm trying to say is that given the need to do something, and that it's a real need, I will only make a film out of real need, which is always personal, more than usually obviously so. Then, therefore, from that point on it's a question of beginning the process, which in this case the analogy was putting snuff in my mouth, which either shortly I'm going to have to swallow this chewing tobacco, or proceed to find a container that it requires under the circumstance. So, that's my sense of form and function being synonymous along the line of need. I don't even accept the Bauhaus 'form follows function', let alone what you seem to suggest in your book that function should follow form. In fact, for years I had as a banner, and did work out of Charles Olsen's oft-quoted statement by Creeley that form should never be more than an extension of content. Well, very quickly for many of us it came to be there should be *no* distinction between form and content. In fact, that banner had to be put that way because of confusions ... because of the dialectics of the previous generation.

MALCOLM: Okay, what I said, in fact, was that form in many cases proceeds experience. Now, that was put forward in a certain kind of polemicism of the assumption of the opposite. I mean I would much rather present it, at this point, as being experience is a dialectic between the capacity to create a form of relationship and those things which are a more basic motivation of that which we wish to express. I mean, in the analogy of your bottle, one might suggest that rather than operate within the constraint, you might investigate the basis of the constraint. Why you are constrained to be chewing, why you don't feel able to simply spit on the floor, why, in your circumstances, spitoons aren't made available publicly for you. What I'm suggesting is a fairly trivial kind of metaphor in a way to follow up and it will lead us to a lot of wrong roots if we follow it up too precisely but ...

STAN: You're doing great so far.

MALCOLM: My own position in film has been towards the investigation of what seemed to me to be the constraining factors. When I say 'constraint' I don't see this as being outside of creativity because that which is a constraining factor, like the apparatus, also has extensible factors. I mean there are factors which are, as it were, latent within the capability of the medium, which have not been developed towards their expressive capacity. So, those factors are there to be discovered through working on—

STAN: Yes, but for instance, as a follow-up to what you're suggesting, which is perfectly true, I mean in that it's interesting, that one could then question why I do need to chew tobacco, or why don't I spit on the floor. One has to ask also, in your book and in your statements, why do you feel that you must escape the previous forms and the previous habits, and are so moved to accept that as a given … and then to suggest that the only way to do it, which I could also argue with, is to invent a distinctly different form (that's begging the question that that's possible), in order to escape those previous habits. Again, let's use some analogies to previous arts and artists of this century. The interesting thing about Schoenberg, for example, is that he felt the weight of the harmonies of the previous time upon his music and really consciously, and over many years, evolved a system to bust out of it. But, people who study twelve-tone music, assiduously, tell me that there are very few, and some even argue, if any, pieces of Schoenberg that can be described as twelve-tone throughout. In other words, he broke his own system. But what he did do, in the meantime, is he, through his polemics, left a system of music writing which has been deadly, in my opinion, to thousands of music students in the schools. I feel, also, it was destructive as it operated on Webern, for example, so strong a man as Webern, who came finally too much under the sway of Schoenberg.

MALCOLM: What I would suggest though is that there's no alternative to this process culturally, in the sense that the area in which we work is a mediating field. We engage with that mediating field and the results of what we do then become constrainers within that mediating field. To bring it back personally, your work is one of the components, a very strong component, in the mediating field which any person making film at the present time must come into some kind of relationship with. I mean, I would suggest that your capacity to treat the area in which you function as being a contained area of language possibility is largely based on your own previous historical intervention in the constraining field that operates on you and that you implanted into that mediating field so much of your previous historical engagement with it that it now becomes a major component in the mediating field in which you operate. So, what I'm saying is that your aesthetic and, it isn't for me just your personal aesthetic, but the cultural implication of your personal aesthetic has become part of the language system in film against which not just I must operate, but also against which you must operate.

STAN: I disagree because I think in the first place that to the extent that I have
been enabled to tap physiological resources out of necessity in making my
films, I've touched physical possibilities in all people and mine will show forth
distinctly unique from theirs within the works, but there will be something of
process in there which we share. We don't share it because I invented a form
and then that's been stamped onto society at large, but rather, because there
are inherent physical possibilities which we all share and which most people
aren't aware of. Now, I am also aware, and it is a horror to me, that it is
possible to take evolutions in my work – one or another or all of them –
though that would be tough because there is such a variety of involvement, but
even eventually all of them perhaps, and certainly any one or another of them,
and teach those to others as a 'good way of seeing', or the 'way to do it' or the
way to begin, or as intrinsically necessary form within the history of film and
create a lot of people who avoid their own personal relationship with their
work by way of taking what's occurred in my work as dictum.

MALCOLM: Yes, you see I don't think … my conception of the way in which it
functions as a cultural process seems to me to be different to that. I have to
entertain the possibility that your conception is righter than mine. I mean that's
something I have to do.

STAN: Why? Because from my viewpoint that would be impossible. It couldn't
possibly be.

MALCOLM: Okay—

STAN: I'm speaking now of the depth of involvement out of which I think creative
work must arise, out of which that could not possibly be, what you just said,
that any way that I would have could be righter than yours.

MALCOLM: Well, let me—

STAN: For you.

MALCOLM: Yes, what's coming up between us is that I am proposing broadly a
cultural model and you're broadly proposing an individualist model, where the
primary question for you is the identification of the individual – where the
primary question for me is the identification, or not the identification, but the
function of the individual within the cultural. Now, that makes it suggest that I
am talking about a condition for practice which is what I would think of as
being like a theory of practice. At the moment I'm not really wanting to go to
that point of making a theory for practice, so much as an analysis of the way
that I see the cultural condition within which we work. See, with your own
work, for example, when you talk about and when you think in terms of
perhaps the devices within the films, the things which are identifiable as, if you
like, your handwriting within the film, and you have specific devices which you
might use – I don't think that those are entirely explicable in terms of your

individualist and your special personality. For example, it seems to me that a lot of your work functioned in relationship to the elimination of not just repression within film, but an elimination of a certain kind of repression within the culture which was a repression on the development of our sensuality and the relationship of our sensuality in a much more open way to our sexuality and this was, in some way, a kind of breaking out of a constraint on our behaviour, which, in a sense, your film work mediated some kind of way of coming to terms with through the mediation of cinema. So, there isn't just the question of the meaning within the film in the way of trying to find some kind of novel or totally individual cinematic form; there's also the question that you, as a being, are yourself functioning within the historical constraints of your culture. And I suggest that you do, we all do, attempt to break out of those constraints which we feel to be inadequacies within…

STAN: It isn't so much trying to break out of those constraints as it is to try to use them. I think in almost every film I've made there are easily explicable examples of influences of the whole history of not only cinema, but of all the other arts that I've experienced and my involvement in social habits of the time in which I live, my ordinary exchanges with everybody else, including all that Conner puts in its primary place in *Cosmic Ray*. It's all at work in there. I see nothing wrong with that; I see nothing at all wrong with that. You seem to imply in your book, which brings me back to my question again, that one must break habits with the past, which has been a particular polemic of the twentieth century. I think that we do have to, at some point, consider that this term, 'structuralism', which you don't want to argue, and you can call it anything you like, but there has been a drift which has caused that very term to arise earlier in this century in Russia – the group that were banded around, generally grouped around, the term 'constructivist', which might be loosely translated as structural. There again, out of scientific studies of the nineteenth century, there was a conscious attempt to be aware of the physiological effect of colour, for example, on human beings, and Matyushian's great colour charts are certainly a marvellous study to discover that, for instance, there was an effect to the eye of dissonance by near-like hues being adjacent to each other in a painting. So, he made a marvellous chart of these and an extraordinary number of painters attempted to, either, create these dissonances or avoid them as they chose, until, of all people, Malevich came along and pointed out that this was just dealing with the physical eye. This wasn't dealing with the mind's eye at all, which was not subject to this chart or any of its effects and then you busted open into what might loosely be called psychology: you're back in the grounds of an immediate recognition of extraordinary differences in people. That's not to say that I'm trying to create something absolutely unique on earth that has no influence of anything else or anybody else. That's quite the opposite; that would seem absurd and senseless to me, unless I indeed decided to inhabit the last uninhabited island on earth, and then there wouldn't seem to be any point in making film. So, why do you feel the necessity to break with these past habits? I ask you with homage, the same as I would ask that question of Schoenberg or John Cage. Why was it so bad to take something of Tchaikovsky along with you that you had to cast dice in order to avoid it.

MALCOLM: Well, I've come out often very much against the Greenberg tradition, which really seems to me to be a theory for a kind of hot-house development of language in a situation where no underlying ideological cause for change can be found. I think that a concept of change without necessity is completely inadequate. In other words, I would say that I'm not interested in any way in the idea of change for its own sake. I'm not interested in the concept of the avant-garde, which is only concerned with the novel and in keeping itself moving. It seems to me that why I found your own work an extremely important frame of reference for me is that it doesn't operate – its innovations have not been innovations which have been arbitrary, but they've been innovations which, in a sense, have had significance. What that means is that there is within your innovation a cultural component ... a component which has significance beyond you. If we are all different, which obviously, in the particular sense, we obviously are all different. There's no doubt about that kind of concept. We aren't all the same – we all have individual and particular lives. If that's so, then there really isn't any value in the communication of our differences. There is perhaps a value in the communication of the value of our differences, that we value those aspects of ourselves which are individual. And it may be that one of the things which is communicated through your work is the value of individuality and that we recognise the value of individuality and even of the idiosyncratic. But, for me, the major component that makes your innovations important is that it's significant outside of those things which are particular to your being – outside of the idiosyncratic and are related to our condition as a whole, our social condition. They relate – the elements of your work which relate to me are those elements which are impinging on the problems within my cultural condition, where our cultural conditions interrelate with each other and where there is a point where any kind of innovational change or realisation which you bring about becomes significant for me.

STAN: Well, this presents a real problem for me as it did reading your book because it is – you are very complimentary to my work in your book and yet it is all within – it seemed to me, and maybe I misread it, an assumption. I'll put

it the way I felt while reading the book – what you were praising me for was as
if I were someone who had invented a nut or a bolt here or there along the line
of the construction of this great movie art machine. That, presumably, would
be some day entirely self-contained, particularly if it ruminated enough on itself
and would then just proceed to manufacture art. That I would be one of the
inventors of some part or other of this, and in fact, you were kind enough to
say some very crucial parts. But, I was deeply offended by that image and
horrified in fact; because – I have to say that one reason that I really agreed to
go out on the stage, rather than talk with you in my living room is that I regard
a certain drift of attention to film in our time, which is receiving a lot of
academic endorsement and intellectual magazine endorsement, as not an
impossible aesthetic under which to make films – quite the contrary, there are a
number of very obviously defined structuralist films or film – conscious films
which I think are masterpieces. *Tom Tom, the Piper's Son*, Ernie Gehr's *Serena
Velocity*, a great deal of Hollis Frampton's work, *Critical Mass* and *Travelling
Matte* to name two extreme examples and so on. I have met many more than I
could name, but they seem to me absolute masterpieces, but they seem so to
me despite the limiting aesthetic under which they developed. What worries
me additionally is that this aesthetic is an easy one to teach and therefore very
available to the large sort of teenage baby-sitting problem that the colleges
have: how to keep the kiddies busy and feeling creative without really getting
too involved with them or they with you is essentially the professor's problem.
Therefore, this aesthetic, and for this reason I believe, is raining as a kind of
deadly poison across the scene. I feel that way, I must say, about you and your
work also. You may not understand that it's a compliment from me but I mean
it as such – that I was so moved by much of what I saw in *Blackbird Descending*
that it was all I could do to keep from performing the socially far more
unacceptable act than spitting on this floor, of cutting it down to twenty
minutes of an absolute masterpiece, and handing that to Don with no other
words as I returned it to him. This is the first time that I have been so moved
with a work of that length and that persuasion, so you'll forgive me if I seem at
times … I do mean that as a compliment, that I thought there was that much
in it and rather fancy that this aesthetic that out along a line of shaking their
hands in the air and so on and it sort of died out at the end of the 60s, but
unfortunately even that could become a deadly form of … I could see certain
students who couldn't make it with basketball being shuffled over to the 'hold
the camera and learn how to hold it' form of an alternative to the fencing class
or something, or along the line of piano practice. It is true that there are
certain things that are going to be needed by all people who hold the camera in
hand when they take film. Or almost all people whatever their persuasion of

making. So, just as you can certainly teach very well piano practice, you can teach certain rituals of handling the camera. Then it occurred to me that it would probably produce that kind of Paganini of the art world, shaking movie camera school which would embarrass and horrify us all.

MALCOLM: What you're saying suggests that one of the important things we must do is understand the cultural process. I think part of which is the process of inter-influence and the way in which any of our procedures can become influences on other people, on the way in which they can become tenets within film practice, within the academy. It seems to me that one of the major—

STAN: Again, why must we understand that? I'm against the academy. I am against teaching the arts you've become committed to in writing ... it does hold you back as well as many others. Furthermore, that as an accepted polemic within the academies it will hold on. It's such a natural for that situation that it would tend to hang on intolerably.

MALCOLM: I have great difficulty in many of the things you've said. I find myself agreeing with you. I mean, I'm also not interested in the copyist sense of academic ...

STAN: Okay, we agree on that.

MALCOLM: I absolutely agree with that and I would point out that your own work has been a major part of the academic dependency within students I have met. I would say inevitably so. I can't imagine how it could be otherwise because when I was a painter I painted like the Impressionists and then as a student I painted Cubist paintings and then I moved from painting Cubist to painting abstract – certain kind of abstract paintings, all of which were not exactly copying the history of art, but in a sense were inevitable routes through which I had to move because it was, as it were, the history of the mediating field. It seemed to me there was no alternative but to go through those routes; but I find myself, in a way, very concerned with the academic in the real sense. One problem we have to face is that more and more our real arena of action is becoming the academy. We don't have a presentation and distribution system of any significant proportions outside of the university framework.

STAN: I think that one reason for that is that we have ... again, one real difference between us, and I'm sort of reaching out to you by using the editorial or pusher's 'we', but actually I do want to make that distinction. You tend to use it far more than I can comfortably tolerate. Again, the 'we' – to say 'we this' 'we that', as if again, this to me bespeaks the assumption of this great machine of art which is being developed by *us* which is not my picture, or not my model for the situation. I do agree with you that it's a horror to me to see certain theories derived from my work. Let me take a simple example: the Shaky Camera school of film-making is perhaps rightfully enough laid at my door. It

bloomed full blossom in the 60s and the only thing, perhaps, that saved it from
a solid academism was:

1) that it required too much muscular involvement, even along a line of chance
   operations for the ordinary academic scene, and,

2) that it was the property of the hippies so they ran it even in grade school, let
   alone in colleges and universities and the academy.

I say this in full recognition that if my wishes in the matter came to pass my
last source of rentals and of making a living would disappear from the face of
the earth, and I'd have to find a new way to make a living is the undramatic
way of putting that. But I'd easily swap that to see the arts actually out of the
institutes and the academies altogether because as they exist now, it's a poison.
I say that with experience of years of teaching. I have turned down all jobs to
attempt to teach creativity in colleges. I do think that something of aesthetics
can be shared. I can share with people my love of certain movies and give
some expression as to why, but the attitude of being able to teach creativity
within the college is so obviously, to me, nonsense that I wait with bated breath
for someone to sue the art schools and the art departments of this country for
fraud.

[Audience applauds]

MALCOLM: I mean it's a very nice rabble-rousing kind of statement to make. But
    it's, within our cultural condition, completely unrealistic without a level of
    revolution within our cultural framework and our economic framework that to
    actually state it without going in for the kind of political action which would be
    necessary to bring it about is an indulgence.

STAN: You peg it as 'rabble-rousing' without realising—

MALCOLM: Well, it led to rabble—

STAN: Yes, but it did so within a college where presumably most of the people
    who are out there are either students or teachers and involved in the arts. I'm
    saying that short of teaching aesthetics, I think they are performing a mis-
    service to the arts. So how can that be rabble-rousing? That's surely not
    calculated to please the artist.

MALCOLM: Alright, but we have to analyse the problem …

STAN: It's interesting, the extent to which it does though, isn't it? Who are better
    authorities as to whether they're wasting their time?

MALCOLM: What I'm saying is that we've got to understand the problem and work
    in a dialectical relationship to the problem. Not simply make, in the air, a wish
    about it being otherwise. It seems to me that we are faced with a certain kind
    of cultural situation. We're faced with a drift for the artist, not just for the film-

maker, into the public institution, mainly the university. We're faced with a drift to public funding, which seems to me to be broadly irreversible in the kind of cultural-economic conditions we're going into. Now, we're faced with those kinds of problems as realities of our context. Now, taking that into consideration, I'm as unhappy as you are about an academic condition which encourages mindless following and copying of artists' styles. It seems to me one of the major methods we have for resistance to this is some kind of strong analytical theory which doesn't create a condition where the student is taught how to use a hand-held camera, or is shown your work and it's suggested that the hand-held camera is the way of the new film and the camera on the tripod is like the way of the old film – but the implications of meaning, the ideological implications which are contained in that inscription of the camera action be examined so that the person who sees your film can understand that which is graspable in analytical terms of your practice. Okay, and from that then, their relationship to your work and their relationship to my work will become one in which criticism has a real component. And it's only out of critique and understanding that we can avoid the thing which I think I fear and that is an uninformed copying. It seems to me that we can't avoid the cultural process.

STAN: Wouldn't you prefer, if you're against copying, an uninformed copying to an informed copying?

MALCOLM: Well, I did a lot of copying as a student. I actually took paintings from other people and copied them …

STAN: Yes, younger people do tend to have the need, and I certainly did, to copy. It tends to be much less informed copying than older copying, So, I'm suggesting that uninformed copying is less inhibiting to the growth of a person than informed copying. So the conclusion is that the more information that you bring to the student, or that he or she is able to grasp in this copying, the less likely they are to … I really think that when I was younger it was my misunderstanding of a great deal of what I thought I was imitating that really formed the first slits in the net, so to speak, through which I could begin finding my own roots for perceiving and seeing and searching. That would tend to argue against increased … I'm not against criticism, I might be against critique. I don't know how you divide it.

MALCOLM: I'm suggesting that we're talking about a very particular problem. We've moved to the problem of the academic aspect of our work and the way in which this leads to influence. I see that as part of the cultural problem which we face and I'm suggesting that we move towards a greater degree of rigour in this, in as far as it is impossible … I'm not even sure that it's desirable … I don't think I share your desire to eliminate formal education …

STAN: I did say at this time and under the existing institutes as I've known them.

I'm certainly not against education and I'm not against deep involvement of younger artists with older artists. And of older artists being able to see each other instead of all the time flying around the country and lecturing to students and so forth. It has gotten to a point where the only use that society seems to be able to make of its artists is to keep them so busy talking others out of doing it, in some curious sense, than going on and making it themselves. Almost all of us are either teachers or earning a living tangent to the teaching field and that may, in itself, be one of the great wrongs of the time. It's certainly bizarre. I have the dream that sometime in the twenty-first century they'll look back and regard as one of the most bizarre things of our time that people who had come to be recognised as artists were really only allowed to make their living teaching, in one sense or another. It's really kind of shocking if you can get that perspective.

MALCOLM: I wonder Stan, if we're following a line along in a way that's going to leave you frustrated about having discussed, perhaps, the wrong topic. It's a very interesting one, but is it the thing ...

STAN: Here's how I think it's to the point. Let me ask you, do you think my definition of a film – let's leave the word structuralism out of it for a minute – my definition of a certain drift or persuasion of film-making, which I see you to be very much a part of, as that the films that are made are primarily, not totally, but primarily involved with that film's own coming in to being, and being existing. Does that strike you as a reasonable definition of the drift, at least, which you're tangent to?

MALCOLM: Yes, I think that it does. I think it's also a good way of putting the question in some way.

STAN: Well, isn't that, in itself, extraordinarily collegiate?

MALCOLM: Well, no. I think that film is not life. Film is a particular and special intervention within life. It's not the thing itself.

STAN: I don't buy that.

MALCOLM: You don't buy it?

STAN: No, not any more than if you said this isn't life [points to water pitcher]. This is a pitcher. What's existed on this film, on the screen, has had its own life and to the extent that it's remembered in these minds and it has had its own life. I deny a separation of the creative process from everything else in life other than the way you'd separate anything.

MALCOLM: I'm not saying that. I didn't mean that. I'm saying that film, as a mechanism, is a special form of intervention with its own constraints and capacities. It doesn't, it's not a system of relationship without mediation. We don't have any systems of relationship without mediation unless, perhaps, there is some kind of telepathy. All of our mediations, all of our systems of communication-relationship come through some mediation. Each of those forms of mediation has its particular constraining factors. We're now mediating through the use of words in a very particular kind of framework, which is actually operating as a conditioner on us. Film is a similar kind of state of affairs. When it deals with what it deals with it deals with it in relationship to the specific mediation. The mediation is part of the intervention of the mediating machinery. Not just the machinery, but the whole kind of conceptual apparatus which is behind the machinery is part of the act. You can't simply identify the thing of the act as being that which is out in front of the camera. You've been aware of this in things like spitting on the lens and so on as a way, in a sense, of shifting the constraint which you seem to be under, by the medium. It seems to me that at the present moment it seems necessary to know more about the thing which is doing the mediation; that it could become a total content in itself, in a tautological sense, I have no real interest in.

STAN: But then, you see, that also was extremely unique to my person and personal; that one thing that constrained me very much growing up was Renaissance perspective. Therefore, the whole Renaissance is very disturbing to me, so I took arms against it and spoke very strongly, very polemically in *Metaphors on Vision*, against the Renaissance and Renaissance perspectives, particularly. There's a very specific reason why this … Being a little tiny kid I had a co-ordination problem. It wasn't at that time understood except as a faulty eye problem, so the solution of that era was to slap glasses on any kid who couldn't see well enough. Now, I learn through my youngest son, a number of years ago, now they have new approaches to this, that many children who are regarded as having eye problems are having whole body co-ordination problems, which he did have, and I imagine did inherit from me. He never has worn glasses – he was given a set of exercises to perform which enabled him to not only see without glasses, but to ride a bicycle. Something I'd never been able to do. For me, they just slapped thicker and thicker glasses on me until they got so heavy that at about 17 I threw them away. Those glasses were ground along lines of Renaissance perspective, which were evolved in the Renaissance and the optic system, which in itself you can take [inaudible] question. So my need rolls out of physical necessity, and my need, perhaps, would be a hand-held camera film-maker, also rolls out of that continuing struggle with the whole system's imbalance.

MALCOLM: Yes, but your resistance to the Renaissance perspective has a number of parallels in twentieth-century art. You can see one of the major developments of twentieth-century art in terms of its resistance to Renaissance perspective, but also in the kinds of solutions it makes through that resistance, and that was to bring the picture space closer and closer to the canvas surface to deal with, to gradually come to deal with spatial relationships which were within tactile space – to concentrate heavily on things which are very close, finally, to the point where the picture surface itself became the surface in question and in your films and in the Bruce Baillie film we saw tonight, and to some extent the Marie Menken film. You know there's a consistency in the way in which space becomes increasingly a tactile space. The correspondence between your aesthetic development in this and that of DeKooning and Gorky and Pollock to some extent seems to me to be very evident and that suggests that we're not talking about something which is explicable in terms of the fact that you had difficulty with certain problems, particularly your glasses, and so on. It may be…

STAN: Why isn't that explicable?

MALCOLM: Well, it might be that the cultural impetus which you were responding to was translating itself within you within those physical …

[End tape]

STAN: … the particularities of my creative evolution is useful to the society, or recognised as being useful at this time of my living, which is happy at least in the sense that it gives me some public forum in the society, and it is unhappy to the extent that public forum gets misunderstood. The cart gets put before the horse and you end up regarding me as the inventor of two or three nuts and bolts along the line of this great machine which will bear just as heavily, far sooner, on the society I feel as the overwhelming assumptions of Renaissance perspective have constricted human sight.

MALCOLM: But I would say that we can't get out of that system of the constraint of the mediating field. We can only dialectically keep engaging with it and bring it, you know, taking it … I mean, I don't want to set … you'll attack me for just suggesting that we just have to be novel, but it seems to me we have to keep pushing the mediation forward in one sense. Where Renaissance perspective was an inevitable constraint on your practice at one point in time, your practice and your achievement and to some extent the direction I've been going in will become the constraining field.

STAN: You're misunderstanding me. Not on my practice. Renaissance perspective as it came to bear on my eyes with glasses and lenses ground along those optical prescriptions was physically forcing me not to use the ways of seeing that I had inherent in me that were different and unique and that were perfectly capable, as I later proved by passing driving tests without glasses and driving cars without glasses all these years, perfectly capable of permitting me to, in my own way, to survive on the roads without killing anybody. There is an extraordinary wonder in that to me. That's one of the great discoveries of my life – that I didn't have to … I'm sure if the people who test my eyes had something to plug into the brain and saw how I was keeping on the right-hand side of the road and avoiding hitting anybody and reading those signs, they would probably take my driver's licence away from me, but the fact is that I've been able to drive and see carefully and to move through this society in my own ways, which has convinced me that countless others can. Let me give you another example, there is a man I met recently who discussed with Jane, first of all, at some extent and later with me, that he was always colour blind. He's been told always since they first took him to a doctor that he's colour blind. Now, I've heard this term for years and have assumed, without thinking about it, this meant that people who are colour blind see things very grey and very pastelly and don't have a clear differentiation, that colours all merge into each other. Not so! He can point at our Mexican bag and differentiate every single one of those bars and speak of them glowingly in a way that makes me wonder, what does he see … and they are extraordinarily bright he assured me and very distinct, only they do not conform – he can't easily, without going through an extraordinary mental process, name one colour blue and another colour red. He can't communicate this world of colour that he sees, so he's tabbed colour blind. Similarly, I met a woman who had been persuaded that she was blind for the rest of her life because she had cataracts removed, she had to wear dark glasses to be sure, in the daytime, not to burn out her optic nerves, but she can see in the dark by [inaudible] of things. But she was going around saying she was blind and she wasn't exercising this as a joy and a speciality of her vision. Similarly, people who absolutely see nothing, they say, I've had many conversations with blind people who have extraordinary life with hypnagogic vision who have that so refined to a process that they can tell when they're approaching a wall by the flicker of the hypnagogic vision reading the echo off that wall. It sharpened their hearing, as we do know, but also that that comes as a visual read-out. What I'm suggesting is that in the face of this, the deadly enemy are those who take the expressions of even these few people who manage to express these other possibilities of seeing and create systems for everybody's teaching of what is the art, or some-such, that we all share. That's what I fear so much in your book and I fear it constrains you. You seem to me a very gifted film-maker from the few works I've been able to see of yours. I feel your almost pedantry, a desire to exhaust the means, to always be referring to film in a structure much as in colleges. They're always there referring to film. They are not referring to people's lives or to real human people making these films. I wish to know more about you and less about film in your films.

MALCOLM: Yes, but it seems to me that you can't know whether you're knowing about me until you know what the component is that is the constraining ... In a sense, unless you have some method of clarification of that which constitutes the, as it were, the observational method or the observational apparatus, separate from that which is being observed. That makes it sound like they're two separate things. I don't think they are two separate things. I think that there's an interchanging dialectic between the apparatus and the thing with which that apparatus intervenes. The apparatus I want to put in a broader context than simply being a machinery. It also includes a number of the contextual habits of usage, or habits of understanding that we have from its previous usage and previous understanding. It seems to me that ... I won't make a prediction in the development of this practice, I have no idea where the development of this practice will go. It seems to me that at the present point, it is necessary for the film to investigate elements of its practice which have been, as it were, unconsidered within the medium, within the language of cinematic practice, that have not been defined as within the compass of the medium. They have only been exploited, but not examined.

STAN: But, alright. Malcolm, you say in your book again, you name all kinds of films, all kinds of film occurrences, particularly happening occurrences where film and live action and other things meet on the stage; you name many of these as 'firsts'. Like this first occurred in Europe, or it first occurred in your film, or in England, and so on. Right away, I was embarrassed for you because there wasn't anything, by your description that you made in your book, that I hadn't seen by the mid-60s in this country in countless happenings in New York City at the Cinemateque and on the West Coast. I was offended that you rather dismissed the vortex concerts as if, while they were an event, they weren't really pertinent to these considerations and then the amazing thing was there were techniques that you came out and named as a first, which occurred first with Méliès.

MALCOLM: With Méliès?

STAN: Yes, but before 1900. For instance, the mixture of live action and a motion picture in relationship to it on the stage: I mean, he started that. Movies were just an addenda to his magic act when he started. So they started as an adjunct to a happening. Well, we won't say started because the Lumière Brothers were there first. Actually, it's hard to say which was first in anything in this. You have the first banned movie in the United States in 1827, I think it was, I think it was a small child reaching in a cookie jar being grabbed by the devil and thrown into hell. This was the first film censorship. You have that poor man who designed those stained glass windows in a drum and whirled them and was so disillusioned by, mainly by the Lumière Brothers getting on the stage first with their movies, that he threw all his drums into the Seine except one, which is extraordinarily beautiful there to haunt us of the tragedy of being involved in the arts with invention and with firsts. Anyway, like so many zealots in this respect, you are wrong – you name all kinds of people, credit them with these inventions – perhaps even me – who don't deserve this tab, but do deserve your attention to the extent that they made something personally meaningful to you and, therefore, of lasting value to you.

MALCOLM: Okay, in some respects the question of the 'firsts' really doesn't interest me terribly much.

STAN: Bravo, I'm glad …

MALCOLM: It doesn't. We have to see that book to some extent …

STAN: Then you must write another book where you approach my films from another standpoint sometime because …

MALCOLM: You've got to understand that book in a certain kind of polemical situation. It's a situation which I don't think exists in the same way now as it did at that time. There was a very difficult polemical situation of complete lack of knowledge in America of work that was done in Europe.

STAN: Yes, and that, unfortunately, still exists.

MALCOLM: Also, a complete lack of understanding of certain kinds of aesthetic drifts and tendencies that came out of Europe and the European situation. There was, in my estimation, a major body of work coming out of European film-makers which was of at least equal value to work that was being done and given considerable attention, by our standards from Europe – considerable attention, both in America and in Europe, while work of equal value was being given no attention at all. So in that respect there was a polemical implication to the book. In one, I quoted some things of the Futurists and while I quoted them, I had some amusement to myself. The chauvinism of the Futurists in relationship to the Cubists and the amusement was that I knew that I was doing the same thing at the same time. I was doing the same thing in relationship to the European, in respect of the European artists' relationship to the American artists. I understood why the Futurists had to do it in their situation and I did it with a certain amount of self-consciousness. I was aware of that polemical problem.

STAN: But isn't part of the problem being a banding together? I mean, the only sense that I can see which American film-makers have banded together is the really practical one: to form a co-operative so that they can have a distribution of work of people who don't agree with each other at all. I must say that all the terms and movements that have been placed upon us, with the exception of one, were entirely engendered by the press, and to essentially put us down. To clump us together in what is called the 'great journalistic herding process', get everybody together so that they can be more easily all eradicated. I think the strength comes in resisting all such herding processes and being involved, certainly, nationalistically. I'm very grateful, by the way, you've interested me very much in Kurt Kren by the way you write of him. I'm a little annoyed that, after all, he's Viennese and I think Kubelka should have taken more responsibility to perhaps bring him over here or someone should be taking more responsibility, not just to put it on him. Maybe he doesn't like Kurt Kren's work at all. Someone should be, actually, making a pipeline to get some of these works over here.

MALCOLM: Well, I think I don't put the blame for the need for this kind of polemical ... on the shoulders of the film-makers here. I think that the things that gave rise to it are very much outside the film-maker's control. First thing is an economic question. The development of an American art machine, like the strength of Castelli and all those people, really came out of an economic ... out of affluence in the American situation which didn't exist in Europe after the war.

STAN: You can be grateful for that because Castelli and his ilk practically destroyed the validity of American ...

[Inaudible conversation]

MALCOLM: ... the American art suppressed European art even in Europe by the extent of the power behind publicity for American art. Also, there's a provincialism in America which I find very disturbing. In Europe we know what's going on with the East Coast film-makers, we know what's going on with the West Coast film-makers and most of the things coming out from in-between. Now, I find myself going to the West Coast and informing the West Coast film-makers about what's going on on the East Coast, I go to the East Coast and often find myself informing them about what's currently being done on the West Coast. You know, the only place where you can have a general perspective of what is going on – East, West, Germany, France and England – is in London. It's the only place where you get a broad spectrum of all the current work that's going on because there's a degree of provincialism, of concern only with that which is going on within immediate geographical regions where one works.

STAN: I agree with you in a way because all my life I've had to struggle to get East Coast, and have been successful often, to get East Coast recognition of someone from the West Coast and so forth. There are regional problems which are very abrasive that come into play here. But, to me the most provincial thing of all is to be concerned in what's going on in that sense. That's not a problem, it's always been to me person [inaudible] not that the East Coast be aware of the West Coast, but that people be able to travel and show each his and her work free of these geographical, national and absolutely of these aesthetic predispositions.

MALCOLM: I'm not in the least interested in a nationalist concept. I mean, I am interested in a kind of socialistic-Marxist concept but I'm not interested in a nationalistic context. Going back to the book, I think all of the factors which suggest that were, on the whole, polemical. So, I would set myself to defend …

STAN: What's very sad to me in this is that actually most American film-makers who sent films to the London Co-op, and a great many of them did, did so in an absolute sense of lend-lease. They never expected to break even on the expense of those prints. They had no reason to expect that they would. They were, in fact, told that they probably wouldn't. They did so reaching out because there was a co-op in Europe and they wanted others to be aware of – to give their films to them – and it is true that that will act as it gets into the social level as a suppressant, or be very irritating. That's so sad because the times when we really didn't know where we were going to get next week's money from, we sent films to England.… .

MALCOLM: I wasn't totally against the films being there. I did more than anybody else to make sure – or I did as much as other people like David Curtis, the people who began the film co-op to try to be sure that we knew what was going on with American film-makers. The opposition has never been to American film-makers, it's been … Again, I come back to the thing of seeing this as cultural processes. A lot of my concern has been contextual in terms of the cultural process. I think we got someone wanting to ask a question.

QUESTION: I'd like to pinpoint one particular … [This was a long question only partially audible] … which may be indicative of a general aspect of some of the personalist school and it might somewhat change the character of the discussion. One of Stan's films in particular highlights this. They were all beautifully done and very [inaudible]. I think a lot of people have expressed the desire to get out of dry formalism. It seems to me that the only way we can get into content is to go to human practice, to human [inaudible]. I think Malcolm is abstractedly – [inaudible] *Cosmic Ray*.

STAN: That film is not by me, it's by Bruce Conner. You mean *Cosmic Ray*.

QUESTION: Okay, I don't know to what degree that film represents the trend. I suspect that some of the suppositions of personalism lend themselves very much …

STAN: God, I can't stand this! You say 'personalist', 'personalism', I now also inherit this. When I speak for personal films I'm sincerely not hoping that this too will shape itself into some goddamned movement which will now become something that everyone will go to college to learn … personal one, personal two, personal three, freshman get it this way, someone else – seniors – get it up the ass and that ends it and it's all over. I hate your language!

QUESTION: Well, I would like to express the point. I have to catch a bus, I'd like to point out that I think that people in [inaudible] social world, they see feminism as a very very important world historical trend outside of the [inaudible]. Whether I believe that or do not believe that, or people who are involved in personal or existential or whatever trend, I think that that particular film caused the trend to be precisely 'gang-bang'. I think it's a perfect example of what Malcolm calls 'emotional manipulation'. This particular medium or particular trend lends itself to a kind of ethical agnosticism and social irresponsibility that leads precisely to 'gang-bang', etc.

STAN: Well, I suppose if that's where you personally want to lead it, you certainly can probably be a very strong influence in that direction, but ordinarily speaking I don't really know what you're talking about and I don't think you yourself – when you go to catch your bus, which was the clearest way you put your language – can do so along an anti-feminist or a masculinist way as you perambulate along the street shooing structuralism or supporting it, etcetera and so on. That's just my view. If you can put it in a way, like you're going to go catch your bus, then maybe I can deal with it as one human being to another.

QUESTION: … put it in very explicit terms. They're going to tend to be somewhat polarising. It seems to me that a great deal of the artists and aesthetic critics tend to be very much isolated from real society and humanity and develop elaborate linguistic architecture and they tend to relate in terms of that architecture, and even though other artists, from what I can see for instance, Malcolm, may not need certain vested aesthetic criteria, I think that there is that root in the real world which, in the final analysis, will make for a much more meaningful artistic advantage. It's real.

MALCOLM: I think I should come in just a bit because I think we do have a major problem that we can't follow up the discussion that you bring up with the sort of time, you know Stan and I have had a fairly good bit of time tonight to talk about a few fairly simple, limited problems. We can't go much beyond that. If we were to engage with what you're saying, I think we would have to have time in which to do it. I do have a sympathy with what I think you're saying about the Conner film. I mean, I was rather surprised that Stan put that film in because I thought that it was, in some ways, the least strong of the films that you showed tonight. I had a great difficulty with it in as far as it seems to be just as spectacular as the thing which it seems to be satirising. Just as much a spectacle and an impotent spectacle, and it is such because it doesn't engage itself with any of the issues which it brings up. It only, in a sense, expresses them in some kind of paranoid way or some impotent, ineffectual way. It seems to me that if art has a capability of engaging with the real it can only do it within the limitation of our effective engagement with the real. A lot of Stan's work's appeal is, in a way, in its narrow compass – the narrow compass of dealing with that which his life comes into contact with and which he engages with. Whether the film expresses that or what, it seems to me that the work had this thing, which I consider one of the major elements of, for the moment, a provisional definition of real or realism and that is a dialectic between our conception-perception structure on the one hand and our effective relationship with the world on the other hand. It's an interchange between perception and effect and one of the problems with the dominant culture, as it comes through cinema and through television is that the dominant culture actually creates a schism between those two elements of the dialectic, having information function entirely on the level of external spectacle so that artistic response to that is often as Bruce Conner's is: an expression of a kind of impotent relationship to this kind of bombardment of spectacle – telling us of problems in our society but at the same time implicitly telling us that we can't do anything about them. Conner's film is, for me, kind of a paranoid expression – and I think it comes through in its paranoia about sexuality … the symbols like the skull on the woman's vagina, those kinds of symbols. The sexual impotence implied by the way that the gun droops – all those things are to me part of a very justifiable paranoia. I think that paranoia is one of the almost inevitable responses of people to the control which the social condition has over them; but I don't think that art can be effective simply by expressing the surface of that paranoia.

STAN: But, you see, there you go again. Art being effective. That sounds so mechanical to me and I must say, I mean I value what you say about Conner's film. Your reading of it … but the very things you criticise about it, to me, are its strengths; that for instance, there's no reason why what he deals with, those images he deals with in those films themselves as – what the light once bounced off of in that Spanish building or anything else and even more, might they be called *real* if you want to use that word in the sense that they are more a part of everybody's experience. Here comes someone, masterful enough and enough in control of his own paranoiac recognitions and his own 'schiz' to deal with that material. Very few artists can. Very few living artists deal with automobiles or airplanes or television or skyscrapers for that matter. They tend to always be dealing with things where they can, indeed, lean on past aesthetic experiences. He confronts, as far as I'm concerned, one of the major dragon-mouths of our time with taking on that material. To me … how many times have you seen that film?

MALCOLM: That was one of the first films that got to London and I've seen it, maybe, twenty times.

STAN: But, do you actually follow through? I mean, there's one way to see it which is, indeed, to be as overwhelmed by those images as one might be confronting them on TV: that is, something that divides the self. There's another way to follow his incredible, to me, and powerful editing throughout, to follow all the different levels of that film where you don't get ... I don't read this skull on the snatch as a sign of impotence at all.

MALCOLM: No, I didn't say that. It was a paranoia about it. An expression of a kind of paranoia about sex: a linking of a symbol of a death wish to feminine sexuality. That's a kind of paranoia about sexuality which I think we might find does derive from certain parts of the – certain conditions of sexuality which emerge out of our culture.

STAN: On the contrary, sex and death have been one of the major combinations of themes in the whole history of human expression. Here's a modern example of it.

MALCOLM: We now have a problem of what element—

QUESTION: [shouting] Hey, buddy, you're a sexist pig! Snatch is something you take when you want. You're also heterosexist! I'm not going to sit here and listen to this bullshit.

STAN: Okay, go! You're going to miss your bus.

QUESTION: Snatch is a sexist word. Admit you're a sexist pig. That's right, you're a dragon-mouth, from a privileged position wallowing in mediocrity ... cutting a new original *art form*.

STAN: You are chicken shit because you are attacking the wrong thing. If you think about it, you'll know you're attacking the wrong people and the wrong thing.

QUESTION: You're saying you're not responsible for your language?

STAN: I'm certainly responsible for my language. You come here because this is an easy place to have a blow-up.

QUESTION: No.

STAN: And, in fact, you blow up because of the same reason I do. Because it's easier to blow up sometimes than to be patient. But it suddenly comes clear to me as I've encountered this over and over again. When you call me a privileged person – you call *me* a privileged person? You know who the privileged are in this society. You don't have any argument with me and you know that the real world is something we all inhabit. You have no right to assume that my world is less painful than yours. None whatsoever.

QUESTION: We all suffer. Nevertheless, women suffer from sexism...

MALCOLM: I think it's very important to come in with the question of the conditions of a debate. It seems to me that the function of a debate is to try, for all of us to try and move towards a greater understanding of problems. I never really have found any value in taking a debate into anger … of any kind.

STAN: Oh, I disagree. I think his anger is very valuable. There is an eruption of something that otherwise gets lost in highfalutin language.

MALCOLM: But I think it gets lost in the kind of eruption of anger.

STAN: Well, it will all be lost in the end anyway. Why can't we have both? Why must everything always be so polite?

MALCOLM: I have a great desire for politeness. I get much further with a degree of politeness. I don't know how you feel, Stan, but I actually do feel that we've gone on for long enough. It's quarter to eleven …

STAN: We only had one question and I do have that sense of responsibility. Some people maybe came expecting to ask some questions so that if there are more …

MALCOLM: Okay, let's have a period of questions.

STAN: Yes?

QUESTION: I have a question for each of you; and that's to ask you to elaborate on points that seem to differentiate these two sides – and that is to ask Stan to talk about risk-taking and how he sees the nature of risk-taking. Under what conditions is it possible to take a risk, or what conditions might preclude risk-taking – and for Malcolm, I want to ask him about – if I were to want to make a materialist-structuralist film, how would I be able to bring those aspects of my intelligence other than my rationality or my analytical mind to the work? For instance, my sense of humour, or my imagination, or my …

MALCOLM: Could you ask the questions separately, because they seem to be separate questions? Can you ask me that one again after Stan?

STAN: Okay, ask me mine again because I got lost and intrigued with his …

QUESTION: Your idea about risk-taking as a part of …

STAN: Well, risk-taking is something that that young man just did. He took it in a very sheltered way in my opinion. I was criticising him – that was a critique on risk-taking actually on one level. That's a good example of risk-taking and, yet, risk-taking within limitations. Maybe now he can take a greater risk. Maybe I don't agree with the terms of his risk. But aesthetically speaking there is a risk involved, for instance, with Larry Jordan when he is at a table and is surrounded by nineteenth-century engraving cut-outs which he's been already moved to cut out without any real clarity. He, by the way, had never seen any of Max Ernst's work.

MALCOLM: He should have, though.

STAN: You see, this is the kind of European shit we get all the time which I will … you know, we are tired of … your sense of American provincialism is so pathetically provincial that I haven't even brought it up.

MALCOLM: I rather suspect that ninety per cent of Ernst's works are in America.

STAN: Risk-taking. He takes a risk when he lays these engravings out before him and insists on them moving him to move them. Because he does not know where they are going and that's a quality of risk that comes from a lack of preplanning, which I respect. You know, a lot's been made of my statements in New York as to the limitations of preplanning. It is not that I'm not perfectly aware that everyone pre-plans and also some of the greatest works in the world have been made as an absolute result of meticulous preplanning and following it through. I do know this. But there are certain directions in making that have limitations built in, and one of them is the extent to which a person preplans, puts the creative impulse into that preplanning and it shapes itself up very much more safely than at risk-in-making and, indeed with, if we're talking about scripts, very much less expensively, but much of the creative energy can go into that preplanning so much as I suggested in this one case it might be that *Arnulf Rainer* by Peter Kubelka is more interesting as a script, finally, than as a film. Another thing that can happen is that, though I still respect the film very much – that brings up another thing: so much energy can go in and be misplaced in preplanning that it can leak out altogether and produce an extremely dull and pedantic work. Then, people tend to want to do this because it's so terrifying to take the risks, either in any aspect of life or in the speciality we're talking about – film-making. To take the risks of not knowing where anything is going and to keep track in the memory of where everything went and has been going and is going and to stay with it on multiple levels of making 'til the brain feels like it will crack and the whole system – and to maybe have this one route into absolutely nothing – that something that doesn't make a world unto itself, or cohere anywhere inside itself and which, indeed, leads to a kind of madness. There is a risk of madness in intensive, meditational, creative making. But it's a risk, in a way, like falling in love. We call it falling in love because it's an enormous risk. There is an actual fall that seems to occur. A feeling of fall that occurs in that and there's enormous risk in giving yourself over to another person, as there is to giving yourself over – especially when there has been preplanning, to abandon that pre-planning at all stages as it crumples around you – it's something like running out on a diving board like you thought you had water, like in the cartoons, then jumping up and down twice and looking down and seeing there is none and then beginning the work. That is abandoning that diving board or whatever and trusting to the evolution of this work or the evolution of this loving – that's what I mean by risk in creativity.

MALCOLM: You want a comment from me?

QUESTION: Do you think of risk as being part of your working process?

MALCOLM: I'm aware that when one commits oneself when one's making work and that involves – there's an incredible amount of uncertainty in spite of any things which you might have clarified for yourself, but at the initiation of any work there's uncertainty and I guess I subscribe to the kind of myth that my work – when I start to work, I must be on the edge of what I know and that the work has to take me into territory where there is uncertainty.

QUESTION: Or danger?

MALCOLM: Well, danger. Well, I don't think we can talk about danger. We're applying an almost military analogy. I think there is a danger, as Stan says, wherever you commit yourself. What you're doing – we have so much time and space at our disposal for our lives to live in and any way in which we utilise that time and space is extremely significant to us because we don't get that time and space back again and there's no way of going back over things which we have done in the past, so that I'm very aware of the intensity of the first time of doing something because it may, in a sense, it's always the only time of doing it. In that way, I guess I subscribe to the concept of risk. I certainly don't think it's an aesthetic aim, though. I don't think it's a test. I think one can take risks which are ridiculous risks. Risks that have no significance. It's possible to build risk-taking up into a system where the – for example, I'm not very interested in mountaineering because I think the motive, the transformation that takes place, where one can see that as a risk is a kind of deviation from applying one's, if you like, heroic activity into an area which really isn't terribly important. It isn't terribly significant. It may help towards one personal transformation – to do something completely meaningless in terms of risk. I am interested in significance. I'm interested in an attempt to get towards some kind of system of value and the willingness to take risk, to put oneself on the line, to act, to some extent, heroically is in relationship to a concept of value and significance … I'm not a nihilist. I think the nihilistic concept of risk is another one of those impotent responses.

STAN: But you seem to speak of risk so much as a tactic … don't you recognise that, for instance, by the vulgarity, what would ordinarily be considered in polite society, the vulgarity of my language, I moved that man to an explosion in kind which revealed something which otherwise would not have been revealed. We don't have a way to make that a whole world in itself which would require searching out, which would require a great deal of time or else a more magical, immediate encounter than occurred. Still, things were revealed, in that they cannot be revealed along the line of tactics…. What is more ordinarily, maybe, called inspiration. It seems to me that you and many others try too hard to have a structure that will, by God, give every eruption that occurs meaning within it no matter what it is. I don't doubt that this may be, ultimately can be accomplished; but frankly that would seem to me to be life making some vast cookie-pushing system.

MALCOLM: But, I'm more concerned that before something like that happens that we have a useful follow-up system for it.

STAN: Everyone will have their own follow-up.

MALCOLM: Well, maybe they will and maybe they won't. It seems that part of – to say it is part of the responsibility of the risk to actually take responsibility for the consequence of the risk. Part of the problem here is to take responsibility for the consequence that that, which has erupted, then becomes … you know, that we follow it up … that we actually sit here and discuss your use of the term 'snatch'. We actually go from what he says to a discussion as to whether your language is sexist. He asked a very good question. Are you not in control of your language? Can we change our concept by a change of language? The feminists have been attempting to do this and with some success. I was very careful about how I expressed that concept. I was very careful about how I expressed the concept of the skull on the vagina.

STAN: … Which moved me to hurl out 'snatch'.

MALCOLM: In an interesting way we've now done a little analysis of the rhetoric and the psychological relationship of … and I find that really one of the more fundamental things we've done tonight is to find out how *this* process is a system of mediation at that level. I think that's a very interesting thing to do …

STAN: I tend to think that you put the cart before the horse very often. That is, the process of … I don't like divisions or dichotomies of thought and feeling, for instance, but because they exist we inherit them as a tradition. I will use them in the broader sense; that at some moment I'll abandon, and in fact quite often, any carefully thought-out … to open to a possibility of feeling – and there's something I tended to think was like a rising volcano there that was not expressing itself. First of all, I had these words that for all his attack on the college; in one sense he stayed too long even as a freshman, that he had to express himself with these four- or five-syllable words wherever possible. I called for some direct speech because I think that it was really, I sensed or intuited that that's what he's wanting of himself – to shed this aspect of collegiate life and that's what he means by the real world. Straight talk. So, in eruption we got a little of it. It was hurled, primarily, at me but that was a risk-taking, in fact, that involved both of us, which could not happen by insisting on careful dialectics or by being careful not to step on anyone's toes or not to offend the ladies present.

MALCOLM: Oh, no. I have no objections as long as we have a follow-up.

STAN: I might say, by the way, apropos feminism, as it reared its ugly head, that all my life I have been particularly involved with the field given to me to care for, to fight for women artists. Marie Menken is certainly a case in point. And Maya and Gertrude Stein. One of my major struggles all my life was to get the institutes to teach Gertrude Stein because I've always been convinced she is the greatest writer in the English language in almost any way you care to define 'great'. She continues to be taught in all institutes as if she was an influence on Ernest Hemingway and that was the summit of her achievement. Now, after all that fight and that involvement I think I have some right to note that the feminist movement, as it has affected the arts, has been devastating. The presentation of women's film is not along the line or recognition of the genius of certain women and how they struggled despite the considerable disadvantages that they've had in their work to achieve a prominence and give their work to the public, but to present them along with a lot of totally shoddy, fake artists who happen also to be women within which they are represented simply as women, which is a denigration of the greatness of their struggle to rise above and to the extent that the struggle has diminished for women, they inherit the same problem that all people do for whom the [...] in this country. I mean all people all over the world do, to the extent that things are made easier for them socially, that they have a podium for social easement. It shows up first in the arts, that the quality of individual involvement and expression diminishes and we're living in a devastating time in which it is much harder to find a woman capable of extricating herself from these imbalancing polemics in order to make a self expression of any kind.

QUESTION: Stan, I have a feeling that we're being led around the bush a bit. Is it possible that people who use the word 'sexist' are predisposed to use the word 'sexist?' I've always considered the Conner film one of the most brilliant anthologies of American culture. I don't find it paranoid, or that it produces paranoia. It is a description of what lies within it. I've noticed that structuralist films very often present a sharp idea, but after fifty frames there's no more to it; it's boring –

MALCOLM: I don't think I want to comment on it. I said what I think about ... I think my argument would be the same as I brought out earlier. I don't think I could go further.

STAN: One of the first clarities I had about that film of Conner's and other works of Conner is that it was always impossible for me to, in any sense, masturbate to those films or anything that came out of them. I knew they were balanced; the sex was balanced and was thoughtful. Whatever might be called sex ... if whatever was in it was within a balance, that it was for the eyes and the mind's eye and it was a moving visual and it seems to me always then, a really brilliant ... it's like all these images are poured into the mind and what does the mind do with them? Most of them are made for ... they're really tough to deal with,

rather than as many people just dismiss as being easy to deal with and just
don't look at them, just forget them. They're *not* forgettable. Particularly, many
of the choices he made for *Cosmic Ray*. Only the process, only the thought
process is what gets explicated in that film ... his mind coming to bear in these
unbearable images. You gave a kind of riff on it as if maybe the film was
exploitive or caused, as if that film caused the same kind of exploitive
involvement that the images had originally in whatever their context was and
that's what made me think that you just hadn't really looked at it in detail.
Like you were too involved in the more easily... Maybe some of the things that
you point out are, indeed, some of the weaker points of the film. That's a fairly
easy joke that collapsing cannon, and while I think it works okay, it gets a fairly
easy laugh in the audience. I know that Conner's weakness ... he runs a risk
socially, I think not personally at all 'cause he doesn't give a damn ... but he
runs a risk socially that because he deals with that kind of image that everyone
has been so used to masturbating to in one way or another they will continue
to do so in spite of his brilliant art and his real use of them in setting them in a
perspective, because that will always be the surface. You have certain social
problems. I remember in the early 60s that if you ran a camera down a street,
you had fifteen other things happening: a mugging, a car wreck and everything.
But you passed one window with one tit showing, that would be all that the
audience would remember, certainly in 1959. It would obliterate whatever else
was in that section. Who can even make a balanced work in dealing with sex,
for an audience in a time like that? In fact, forget the audience. Who can make
a film himself, because we're all subject to some of those constraints? I will
agree that there is ...

QUESTION: In spite of the audience, I don't see the film that way. I see it, actually,
as a quick collection of found objects or quotations, or—

MALCOLM: But why are they significant? They're significant as Stan's ...

QUESTION: [inaudible] —has such in it; it seems to be a description of certain
paranoiac aspects obviously. I mean I don't even get paranoia out of a
discharged gun. I just see it as ...

MALCOLM: Stan is suggesting that the strength of the film, which I agree with, is
in the power of the imagery which is taken in the sense that the imagery is
loaded, it's loaded in by being part of a cultural system which gives those
images—

QUESTION: Or it comes from the history of certain industries of this country.

MALCOLM: Yes, I know. But, the problem is that the film only expresses the
surface of that kind of industry. The thing to which the artist is subject, it
doesn't do any work on those problems. It doesn't go beyond the question of
the surface.

QUESTION: It does the same kind of work a steam engine does when it compresses that kind of pressure and releases it. It's quite a working film in that sense.

STAN: It's certainly full of cuts and—

MALCOLM: I'm saying it doesn't do any work on that area which is the thing which creates our subjectivity to the imagery. Like the atomic bomb image, for example. It is an expression, primarily, of a region of the economic, world, political situation which Conner has no method of having a control over, so it's an element of his spectacular universe.

STAN: What do you mean? He can control it absolutely. First of all, he can control it, if he can, in his thoughts about it. Second of all, he can – and has demonstrated to us – he can control it magnificently along a strip of film. In addition to which is more than just … you're attaching words to that image and that's all we can do in a discussion but it is also a shape, it occurs within that film as a shape in a particular form of intelligence which can be read as a series of moving shapes to shapes throughout the film. In other words, in that sense I disagree – well, not disagree – but I suggest that it cannot just be thought of as a series of found objects because the placement of those objects to each other: those shots and the rhythm with which they are placed and the order that they're placed which makes certain shape-to-shape rhymes throughout that work are what make it very much more to me than a collection of found objects.

QUESTION: The point is he didn't invent the classic gun or the oscillating skull or any of that. They're not his. The power is in the organisation; that's the art of it.

STAN: But the correlation is as with Pound. I think it's part of that aesthetic which was determined to quote 'so that poem and document would be one', so that poem would cease to be about something and this film is not about…. For instance, you make a sequence which rhymes with Lumière's first humorous film is what they always told me that was, probably not the first, but one of his early humorous films, one of the Brothers' earliest humorous films, so you re-enact that. Now what Conner does is wishes to get closer at the handle, and I sense the courage of this – the risk involved almost like handling uranium itself – to take this thing itself and by his rhythms and by his order and by his ordering of them and the very cuts themselves to string them along a line where they can be read, without dominating. The risk is that they're also so loaded that perhaps many people can't see them.

MALCOLM: I really didn't want to get involved in a discussion about the Conner film because it's not one that interests me. It was very exciting to see it when I first saw it because I made a film which was similarly a montage of found material at the time that I saw it. It wasn't the kind of material which is in here, but it was a lot of montage of found-footage material and had something of that kind of pace and that kind of feeling and so it was very interesting to see that and to see the kind of material; things like he included countdown leader and my film included countdown leader. There were a number of points where I found a sympathy with it, but my problem with it is on another level now. For example, the aestheticisation of the atom bomb image can only, at best, become a kind of satirical irony – it becomes an abstraction.

STAN: Have you seen *Crossroads*?

MALCOLM: No, I haven't.

STAN: It does not exist as a satirical irony there. The whole film is one hydrogen explosion after another and it doesn't exist in a satirical ... I don't believe. Would you say there is satire involved? Certainly not primarily in Conner's *Crossroads* and that makes it the first possible view we've had of that material of the explosion of that bomb ever. But I must say one thing you said puzzled me because you said you didn't want to talk about it because it didn't interest you and I must say that if I were to follow that dictum, apropos structuralism, I would not be here at all.

MALCOLM: At this point in time it seems a little late to go onto a particular sidetrack like that.

STAN: Point in time is an interesting provincialism I think you've picked up from the Watergate tapes. It's a curious phrase over here because we heard it over and over again and it's been the number one example ... well, people puzzle over it anyway. What does it mean: point in time?

MALCOLM: Well, it means that I'm catching a plane at 10:00 tomorrow morning.

STAN: I'm sorry, I'm being maybe rude, if you really want to quit.

MALCOLM: Yes, I wouldn't mind having a couple of more short questions and then I really...

QUESTION: You talked about a mysterious force – that film arises out of personal need. Can you explain perhaps a little bit more about when you introduced those films, the four films in a row, you introduced negative need, must it always be a negative need?

STAN: No, I said at one point that, out of an overwhelming joyful need or a crisis ... I said an overwhelming crisis in the joyful sense, or as we usually use that term of a sad nature or of, in fact, any other motion in between, including those we don't have words for. But the crisis, to me, doesn't have to mean a sad or a terrible thing that you deal with in the standard cliché romantic tradition – you paint and just cut your ear off on the worst morning of your life and now all there's left to do is paint an image of it is one kind of crisis that's been overwhelmed in the arts. There is another use of that word that I think should be as authentic that's like when you can see very much in caring for children. At the birthday party everything will start getting so joyful that any reasonable parent will know that if this doesn't cool down a little someone will cut their lip, the table will fall over or vomit ... it's just all become too much for them. They're all red in the face and hysterically happy. Well, there are crises of this order which I think I work out of and I think many artists do too. They just haven't received the attention that the Van Gogh ear syndrome has.

QUESTION: ... First I'd like to ask you Stan if that need – does that presuppose some effect on the viewer when they view the film that arises out of some need in the maker and how do you, as a film-maker, deal with that problem?

STAN: I don't postulate the viewer or viewers when I'm making and then later it is interesting to see to what extent people have kin feelings to those I had about the film or certain images, but often they're quite disparate and I think that's proper because the work, my business is to make the work – to attend the work coming in to being so that it's a world. It has integrity, everything in it if possible is in integral relationship with everything else, it's a world and then that spins for anybody to look at.

QUESTION: That's really what struck you as a need. Like archaic man had his whole cosmos, that everything had its place and a particular structure; I'm not criticising you for saying it. I'm saying that people who make a lot of structural films are trying to get back to that.

STAN: It's just that – I'm not opposed to ... I think that every art work should have a constant reminder in it that it's, for instance, a painting – not a window, that it is a film – not a window. But I do not, I am not deeply moved when that is the primary, or the entire world of the film and I don't in any way see the necessity for that because that kind of clarity does and can go continually through the work as one thread of its being along with everything else and it just seems to me that the ordinary tenets of structural aestheticism is that that's a narrowing down to that possibility.

MALCOLM: Except my experience of that project is that it seems to be expanding outwards in the sense that investigation on some of the issues which seemed at one point to be a kind of narrowing down now seem to be a very expanding area of question, like the whole question of the issue of speculation on what is half seen, what is outside of what can be currently seen and the role, the element of one's own understanding of the reality of a work that is constituted by that kind of reflexive speculative work on the film as the viewer. And when I postulate the viewer, in a sense, I don't see the viewer as separate from myself, I mean I see myself as the viewer. In some ways I've been very interested that it's possible to set up a film where I become more of the viewer of the film, that I can set up the film which I initiate and carry out, but where my primary role is more of that of the viewer of the work than the identification of myself as the maker. That actually interests me as a kind of development from the attention to process. I reacted very much against process. The illustration of process just taking over from another kind of narrative content. The illustration of process is not really interesting to me – it's only interesting in as far as it leads you to, I think, to speculation on those elements of the work which are part of its substructure of coming into being and the substructure of coming into being is as extensible as any other aspect of inquiry. It's extensible as far as it is a complex – any one situation is a complex universe and any point of entry into that in an inquiring way tends to lead you along the consequences of that inquiry and that seems to be extensible, not reductive.

STAN: That would interest me very much … I'm not in disagreement but that's a possibility for a great film. I would still say that I think it's more than usually dangerous as an aesthetic. It's almost like this. Maybe we can agree in this sense: that certainly very many great sound films have been made and I think I showed some examples here this evening. Mostly I make silent films but I feel that very many great sound films have been made, but that the process of combining sound and picture was extraordinarily underestimated and maybe that's what's bothering me generally in the scene these days: that the difficulty with this extremely difficult aesthetic that I feel you're proposing has been grossly underestimated.

MALCOLM: I do as well. I agree with you absolutely about that and that comes back to your question, how do you make a structuralist-materialist film? I think you can't make it as long as you follow in terms of being a category. I mean, you have to follow it in terms of being a question, in my understanding, a question of investigation. I do not think, also, that you can't follow it outside of the question of, to some extent, understanding the theoretical and critical basis of that direction of work, because if you follow it without that it seems to me you do run a risk of simply echoing an investigation as a form and that seems to me to be quite faulty. The investigation has to be a valid area of investigation. You have to go into … I really can't make those kinds of statements. I think you have to know the field you're operating in. You have to know the history of cinema, it seems to me. You have to understand your cultural framework and then you can begin to grasp, in a sense, your point of entry to that cultural framework. But, I agree also with Stan that it isn't a simple question of intellect in that. One learns to read the language of cinema by being exposed to cinematic works. It's not something you can simply position yourself to out of a kind of desire or theory. I mean, I know a lot of people who have very interesting theoretical positions, but who in my opinion do not articulate cinema in relationship to those theoretical positions at all.

STAN: I also have to interject here that I know kids who have just sat down with no introduction whatsoever and looked at some of the most difficult films in my collection and then just overjoyed and deeply moved me and made just astonishing statements about them. My experience is that with children that this is abruptly diminished as they enter public schools; this ability. Within a matter of weeks. It's an enormous struggle to maintain at all at every stage of increasing education under the existing institutes. That's why I would like to have art, or anything in relationship to it, taken out of it altogether. Not because I'm opposed to teaching or understanding. My feeling is that art actually could also be taught in a way that would be as difficult and as exciting as the most thrilling science class you can imagine. The history of what we call arts is certainly older than the sciences and the diversity of means that have poured into that great body of work east and west, the wide world over, is certainly a largesse so enormous that it could be one of the most fabulous disciplined and greatest studies of all and I would love sometime to teach in such a marvellous institute where it was given a modicum of that respect. But, again, even there I'm convinced that would be for specialists and scholars and doesn't really happily touch the life, as I sense it, of the arts in relationship to most of humanity, which is more or less arrived at more happily, less theoretically. The less theory and the less education in my experience.

MALCOLM: Okay, I only suggest that historical conditions change certain sorts of problems. I feel, myself, a great necessity at the present moment to relate to a strong analytical and critical theory. It seems to me that my grasp of the problems of practice does require other people. I think there are problems in cinematic practice which are outside of the range of my individual capability of understanding and any kind of assistance to a grasp of that problem from a good theory and a good critical analysis is very useful to me. It's also very useful in actually defining where it isn't going beyond the point which is like categorisable within existing theory.

STAN: That's what really troubles me. That's where I feel you misread the real. If there is any social use to you in work given to me to make a very limited one in that sense. Myself as an innovator seems to me questionable and, anyway, a very small part. So you tend to preclude, it seems to me, as a viewer just exactly the subtleties and the varieties of occurrences which tend to happen within films that actually don't look particularly avant-garde at all. I mean Baillie's film *Valentin de las Sierras* is a film that actually could run over here at the Fox Theatre as a short to begin the programme and would still exist with all the integrity it has. I mean, it doesn't have anything in it that comes on as 'I am art, I am avant-garde, I am a film, I am about film', and yet all those things are also there. That is a more shareable, outreaching possibility out of the privacy of a person's need to make.

MALCOLM: Yes, except I have great difficulty in defining my location in relationship to the time and space which is constructed within Baillie's film. As a viewer of the film I can't develop a coherent location for myself in relationship to it.

STAN: Maybe if you took something like the *Upper Left Hand Corner* and just gave that a run ... some means that you might provide that would make you feel more comfortable academically would enable you, at least, to follow through to see that, indeed, there are startling newnesses on earth in this work that are integral and behave within that world of that film with absolute integrity...

MALCOLM: I see the co-ordination ... I'm aware of the co-ordination very strongly.

STAN: Do you go to the movies?

MALCOLM: Not a lot.

STAN: Ah, well that's perhaps your problem.

MALCOLM: I mean, I find it impossible, at the present moment, to handle any shift of the camera in editing construction because it breaks any reality dialectic within the cinema. I mean, the operation of a time-space structure with a camera location which doesn't have a relationship with our bodily dialectical limits seems to break any kind of dialectical relationship between the film and our conception of reality. So it's always thrown off to an area of spectacular fantasy and that's to me a very fundamental problem.

STAN: Isn't it conceivable to you that that level of what you call spectacular fantasy can also exist with absolute integrity along with everything else within a given work and be of value? Do I strike you as being greedy in that I envision a film that has everything in it that it can have – all the possible aesthetics and then some? I mean that all of them are running consonant and that it's just that much bigger a world of possibility, that much bigger a film, having fed into it, as in fact yours did too. You did look at movies as a child and, therefore, that's ever with you and for all that you confront it, you're never going to be able to completely get rid of it any more than I will the Renaissance. I mean I complain about it, confront it and bitch at it in various ways, but it's always there.

MALCOLM: It seems to support my argument.

STAN: Yeah, I think we got the tail into the mouth of what you started with except that you seem to draw such pedantic, forgive me, narrow and academic, and from my viewpoint, poisonous, culturally speaking, conclusions from that.

MALCOLM: That sounds like a good note to close on.

9

Letters from Gidal and Le Grice [1978]

The [Millennium Film] *Journal editors invited Peter Gidal and Malcolm Le Grice to respond to the following questions:*

1. *In the history of the American avant-garde cinema it has been possible to define periods of development. For example, the 'trance' film, the 'lyrical' film, the 'mythopoeic' film, the 'structural' film. While these classifications are not considered absolute, they present possibilities for approaching and defining the product of the first generations of work in the American avant-garde film. Is it possible to locate comparable groupings in the British avant-garde? Is it possible to identify an evolution within the history of the British film?*

2. *To what extent are the creative methods, the production, financing and distribution of the avant-garde antithetical to the commercial British cinema? How does the monetary cost of film-making affect and set the conditions for the kinds of films produced? What is the difference between the avant-garde and that group of 'non-commercial' film-makers whose films appear in commercial theatres: Godard, Straub, Resnais, Antonioni, Herzog?*

3. *In general the tradition of the American avant-garde has been one of a single individual independently responsible for all aspects of his or her film-making. One could argue that this tradition is part of a larger American tradition of individualism. Does a similar aspiration dominate the British avant-garde, or does the collective film-making, distinct from the Hollywood guild model, offer a stronger impetus? What specifically British cultural conditions have shaped the evolution of one or the other mode of production?*

4. *Recent articles by European film-makers suggest that the American avant-garde has had little effect on the development of the European avant-garde. Is this position accurate or does it represent, as various Americans have suggested, an attempt to justify those films which duplicate earlier American work?*

5. *Has the British avant-garde produced political films? Does the form of these films differ from the propaganda/documentary tradition of film-making?*

6. *What polemical and critical literature, and what knowledge of the history of cinematic theory sustain the British avant-garde film-makers?*

7. *What relation does British avant-garde film have to contemporary work in the other arts in Britain, particularly theatre, painting, photography, and literature?*

Peter Gidal Replies

1. It is possible to locate 'comparable' groupings in the British avant-garde. Such groupings would have to be seen as deriving from influences such as the early showing of Vertov's *The Man with a Movie Camera* shortly after it was made, Eisenstein's *Strike*, various products of the documentary schools of cinema in the 30s and 40s, Len Lye's work, Continental painting and Anglo/Irish (more Irish than Anglo) writing, as well as the strong connections between Paris and London before the war. After the war, the early development of what later was called a pop-art sensibility, happenings, etc., came from the dual influences of e.g. Dada/Surrealism (a pre-war influence carried over) and work on art and design by the British 'pre'-pop artists. Design research and exhibitions which related art and design were important in the works of several British painters and graphic artists; later, the critical tendencies of British and French literary criticism had their influence, as well as the pre- and post-structural work of various Marxists in England and France, as well as the films and plays of such artists as Beckett, Genet, Dürrenmatt, Frisch, Peter Weiss, Grotowski, the Living Theatre, Jack Smith, Andy Warhol, Kurt Kren, Ron Rice; as well as paintings predominantly by Rauschenberg, Warhol, Johns, Twombley, Giacometti and the earlier Malevich, Moholy-Nagy, Duchamp, Klee, Schwitters, etc. This was all assimilated influence before 1966.

   Thus it is possible to identify an evolution within the history of the British film, one that becomes especially clear when taking the following periods (in terms of the recent avant-garde): pre-1966, 1966–8, 1968–71; 1971–4; 1974–7. The specific classifications have been brought out in various forms, explicit and implicit in various writings, such as articles in *Afterimage* 1–7, *Studio International*'s Film Issue (November 1975), Peter Gidal's *Structural Film Anthology* (1976), *Abstract Film and Beyond* (1977) by Malcolm Le Grice, in books by the Heins, David Curtis, Steve Dwoskin, and in the unpublished but available Slade School of London University M. Phil. thesis of Deke Dusinberre, as well as in various bits and pieces in *Screen* (Winter 1976/7; Spring 1976; Summer 1976; Summer 1977: Brewster, Wollen, Dusinberre, respectively). The programme notes published as a catalogue by the Arts Council of Great Britain for the Hayward Gallery (February 1977) show on avant-garde film is most useful in the respect of groundwork for a classification.

2. The answer to this seems self-evident if one reads the question carefully. (Which does not mean to say that the answer wouldn't also be a very long one.)

3. Individualism and making films individually, i.e. on one's 'own', are not the same thing. Two or three people working together don't automatically make the product a collective product. And there shouldn't be a fetishisation of such a pseudo-collectivity which assumes that five is less individualistic than one. The above statement reflects, I think, the thoughts and feelings on the subject of most independent film-

makers in Britain. Obviously shaping the idea of a film co-op which has facilities for production is the economics of film production and the not necessarily middle- or upper-middle-class status of those who wish to make films independently.

In that sense a collective work has been existent in London for avant-garde film since 1966. I don't know enough about work prior to that period to say any- thing on the subject. But the co-op aesthetic/ethic (both problematical terms) was and is decisive in such a formation of anti-individualism. I won't here go into detail on the co-op's production, distribution, and exhibition set-up; it has been handled in several papers by William Raban and Malcolm Le Grice and also somewhat in the intro to each LFMC catalogue.

4. The American avant-garde has obviously had an effect on the British avant-garde, only it hasn't been to the extent that has previously been assumed. Obviously Warhol was a dominant influence, even Anger and Deren were influences, but one mustn't forget that in England and Europe one has grown up in (or closer to) a culture which has imbibed the works of Brecht, Piscator, Eisenstein, Godard, Valentin, Klee, etc., etc. ... not to mention writings by Joyce and Beckett and many others. The Berliner Ensemble and Therese Giehse were not hard to get to see; each new Godard as it was released was seen, and not ten years later. At least this is the case in Europe and for some of the British this was reality as well. Obvi- ously after *Wavelength* and *Back and Forth* by Snow, the influence of the Viennese school of art (in all its forms, with its specific history) and of European (specifi- cally Parisian) work, waned, and thus the influence of specifically those two films cannot be denied, though I would say this influence affected the work of the sec- ond generation of British structural (in the broadest sense) film-makers, and not the first generation, whose influences I have traced in the answer to the first ques- tion. (I think I forgot *Tristram Shandy*, Kafka, and British music hall exemplified by Max Wall: it is no coincidence that he is *the* great English-language monologuist in the tradition (not specific influence) of Karl Valentin (who in turn influenced strongly both Brecht in his early days, and Beckett in his (most specifically). British music hall has been a great influence on the sensibilities of British artists, as well as the way such has been transmitted on the BBC both in radio and television form in the 1940s and 1950s.) So a straight answer to the question of the great or little effect of the American avant-garde on the British would have to be answered mechanistically as follows: pre-1966, about fifty per cent of the film-makers obvi- ously partially imbibed American culture, possibly co-equal to the influence of British and European culture, while another fifty per cent were influenced by two or three strong American figures (or works by such) but in the main did their work out of a more specific context of Britain and Europe. In addition, of course, one must take into account that all influences are transmuted through the culture and history of the social position from which they are 'received'.

I don't think there are *any* films in England that have been in any way seen as acceptable or interesting, let alone important, by the community of film-makers themselves, which duplicate earlier, American work. The films where overt influence of any sort is a straight derivative seem to disappear quickly. Presumably this is the case as well now with the Straub/Huillet and late-Godard influence both here and in the United States and in Europe as well.

5. Yes, there are avant-garde political films in Britain. Yes, the form of these films *sometimes* differs from the propaganda/documentary tradition of film-making. More often than not, though the intention differs, the actual films fall short of their goal. But the problematics of advanced political film have been critically engaged by the film-makers within this field and by those without.

6. Polemical and critical literature that sustains the British avant-garde includes much work by Marx and Mao, Althusser and non-idealist critiques of same, writings on film by Brecht (a bit), some of the polemics that appeared in *Time Out* in the years 1970–4 by John Du Cane and myself, as well as some of my other writings in *Art and Artists*, *Studio International*, *Screen*, *Journal of the Royal College of Art*, and Le Grice's occasional writings in *Studio*, *Afterimage* and *Art and Artists'* Film Issue, and more recently, Dusinberre's notes at various film shows at the London Film-makers' Co-operative and for the Arts Council shows in various places. All this adds up to a kind of polemical/critical literature which sustains the film-makers. But I should mention that in terms of the past, there was of course the polemical/critical writing of Annette Michelson in *Artforum*, and well as P. Adams Sitney's pieces in *Film Culture* and *Film Culture Reader* and *Afterimage*.

Obviously there is other polemical/critical literature, but I am not knowledgeable enough to say who reads the odd bit of Roland Barthes and is influenced, who immerses her/himself in Foucault, who finds sustenance in critical readings of Wollen's *Signs and Meanings* book, who finds real use as critical/polemic sustenance in psychoanalytic readings.

I think the film-makers often have huge gaps in knowledge of cinematic theory (I include myself vehemently in this category). This is partially due to the art college education in Britain, partially to other factors. Similarly, the academics at university in Britain often have an incredibly parochial and provincial knowledge and experience of avant-garde film, let alone any culture other than the literary one prescribed to them in youth. (I think it only fair to add that nowhere else have I experienced as *extreme* a parochialism as in the United States vis-à-vis any advanced film practice or theory, in spite of the obvious *access* which seems to exist. Perhaps your journal will force this contradiction productively.)

7. British avant-garde film's relation to theatre, painting, photography, and literature here is extremely minimal.

Malcolm Le Grice Replies

Something of a reply to your recent letter … I am reluctant to reply in detail as it would become expansive and cover an area which is largely covered in my book *Abstract Film and Beyond*. I also have the advantage of a copy of the reply made by Peter Gidal to your same letter … Taking points out of order, but in relationship to what Peter has written, I can begin by making a complete endorsement of his views on individual/individualism/collective/collectivism expressed in his response to question three. I would like to add a footnote to his formulation, as follows: One factor which has distinguished the development of the avant-garde film in London has been the close proximity of the film-makers to each other in their working and screening situation through the unique form of the London Co-op. Almost as a by-product of the form which the Co-op took, the film-makers developed a critical community of practice and inter-influence which allowed it to develop in a way which could rightly be termed a 'school'. (In the way in which Impressionism was a 'school'.) This should be seen together with the influence, at quite a deep level, of broadly Socialist philosophy, in contrast to the individualist anarcho-capitalist myths which inform the predominant American psychology. The young British film-maker is less disturbed by having been influenced by work of his/her contemporaries than the American. I would similarly endorse his reply to five concerning political work, and point out that the film-makers surrounding the Co-op have, from the beginning (1966–7), frequently considered and discussed their work in political terms, resisting the schism between advanced art and advanced politics. This fact (however misguided or flawed the arguments may seem in retrospect) (which is not to say that they are), together with the historical primacy of the Co-op as an organisation in England over subsequent groupings of a more overtly political kind, has eliminated much of the schism which is forced between the aesthetic avant-garde and the advanced political film-maker … this is at least true at the level of dialogue … the Independent Film-Makers' Association, which represents all persuasions of British independent work, currently reflects the assumption that there is no strict division in the two elements of practice.

As for question four on American influence, I do not understand Peter's concept of fifty per cent influence before 1966 etc.: it is simply unclear what he means, but Peter was not directly involved in London at that time (I don't think he arrived till later) … in my view the situation was as follows … Not forgetting the almost completely self-directed Austrian work of Kren, Kubelka, Adrian of the 1950s and early 1960s, and some early German work by Lutz Momartz (1962) … there was almost no avant-garde film in Europe before 1965–6 … when it began in the period between 1966–8 little was known directly of the American film but some of the indirect influence of the 'underground' culture sustained certain motivation … but the influence of the American films themselves before 1968–9 (certainly in England, but also I think in Europe) can almost be discounted ... it influenced less, curiously, than did advanced American painting and music. As I point out in my book, the already established tendency towards formal experiment in the European film (loop repetition, editing system, camera strategy limits, concern with duration, concern with the screen as material, etc.) conditioned the reception of the first American work seen in Europe which was read more for its formal concerns than it warranted (particularly the interpretation of Brakhage filtered out much of his retrogressive expressionist symbolism and overstressed the formal grasp of his work). So, the American work was received more in the sense in which it confirmed the already established direction of the European tendency. The question of phases of development which is number 1 on your list must be seen, it seems to me, in the context of this development. We must realise that from 1966 to 1968 there were only about fifteen to twenty avant-garde film-makers in Europe; from 1968 to the present there has been a sliding scale of increase (since 1971 almost all concentrated in London) in the number of film-makers ... the development has been considerably telescoped in relationship to the American, relatively gradual development stretching back to the early 1940s and really getting off the ground in the mid-1950s.... I think some phases might be identified, but should not be stressed ... Except in work since 1972 where there has been an increasing clarity of theoretical relation and a consciousness of the advanced place certain aspects of the British work had in the general field of aesthetics (an awareness by the British film-makers that their concerns were broadly in advance of any other film work currently being done, with the possible exception of Snow) and also an awareness that this aesthetic was also advanced in relationship to developments in other fields of art ... like concept art, body art, land art movements) ... Except in work of this most recent period, I feel that a simultaneous model of classification of various threads of exploration is more appropriate to the early work of 1966–72 than a sequential-phase model.

Peter's very catholic and broad concept of the general influences which form the context of European film-thought seems to me to point out in general the more socialistically orientated culture which exists as a matter of course in Europe ... Few theorists or artists worth mentioning in Europe throughout the twentieth century have not seen themselves within a generally socialist framework.... .

I have already written more than I expected to, but do feel that the most sensible course of presenting any thoughts which I have on the subject should come from the book.... .

10

Narrative Illusion vs. Structural Realism [1977]

MALCOLM LE GRICE: On a number of occasions, I've made an attempt to be more precise about what I understand by the term 'structuralism' and where I think the notion falls down, and where I think some other ontological descriptions are better. One of the more useful general terms I've come up with is the term 'material'. And in using the term 'material', I've been very unwilling to put the 'ist' on the end and turn it into 'materialist'. I see in the development of recent avant-garde work something which is parallel to some of the things which were happening in painting at the beginning of the century, coming out of Impressionism – and that is a gradual awareness of the material of the medium itself. In the most obvious sense, the notion of 'material' refers to the physical substance of the film. What I mean by that is the acetate strip on which the film is supported – any things which happen on the surface of that material, and perhaps, if you like, the material of the screen on which a projection is made, and so on. The processes which go on in the transformation of the surface of the film.

The first extension on the idea of 'materiality' seems to be from the physical substance to the physical, chemical processes. As soon as we open up that possibility we've got to ask about how the photographic constructs an image, looking for example at the system of light falling onto an object and being reflected from that object and taken through a focusing lens onto the surface of the film. This brings about a physical change which is fixed by a chemical process as part of the material of film. What I'm suggesting is that one might see a continuum of causality from the event which takes place in front of the camera through the physical properties of light and the apparatus which makes the document of that event as being incorporated within a materialist understanding of the medium. This all has to do with the material aspects of the filmic document and the pro-filmic event.

The other question we've obviously got to ask has to do with the material processes of viewing. The most obvious and accessible of these might well be the optical mechanism which we operate. I am putting forward this schema because we can relate a number of these concepts to things which have been done as part of the so-called 'structuralist film experimentation'. There have been a number of films which have examined the processes of visual perception in so far as they are part of an optical process. If we then take the materiality of the optical process, we move very quickly from what I have termed the 'autonomique' – that is the area of visual perception which is not related directly to conceptualisation, but which is related only to physiology. In other words, things beyond the immediate functioning of the optical system have to be brought into play, and then we enter the much more complex area of reality construction.

In terms of the notion of structuralism, in my definition, I've located the structural activity more in the area of the conceptual, constructive process which goes on beyond or behind, underneath the optic functioning. It is a question of the mode of structuring that is entered into by the viewer in looking at any work; and there are two aspects of this which I have schematically stressed. One is the dual activity of the reflexive and speculative behaviour patterns. That is: the viewer's perception of the work as part of reality involves treating it as material which is to be structured, then quickly moving to the storage of the perceptual material in memory and the use of that material stored in memory – this one might call the reflexive behaviour, the looking back to the things which have taken place but which are not currently being presented. From that emerges a speculative behaviour: in the currently presented image what is of significance, what is to be paid attention to? This will be needed subsequently in order to continue the conception of reality and in order to make sense of the things presented in the later parts of the work. I think, in fact, it could be applied to static works as well, but obviously I'm talking mostly about works which take place in a temporal form. That's a broad description of where I find myself at the present moment.

This brings us to a question which I'm just beginning to think about. That's the question of the dialectic of the reality principle, which is a very provisional description of a concept. I'm not at all sure that these are the best terms. The way I described it last night was to suggest that in our engagement in a day-to-day world, I mean outside of any art perception, outside of any film perception, our perceptions are constrained by the bodily binding of our nervous system and by our relationship to experience. In other words, if I want to change my perception then I have to do some work – I move my head from here to here, there to there, etc. If I want to change it more drastically, I have to get myself up and take myself to another space. However I do it, my perceptions are constrained by my capacity to engage with the world. This sets up a particular kind of concept of reality, and for simplicity I'd refer it broadly to the concept of reality structuring which I understand Piaget has put forward.

Now, what I'm suggesting as a condition in film, before film can move from material to materialism, is for some dialectic in the construction of reality, in the sense of the body binding of access to reality. A dialectic in the way in which the camera intervenes in the event which is filmed, which is why in a number of recent works that I have done, the camera has tended to take up quite a specific relationship to the thing being filmed and for relatively long periods. Generally what I'm talking about is the question of point-of-view continuity being dialectically related to the point-of-view continuity which we use in our engagement with reality. Now, the confusing problem here is that we have in our mental apparatus a number of possibilities for conceptual and imaginary function, which do not involve body binding. We have a mental apparatus which can, while I'm sitting here, project or conjure a thought which sees myself tomorrow morning in London, or yesterday in San Francisco. I can conjure up images which are not bodily bound and can make reconstructions of past images and events, both in a conscious waking state and out of conscious control, in a dream state.

The capacity for rapid exchange of point of view seems to be located in that area of fiction, dream, fantasy. Film which operates with this kind of rapid exchange of temporal, spatial point of view would then almost inevitably locate itself primarily within this range of experience. Part of the thrust of my argument is actually to see if it's possible to counteract the inevitable location of film in the area of fiction by the establishment of some kind of reality question based on the material-materiality continuum I have described. It brings up questions to do with the status of realism – questions about analytic realism, the elements of underlying substructure to the surface of our reality experience. In other words, how do we analyse from the surface of experience to the underlying, obviously historical material realities which give rise to those conditions, but which can't be simply described by a presentation of the surfaces which require a degree of analytic structure beyond what normally goes on in the use of verbal language. How do we have any kind of integration of the concept of historical materialism with the materialist, that is, the physical property material continuum which I have described? And can we ask questions like: What is the function of fantasy? Can there be a social function for fantasy? And can fantasy and imaginary structures themselves have any kind of dialectical relationship with perception of reality or with the reality principle? I hope that's not all too complicated. Was that more than ten minutes?

MEDIATOR: Yes it was, but it's okay.

P. ADAMS SITNEY: You're not going to believe this, but this all started on West
Broadway, as far as I'm concerned. I went there on Saturday. I never go to

West Broadway on Saturday; it's insane. A friend had a show in a gallery; I looked at the people in the show; walked out and went to a yoghurt bar, believe it or not. There were Vicki Peterson and Taki Iimura. Vicki said to me: 'You're debating Malcolm Le Grice at the Millennium.' And I said: 'Oh yeah? For how much?' So, that's how it started. Later, I got the word that it was true. So I said, 'He's a guest; he's from that island over there', let him pick the topic. I was told: 'Narrative Illusion and Structural Realism'. [To Le Grice] You know a lot about that, do you? That's not anything I would choose to do, even on Hallowe'en: play narrative illusion. I was in a saloon, not the same day, when someone came up and said: 'How can a critic debate a film-maker?' Oh God! I knew I was in trouble before I even came here. But I prepared a statement in any case, in answer to this preliminary interrogator in the saloon. It's in three parts, but it's brief.

Narrative Illusions and Critical Delusions. One: All artists are also critics: a proposition that is not reversible. A powerful artist will turn out also to be a volcano of strong opinions about this tradition and his contemporaries. Two: Criticism, I mean written criticism, is the eccentric ambition of finding language adequate to perceptions. Tonight we meet as critics for a clash of language. Three: Narrative Illusion. The rubric is from Malcolm Le Grice. I willingly accept the role of championing illusionism. So little of high value has been created in cinema. So much is dross, that the achievement of the great narrative illusionaries, or the illusionary narrators: Dreyer, Eisenstein, Bresson, Buñuel, Dovchenko, cannot be sacrificed for polemics. (You notice how polite he was, by the way; he didn't say anything nasty about me in his opening remarks. Well bred!) Four: Le Grice has emphasised the international avant-garde in his recent writings. This is truly laudable, but international does not mean one world without nations. One critical task we must face is tracing the intricate and subtle ways in which local aesthetics have international import. Take an example from the realm of theory. A literate American, if that's not an oxymoron, would have to situate the writings of John Cage in the tradition of Emerson. Here Cage reinforces our native polemic. Abroad, outside this tradition, Cage is understood differently and the angle of his influence would be, accordingly, different. So ends Narrative Illusion and Critical Delusions.

The Battle of the Books now. The issue boils down to a question of genre. Le Grice, in *Abstract Film and Beyond*, tried to invent an international genre to fit his polemics. An energetic, critical act. A nice try, but doesn't come off. It depends, in part, on the mobilisation of a conventional art-historical fiction, that the early years of the twentieth century marked the significant, even fundamental, reorientation of the entire art world. Unfortunately this model is almost always tied to a pathetic reduction of nineteenth-century aesthetics.

Romanticism and the Victorian novel become 'fall guys', which is only possible when one doesn't know the dialectics of consciousness in romanticism or the vertiginous voids inscribed in the great novels of George Eliot, Conrad, Dickens, Henry James, and Hardy. *Abstract Film and Beyond* is peppered with these commonplaces. I came under attack several times in that book. Fine! I regret even more than Malcolm Le Grice the fact that the term 'structural film' has become a slogan more than a tentative critical-historical term. But in writing *Visionary Film*, I set up a large target. Le Grice has taken some well-aimed shots. There are a few instances where it was wrong. But basically his criticism is justified if you accept the premise that the critical perspective must be international. I do not. I'm prepared to argue that there is at least one characteristic American avant-garde cinema, and that there are different points of focus for independent cinema in Germany, France, and England. So ends the 'Battle of the Books'.

Here comes the 'Confession'. Don't get too excited. I love stories and illusions. *Visionary Film*, like any sustained critical history, if it is one, is a story book. It begins with a mystery of two odd couples. I'll quote the first line: 'The collaboration of Maya Deren and Alexander Hamid shortly after their marriage in 1942 [romantic story] recalls in its broad outline and aspiration the early collaboration of Salvador Dali and Luis Buñuel in *Un Chien andalou*.' But *Abstract Film and Beyond* has an even wilder start. It begins with an assassination, in order to establish the birthright of a bastard in the name of art. And I'll read you the first line: '*The Assassination of the Duke of Guise* was the first production of a company called Film d'Art, which in 1908 tried to elevate the cinematograph, a bastard of the circus and side show to the level of high art.' I didn't make it up. That's the start.

Le Grice has his favourite stories, which he likes to repeat throughout his book. I noticed three of them. They are: The first story that we find, it's a good story too; I like it a lot: the film tells how it got made. It's one of his favourite stories. There is also another story he likes to tell: What happened when the viewer wised up. That's another. And at the end we find the best of all: Something was happening in the room while the film was on. For my part, I guess I prefer the 'Battle of the Titans'. Those who know me intimately know I would even prefer to say it in Greek: Titanomachia.

My favourite of all, which I tell again and again, whenever I get a film to play it upon, is the story of how the spirit came to name itself. I must also confess that I was more moved by the great poems of Dante, Homer, and Milton or the novels of Melville and Stendhal, or the paintings of Vermeer, Titian, or Cézanne, than by any films. Furthermore, those films which excite me, by Dreyer, Brakhage, Harry Smith, Vertov, Michael Snow, etc., seem in a class far, far beyond the most interesting recent avant-garde films from England and Germany. I should, and eventually will, know the new European avant-garde better than I do. I only wish I could admire it more. I hope I've stirred up something.

MLG: A film-maker who is a theorist after a theorist who is a humorist is a hard act to follow.

PAS: I am more serious than I have often been.

MLG: You make a point of national criticism as opposed to international criticism. Now I'd like to point out one of the implications of that: that it relates to a historical condition where America was an escape from the social constraints which were inevitable in a European situation of limited space, limited resources. The inevitable situation where priorities had to be defined within society. The American nation has very largely been peopled by groups who were incapable of finding room and resources in the European situation. They came to America, which was an unexploited land with seemingly endless resources which allowed a historical development to take place, which was not possible for a period within the mainstream of European tradition, because it didn't face European conditions of shortage.

Now, my understanding of the reason why the American condition must at this point become more international, and reinvestigate itself in relationship to the international tradition, but in particular in relation to the European tradition, is that it now faces the same kinds of conditions of shortage of resources which are no longer available for endless exploitation. It's facing a rigidification in the class relationships within society. And out of that position, it must take up the problems of priorities – the understanding that there has to be a degree of planning, restructuring of resources, and so on.

It seems to me that a large part of the impetus of the structural, formal tendency within European work is related to the grasp that there are not endless idiosyncratic possibilities available within the culture. And I think that American criticism, which remains specifically American, and specifically related to a particular kind of American romantic frontier mentality, is really doomed to be a pointless task in the long term. What interested me about the development of parallels to the formal tendency in European work in America was that there was a beginning of a grasp of the inevitable cultural limitation by some of the film-makers who worked here, through their focusing on definable and narrower problems, which were more fundamentally materialist and less romantically expansive than was characteristic of the earlier period of American culture and American myth.

PAS: I'm in almost total agreement with everything you said. I mean, I'm not in agreement with the hyphenation of a romantic-myth theory, because 'romantic' and 'dialectical' are practically identical terms. But I just have to reiterate, I think you have used 'romanticism' as you have used the Victorian novel in your argument here and in your book, without enough examination of its ramifications. In other words, I don't think we are out of the romantic era in England, in Germany, in America. Two: when I spoke of national, it was not America versus Europe, but I push for a criticism that recognises and faces the nuances of difference between what happens in England and what happens in France and what happens in Germany. An international criticism is not to be had by simply proclaiming a fiat. Thirdly: a word on the word 'structural'. I enjoy this opportunity. I made a mistake when I came from Europe in 1969, naively thinking I had the right to use whatever word I found appropriate. I had no idea that American universities were predicating themselves upon a cesspool of French thought that was about to swamp all the academic departments. I had no notion, at the time, what was going on in this madhouse where every second-rate academic had incorporated a Lévi-Straussian vocabulary. This is a particular American frontier and a very unromantic phenomenon.

I used the word 'structural' to describe a tendency in certain films. I never spoke of structuralism. I never spoke of structural film-makers, but of particular tendencies in particular films. The use of the word meant to have nothing to do with anything in Lévi-Strauss, or French structuralism. I had no notion, at all, that this article would catch fire, more than anything else I had ever written; that it would become a disease; that it would come back to haunt me. It was hopeless. But it's a word that has stuck, and I'm stuck with it. You're right, I wish I had thought of a different word at the time. I want to state my total agreement with you on this thing – that that was a mistake. I am sorry about it, but the mistake of associating structuralism with structural film was not in the text of mine.

MLG: It was an inevitable kind of move from using the title. I'm not going to pillory you on that one anyway.

PAS: You already have done it.

MLG: I think that one is cleared up. I don't think there is any real confusion left about it. I think we've begun to get, perhaps not better generalisations, but a better set of less fundamental classifications. I think what you started to do in defining the characteristics of what you call a structural film, in some ways, has been extended. I think I've extended what you see as its characteristics. It seemed to me that the problem was not your characterisation, but moving too rapidly from the characteristics to a general description or a general category. What I tried to do in the book was not give a general category but take the various characteristics and see it as a broad formal tendency. Any work or groups of works might be a combination of a number of characteristics or parameters of inquiry. So my analysis was, in a way, less ambitious.

PAS: I can comment on that. I thought both your arguments and Gidal's were fine, and they added nuances and as such I fully accept that they seem to be engaged polemically in an argument that said, basically, that this particular moment had to be treated internationally. However, I think that the description I gave of structural film is certainly not applicable to most of the films made by any of those film-makers today. Therefore, they are not, nor were they ever, 'structural film-makers'.

MLG: I've seen another confusion in the discussion and I feel slightly guilty of this confusion because it was an articulation which I didn't have at an earlier point, for example, when I wrote the book. This is a confusion between analysis, criticism, and theory, and does relate to some of the polemicism which you see in Peter Gidal's, and my writing. Incidentally, I think Peter Gidal's writing is more ambitious than mine, because he does attempt to move clearly into the area of theory. It seems to me that you were putting yourself, as a critic, into the position of doing historical, cultural analysis. In *Visionary Film*, I think that the work you did on the early period up to what you called 'structural' is the most useful and best description of the cultural processes which took place and gave rise to the films which came out of that period. There is no doubt in my mind that there isn't another work which does that job as well as you do it in *Visionary Film*. That is in the area of a historical, critical, cultural analysis.

Now there is another level of analysis which is not an analysis of a cultural development so much as an attempt to find an analytical system for the description of films and which you've also kind of half-way attacked, and that's the analysis coming out of semiology. I mean, to attack the universities here is not to attack fundamentally the way in which semiology attempts to form an analytical system for the examination of films. Okay, that's two different kinds of analysis. Now the next question is that of criticism. It seems to me that criticism, at some level or another, must set up a value system. It must in some sense develop a degree of judgment. This is the difference between the critic and the analyst. The critic must define values in the things which are judged. An analyst may do it by implication in those things he analyses as opposed to those he doesn't analyse. This gives a kind of implicit value judgment. But it seems to me that a valuable development of criticism would establish its frame of reference for value judgment more overtly than by implication within the level of what is chosen for analysis. Criticism is always veering towards the polemic because by making judgments it's suggesting that within a cultural situation some things are more significant than others. Critics have been absolutely frightened out of their wits to do that kind of work because it puts them in a polemical position.

Now the next thing is theory. Theory is not just a question of analysis or judgmental criticism but is to do with setting up conditions for the development of further practice. Whether the theory is a theory of film-making or whether it is a theory of some other kind, it is concerned with defining or indicating the extension of practice. It's very difficult in a pragmatic situation of any real cultural framework to separate the production of theory from polemic, because theory comes out of a commitment to a cultural development. As a film-maker I can't be a liberal – as a film-maker I can't incorporate all possible directions. As a film-maker I have to develop a concept of what I think of as a right direction. And so the theory that a film-maker or any artist develops is always suspect, because it's always partisan. We don't live in a cultural condition where all developments are possible. So that it's very hard to get to a point where theory – I mean functional theory, a theory which bears on practice – can be separated from polemics. And I think we do have a problem here, that critics almost reserve the right not to involve themselves with the polemic, trying to step out of the polemic and act more as analysts than critics. I don't know where I'd place you. In broad terms I'd place you primarily as an analyst. A very perceptive kind of analyst in a certain sort of area.

And where do I place myself? I'm even more confused. I'm sort of trying to wear two, or maybe even three hats at once. I am a film-maker who has done theoretical and critical work, which is very suspect because inevitably I'm going to be partisan – I'm going to be concerned with changing the situation polemically. And in writing *Abstract Film and Beyond* I was very aware of this polemical function. It came out of a historical situation where particularly the work of the European avant-garde was not known about and was not valued in the international situation. Where the relationship of the early European experiments in cinema and art, a historical mainstream of European art development, was not seen in relation to work that has come out of America. And so there was a conscious polemical function in the writing of that book, which puts me, not in the same kind of category as an analyst, which I think I'd tend to put your work in.

PAS: I miss in your writing the question of interpretation: for instance the question of the status of nature in any number of British films (by Welsby, Raban, or yourself). It is a different world than Klaus Wyborny, or Nekes, or Dore O. are showing. My argument has consistently been that the only way to understand these questions is in terms of our artistic and philosophical heritage, which is that of romanticism and the various things called post-romanticism. However, among people interested in film, there is a tremendous influence of art-historical education. And only in art history is this myth of twentieth-century cleavage so strong. When this perspective is abandoned, suddenly films that look obscure become visible. German, British, and French films of interest will become much clearer. Criticism will no longer just be descriptions of how the film came to be made, once the films are seen in the light of these deeply powerful visions of nature, consciousness, self, development, and dialectic. Therein is what I find fundamental, and polemical, in my work.

MLG: One of the problems we have at the moment is that we're going into a phase where there are thousands of artists. The reason is that the real arena for art activity is the educational institution. The real supporter of art financially is the state via the education budget. So what we have now is a vast number of artists who are still trying to apply systems of value, which suggests that some artists are better than other artists. I would go along with the attempt to develop systems of value, but what we're not doing is understanding that in society we're opening up the base of art production by inevitable forms of socialisation within our culture. And it's a socialisation which in America is not understood ideologically. I keep saying it on this trip, that America is going ass-backwards into socialist structures. And the whole construct, the whole context of art activity is moving into the institutionalised area of the educational system. The NEA [National Endowment for the Arts] is part of the education system. The capitalist corporate financing of art in proportion to what is coming from public financing is evidence of a shift in the financial base of art, and this is going to have its effect in the conception of the base of the artistic process and will inevitably feed itself into certain aspects of the language of art.

PAS: But we have come to the point where I think I can begin to address myself to your first initial comments. The rhetoric of Marxism which underlies your historical vision also underlies your vision of the real. It is a very persuasive story. As I listen to a film-maker describing his vision of reality even in classical Marxist terms, I am fascinated. It is the kind of thing which I spend most of my time trying to pay attention to – the ways in which film-makers postulate the world both in their films and in their theories. Yet, from a theoretical point of view, I find it very questionable as a general theory. It certainly is a mode of privileging certain kinds of films, primarily narrative films, or films which are involved in some 'love me/hate me' relationship with narration as opposed to optical sensibilities. There is no question, one has to pay attention to the influence of Marxist theory variously conceived, misconceived and reconceived in order to understand a number of developments important in cinema today. That's hardly the whole story though. And I don't even think it's the major part of the story. It's not a view of film. It is a view of the material object and, for me, material plays no role at all in film. Material is like a metaphor. It is one of the metaphors which is interesting in this particular time. Like the metaphors of the self, the mirror, and the empty frame, which were so interesting in the 50s, or like the 60s' out-of-focus shot as a sign of the optics of the film-maker. As illusionistically illustrated in the film, the metaphor of material is fascinating. It is dominant. It is also a self-blinding ideology and that's good; you can't make films unless you believe you have something to contribute.

MLG: P. Adams has put me into a position of putting forward a Marxist viewpoint. I don't think what I'm at in my theoretical work to …

PAS: You don't feel that's what you are doing?

MLG: I do, but I don't think I've developed that as well as other people. I think I've always resisted the shift from material to materialism to historical materialism. For me it's not so much a question of whether it's right or wrong, it's whether at this point in the handling of this problem it is an integratable question. Because quite plainly, as a substructure to the question of the material is a whole economic historical materialist facet. And by stressing the definition of material simply as tactile substance is …

PAS: But you don't touch in the movies.

MLG: But …

PAS: You don't touch the movie.

MLG: No, that's a different thing. I was defining the material in terms of the tactile sense. Which is a very limited, narrowed interpretation of material. When the light strikes our eye, there is a material interchange.

PAS: You are talking about the metaphor of light. We're back in the Romantic period. [MLG starts to say 'No it's not …' – PAS interrupts:] I'm deeply moved. I mean I agree with you. [MLG again tries to say 'No, but …'] We're closer to Wagner than to Marx.

MLG: No, I don't think it is a metaphor. I mean in the sense that the light which strikes the eye is the product of a certain kind of economic situation. That light comes from the projector is produced by the conversion of material by people into electricity. It is very difficult, however, to move from the experience of the light on the eye to its underlying economical and historical base, in terms of its mode of production. That's the problem of integration.

LENNY HOROWITZ: P. Adams, I'd like you to clarify something in my mind. You know I find your interpretation of history, of the history of certain elements in art very interesting, just like you find listening to film-makers very interesting. I would agree that maybe art or theories of art or practice of art or the process of art does not improve, however it seems to me that it certainly changes and those shifts, as Malcolm said, certainly have a tremendous effect on the process. And as you mentioned Cézanne as one of your favourite artists, certainly Cézanne was very influenced by the Impressionist revolution and improvisation. I was a painter for a long time before I was a film-maker. I changed through this horrible thing that you call modern art.

PAS: Wait a second. I have nothing against modern art; I have something against the ideological results of modernism. That is where you begin to define the 'characteristics' of modern art. You invest very heavily in your definitions, and then you have to sit around writing why everything that happens from then on is not modern art, and is wrong. It is known as 'Greenbergism'.

MLG: How do you get out of this by not identifying the characteristics? I mean, it seems to me that you replace this by a-historicism, which suggests there is more freedom in *not* defining the characteristics than defining the characteristics. I think the definition of the characteristics actually allows you to get to a position of greater freedom than the resistance to defining the characteristics. So I don't attach myself to Greenberg, because it seems to me that Greenberg was providing a formula for avant-garde development outside of the context of a broader ideological question. So I don't apply myself to Greenberg any more than …

PAS: I meant Greenberg as a paradigmatic case of what happens when you create this. I'm against the ideology of modernism, not against the work of the twentieth century. There is a major difference.

MLG: But do you see the work of the twentieth century as an advance over the work of the nineteenth century?

PAS: No.

MLG: So why do you attach yourself to it more than to the nineteenth century?

PAS: That's a trade question. This has for various personal circumstances become the area of my publishing and public life. It is for certain reasons, well, one can be frank, why not? Sure, with the help of Jonas' *Fundador* I can say anything. The problem is that there is a lot more space for a person of my peculiar mentality talking about twentieth-century film than talking about nineteenth-century paintings that are richer. This is a field in which there are giants.

AUDIENCE: My name is John Hagan and my question is to Mr Le Grice. I was wondering if you would address yourself more specifically to the question which P. Adams raised about the dialectical nature of romanticism, because starting even with a film-maker like Maya Deren, in whose theoretical writings and films you find very explicit attempts to combine the tenets of Gestalt psychology with Freudian analysis, there does seem to be an attempt at a dialectic, at a combination of what I think you in your book call 'pure experience' or 'existentialism' with structuralism of some sort. You find this starting with Deren, in Brakhage and in many other film-makers which I have the sense you ignore somewhat both here tonight and in your book.

MLG: Okay, I'm not sure if I can address myself directly to the problem because it depends a lot on the definition of romanticism. My conception of romanticism is a split between fantasy and reality, a separation where there is no dialectical relationship between fantasy and reality. In other words, fantasy functions as a substitute for reality and not as a dialectical operation in relationship to it, which demands that fantasy affects the way that the world develops. It expresses the discrepancy between the requirements of a being and the conditions within which that being exists. It expresses the difference, the mismatch between the two. And where there is no requirement for that mismatch to address itself to the change within the world which gives rise to the mismatch. And so for me the question of romanticism is couched in very particular terms of that schism between the fantasy function and its effective relationship to the world.

The non-treatment of Deren is another question. I only knew two of Deren's films. My feeling about Deren as a theorist is that Deren was probably the most, probably the clearest film-maker-theorist that's come out of the American situation. In terms of looking at what she said, I think Deren has said more of real interest than any other film-maker in this situation. On top of which I think that an examination of her films in terms of some kind of formal questions actually does reveal more than I realised at the point when I wrote the book. If I were to rewrite the book, I would certainly include Deren because I think that I was, like a lot of critics at the time, over-determined by the Freudian symbolism of the objects within the film. There is no point in denying their existence. They are there and they do over-determine the relationship to the film.

On the other hand there is an underlying formal structure, and particularly in *Meshes of the Afternoon* with the reviews and repeats of the action which develop in different ways which are thrusting in a direction different from the thrust of the Freudian symbolism. And I think there are a lot of confusions in Deren's work and I think she suffers more than a lot of other film-makers by being, in a sense, one of the first avant-garde film-makers of her period, where there was no other work for her to build on top of. She could only relate herself to a very scanty tradition other than that of the commercial narrative cinema. We are now in a much more developed cultural condition alternative to that of the dominant narrative cinema. So it seems to me that we are much better placed to clarify certain relationships which I think Deren's work was not able to clarify but I do at this point rate Deren's work extremely highly, and when I say formal, that's a shorthand, what I mean is in terms of the plastic implications of time, space, construction in relationship to viewpoint; I don't just mean formal games.

PAS: I must make a comment on that. Your historical vision is more limited than anything else. It is a progressivist model that I cannot possible accept. Secondly, your definition of romanticism is the romantic definition of fancy as applied to seventeenth-century thought. In your book, you describe *Sirius Remembered* as having two elements. The romantic element being the dead dog, and the formal element being Brakhage's manipulation of the camera. What is romantic about the film is, unquestionably, the dialectical relationship between the kinds of camera movement, the presence of the film-maker, the seasonal change, the temporal ambiguity and even the ridiculousness of the image as an effigy. That image is romantic, not because one loves the dead dog, but because it seeks to create out of the material fact, a sign that is so transparent that it becomes a sign of the movement of consciousness.

MLG: I don't agree with you. I think that the use of the dead dog over-determines the material relationship to the way in which the camera investigates. And it actually turns, not completely in that film because some of the formal aspects of the film are extremely strong, but it turns the movement of the camera towards being an expression of the relationship to the subject matter.

PAS: The subject matter is the image: the dead dog as an image and as a sign.

MLG: If that's so, Brakhage confuses it very greatly by over-stressing the personal relationship between him and the dog. I mean, if he wants it to operate as a kind of sign which is illustrating its flexibility in the way which you suggest it does, then he should talk about it a little more carefully. But it's curious he resisted me on exactly the cultural model which you seem to be resisting – the cultural historical model, that takes film as a mediating field, a discourse with something which already exists, which is the condition of cinematic practice. The film-maker operates on and with existent film-making.

PAS: So Deren made leaps.

MLG: I'm not denying the capacity for the individual to bring about major changes within the discourse and to implant those changes within the discourse, that's what made Deren a more important film-maker than another film-maker. I'm not denying the responsibility for the leap. But Deren's responsibility for bringing about the leap does not mean to say that I have to turn Deren into a hero for that leap. I have got to identify with the text of Deren's work, not with Deren as the hero.

PAS: I'm not suggesting that Deren was a hero either.

MLG: I'm not denying the leap. But it is curious that it is the model of cultural restraint through the mediating field of the language and conventions of the cinematic practice at any one historical time that you and Brakhage have both resisted me on. I just bring that up.… How do you kind of deal with the problem of the shift of the material question to the mode of operation of functioning of the mental construction of the viewer of the film? It seems to me this is a major shift which does not fit within any of the conceptions of Brakhage. All of the critical or analytical work which you have been involved with has been to do with the function, the operation of the film-maker on the construction of the medium, but has not seen the relationship of the medium in its mediation with the viewer.

PAS: Now I would see my work differently. What I'm really interested in is the way films – like *Meshes of the Afternoon* – talk to other films in two directions – like *Un Chien andalou* in the past, or Brakhage's *Desistfilm*, or Michael Snow's *Wavelength*, or your film. It is not between the film-maker and the film. The film-maker sometimes throws a lot of light and gives you very helpful suggestions.

MLG: The concept of the film talking to other films: what that really means is that the films define themselves through their differences from other films – through their extension of and their difference from other films.

PAS: Differences and similarities.

MLG: Difference and similarity, right. I would accept that, and I would also suggest that it is progressive, it is not just a question of differentiation. The significance of its differentiation is related to the advance that the differentiation makes in relationship to what has gone before. That the rejection of what has gone before within the mediating field by the artist has to do with a wrongness of what has gone before and the rightness of what one supplants it with.

ANNETTE MICHELSON: I have a question, it is rather simple but I think the question arises from some doubt about your method of analysis in this particular discussion. Do you remember that when you came out of the discussion between P. Adams and you on the 'structural' versus the 'structuralist', a verbal dilemma heralded by that theme involved the material versus the materialist? This might have perhaps been long resolved by the recognition that both of these are dilemmas of work predicated upon an application of art-historical descriptive terms and categories.

MLG: I'm suggesting that some of the myths which informed the concept of art activity in the American situation are similar to those which inform the frontier mentality. The assumption that if there is not enough, we go somewhere else and we find enough to exploit elsewhere, and it's only a question of how quickly we can exploit it in order to support the lifestyle. And it seems to me that the myths which propel that kind of psychology within the social order also inform much of the psychology of the avant-gardist direction of American art, and it seemed to me that there is a concurrence, in the middle 60s, when there is a beginning of awareness that the social structures, particularly in the urban areas of America, have to be dealt with in terms of a planning of development. So we move towards a concept of art which does not see endless idiosyncratic possibilities for art's development. It's curious to me that one of the major innovators in this way is not an American at all, but is Michael Snow who is a Canadian.

PAS: How so?

MLG: Because I think that perhaps underlying the education of someone from Canada is a much greater awareness of the socialising process.

PAS: But how is he an innovator in this particular scheme?

MLG: Because his work defines the manner of the structure in intervention, as well as the experience of the product of that intervention. I mean, particularly in something like *Back and Forth*, the apparatus is defined within the inscription of the film, in a way which the apparatus is obscured in similar operations, for example, in Brakhage's *Sirius Remembered*. There is not such a great difference in the effect of both of those things, but in Michael Snow the apparatus is inscribed, in *Dog Star Man* it is not inscribed.

AM: Your answer raised one or two more questions; I think the reply was interesting. I think it is true, for first of all I am aware of the mix of film-making and other forms of art practised in this country, there are many and not all of them are well-defined and laid bare, as it were. But it is certainly true that by the mid-60s there begins to be, not only in film-making, but in painting and visual arts generally, a specific emphasis on a kind of concern, which is also yours, in fact. And which is that of art as a series of tasks to be done, or problems to be solved. And as you said of Deren before, of clarification. It's very interesting because that word is obviously of Maya Deren's generation and even beyond. Deren is after all a contemporary of, say, Barnett Newman. The category of the imagination is central, and one has the feeling, by the way, that the leaps of which P. Adams talks are not admitted really in your schema, because, as you said, Deren was not able to make certain things clear. And, of course one does not feel that she was able to make anything clear, that she would have seen it in those terms. Her films, like many significant works, make things clear to us, but in ways which are very special and which come much after the period. There is at that point in the mid-60s an emphasis on problem-solving, on task performance and so on. But I'm not at all sure it has to do with a recognition of the task performance in the problem-solving that has to be undertaken by the society, because if one proceeds, and obviously we can't here, to any kind of intensive analysis of the socio-economic period, I think one would find a certain tension, a certain variance between the artist and that particular moment.

AUDIENCE: Do you think that a work interesting to you is anything but idiosyncratic?

MLG: Yes I do, because it doesn't have historical and cultural significance if it's other than idiosyncratic. Because idiosyncrasy is significant in as far as it supports the capacity to be idiosyncratic culturally, so that the idiosyncratic becomes significant as a cultural stance.

PAS: There's a real political problem. I care very little about the metaphor called society. This may be my doom. I have no respect for leftist ideology. I am seized, at certain moments, by what I would in crude terms call certain powerful moments of the human spirit. I'm seized by such things when I see a film like *Wavelength*, Brakhage's *The Art of Vision* and Harry Smith's *Heaven and Earth Magic*. These things grab me not as idiosyncracies, but as fundamental ways of apprehending what we would call the world. When I think of what is real, whatever reality is, it isn't selecting an image out of *Heaven and Earth Magic*, but *Heaven and Earth Magic* has somehow fundamentally affected my vision of the real, as has *Wavelength*, as has *The Art of Vision*, as have numerous poems, many of them by great artists who are much more leftist than anyone in this room. This just isn't my discourse: to talk in these socio-economic terms. I am deeply moved by Eisenstein and Vertov, but I am just as deeply moved by Brakhage and Dreyer.

MLG: So the question really is not the work but how we interpret the mode of cultural intervention of that work. We seem to have a number of points where our sensibilities of value coincide, a large number of points. You and I are in the minority in relation to the dominant cultural practice. We would not be sitting here if our points of reference weren't largely similar. The problem, it seems to me, is in the interpretation of the mode of cultural intervention, the form of analysis which we use to relate the work of art to the social situation.

I'm the first person to admit that there is a real paucity of analytical, critical, and theoretical work done on this area of cultural practice. The fact that I as film-maker have put such a large part of my energy into working in the verbal, analytical, semi-critical polemical area is because no other person is doing it, in the situation I find myself. I'm doing it by default, not because I'm the best qualified. It seems to me that we must determine some cultural priorities, for the development of our practice. I happen to see some cultural priorities, and one of them is an advance and improvement in the analytical, critical, and theoretical work done in relationship to cinematic practice. And a liaison between people whose main practice is criticism and theory, and of people whose main practice is film-making.

PAS: Hold on a second. How do you think such a thing could come about?

MLG: In one way it can come about by film-makers actually approaching the theorists and critics, in a condition where they don't feel egotistically threatened by the operations of critics and theorists.

PAS: At this point another breakdown occurs. As if there were this sensitive, intelligent body called theoreticians, critics, and historians who only have to see good, serious films in order to be converted. This is the offensive critical myth: as if writing criticism were not almost as perverse a passion as taking all of your money and buying celluloid to show it in a room full of a hundred people, across an ocean, for next to nothing. I mean, there are not 'critics', there is only human intelligence, which is rare and I wish I had a hell of a lot more of it.

MLG: Is anyone going to come up from the audience and rescue us?

PAS: Okay, is there a final question? I feel I have been picking on Malcolm a lot.

MLG: That makes you feel bad?

PAS: Yes, this is America. You are a guest, I mean.

MLG: Wait a minute, there is more to be said. The polemic has gone on, as if I'm on the left and you are on the right. But there should be people sitting here who consider themselves more on the left than I am.

PAS: And more on the right than I am.

MLG: Are we going to have any intervention within the body of the discourse, or is it going to be … ?

PAS: They are looking at their watches.

MLG: One of the things we should suggest is that there is no reason why the intervention should not be couched in terms of the statement.

AMOS VOGEL: [to P. Adams Sitney] You made a rather interesting statement earlier to the effect you're not at all opposed to modern art, but that you are opposed to the ideology of modernism. Or rather you're not opposed to modernism but to the ideology of modernism. Now I would like you to clarify this further along several lines. What is the ideology of modernism that you are opposed to? Does modernism have an ideology? Are there developments in the arts, we are only talking about the arts tonight, that can be considered non-ideological in nature, etc.?

PAS: Modernism as opposed to modernity: there is a linguistic distinction, but I think it has meaning. Especially within painting criticism, and by osmosis or seepage into literary criticism, there is a notion that there are works which crucially define the modern and that those works will absolutely and fundamentally dictate the conditions of future modern works, in a system of reduction. Now this ideology comes into *Abstract Film and Beyond*. At the same time there is the Vertovian model and the self-reflexive film. These two things are represented in *Abstract Film and Beyond*, as if they could somehow synthesise. I think they are not synthetic.

MLG: What I tried to do was to bring the structuring of meaning within an ideological question. The fault of Greenberg is that his method of description of the work does not attempt to bring the structure of perception to conception within an ideological description. It does not mean to say that some of the works which are described by Greenberg are not advanced. My rejection of Greenberg is not to do with the work which he supports in total, but to do with the form of criticism which he applies to those works, which in extension feed into the cultural development, which is where it is dangerous. Where what Greenberg misconceptualises, in critical terms, becomes a basis, upon which further art practice develops. This is why it is necessary to do work on the critical ideology, because the critical ideology is effective in the subject. And my attempt to bring some relationship between work at the abstract level as being concerned with perception and conception into some kind of political and ideological framework is to do with establishing within a critical theory, a form which can apply itself to advanced art which is not directly, overtly representational of some kind of political ideology.

PAS: Well, I should add one thing: that the reason Greenberg's name comes up so often is because he is a fine writer: he is an incredibly persuasive writer, and therefore he makes his mark.

MLG: I'm suggesting that there is a determination within the Millennium of a similar kind. And my assumption is that if I come to New York, the first place where I request to do a show is the Millennium, because of that ideological framework.

PAS: Okay, there is an applause; I think it's over. [laughter] See, that's what applause is for: not meaning you are right, but meaning 'Shut up!' Applaud!

IV

GENERAL THEORY

11

Real TIME/SPACE [1972]

From my own film work since 1966, I have gradually been developing ideas which lead me more and more to the consideration of the film in relationship to the conception of 'real' TIME/SPACE. The term 'real-time' has grown in use from the field of computers, but has much wider implications and significance than the way in which it is used there. In computer terms, an operation in 'real-time' is one which is going on as results are calculated and output, rather than one where results are stored 'off-line' for future consultation. 'Real-time' is *now*. Real TIME/SPACE is *now* and *here*.

Though this seems simple, it is far from obvious how such a general notion can be applied to film. First of all the whole history of the commercial cinema has been dominated by the aim of creating convincing illusory time/space, and eliminating all traces of the actual physical state of affairs at any stage of the film, from scripting, through shooting, editing, printing, promotion to projection. However, largely through developments in the underground film, it is possible to see an increasing concern with the problem of 'actuality', 'reality' at the various stages of film production and presentation. I would like to introduce a diagrammatic scheme for applying the notion of real TIME/SPACE to the processes or events of film.

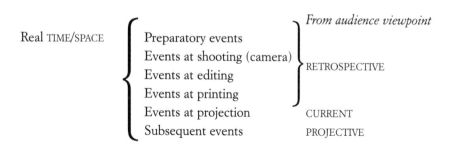

In the third column, I have carefully included the way in which the various aspects of 'reality' in the film relate to the audience or more precisely the individual viewer. His point of access is through the projection event only, and that for him is the current confrontation. Certainly this factor has been a prime consideration for me, and I have given a great deal of thought to the kind of condition, role and behaviour which is available to the audience, to the 'credibility' of what is presented as some form of, or relation to 'reality'. I have considered the situation of the audience politically and ethically, and have reacted strongly against the passive subjectivity to a prestructured substitute and illusory reality which is the normal situation for the audience of the commercial film. The language structures developed in this aspect of cinema have conditioned film-makers' and audience expectancy, in such a way that even the 'realist' documentary, the politically and socially conscious film and much of the alternative cinema of the underground, operates in the same ethos of audience passivity. In this situation, there can be no credible relationship between the current presentation, the events which it purports to be 'about', and the method by which these events are selected and structured by the film's process. In other words, the techniques of film have been primarily developed to 'manipulate' a recorded (picture and sound) 'reality' into structures and events which never happened in anything like the terms which the language tells us they happened, while presenting the result as a 'representation' of reality. As a result of this, whatever the motivation, if any of the methods of 'narrative' (manipulative) editing and shooting are used, even in relationship to 'newsreel', or documentary material, the result is inevitably suspect. Before any film can relate itself to events in retrospect of its presentation to an audience, with any credibility, it is necessary to develop language and techniques which can clarify, within the film's structure, the actual processes which are taking place.

The complexity of this problem defies any obvious solution in filmic terms, however, I am not the only film-maker who has identified and reacted to it in some way.

Primacy of the Projection Event

The direction of my thinking, and the tendencies in my films, keep returning me to an affirmation of the projection event as the primary reality. In other words, the real TIME/SPACE event at projection, which is the current, tangible point of access for the audience, is to be considered as the experiential base through which any retrospective record, reference or process is to be dealt with by the audience. This reverses the situation common to the cinematic language where experience of the real TIME/SPACE at projection is subsumed by various aspects of manipulated retrospective 'reality'. My own awareness of this problem has developed gradually, and though other film-makers' interpretations of their work may not correspond to mine (it is not important if they do not), I see a fairly clear historical direction.

The Camera and Shooting Event

Perhaps beginning at the cinéma vérité movement there has been a tendency to seek (mostly only partially conscious) some form of TIME/SPACE equivalence between the events before the camera, and those presented to the audience. The greatest obstacle to forming some kind of interplay between the real time and real space of the cinema-viewing situation, and the recorded or implied time of the film's action, has been the enormous discrepancy of scale between them. One and a half hours in a roughly rectangular cinema interior to be related to the portrayal of a lifetime in Russia … . They are so far apart in scale as to be unrelatable.

Andy Warhol was the first film-maker to find an extreme enough base from which to deal with this problem. His work from 1963 to 1965 including *Sleep*, *Empire*, *Couch*, *Blow Job*, *Harlot* extended the realist tradition. The deliberate use of unfakeable continuous takes, the inclusion of white flare at the end of reels, background noise and director's instructions on soundtracks allows the series of recorded images to stand as a credible *equivalent* for the events before and in the camera – the processes and actual state of affairs at all stages are made fairly clear in a matter-of-fact way. However, Warhol seems to have abandoned the more fundamental implications of this earlier work in favour of a return to a narrative/documentary style, leaving its extension to others. Of these, the two who have explored the possibilities of 'equivalence' most thoroughly have been Peter Gidal (*Room*, *Focus*, *Takes*, *Bedroom*) and Larry Gotheim (*Fog Line*, *Barn Rushes*), all these works, particularly Gidal's, have a determination to work with a 'shallow' camera TIME/SPACE – shallow space in that the camera is either static or its movements are limited and formal, the arena for filming (frequently a room interior) is directly relatable to the space in which the film is to be seen – shallow time in the basic use of continuous takes where the shooting time can stand as a direct equivalent for the projection time.

From the introduction of the notion of equivalence between the shooting (camera) and projection TIME/SPACE, the possibility of other forms of relatability must arise. The work of Michael Snow, beginning at *Wavelength*, draws on Warhol's TIME/SPACE equivalence as a starting point, but this film and ↔ (*Back and Forth*) develop more complex kinds of relationship. In both, some strict continuity allows the real TIME/SPACE of projection to become a 'concrete' experience in its own right. It is clear though, that neither film is shot in one take, or one camera 'set-up', but that in both the 'shooting' TIME/SPACE is shallow enough for the experience at projection to become an analogue or be used as a metaphor for it. A complication arises in that both films try to form a compatibility with a more conventional illusory, narrative TIME/SPACE, I think in a confusing and detrimental way, stretching the tenuous thread of relatability with the 'concrete' projection experience beyond its limits. This is unfortunate as a new kind of possibility emerges, particularly from ↔ (*Back and Forth*), a product of the special camera procedure. This also involves illusion of a different kind, it is non-retrospective, a physical/psychological product of the 'concrete' experience. The repetitive movement of the camera side to side, as it speeds up, brings about a visual transformation of the portrayed and actual space experience, among other transformations seeming to widen the screen, so that the screen wall takes on the identity of the wall and windows before the camera, and the filmed room space flattens to the thinness of the screen or the photographic celluloid. Mattiejn Siep's film *Double Shutter* also explores this area of perceptual transformation of TIME/SPACE brought about by extreme processes of selection/sampling at the camera event (camera on a swing, with a secondary rotating shutter in front) continuing the development of a 'Cubistic' film TIME/SPACE. Roger Hammond's new film, *Erlanger Program* also extends and makes clearer this 'relativistic' conception of the camera event, and the way in which construction of 'reality' is directly related to the methods and procedures of observation. However, his film raises so many interrelated questions and new thoughts that there is no value in any short cursory analysis. I will save myself that pleasure for another piece.

The Printer

In the earliest stages of film's history, the same piece of equipment was often used as camera, printer and projector. The similarities of functioning provide something of a 'mechanistic' basis for the 'equivalence' idea. Until recently, printing has been the area of retrospective TIME/SPACE (or content) which has involved me most. I have been interested by the way in which it allows physical aspects of the medium, the reality of the celluloid, emulsion, sprockets, the nature and capabilities of the machinery to become the basis of experience and content. Though I am not completely convinced that printing, being less 'retrospective' in the whole film process, gives it an advantage in relating to the projection event over involvement with the camera, it does seem to help with the elimination of narrative, and psychological portrayal factors. This assists the gradual focusing down onto the nature and processes of film. Historically (certainly for myself), the relationship between the printer and projector has helped to develop awareness of the components of the projection event. (Although I now see some of the involvement in this area as an inhibition to a more thorough concern with the projection event itself.)

The earliest direct references to the film *material* as *content* (celluloid etc.) came around 1966 with George Landow's *Film in which there Appear Sprocket Holes, Edge Lettering, Dust Particles, etc.* It started its life as a loop film performed by Landow (live projection situation!), as did my own *Little Dog for Roger* (two screen loop film, 1967). This film was printed by me on a converted, old projector, printing 9.5mm direct onto 16mm. It caused so many difficulties in the printer/projector that the resultant film referred very strongly to the various aspects of celluloid, sprockets, scratches, and projection. The projection slip printed on the film still causes projectionists to stop the film to correct the fault. The other film which most contributed to a developing awareness of these areas was *Rob Film* (*Raw Film*, 1968), by Birgit and Wilhelm Hein. Again the production was closely linked to projection activity, being refilmed from the screen, pushing all kinds of pasted-up 8mm and 16mm material through a very accommodating Siemens projector. These films were produced unaware of the others, and though all very different from each other (I still have never seen Landow's film, but reports indicate many differences), their independent emergence supports the idea of some coherent, more than idiosyncratic direction. Recently the possibilities of the printer, and material aspects of film as content, have become the basis for a wide variety of work. It is premature to define 'movements' in this area. It is complicated by a number of factors, the first of which is that so many possibilities have been opened up in a previously neglected area that it is difficult to see which are fundamental and which are peripheral. The second is, that though the 'tactile' direction of the first three films has been extended in films like *Green Cut Gate*, and *Maja Replicate* by Fred Drummond, and *Slides* by Annabel Nicolson, other areas have emerged exploring time-based structuring, permutation of loops or other mathematical ideas, films like *Film No. 1* by David Crosswaite, *St Pauls* and *Clock Time* by Stuart Pound, my own *Reign of the Vampire* and *Love Story 2*, and *Shepherd's Bush* by Mike Leggett. The last two films in particular show some of the difficulties of classification, being strongly concerned with 'duration' in the projection event. Though both the films are dependent on structuring at the printer, this aspect is given some kind of 'neutrality', so that the current time experiences at the projection can be dominant. For myself the concept of 'duration' as a concrete (quasi-sculptural) dimension has recurred, being included in the titles of three of my films, *Blind White Duration*, *Blue Field Duration*, *Whitchurch Down* (*Duration*), and is a notion which seems to play a significant part in the Michael Snow films, particularly *One Second in Montreal*. Another direction has emerged out of concern with film copying procedures, which creates many new ideas of 'content', and uses highly 'retrospective' material, and does so in a way which completely declares the process, treating existing film as raw material for transformation. Though I was vaguely aware of this direction in *Little Dog for Roger*, Ken Jacob's *Tom, Tom, the Piper's Son* (1969) is a clear and deliberate exploration of the transformation and methods of transformation of a small piece of very early silent film. My own films, *Berlin Horse* (1970) and *1919* (1971), have similar concerns: *1919*, taking a short piece of Russian newsreel from the date of the title, attempts, through printing transformations, to build an insight into the changing function of a piece of film as it relates differently to the world throughout its history.

Much of the work that has been described has a degree of conscious awareness of the real TIME/SPACE of the projection event, is aware of some of the factors of audience behaviour in assimilating or structuring the film's information, and is influenced by this awareness at some level in the film's construction. However, there is yet another important direction which has emerged, which depends almost entirely on the physical events in the projection situation for its 'content'. This is the direction opened up around the notion of 'flicker'. Though *Arnulf Rainer* (1957) by Peter Kubelka is clearly the first film to use alternating completely white and black frames, and is an exceptional and prophetic film, it has a musical, compositional structure which inhibits developing 'content' out of the fundamental perceptual and conceptual mechanisms of the audience. *The Flicker* (1966) by Beverley and Tony Conrad on the other hand, using the same black and white frame limitation, works almost completely with the 'autonomic' nervous system as the basis. The film develops higher-order perceptual (rhythm 'Gestalts') and conceptual structures but is careful to maintain a 'neutrality' in the film's internal structuring, so that the viewer can be more concerned with his own transformation of awareness, than with discovering the film-makers' structural intentions. The viewer's own behaviour is his content. *The Flicker* has opened up the possible, more precise, understanding of human response to different orders of periodicity in the visual field, from events of very short duration 1/24th of a second, to controllably long durations, and various stages between. Also in 1966, Paul Sharits, with *Ray Gun Virus*, began to explore a similar region, using colour frames. Though his work has never had the 'neutrality' and strict limitation of *The Flicker*, the viewer is frequently able to adopt a similar role in relationship to his own responses. Between 1966 and 1968 he made a number of statements which show that he was concerned with the development of a new concept of cinema, with its base in the sensory and conceptual mechanisms of the audience, and the physical realities of the material and equipment of film production and projection. His most recent films, *S:TREAM:S:S:ECTION:S:ECTION:S:S:ECTIONED*, and *Inferential Current*, show a concern with the celluloid, scratches etc., an area of involvement already described, but there is another direction which he has frequently (at least since 1969 or 1970) expressed a desire to explore: the conception of film as the basis of an 'ongoing' gallery installation, and which he recently was able to realise in one work. This direction brings up some questions and ideas which are crucial to my own work, but because of the developments I have been describing and recent work by other film-makers, I consider many of them to be more generally valid. Increasing awareness of the projection event as a primary reality has led to concern in five interrelated areas of exploration.

1. The relationship of the audience to retrospective filmic reality.
2. The nature of the medium: materials, equipment, processes.
3. The nature of behaviour and experience available to the audience in relationship to a current 'concrete' reality.
4. Time or duration as a 'concrete' dimension.
5. Notions of the spatial or TIME/SPACE structuring of the projection event.

I have discussed the first two areas, and touched on an aspect of the third and fourth but work in those areas and the last is at a formative and uncertain stage. Although exploration of perception and duration can be continued in the present projection format and context, my own feeling is that significant further development is being inhibited by the physical structure (and cultural conditions) of the projection situation, even within the more flexible 'underground' context.

My own recent work has drawn me into an overriding concern with the projection event itself, and an increasing desire to limit retrospective input to that situation, or at least to have it clearly subservient to the current reality. By considering the nature of the film event at projection in more general terms, a wide range of new possibilities of filmic structure and audience relationship emerge. In addition I feel that many existing films could be seen and understood better if the audience and projection relationship could be re-specified. I have always encountered difficulties in presenting my double projection work, but it has just been possible to contain it within most cinema formats. However, my most recent work including live shadow action and spatial distribution of projectors is usually impossible, or forced into a compromise form. I see film as the basic component of a TIME/SPACE event structure, where time can be thought of as a dimension almost in a sculptural sense, and the distribution of projectors and sound sources can be specified as part of the work. In this situation, projection serves film, rather than acting as an unconscious determinant of it. As well as my own recent film pieces, other film-makers have either produced work or have presented ideas needing a new cinematic format.

Tony and Beverley Conrad recently showed in London (under very inadequate conditions) two works for spatially distributed projection. *Four Square* is a film designed for four screens surrounding the audience. Through its spatial distribution of abstract image and sound it begins to build up a TIME/SPACE experience where the mental construction of the events do not clearly differentiate between separation/distribution in time from separation/distribution in space. A unified field TIME/SPACE experience. Their second (untitled) piece using four loops of identical and very simple slightly oscillating vertical stripes was projected for one and a half hours, with gradual changes in the projection format. This always allowed the audience time to experience internal/subjective perceptual transformations to basically simple and stable external phenomena. The recent Paul Sharits installation also involved four projectors, where the images were rotated through 90 degrees (into a tall narrow screen format), projected side by side. The film was printed to incorporate sprockets, frame lines and soundtrack within the image, the total result of the projection being like a shimmering section of film viewed from the side. His expressed intention for this format is largely in terms of creating a situation where the audience can enter or leave the work at any time, viewing from any angle.

In my own shadow pieces, though the inclusion of people performing some action introduces a theatrical and imagist aspect, my main concern is still formal, and has a strong sympathy with the Conrad work. I have four shadow pieces, but *Love Story 1* has only been performed once, was exploratory and improvised, the most successful elements being incorporated into *Horror Film 1*. This piece has very simple components, a sound loop tape of breathing, two movie projectors with loops of pure colours fading in and out of each other and a larger frame slide projector, with one fixed colour. All are superimposed on each other with the projectors aimed from different angles. The superimpositions create a continually changing colour light mix. I interrupt the beam with a series of formal actions creating a complex set of coloured shadows. The final section involves focusing a pair of skeleton hands onto the screen in relationship to my own hands. The intention with this, as with my other shadow pieces, is to build a complex visual experience out of simple and readily available aspects of the projection situation. *Horror Film 2* uses a back projection screen with a variety of projection sources, including a red and green source close together. The space and action behind the screen is revealed piece by piece by the shadows from discrete light sources (searchlight eyes, an analogue for the camera). The information which is given is continually contradicted by further information from different light sources, including the red and green stereoscopic source (the piece is viewed with red and green glasses). It is an illusionistic piece; in much the same way that the tricks of a magician are illusionistic, all the components for the illusion are concretely available. It explores some of the primitive mechanisms for dealing with information from sometimes contradictory traces, but which none the less are known to be being produced out of an 'actuality' in current real TIME/SPACE. *Love Story 3* is also a simple piece in its components. A person walks backwards and forwards across two white screens casting a shadow, later his actual shadow is joined by pre-filmed shadows performing the same actions. Gradually the actions within the film deviate from what is directly possible for the shadow cast by the person in real TIME/SPACE, but the two 'realities' are kept closely relatable as references to each other. Similar to the problem of illusion touched on in reference to Snow, there is an important difference when the determinants for illusion or TIME/SPACE manipulation are concretely available, and when they are hidden. In my 3D shadow piece some of the anomalies of perception and illusion would have no structural significance (or tension) if the same effects had been pre-printed onto film, with all the manipulation tricks which are possible in this. Their significance lies in their being in a concrete referential situation, the product of a current reality.

Sally Potter's double projection film and live event, *The Building*, explored (earlier than *Love Story 3*) some possibilities of the comparison between pre-filmed action and their current live reconstruction, but her film work, recently including dance, extends much more towards theatre than my own. Film inserts have been 'used' in the theatre situation from time to time, particularly since the multimedia direction, however, Sally Potter's work integrates the film and theatrical action in a way which does not relegate the film to the role of moving backdrop, and extends the formal possibilities of film and theatre. The work of David Dye represents another direction, mostly based on the physical manipulation of 8mm projectors in some near one-to-one equivalence to the camera handling which gave rise to the film in the projector. Small differences in the nature of the two events become significant content in the 'idea' space between the image and the projector handling. Some of the 'semantic' aspects of Dye's work are similar to earlier film and live action pieces by Peter Wiebel and Valie Export, isolating specific discrepancies between the nature of film and 'reality'.

Recent work by David Crosswaite, Birgit and Wilhelm Hein, Mike Leggett, Annabel Nicolson and Tony Hill has all stretched the conventional projection situation to its limits and beyond.

We have now reached a situation where it is necessary for projection events to be defined and specified at a more general level, controlling the component elements, their space and time distribution, and audience relationship as an integral aspect of the film structure.

The biggest problem to be dealt with is creating a physical 'venue' for this kind of work. The most suitable existing possibility must lie in performance or installation in the art gallery situation, and this requires the back-up of a pool of suitable equipment which can be transported, with performance or installation, for longer than a one-night stand. Meanwhile the work will continue to develop and be seen under inadequate conditions.

12

Material, Materiality, Materialism [1978]

Preamble

I am primarily a film-maker and artist, my inclination is to work-things-out, or work-things-through by making films. At the same time, my praxis has always involved a significant proportion of time spent on theoretical and critical consideration. I am aware that none of my theoretical work has involved the depth of study which is rightly expected of a person whose main practice is theory. On the other hand, I have the advantages of insight which comes from an involvement with the practical problems of film-making. Being deeply concerned with the problems of immediate practice I hope allows me to avoid the worst aspects of abstract academicism.

As a film-maker, my analysis and theory also inevitably relates very closely to my own particular work, but as an artist I have become increasingly concerned with art as a social and cultural rather than private and personal activity. As an artist, I am not only constrained by my own social history, but perhaps more importantly, by the historical context of the medium I use and in particular the current state of its 'language'. ('Language' in this sense implying the specific preconceptions and habits of usage within the medium.) Artists work against the enculturated determinants of their medium. The results neither free the individual, art, nor society from enculturation, rather they continually modify the determinants within the effective range of the medium/language in question. In the same way that I view my film work as 'cultural' and 'historical', from a critical point of view, I draw no clear distinction between my own films and those of other film-makers. I am aware of large areas of overlap and influence between my work and that of my contemporaries.

Artists contribute to change in society through the modification of the preconceptions and habits of usage in their medium or language. More difficult to establish is when these modifications represent advances or regressions in social-artistic terms. It is certainly not possible without recourse to questions of ideology, politics or ethics within the critical theory. Even if an ideological stance can be agreed for criticism, there remains the problem of 'reading' the meanings and implications within the works themselves. Both are major and crucial issues of art criticism confused by the East/West polarisation identifying Marxist art with Socialist Realism, and in reaction, Western capitalist art with a false a-politicism.

In this paper, even if I were capable, there is no space to go into these general questions in depth. The ideological stance will remain mostly implicit though it is clearly orientated towards a Marxist–materialist position. The paper will tend to concentrate on some aspects of the second issue, that of 'reading' and in particular on the issue of materiality in avant-garde film. I shall outline a broadly historical schema with a definition of some areas of problematic as the basis for discussion.

Materiality in Avant-Garde Film

At this stage I use the term 'materiality' so as not to preassume its relationship to 'materialism'. In its simplest sense, the question of materiality is seen in relationship to the: *physical substances* of the film medium, the film strip itself as material and object. Work in this area drawing, and paying attention to the physical base (acetate), emulsion surface, sprockets, joins etc., easily shades over into an awareness of: *mechanical and physico-chemical processes*. In this case attention is drawn to the photochemical response and its chemical development, the transfer of image through printing, the transformation of image through these processes and the mechanical systems of film transport in camera, printer, or projector.

The earliest example of this awareness is found in Man Ray's *Retour à la raison* (1922) through his incorporation into film of the direct photography 'Rayogram' technique, by laying small objects like dust, nails, pins and springs directly onto the film before exposure without the use of a camera. Distancing the representational image in this way draws attention to film substance and process as an element of content.

Although the hand-made films of Lye, McLaren and aspects of Brakhage (*Mothlight*, 1963, for example) develop this awareness, to some extent the issue is masked by its incorporation as an expressive means rather than an intrinsic basis of content. The earliest clear explication of this region of attention is seen in three similar works made independently of each other within a couple of years. They are Landow's *Film in Which … etc.* (1966), *Roh Film* (1968) by Birgit and Wilhelm Hein, and my own *Little Dog for Roger* (1967). These three films enlarge on the area of involvement hinted at in the Man Ray film, making greater use of repetition through printing, and exploring the presentation or representation of the substances, film strip edges, sprockets, etc., and exploring the tactic/device of including substance aberrations like dust, tears and scratches, and machine transport aberrations (not in the Landow film) like film slip, jamming and lateral movements.

Another relatively simply definable area of attention to filmic materiality is: *optic functioning*. As with the more serious areas of Op Art, film work in this area exposes rather than exploits perceptual phenomena. Though Duchamp's *Anaemic Cinema* (1926) is the initial historical point of reference this set of possibilities is most clearly developed in the full-frame 'flicker' films beginning with Kubelka's *Arnulf Rainer* (1960) and most thoroughly explored in its own terms by Conrad's *Flicker* (1966) and in a number of works by Sharits like *Ray Gun Virus* (1966). This area of exploration which shifts the question of materiality from the film-material to the material functioning of the viewer, in a primitive sense, is made possible by the location of film's frame/projection rate at the threshold of optical discrimination.

Even with the three areas outlined, it must be pointed out that the schematisation only deals with certain aspects of any works which might be used to illustrate them. From this point the issues become more complex and though in my own work their emergence has followed a developmental pattern (to some extent), I am wary of overstating this coherence as other constructions might be found, particularly from the framework of another film-maker's development. We must now move into the more difficult area of:

Duration as a 'concrete' dimension. The complexity of this issue stems from a number of sources, the first being the extremely strong cultural assumption of cinematic 'time' as a compression, absolutely basic to the illusionist, commercial cinema. Initial grasp of this question emerges as a by-product of Warhol's continuous take films like *Sleep* (1963) or *Empire* (1964). Some development of this awareness comes about in Snow's *Wavelength* (1966), but more clearly in his *One Second in Montreal* (1969), my own *Blind White Duration* (1967), in *Und Sie* by Birgit and Wilhelm Hein (1967) and in *Room Double Take* (1967) by Gidal. Each of these films has some conscious awareness of the factor of actual duration, the period of watching the film, to some extent treating duration as a quasi-sculptural dimension. In an earlier article (*Art and Artists*, Dec. 1972) I misleadingly talked about this notion of duration using the term 'real-time'. While being concerned with the actual passage of time in the viewing situation, the experience of this, even if measurable in the 'clock' sense, must still be thought of in the relative and experiential sense. (The inadequacy of numerical measurement as a correlative for experience of actual duration also reflects on the spatial experience of sculpture.) From these considerations of duration I was led to define three areas of film time (and space).

1. The apparent time/space of the film's interior subject. This is the illusory time created by the construction of the narrative action.
2. The time/space of the film's making (the actual time/space of the pro-filmic events originally considered by me primarily as the film's shooting).
3. The time/space of the film's presentation.

In the conventional cinema the illusory narrative subsumes and obliterates any grasp either of the time/space of the pro-filmic event or the actual duration of the projection. By using filmic constructions derived from narrative cinema, documentary cinema also fails to develop access to experience of duration as a material experience in the region of the documented camera event. Except in rare instances of cinema documentation where narrative editing is eliminated in favour of an un-manipulated presentation of the shot material as in the unsophisticated work of Lumière and early Warhol, there are no examples of access to the shooting durations as 'material', and even in these instances the actual duration of the presentation is frequently subsumed under involvement in the presented interior action. What became evident to me was that the only point of actual/material access to the filmic process for the film's viewer – the projection time and space – was invariably subsumed as an experience by some element of retrospective content.

This awareness leads to the treatment of: *the projection situation as material event*. Consistent with the general tendency to focus on the material aspects of film is the attempt to locate the primary area of cinema reality as close as possible to the actual/material situation of its access – the projection. This motive, as well as having a bearing on the development of reflexive film structures and the minimalisation of 'content', forms a relatively conscious basis for some of the British 'expanded cinema' developments. In my own work I sought to limit images deriving from other times and spaces and even the manipulations at the printing and editing stage. This led to works like my *Horror Film 1* (1970), which attempted to make use only of the simple components readily visible within the projection event itself, working with simple loops of changing colour, directly-cast shadows and moving projectors. This attempt to eliminate the 'pro-filmic' event or to limit as far as possible all elements of 'retrospective' content, as might have been predicted, became a complex project which isolated a number of major problems. The first of these was the impossibility of eliminating the pro-filmic event – instead, what could be considered as the pro-filmic event/s shifted, for instance, to include issues concerning the manufacture of the materials, equipment, or simply power sources for the projection. This issue is examined in 'Principles of Cinematography', 1973, which included a reading describing the manufacture of acetate base. The second problem is that of the control on the meaning of work imposed by context. All works are made and seen within a historical and physical context. The more interior referential content is reduced the more context determines experience. Minimal art initiates the possibility that context can be examined as content (see my *Pre Production* and Conrad's *Yellow Movies* for some of the consequences of minimalisation on context and questions of conceptual information about manufacture, as content within works). The question of minimalisation or reductivism raises a number of crucial critical issues. Peter Wollen, for example, interprets the paring down of concerns and the elimination of the most obvious aspect of the pro-filmic event (the action before the camera) as basically tautological – film, self-reflexivity about film (a tautology?). There is a great confusion here which stems from the strength of the Greenberg critical framework encouraging, particularly in America, a practice, but more importantly a film critical ethos, stressing interior relationships, interpreting materiality in a neoplatonic, essentialist way. This assumes a search for formal purity based on the 'essence' of cinema. It must be made clear that a film which deals with/through grain or scratches for example is no less referential or significatory than one which contains recognisable photographic images. All events are contingent on other events and all carry, to some degree, an inscription from those on which they are contingent. A scratch, in standing as a result of its making, not only refers to the material on which it is made, or the material fact of its making, but also initiates a complex signification through the 'how' and 'why' of the act. Elimination of photographic portrayal does not eliminate exterior reference or signification. At the same time work on the 'signifier' makes it possible for the relative and constructive relationship between signifier and signified itself to become 'content'. A more obvious consequence of the reduction of particular representation in art (abstraction) is the way in which concepts of ordering or structure can be focused on without the limitation of anthropomorphic interpretation. (A Kandinsky abstract is no less a 'self-portrait' than a Rembrandt with that title, and in a sense, allows a more direct access to certain aspects of human functioning.)

Even if part of my own initial motivation in concentrating on the projection event was the elimination of the pro-filmic and exterior signification, the result of this stage of work was to develop other areas of problematic. Establishing the primacy of the material access to the work at projection and extending the notion of what constituted the pro-filmic events as well as grasping some of the issues of signifier/signified in the 'phenomenological' situation of confrontation with material shifted the problem to that of the integration and conditions of access to the pro-filmic.

Both my own *White Field Duration* (1973) and William Raban's *2 minutes 45 seconds* (1973) were made with a conscious intention to reintegrate the pro-filmic event of the camera while maintaining the primacy of the projection situation. The changed frame of reference made possible through the primacy of the projection as a material situation allowed the re-examination of film as a recording or representational medium focusing on this, not as an assumed capability, but as a *problematic*. In what way, and to what degree can film bring to the material-present of the screening elements of experience of information deriving from another (prior) time and space? To what degree can the cine-photographic capability of recording be integrated into a material (materialist) reading of film?

The development which is represented by these two films involves a shift in the way in which issues of materiality and 'form' may be viewed. The awareness of materiality has been established through attention to physical substance, projection beam, screen surface etc. Where it has focused on process, it has concentrated on the mechanical and photochemical. At this point, what comes into question are the *procedures*, both those of the film's making and those of the film's viewing and their relationship to each other. It is necessary to consider this concept of 'material' procedure in relationship to structure and form.

In some senses, the term (which I have avoided so far) 'structure' or 'structural' has become, for many people, including film-makers, synonymous with form. Leading to a concept of film's structure as a set of describable internal relationships or consistencies. This is often made respectably 'objective' by using numerical systems. In this situation, the false dichotomy between form and content is perpetrated, where the form/structure can be read as the set of internal relations or general consistent 'shape' and the content as the signification of the images and depicted actions or objects. Masked here is the need to question the signification of the chosen system of relations or form as the issues of meaning and implication carried at the levels of structure and plastic construction are more fundamental than those at the level of object or action representation. The reduction of the concept of structure to that of static a-temporality (effectively equivalent to form) reinforces the formalist reading. This can be opposed by a dynamic concept of structure (better considered as 'structuring') which can be accessed by the development of a critical language based on an examination of procedures. Concentration on material procedures, those of the viewer (e.g. perception, differentiation, conception) and those of the film-maker (selection, collection, structuring and presentation) promises a potential terminology more suitable for dealing with duration, transformation, cine-recording and perception-phase (attention changes in the viewer). In this case, form or structure can be viewed in the dynamic sense following as an aspect or 'residue' of procedure or as the initiator of a viewing dynamic. The concept of procedure does not dispense with that of signification. In criticism, questions of the signification of procedures within a work must be asked, but at the same time the dynamics of the processes of signification must be seen as part of the problematic of works themselves.

Some recent work by myself, *After Lumière* (1974); Gidal, *Condition of Illusion* (1976); Dunford, *Arbitrary Limits* (1974); William Raban, *At One* (1975); and Tim Bruce, *Meeting* (1975) all deal in some way with the relationship between procedures of film viewing and those of film-making as a conscious problematic.

They all initiate a reflexive speculation on the acts of viewing and the integration of the material acts which have preceded the current state of the work and upon which it is materially contingent. Access through the work to speculation on its chain of contingencies isolates the particularities of film's capability to refer to events not materially present through those traces which are the residue of its material processes. This is not an isolation of the 'essence' of cinema, as those procedures which can be accessed and integrated are extensible and not the result of some intrinsic 'nature' of the medium. Though at any historical point, access and integration are conditioned by the enculturated habits of usage.

Underlying this concept of integration and access are a set of assumptions concerning the ideological relationship set up between the viewer of the film and the film itself (or with the film-maker through the work). The intention to locate the primary reality of film in the time and space materiality of the viewing situation and its extension to seek a traceable relationship between the verifiable material of that situation and the pro-filmic events on which it is contingent must also be seen in the same ideological framework.

As I indicated in the preamble to the paper this topic is beyond the scope of this paper to examine in detail, but some points must be made (rather as contentions than arguments).

The aims of realism and (Marxist) materialism have always assumed the need to present and take account of the actual state of affairs. Marx's concept of historical materialism clearly and simply is concerned (in opposition to the idealists and Hegel) with establishing 'the real process of production, starting from the simple material production of life, and the comprehension of this form of intercourse connected with and created by this mode of production … as the basis of all history' (Marx–Engels' *Gestamtausgabe* Vol. 1 Part 5 (1845–46)). However, the question of what form of artistic practice is consistent with this concept of history is confused by the attempted utilisation of art for specific propaganda aims within revolution. While the materialist view of history opposes illusion and fantasy, the exigencies of revolution paradoxically encourage the incorporation of illusion and illusionism within propagandist art. The paradox between realism and illusionism is unacceptable as a basis for materialist art as ultimately is the conditioning function of propaganda (bearing in mind that our consciousness is already conditioned by social circumstances and its prevailing propaganda). I take the view that the development of a materialist consciousness is not consistent either with illusionism or conditioning but is only possible through the individual's active, participatory structuring of actuality. Within this framework film should be considered as an element in the experience of actuality for the viewer. Examination of film's reality involves attention to its materiality/actuality as the basis of the film experience. In this respect, apperception of the current reality within the film viewing situation might be considered to serve as a model situation in which materialist consciousness might be initiated. Engagement in the problematics of, meaning, signification, structuring and material process etc. extends the rudiments of awareness of substance into material reflexive attention. Illusionism, on the contrary, draws attention towards a condition where perception is divorced from the possibility of making effective choice, turning experience (information) into exterior spectacle. Within the art work effective choice can only take place through the integratable relations of substance and processes. The only art which deserves the term realist is that which confronts the audience with the material conditions of the work. Work which seeks to portray a 'reality' existing in another place at another time is illusionist. Confusing the issue of illusionism in cinema is its base in photography. As a photochemical recording system there is a chain of contingency (material consequence) between the record (specific and particular) and that of which it is a record. The tendency for identification of the 'image' to go beyond the specific to an assumption of 'standing-for' aspects of the situation for which it is not a material record must be engaged as an active element of the material(ist) problematic, within the works themselves. In this respect the issues of illusion and documentation become aspects of the material(ist) film problematic. Issues impinging on narrative also become aspects of the problematic both through the recording of incidents of action which have development (consequential structure) and more importantly where the organisation of presentation has a developmental sequence.

As the mainstream of cinema practice in both narrative and documentary fields remains illusionist and antithetical to the development of a materialist cinema, care must be taken in the development of a terminology whereby the questions of cinematic documentation, illusion, incident, narrative and narration are dealt with in the context of work which has established a material basis for its practice.

13

Problematising the Spectator's Placement in Film [1978]

Since I began making films in 1965 much of my theoretical concern has been with the role and condition of the spectator. The shift towards a similar concern in Christian Metz's writing represented by the article 'The Imaginary Signifier'[1] enables (and demands) a relationship between his work and my own practice. This paper addresses some of the concepts Metz presents in that article from the position of a film practice which seeks to transform rather than exploit or simply analyse the condition of the spectator.

A major object of Metz's article is to define that which is special to the cinematic signifier. More precisely, he terms this a signifier effect (already introducing the spectator subject by implication), which he defines as 'a specific coefficient of signification (and not a signified) linked to the intrinsic workings of the cinema …'.

In discussing signification in general earlier, Metz quite clearly aligns himself to the awareness that signification is not 'just a consequence of social development' but becomes 'a party to the constitution of sociality itself'. While quoting Lacan as a footnote, 'The order of the symbol can no longer be conceived as constituted by man, but rather as constituting him', he still makes it plain that he sees, by what he nicely calls 'the partial "uncoupling" of the laws of signification from short-term historical developments', the capacity of the semiotic to function as a radical, definitional, sociality. In other words, he makes it evident that the conditions of signification are not immutable, however deeply determined.

In approaching the definition of the intrinsic condition of the cinematic signifier, Metz is forced to go by the route of the only form of cinematic practice which he knows, namely the dominant industrial fiction film. He defines the fiction film as 'film in which the cinematic signifier does not work on its own account but is employed entirely to remove the traces of its own steps, to open immediately on to the transparency of a signified …'. However, this 'intention' of transparency applies in structural terms to every film which Metz might quote, including his non-fictional genres like documentary, coming as they do from a context which has an investment in maintaining the transparency of the signifier. This in part leads Metz to the notion: 'Every film is a fiction film.'

Without positing the whole avant-garde cinema, or even structural/materialist film, as some *absolute* alternative to the cinematic form which provides Metz's historical reference points, it is none-the-less a polarity within which instances can be quoted providing some embodiment of what is the implicit obverse of Metz's definition, namely 'film in which the signifier *does* work on its own account'.

When Metz says 'attempts to "defictionalise" the spectacle, notably since Brecht, have gone further in the theatre than in the cinema ...', he helps to obscure substantial cinematic developments which have aimed themselves directly at this problem. I see the predominance of the fictional in cinema as a historical problem related to the economic/social function cinema has been called upon to perform and the deep effects this has had in the development of cinematic conventions. Metz, on the other hand, unaware of films which have attempted to 'work on the signifier' and 'defictionalise the spectacle', sees it as a product of intrinsic conditions of the cinematic signifier itself which is from the outset 'fictive and "absent"'. In spite of his own earlier concept of the partial 'uncoupling' of the laws of signification, which he would evidently consider to be at play in Brechtian theatre, his argument on the cinematic signifier sails very close to naturalising it as an immutable essence of the cinematic.

In support of his argument of the intrinsic fictiveness of cinema, the concept of a special condition, or degree of 'absence', for the cinematic signifier is fundamental. He supports this contention of 'absence' in various ways – from a demonstration that a can of film does not 'contain' those 'vast landscapes' which are the subject of its images to detailed comparison with theatre where the actors (here seen as synonymous with the signifiers) are really there in the real time and space of the theatre. He points out emphatically that everything in film is recorded and that what is recorded is by definition absent. In both the comparison with theatre and in the issue of recording, Metz's argument for a special 'absence' of the cinematic signifier is faulty. If, in the theatre, the actors (or props) are considered either as the signifiers themselves, or their 'real' presence somehow resists the transparency of the theatrical signifier, this is no more than an argument of an awareness of the material reality of the signifying substance. It is parallel to those movements in painting which drew attention to the material of the painting rather than simply using that material to construct a pictorial illusion. There are more than enough films from the avant-garde cinema which draw attention to, or work with, the cinematic materials like colour, light, screen, acetate, shadow, auditorium etc., to make it quite clear that an awareness of the signifying substance is as possible in cinema as in any other medium. However, even if we pass beyond this concept of the material substance of the cinematic image, and consider it in its state as a record (or recording), even if that which had been the subject of its recording is absent, its recorded trace, like a footstep in concrete, is present. Locked in this terminology, it must be argued that the cinematic image is a real image, within the specific parameters which the recording mechanism is capable of recording. The confusion occurs when the specific limits of the recorded image are read beyond those limits not as a real image, but as an image of 'the real'.

In fact, some of the specific considerations of the cinematic signifier (its 'intrinsics') might best be pursued along the lines of the problematics of the relationship between the substance of the record, the material processes of recording and that continuum out of which it is a recording – for the image is a production and inscribes its production (though these inscriptions may be effaced or attention drawn away from them).

In many respects, the cinematic signifier for Metz is the theatrical signifier at an extreme end of theatrical naturalism (where the actor is also made transparent in respect to the character – which again goes equally for props, vast landscapes or what you will), and absent in cinema because parameters of presence are assumed beyond the specifics of the cinematic image. This condition is only possible while film's specificity is *made* transparent in order to preserve the naturalistic theatrical signifier. However much Metz may argue the extension of perceptual registers in cinema, a factor which clearly assists transparency, these registers (better expressed as the parameters of range and resolution of the recording) remain specifiable.

The direction of this refutation shows simply that if the fictiveness, or imaginariness, of the signifier is counteracted in theatre by asserting the presence of the signifier (or signifying substance), such a condition is equally open to cinema. However, this tempting elevation of the cinematic signifier to the status of its own reality, its presence, is also problematic, rebounding on the assumption that the signifier is 'present' in theatre. In a film which, for example, draws attention to the screen surface, the projector beam, the intermittent mechanism or whatever 'material' aspect might be chosen, is it correct to assume that the signifier is present? At the moment that the signifier functions as a signifier, whatever the medium, it becomes transparent. Attention to the signifier in its material sense (as the signifying substance) does not escape the process of standing for that which it is not. It is incapable of standing for itself in any more than a representation of some *aspects* of its properties. Films which may be described as working on the signifier counteract transparency more by making aspects of the signifying *process* evident (tracing the path of shifts and transformations between signifying substance and signification) than by asserting the unproblematic presence of the signifier. I can see no distinction in kind to be made on this level between film and any other signifying practice. The signifier is neither unproblematically present as substance, nor absent as signification. Its absence, inevitable in certain moments of the signifying process, is not to be demonstrated on the basis of some special intrinsic condition of the cinematic medium.

As to this point, Metz has looked for the special conditions of cinematic signification mainly within the medium and apparatus. More fundamentally interesting is a shift which concerns itself with the conditions of response in the spectator/subject. In order to approach this problem, Metz refers to that general science of the subject, psychoanalysis, and in particular the work done on the specular regime by Jacques Lacan.

Perhaps because of my own inadequate theoretical expression or the polemical function of much of the discourse I have been involved in, there are some misunderstandings about my attitude to psychological investigation which must be cleared up.

Much of my resistance to the dominant cinema has been expressed in terms of demanding or encouraging a more 'conscious' or self-aware spectator. I have argued against the manipulated passivity of the audience to both film and television and have sought devices in my film work to establish what I have called a speculative/reflexive mode in the spectator. The rhetoric and polemics of this enterprise have been interpreted as a denial of psychology and the unconscious. My film work and theory have rejected, on one hand, symbolist expressionism, not as a rejection of the unconscious, but as a rejection of the unconscious manipulation or exploitation of the unconscious so that it remains unconscious. On the other hand, the concept of the conscious spectator was an attempt to break the subjugation of the spectator's ego by the film and film-maker (but more pertinently the subjugation by the multinational cinematic corporations through the agency of the film and film-makers). Neither in any way denies the psychological or the fact of the unconscious. However, until recently, the application of psychoanalysis in cinema has been almost exclusively at the level of interpretation of symbolism, either a psychoanalysis of the film-maker via the film text, or, at best, within the sociological aspect of film criticism, a form of socio-psychoanalysis. Little work was done on the more fundamental psychological mechanisms at work in the cinematic experience.

As an artist who came out of the tradition of abstract expressionism, my early reading of Freud remains an underlying frame of reference. But, except for a reading from Freud's treatise on Leonardo in the performance of my film *After Leonardo*, I have drawn less specifically on Freud in my film work than on Jean Piaget. His concept of the development of the constructions of reality in children has had a considerable influence on my theories. I do not see Piaget as a behaviourist, and though he does not address the basic psychological formations in the language of the subject, but rather in the terms of scientific observation, I see no incompatibility between his work and Freudian psychoanalysis. His work may be difficult to integrate with psychoanalysis, as it does not emerge at all from the verbal activity of its subjects, but it may be its observational basis which has recommended itself to me most as a film-maker, and an artist in the anti-literary twentieth-century tradition. From my limited reading of Lacan, I retain some reservations about the use of psychoanalytic language outside of that practice. Its language is already metaphoricised in relationship to the language of the subject, and confirmation of its theories (in the real sense of one's own experience) is difficult outside the practice. As I am not in analysis, if its concepts are to be productive to me as a film-maker I must relate them to my experience in the cinematic.

Basically, what Metz draws on from Lacan concerns the relationship between the formation of the ego and the image – the way in which fundamental unconscious formations are embodied in the imaginary function – his main reference being to Lacan's description of the 'mirror phrase'. Whether or not Metz's interpretation of Lacan is correct, it leads along a path which provides a number of interesting debating points. Metz sees in the mirror phase a primary identification, the formation of the ego through the perception of the body image, this body image providing an image of completeness through which an imaginary coherence may be given to the ego. In addition, the mirror image in the presence of others (primarily assumed to be the mother) gives to the child its sense of being an other in the presence of others like itself. This likeness is used broadly to explain the basis of the capacity to identify with the other through the image of the other, a fundamental mechanism in socialisation.

At once, in his discussion, Metz encounters a difficulty in relating the cinematic to the mirror phase: the fact that the spectator's body is not reflected in the film image. He overcomes this difficulty by suggesting that cinematic perception is only possible subsequent to the spectator's ego formation in the mirror phase, maintaining the analogy of cinema with the mirror by a special 'implacement', whereby 'the mirror suddenly becomes clear glass'.

In his pursuit of a mirror analogy, Metz misses what might be a productive avenue in the consideration of 'recording', namely film's capacity to 'reflect' time in the way in which the mirror reflects space. Though it is not central, it should be pointed out that in a major area of cinema, the home movie, the subject's image is 'reflected' in the scene.

Taking account of the spectator's bodily absence from the screen, Metz turns to identification with the represented characters, but because he is drawn towards his more challenging formulation of the spectator's 'placement' (my term) in the scene, he moves very quickly over the identification with character in the fiction as secondary to the primary identification afforded by the 'self-identification' of the mirror phase. This is unfortunate for a number of reasons.

It seems to me debatable that the mechanisms of identification with others are secondary and subsequent to the identification of ego with the self body image. Many aspects of the mechanisms of identification either with others or objects in the child's stages of extreme dependency must have a very primary psychological form. Furthermore, in the form of cinema which Metz uses as his basis of reference, because of the transparency of the signifier, identification with character is paramount. His argument that there is no loss of identification during long periods in which no image of a character appears on the screen fails to take account of the fact that identification with 'others' on the screen, as in its social formation, is not simply an identification with the likeness of their bodies to our own, but an intricate concern with the consequences of their actions.

Long periods (which in fact are always short except in the area of cinema I would quote as an 'alternative') of what Metz calls 'inhuman' sequences are always contained within structures of narrative consequence, identificatory response to them being conditioned by their context. If we are to understand the psychological mechanisms at work in the film spectator, we must examine how the mechanisms of identification which form the basis of social relationships function in the identificatory response to images of others, objects, the reading of consequentiality, etc., within the cinematic. This is particularly important in a critique of cinema where the signifier is transparent, opening directly, as it were, onto the scene of the imaginary action. If the mechanisms of identification are in significant development preceding and superceding the mirror phase, they become deeply intricated with what Metz tries to differentiate as the spectator's identification with self. At the same time, even in those avant-garde films which eliminate the portrayed character or even eliminate all photo-recording, the issue of identification in the consequences of the film's transformations is raised by the investment implicit in the spectator's attention. Whatever distinctions may ultimately be drawn between the spectator's self-identification and the identification with the characters, actions and objects of the screen image, it is evident that the 'structural/materialist' films provide virtually the only frame of reference where these issues are raised in the film texts themselves (as opposed to being superimposed by an advanced theoretical stance onto film works which pay no attention to the problem).

In attempting to define the spectator's identification with self as more primary than identification with the screen's characters, Metz turns the lack of image of the spectator on the screen to profit, reasoning that the spectator's ego must therefore identify itself elsewhere.

In one paragraph, in which he talks of the 'subject's knowledge', he outlines a number of factors necessary to be *known* by the spectator in order for film to be possible. After a (metaphorical?) first-person description of a knowledge of being within a cinematic space knowingly perceiving and knowing therefore 'that I am the place where this really perceived imaginary accedes to the symbolic ...', he goes on to what is for him a key concept: 'In other words, the spectator identifies with himself, with himself as a pure act of perception ... as a kind of transcendental subject ...'. He sees this inevitable self-identification of the spectator as a necessary consequence of the very possibility of the cinematic perception. Fundamental here is Metz's concept of the spectator as 'the constitutive instance ... of the cinema signifier (it is I who make the film)'. Of course it is *in* the spectator that the film experience is constituted, but, and it is crucial, to what extent does the spectator make that constitution, and to what extent is that constitution made in the spectator as the final point of the corporate production? Unconscious complicity in the constitutive process has a different status to knowledge of that process, and it must be distinguished from the necessary condition of choice in the spectator before the imaginary can approach the symbolic.

In spite of recognising that this transcendental subject places the spectator into the illusion of deity, in spite of recognising that the state of 'all-perceiving ... all-powerful' is an extreme reaction of the ego to the frustration of its power, and with all his consequent attention to the 'perversion' of voyeurism in cinema, Metz does not attempt to dislodge this condition of the spectator from an intrinsics of cinema. Before we can begin to consider the specific psychological formations of the spectator in relationship to the film, the spectator as constitutive instance must be given a historical and economic description. The cinema's spectator is the unconscious agent of a corporate consumption. While the film seems to be a dream of the spectator, the spectator's cinematic dream is the final point of the institutional production. As this condition is deeply embedded in the form of the cinematic institution (its modes of production and presentation), its apparatus (the machinery and techniques), its conventions of structuring (modes of editing, camera use, etc.) and in the psychology of its audience, perhaps we should avoid over-general conclusions and concentrate on details of its modes.

Metz follows his general concept of the spectator's identification with self by some consideration of identification with the camera. There is a parallel in my own film work; a period in which I attempted to address directly the problem of the spectator's physical (temporal and spatial) location within the cinema auditorium largely by minimalising or expelling the photocinematic from the screen has developed since 1974 into a consideration of the spectator's relationship to the camera and cinematic recording. Metz's transition from the spectator's transcendent self-identification to identification with the camera broadly follows the argument concerning the placement of the spectator/subject in quattrocento perspective and its continuation in the development of the optical apparatus. The spectator, it is argued, by occupying the 'empty implacement' inscribed by the viewpoint of the camera puts the spectator in the relationship to the scene previously occupied by the camera in the act of recording the image. Through the psychological arguments which express the equation between seeing and causing as a reaction of the ego to its inability to possess or control the object of its gaze, Metz interprets this empty implacement as implicitly that of an all-seeing, all-powerful 'God himself'. While I accept the broad terms of the psychological argument concerning the formations in the specular regime, there is a significant sense in which the camera as a definable mechanism is capable of clarifying the limits which the apparatus imposes on the image.

The image can become specifiable in its relationship as a production through awareness of the camera and its properties as a mechanism, thus counteracting the omniscience of the point of view by giving limits to the method of access to the scene. In this way, the viewpoint becomes relatable to a causal agency, readable in a materialist sense rather than as a generalised ideal access (in effect unread through the transparency of its inscription). This point of access need no longer be interpreted as an immutable 'natural' condition before which the subject is powerless, leading in turn to the illusion of absolute power as a reaction to support the ego. It might be argued that the camera as a mechanism, like quattrocento perspective, is more intrinsically inclined toward the materialist specificity of access to (and construction of) the image than the transcendental omniscience which Metz sees as intrinsic. Whichever way this is read, the camera and its functioning in a film constructs the image within a system of production (a motivated causality), and this is inscribed in the resultant image. It is a historical problem if this inscription is suppressed and if film practice fosters a misreading of the historical for a 'natural' or theistic causality, however much this is supported by the psychological compliance of the spectator. Where Metz talks of identification with the camera, I feel a better expression would be identification 'through' the camera.

Before the issue of identification with the camera can be approached as a theoretical or critical problem, it is necessary to consider film texts which can clarify the distinction between identification with the camera and with the narrative thread of the film construction. Except in a small line of development from the early films of Warhol, which includes work by Michael Snow, Peter Gidal, myself and a few other film-makers, there is little to refer to where the camera identification becomes problematic within the film text itself. In these cases, certain constraints in camera movement and edited construction demand some consideration of camera implacement (both in a spatial and temporal sense). In this work, while there is identification through the camera with the components of scene or action, there is also an inevitable shift towards an identification *of* the camera as a spatio/temporal implacement.

In order to make use of a concept like 'identification with the camera', we must attempt to distinguish to some degree an identification with the camera as camera, as mechanism, from the components of the scene on the one hand and subsumption as an agent of the narrative on the other. The camera is a mechanism, and identification with the camera incorporates identification with that mechanism and is not the same as identification through the camera with the agency which controls it. Crucial here is the distinction between identification 'of', 'with' and 'through'. If identification 'with' involves a transfer of the subject's ego to the condition of another object, with all its vicariousness but social necessity, in the same process identification 'of' involves a differentiation of the subject ego from that object. The ambivalence of the subject in the mirror phase might show us that identification 'with' and 'of' are interdependent in the process of relationship between the ego and other objects. In the process of identification 'with' a character, it is necessary to make some identification 'of' that character. In the same way, if there is to be any meaning to the concept of identification 'with' the camera, there must be some element of identification 'of' the camera. Identification 'with' the camera, far from being a common condition within the cinematic experience, is a difficult condition to initiate and maintain, as this involves a conceptualisation of an implacement not represented directly in the scene but inscribed through its effects. In general, this identification is most frequently approached via the personification of the camera in the character point-of-view shot, or its extreme extension as the point of view of the first-person film-maker. In both these cases, identification with the camera, as such, is lost as the identification becomes relocated in the personification, becoming again an identification with a character. In a sense, the more the identificatory process bypasses the conflict implicit between identification 'with' and 'of' and transfers itself to another object, the more we should consider this as an identification 'through'.

In most cases where we talk of identification 'with', because identification 'of' is suppressed, it constitutes identification 'through'. While the most evident identification through the camera in the dominant cinema is with the components of the scene and action, it is mainly because of the continual dislocation of the viewpoint that the spectator has no alternative but to identify through the camera with the source of the narrative continuity. Some continuity in the camera implacement, which begins to differentiate the viewpoint from the scene, also begins to develop some distinction between the mechanism and the ordering authority. Without this continuity of viewpoint, as a consequence of the spectator's incapacity to locate the ordering authority, the ego is forced to adopt an 'idealist' location. The spectator's illusory identification with this unspecifiable ideal location masks that it is in fact an identification with the power of the institutional authority behind the narrative order.

Metz may point us in the right direction of the psychological theory which deals with the mechanisms of this identification, but rather than begin from the general psychoanalytic theory and look for its correspondence in the cinematic, I would prefer to look in more detail at the condition of the spectator in cinema and then suggest some relationship to psychoanalytic theory.

Metz refers us to Baudry's observations in his 'Ideological Effects of the Basic Cinematographic Apparatus',[2] that the spectator is in 'a sub-motor and super-perceptive state'. I consider that an examination of the relationship between the motor and sensory regimes in the cinematic experience is crucial. I use the term sensory here rather than specular, so as to include the auditory aspect, as, for example, the

concept of identification with the camera should be extended to take in the identification with the microphone. Fundamental dissociations between the sensory and
motor regimes are at work in cinema. The spectator is at rest in a seat, and not only
is the more obvious motor activity – that of walking about in the space – eliminated
(it is largely only effective in the initial and subsequent instances of walking to and
from the cinema) but in the cinematic experience in the most obvious way the spectator is unable to enter into the action and cannot influence its outcome by
intervention. The latent desire to do so is maintained through identification with
those portrayed characters who seem able to do so by their actions. By identification
with the characters, the spectator seems to act toward the determination of consequence. This vicarious identification is at the cost of any real implication of the
spectator in the consequence of the film.

In the fundamental development of the relationship between the subject and the
world, the subject becomes implicated in the sensory through the consequences of
general motor engagement in the world. Thus, whatever the fundamental psychological basis of motivation, its transformation towards relative volition is moulded
by the developing capacities of the motor regime – motricity and motive become
deeply correlated.

The effect of this 'implicatedness' in the world is inscribed in the sensory construction of the subject within which the effects of the mirror phase are a stage. In
the cinematic, the question of the spectator's implication or disimplication becomes
fundamental. It is evident that the spectator's sense of implication in the narrative
action itself is unavoidably vicarious and illusory, but what of the more detailed
issues of the specular and auditory response?

In the same way in which motor engagement in the film's action is impossible, the
less evident motor actions normally deeply intricated with the specular and auditory
are also highly reduced. In the specular, the neck muscles are not called upon to
swivel the head as the screen is contained within the visual field of a static head; the
eye has little lateral or vertical movement to make as the pertinent aspect of the
image is normally held near the centre of the screen. As the image is flat, there is
not even a necessity to refocus for various distances. Similarly, no motor demands
are made in locating the auditory source.

For the moment, we will leave aside the auditory issue in its sense of the dissociation of the spectator's voice, and concentrate on the active component of the
specular, 'the look' (for which 'the listen' might be an auditory equivalent). The look
is the operation of the motor regime in the specular. In the same way in which motor
and motive become generally interrelated, in the specular they are intricated through
the expenditure of energy in the determination of the perception. It is evident that
the greater the perceptual shift desired by the subject, the greater the motor energy
required to initiate it. Perceptual changes in the world are deeply related to the econ-

omics of this expenditure. In the conventions developed by the cinema, the disimplication of the spectator under the illusion of implication extends to the look through the dissociation of the specular and motor regimes.

The consequences of this are particularly demonstrable in the conventions of camera movement and action montage. Whatever the basis of specular desire, the initial engagement of the spectator in the cinematic rests on some correspondence between the object of that desire and the agency which initiates the film image. This engagement is maintained in the film by a continuing correspondence through the desired development and transformation. In particular, the conventions of camera movement and montage follow the desire to maintain contact with the development of the action. The camera follows movement or the cut opens on to the pertinent continuation of the action. Though the devices may include sophisticated suspensions, they only do so within the context of ultimate co-ordination. What is important here is the detailed psychological effect of the continued provision of the desired object in the scene. Desiring to follow the consequential structure initiated in and by the film, when confirmed by its provision, the spectator seems to bring about the perceptual change as an act of volition. When a camera follows the action, there is sufficient correspondence with the desire of the spectator that the experience seems (unconsciously) to be one of choice exercised in the look. But, in the same way in which the spectator is unable to enter the action in the crude sense of intervening in its consequence, the spectator initiates no perceptual changes of the cinematic scene. The apparent implication of the spectator – by the apparent responsiveness of the camera movements and scene changes to the spectator's volition – produces a fundamental illusion of choice and control where none exists. If, in cinema, the sensory/motor dissociations are basic, is the dissociation of the sensory/motor from implicated volition inevitable, and in what sense can the spectator appropriate the cinematic experience?

Many of the devices which the 'structural/materialist' work has adopted might be interpreted in terms of making the fundamental dissociations evident or problematic, in this sense clarifying the relationship which exists between the film, the film-maker and the spectator. To this end, the devices and strategies have served to expel the spectator from the text (also attempting in some respects to expel the film-maker) rather than create an unconditional engagement. Correspondences between the film's structure and the expected desire of the spectator have been resisted. However, the various oppositional devices have been developed together with an attempt to permit, encourage, or initiate the spectator's own symbolic activity as the basis for appropriation of the film experience.

Both aspects, which are difficult to distinguish from each other, form the basis of the problematics in my own current film work. My experience from this work suggests that the point at which the two questions come together can be approached through the relationship of the symbolic activity to the motive in the motor aspect of the sensory/motor relationship. In the auditory regime, the symbolic activity of the subject emerges from the aural *production*, the motor activity of the voice. We may note that not only is the spectator's voice not produced in the cinematic, it is invariably subsumed by the film text in the same way in which the spectator's action and perceptual action are subsumed. In the specular the directedness of the look might be considered as an equivalent in some respects to the voice in the auditory. We might then suggest that the development of the symbolic in the specular is directly related to the subject's implicatedness in the act of choice and selection in the look. If this concept of the basis of the symbolic activity is to be seen as a point from which the spectator's implication in the film by appropriation is to be developed, its interiority must be taken into account.

While the concept of the spectator's interior voice may be readily grasped, the concept of the operation of the look in an interior sense is more problematic. However, in both cases, it is necessary to assume that the spectator must *produce* an auditory and specular construction for the film which is not directly that of the film presented – the spectator must be expelled from the film text in order to produce the conceptual construct as an act of the symbolic. In other words, the spectator must *become* the constitutive instance of the film in the limited sense of a relationship to the definition of the limits of the film text. What occurs to me in this formulation is that such a conceptual construct is not synonymous with the spectator's ego in any whole sense. In fact, I suspect that the expulsion of the spectator from the text counteracts the tendency of the ego to identify itself satisfactorily within the form of the body image, via any identification it might make within the screen image. A cinema signifier locked into the form of ego construction of the mirror phase, as a stage in ego development which short-circuits the ego concept into a body image, might be considered as helping to maintain a fixation at that stage. As a consequence of such a notion, we must ask if the pleasure involved in cinema is a regressive pleasure utilised by the cinema institution to maintain the disimplication of the spectator.

These notions are presented more in the spirit of a search for the productive problematics than a rhetorical conclusion.

Notes

1. C. Metz, 'The Imaginary Signifier', *Screen* vol. 16 no. 2, Summer 1975, pp. 14–76; quotations throughout are from this article.
2. J.-L. Baudry, 'Ideological Effects of the Basic Cinematographic Apparatus', *Film Quarterly* vol. 28 no. 2, Winter 1974/5.

14

Towards Temporal Economy [1980]

Generally, avant-garde independent film-making has suffered from being provided with a history of its own (Le Grice's *Abstract Film and Beyond* is not really any advance in this respect). What we need most is a quite different history, radically theoretical, something like 'Towards a Political Economy of Film Meaning-Production and Use'. Structural/materialist film would have its urgency in such a history, a history that the films, and this is their radical, political actuality, ceaselessly suggested in the scope and from the limits of their practice.

Stephen Heath, 'Repetition Time'

Introduction

This article maps the development of some of my most central theoretical concepts which have emerged in the period from 1965 during which I have made films. The lack of critical attention given to the direction of cinema to which I have contributed necessitates a lengthy review of the background to current concepts which inform my work. Even so, many issues are not examined in the depth with which I have considered them in other writings and the more recent concepts introduced here are themselves sketched in for later development.

General Critique of Dominant Cinema

In an article for the catalogue of the Arts Council exhibition 'Film as Film' (London 1979), entitled 'The History We Need', I defined two aspects of theoretical statements on avant-garde cinema: the negation of dominant cinema and propositions for the form of its alternative or replacement. While all art movements tend to define themselves by their negation of previous movements and assumptions, the degree of opposition within experimental cinema to the predominant direction which cinema has taken has been far more fundamental than that which can be said to give rise to stylistic evolution within art. It is not my intention to trace the history of this opposition here, but because of certain developments in my own film work, which are also evident in that of some other contemporary film-makers, I find it necessary to clarify some of the major premises of this opposition.

The dominant cinema is a narrative cinema. Even where it is a documentary cinema its overwhelmingly predominant form is narrative. Statements including my own from within the avant-garde have tended simply to oppose, as a whole, the dominant narrative cinema. I would like, however, to distinguish the problems of its social function from the forms within which the films themselves work. By separating the question of the cinema institution from that of narrative form we can move towards answering a question which I asked in 'The History We Need': Are all aspects of narrative irrevocably embroiled with the repressive social function it has come to serve? As I shall indicate, this question is in no way prompted by a notion of compromise between the avant-garde and dominant cinema but is made necessary by problems which are emerging within the by now substantial body of alternative avant-garde practice.

My main opposition to the dominant cinema institution is to the social effect transmitted through the psychological catharsis of its spectators/consumers. (In this respect I see the cinema institution as including all genres of television including game shows, news, and so on). The narrow limits of experience placed on working people by the forms and methods of capitalist production and their attendant social relationships are recompensed by the substitution through film and TV of a vicarious, specially mediated variety and excitement. Political and social pressures which might arise from these restrictions are released through this mediation, as Dziga Vertov put it: 'Film is the opium of the masses'. There is little evidence, however, that the social function of the cinema institution is significantly different in industrially advanced socialist societies than in capitalist countries – the viewer of film and television is in the position of an equally passive subject in both cases. This effect on its spectators must be communicated by the conventions of film construction, and embodied through the historical development of those conventions. Further the maintenance of this social function and the direction of its cinematic conventions must be supported by the patterns and economic basis of cinema production.

Thus, my other major opposition to dominant cinema has been to its conditions of production, distribution and finance.

The structure of the film and television industry permits access to production only to those individuals already predisposed to maintain that social function. This function is supported by the illusionistic codes of lighting, framing, sound, camera movement and editing, as well as the more obvious ideology of its narrative resolutions. Even though film production is intrinsically expensive, maintenance of the illusionistic codes excessively multiplies production costs. High production costs restrict access to the means of production to state and commercial interests as well as maintaining a division between production and consumption in cinema. Consequently cinema has developed as a mass culture at the point of consumption while maintaining an extreme elitism at the point of production.

The conditions of production within the film industry have ensured that the concept of film form and the development of film conventions have remained within relatively narrow limits. If the avant-garde represents the only major diversification in film form within cinema history, it does so largely through developing significantly different means of production, distribution and finance.

Opposition to the limitation of access to the means of production assumes the desirability of easier access (an end towards which I have worked in the London Film-makers' Co-operative and on various committees), and which I have tended to describe in ethical, political and artistic terms. Ethically it assumes a broad egalitarianism.

Film as Art

Historically, both in my own practice, and I think demonstrably in the avant-garde cinema as a whole, the development of alternative forms has not proceeded by a steady deconstruction or transformation, either in theory or practice, of the dominant cinema conventions. Theory of avant-garde cinema has tended cursorily to dismiss narrative, illusionism and identification together with the dominant commercial institution and to seek a basis for the development of a new aesthetic outside these forms, practices and institutions of cinema.

In *Abstract Film and Beyond* I have demonstrated how both the models for individual-based film production and the search for new form came from fine art practice and in particular from painting and music. Though I have become increasingly critical of subjective individualism as the basis for art practice, my own practice assumes that the necessary integrity (integratedness, not sincerity) of the components of an art work is only possible through the rigorous and critical construction by an individual opposing the cultural coherence of established form. Though the auteur theory sought such conditions in the commercial cinema through the structural, thematic consistency of films by certain directors, it is only the avant-garde which has produced a film form where this integrity does not need considerable decoding from the predominant constraints of the industry. Though financial constraints remain a factor for the avant-garde, the main constraints it encounters are similar in kind to those faced by other serious cultural and intellectual work of the modern period: science, philosophy, literary authorship, fine art and music. They derive from the historical conditions of thought transmitted through language, or embodied in the psyche of the film-maker, coupled with those of the medium, its techniques and preconceptions of construction. I have suggested that the major shift in cinematic practice which formed the basis of avant-garde cinema was through engagement with practices of modern painting and music. A fundamental assumption of modernism is that the forms and conventions of an art should be appropriate and specific to the medium of that art. (In spite of a lack of any modernist work in commercial cinema, its theorists from Munsterberg through Arnheim to Bazin have similarly sought to define this specialness and appropriateness.)

Film and Modernism

There is a paradoxical problem in the early history of avant-garde film which emerges from the modernist enterprise. Painting, assisted by photography taking up its representational function, sought painterliness in the abandonment of representational space in favour of the abstraction of surface, shape, line and colour. Film, the technical history of which is almost directly an extension from photography, first encountered the aesthetics of modernism through the influence of non-representational painting. Despite the liberating influence of fine art practice, I argued, in *Abstract Film and Beyond*, that if a filmic basis was to be sought for an art of cinema it would not to be found in a cinema dominated by forms derived from music and painting any more than from theatre and literature, rather, that if a filmic basis were to be found it should be sought in cine-*photography*, a position which I would now extend to include sound recording, stressing film as cine-*recording*. The main challenge to this position is that the very attempt to define a filmic appropriateness is essentialist. Peter Wollen raised this criticism in his article 'The Two Avant-Gardes' where he countered the concept of the filmic by that of an eclectic plurality of codes. While I also have difficulties with the preconceptions of modernism, this does not invalidate the historical practice which has emerged in those terms. In film, this history (as represented by the 'Film as Film' exhibition and its catalogue) constitutes the only substantial alternative to that of the dominant cinema. In film, as in painting, this development has concerned itself with an exploration, outwards in a sense, from the materials and properties which can be defined as belonging to the medium. The theory which has supported this exploration has frequently reflected an essentialism – terms like pure film and tautologies like film as film echo earlier concerns for 'l'art pour l'art'. However, this is more an issue of faulty theorisation than faulty practice. The attempt to define the intrinsics of a medium is always relative and historical. The possibility of postulating an autonomous film practice already rests on certain historical conditions. For example, the technological development of the materials and machinery is a necessary prerequisite, but as Jean-Louis Baudry alerts us in 'The Apparatus', the form of this technology is already enmeshed in the historical preconditions of its social and psychological determinants. Instead of treating the properties, processes, machinery or materials of cinema as fundamentals or essences, their definition should be considered in terms of their place in the problematics of signification. Just the same, possible artistic functions remain for the denial of historicity. It could be seen as a primary justification for aesthetic activity that it resists meaning and signification in favour of *experience* temporarily outside history and psychology. Of course from the standpoint of historical materialism, such a concept seems untenable as any current phenomenon may be defined *a posteriori* in terms of its determinants (though the occurrence of that phenomenon may have been unpredictable *a priori*). In another respect any phenomenon will come to be seen in relationship to its consequences, in other words the ostensibly meaningless will become surrounded by meaning, will be given – take on – signification.

Leaving aside for the moment the problem of unconscious or unintentional inscriptions in a work, it would seem that the attempt to produce autonomous aesthetic experience depends on the resistance of existent signification. Certainly in my own work, and I think in modern art practice as a whole, there is a fundamental assumption that already existing meanings should be resisted as they flood in to the conception and execution of a work. I have tried to avoid both the Greenbergian consequence of this which tends towards the hot-house novelty of avant-gardist movements without concern for their significance, and the absolutist (nihilistic) demand for meaninglessness – pure presence. While resisting these consequences, I maintain that it is incumbent on the artist to produce a work beyond the predictability of existing meaning and form. While this does not imply a concept of mythical transcendence it does seek far-reaching transformation. Rejection and elimination of existing aesthetic solutions has played a major role in the process of formulating works. At the same time the positive constructions which have replaced those rejected have often seemed arbitrary, irrational, impulsive and insignificant at their inception, even to the artist.

Aesthetics and Politics

My concept of aesthetic experience has also been underpinned by ethical and political considerations. I have argued that politics is not to be sought within the *content* of the work – within its meaning or signification – but in its resistance to signification in favour of creating aesthetic experience. In the process of resisting and negating existing constructions of meaning, a work determines new forms and resolves itself into new meanings. Dislodging the signifier from its expected signification permits a transformation of signification (and the possibility of experiencing some of the process of this transformation itself). Such work on the signifier and its production of new meaning is often a result of aesthetic strategies which stress *presence* over meaning. Here, my political argument becomes extended not just to the creation of new forms but to the *significance* of the new meanings produced. I have asserted that the forms and structures of an art work can become models by which experience outside art can be organised. It has been a commonplace assumption that the forms of art represent the world (as it were in retrospect): perspective represents the condition of spatial relations; narrative represents the sequential causality of human relations. The forms of these representations may be modified and radically transformed as Cubism did for perspective. But understood more radically, Cubism transformed not only the form of spatial representation, but, by implication, the structure which was understood to exist in that which was represented. Even where the pictorial representation is abandoned as in the concrete abstraction of Mondrian, I, and others, have argued that such work can be read in terms of a representation of consciousness revealing an abstract logic underlying structuration. Though I would now avoid an articulation in the terms of consciousness-models, I would still maintain that the structures within art have implications outside art and furthermore that a major historical function of art is its capacity to formulate terms for the *construction* of experience (rather than simply its passive representation). Art forms experience and does not just reflect it.

The Spectator and Politics

From the beginning of my work with film my predominant concern has been with the spectator. My earliest definition of this problem identifies the general ills of audience passivity, undistanced and unresisted consumption and unconscious psychological compliance with the illusionistic manipulations in dominant cinema. I was concerned to produce an active, conscious and distanced spectator. The term spectator gradually replaced that of audience in my writing not because of any implied priority of sight over sound but because of the connotation in the term spectator of addressing an individual rather than collective viewer.

In analysing cinema (and television) as a social-conditioning apparatus, the political validity of a basic demand for the rights of the individual spectator seemed self-evident. This analysis opposed both exploitation of those involved in production and exploitation of the spectator in viewing the film. Film viewers, I argued, have (an ethical and political) right to integrate and form their own concept and experience of the film. Though this view came from attempting to embody a radical notion of democracy, within the aesthetic of the work, it rejected the expression of overt political viewpoints which were seen to manipulate the spectator. The behaviour of the spectator in relationship to the film was thus seen as more fundamental than any particular content. This developing awareness of the problem of the spectator which was particularly evident, though not always adequately theorised, in the European structural films and in Fluxus work for example, constituted the most politically radical development of avant-garde film. Paradoxically it has led to, or reinforced, the reduction of overt content – the minimalist tendency – which, in turn, has brought an accusation of apolitical formalism.

The main obstacles to the active engagement of the spectator, as I (but also Gidal, Dunford and others surrounding the London Film-makers' Co-op) saw it in the late 1960s, were identification with characters, the linear coherence of narrative development and the general illusionism of representation. All these cinematic illusions drew spectators into the action within the screen space and time, and out of the apperception of current reality. Withdrawal into illusory experience in cinema was only seen as an aspect of a more general social problem. Cinematic (and televisual) illusions prevented perception of the actual limits of experience and effective social relationships of the individual and I sought a concept of film structure which could counteract this. My concern was to produce a materialist model of 'consciousness' and perception within the cinematic *experience* using terms like 'politics of percep-tion' (which led to some confusion concerning the priority of a relatively minor genre of flicker films within the overall concept).

In most of my films around 1972 there was a deliberate attempt to remove illu-sionism as well as to eliminate narrative continuity and resolution; the tendency of the photocinematographic image to call up other spaces and times also demanded its gradual reduction and eventual elimination. In the elimination of narrative form (replaced in particular by forms of repetition) and the gradual elimination of the pho-tographically based cinema image, the image source increasingly became the physical materials and processes of cinema themselves – film strip surface, sprockets, dust, scratches, film transport mechanism or the projector beam. While this reductiveness, this negation of cinematic illusion, led towards an affirmation of the physicality of cinema, it was primarily understood as focusing the spectator into an extreme aware-ness of the constituents of their *current* reality (what existed in their immediate presence). This notion sought the subsequent transposition of the capacity to per-ceive the limits of experience and effective relations from the cinematic experience to the political world of the spectator. This motivation resolved itself in some respects similarly to the classical aims of realism. It differed significantly however to cinéma vérité or neo-realism, by rejecting the *portrayal* of reality on the grounds that the nar-rative forms of cinematic construction unavoidably locked this enterprise into illusionism. In the 'realist' cinema the conventions and conditions of presentation retained the spectators' passivity by working through their emotional identification – so, I argued, the *mode* of their relationship to the cinematic spectacle went unchanged. The particular avant-garde enterprise to which my own work contributed at this time based its realism primarily in the spectator's confrontation with the reality of the cinematic itself. I was aware that extreme reductiveness risked the complete isolation of the work as an aesthetic experience within the space and duration of presentation. In my own work, even at the point when the cinematic image was most reduced (about 1972 – *White Field Duration*, for example), my writing did not advo-cate a hermetic isolation of the projection experience but its elevation to primacy within the overall consideration of film. I wrote, for example:

> The real TIME/SPACE event at projection, which is the current, tangible point of access
> for the audience, is to be considered as the experiential base through which any
> retrospective record, reference or process is to be dealt with by the audience. This
> reverses the situation common to the cinematic language where experience of the real
> TIME/SPACE at projection is subsumed by various aspects of manipulated retrospective
> 'reality'.

Though I would now revise the terminology, particularly the simplistic concept of current reality contained in the title, it is implicit in the statement that what is dealt with through the spectator's present confrontation incorporates a consideration of those events which preceded and gave rise to the current reality. In my film work, the attempt to reduce retrospectiveness, which was foremost the *once-upon-a-time* of fiction but extended to the photographic aspect of the cinematic image, served mainly to restrict retrospection to those features clearly traceable to the process of cinematic production. These included, for example, the transformation of the image in printing (as in *Berlin Horse*) and at its most extreme (in films like *Love Story 2*) worked only with changing colour fields on the screen.

My notion of films' content at that time might be summed up as follows: the spectator, within the constraints of cultural history, psychology and psycho-physiology encountered the film experience as phenomena. This then became the 'content' of the work through the process of reflection on materials, mechanisms, processes, transformations and manipulations in production as well as reflection on the spectator's own mechanisms of perception and conceptual structuring. In this respect the most fundamental distinction between this enterprise and conventional cinema became located in the specific mediations of the cinematic process and the active reflexiveness (since formulated as speculative/reflectiveness) of the spectator.

The aim then, of initiating within cinema the possibility of a spectator whose mode of consciousness resisted illusion in favour of reality, seemed consistent with, and to depend on, a film form based on the actual substances, mechanisms and processes of film. Confrontation with reality was to be initiated in cinema by confrontation with the reality of film: its acetate, surfaces, the light of its projector, its screen and shadows, its space of presentation and in particular, duration, its concrete dimension in time. The concept of a materialist consciousness for the spectator seemed equatable with the materials of cinema, as did the materialism of the filmmaker with their manipulation. A political aspiration led to an attempt to demonstrate and elaborate a theoretical relationship between film materiality and historical materialism. My film practice, and that of some of my contemporaries, indicated that the concept of materiality need not be restricted to physical substance, but could be extended to incorporate the material processes of cinematography, the properties of its machinery, the conditions of its presentation and the mechanism of its perception by the spectator. While processes such as printing and developing the film image were not strictly *present* in the substance of the film at projection, their inscription remained (as a trace) at projection. Only in this sense did the retrospective become compatible with presence. Films which inscribed or did not efface the traces of their production made their history and production available for consideration.

Record and Realism

Subsequent to this extreme focus on the materials and material processes of film, my notion of inscription as record (trace) and material presence extended to the (re-)incorporation of photorecording as one of its cases. The concept echoed Bazin's concern to root cinema realism in the mechanism of photorecording. In his essay 'The Ontology of the Photographic Image', he likens the process of photography to a death mask: 'One might consider photography … as a moulding, the taking of an impression, by the manipulation of light'. However, the concept of photocinema which I developed relates more generally to J. S. Pierce's definition of one class of signifiers as indexical.

The indexical signifier is not tied to resemblance, but is none the less characterised by its form being a direct physical consequence of that which produces it. For Pierce, a barometric reading is an example of an indexical signifier. In order to grasp some of the problems of considering photography in the terms of an indexical signification we could pursue the concept of direct impression, say, taking a footprint in sand. If we treat the footprint as though it were a foot (as a representation or evocation through its resemblance) its indexical aspect, namely its condition of materially recording the trace of an occurrence, becomes diminished. This is to suggest that while the photographic recording may be considered as a form of indexical signifier, its condition as such (in the experience) is not simply assured by the mechanism of photography. In the photographic realm this indexicality tends to be (immediately) counteracted as its resemblance encourages the trace of an object (or event) to be treated as the object itself. This might account for the need I felt to eliminate the photocinematic as a representation before its condition as indexical record could be reintroduced to my work through the refilming of the screen and image of scratches in *White Field Duration* for example. This followed a realisation that even the extreme reduction of the cinematic to the materially present did not eliminate its place in a historical continuum, a realisation that its present condition was a consequence of its process of production some, but not all traces of which, remained evident. Instead of elimination then, the pro-filmic became a problem of integration through material traceability. In other words, the primacy of the materially present was maintained over the retrospective through stressing the *specificity* of the trace of the retrospective in projection. Where Bazin assumed an automatic (transparent) credibility between photorecording and a generalised reality of the object photographed, I was concerned only with the limited credibility brought about by particular relationships within the specific limits of cinematographic recording. The physical-chemical coherence of the process of tracing the light pattern (or sound pattern) may demonstrate the material continuity between reality and record, but, however extended the parameters of recording may become (colour, 3D, ultra-wide screen), the recorded trace remains within specific limits. Access from the record to the object of the record is only to those aspects of the real available within those limits. One major level of cinematic illusion rests on treating the limited trace (a specific record) beyond those limits as a representation of a generalised or whole reality. Thus the status and form of cinematic representation becomes *problematic*, not a matter of automatic assumption. Identifying the specificity of the material continuity between a real other-where, other-when, reinforced my argument that if we are to use the terms of realism in the field of representation it is more appropriate to concentrate on the concept of *the reality of the trace* than the representation of reality. My own theorisation, from a similar basis and motivation to Bazin (the desired supremacy of realism over illusionism), has tended towards much more narrowly defined limits for film's capacity to bring cinematic representation into a relationship with pro-filmic reality. This demands distinction between recording (a mechanical, physical, chemical process within specific parameters) and the more generalised concept of representation – document not documentary. Assessing the credibility and veracity of a cinematic representation rests on recognising the specificity of filmic mediation as 'real'. However, any definition of the specificity of film as material and as mediation is itself problematic.

I suggested earlier that a major feature of the avant-garde cinema was its attempt to locate, and locate itself within, the special and intrinsic terms of the medium. I also suggested that while this has been criticised as idealist, essentialist or reductivist (I was mainly referring here to criticisms from Peter Wollen which emerged in a public seminar with papers by me, Gidal and Wollen, held at the LFMC), evidence of working as a practitioner inside this enterprise indicates that the very definition of intrinsics is not fixed but in extending transformation. This transformation proceeds both by the extension of the potentialities of the medium in the practice of film and by a critical (in the sense of crucial) grasp of the condition of its current historical determinants. I have previously predicated my discussion of film materiality on the desirability of confronting the spectator with the reality of film in its presence in projection. I have recently found it necessary to distinguish and clarify the roles and status of film-maker and spectator in this discourse. The attempt to elevate the status of the spectator has required a reconsideration of the authority of the film and the status of authorship of the film-maker. The introduction of this problem into the avant-garde cinema must be seen in its historical context.

Structure/Apparatus/Spectator

Particularly in America (but also evident in the aims of the European *nouvelle vague*), the development of avant-garde cinema post-1940 was primarily supported by the notion of the individual artists, and the personal expressive film. Avant-garde film of the mid-1960s saw a tendency to consider form before expression (loosely dubbed structural film). This was partly a general reaction against the idiosyncratic consequences of extreme subjectivity of the classic underground (Brakhage for example), partly in recognition of the special conventions and materials of the medium and partly an admission of the impossibility of artistic construction unmediated by constraints of history. In my case, this general shift away from romantic individualism was related to an ethic opposing the subjugation of the spectator to the personality of the artist almost as strongly as it opposed subjugation to the authority of the state or corporate cinema. The structural film is rarely understood in these terms because of the residue of the tradition of personal cinema, instead of seeking to express the film-maker's special vision it tended towards the anonymity of a definable structuring concept. In various ways, from the application of strict systems through to relatively determined strategies of film construction, the principles of a film's structure, I argued (in *Abstract Film and Beyond*), could be differentiated from the subjectivity of the film-maker. Exploration of the potentialities of film mediation, rather than the life and personality of the film-maker, tended to become the primary content. By locating content in the exploration of the medium, the film mediates culture for both film-maker and spectator and the film work becomes predominant over the personality of the film-maker.

Predetermination of a system or strategy does not however eliminate subjectivity; instead it tends to shift its terrain. The film-maker must still devise the structural principle, select its form of application in the film construct and the components of its image. Moreover, if these factors are not seen as problematic, or if the condition of the spectator in the whole discourse is not considered, the system or strategy may become no more than a convenient *mechanism* for the generation of a film. In particular, the apparent neutrality of a film's manipulations masks the problematic relationship of authority remaining between the spectator and the film.

Even where the film attempts to locate its content in the exploration of film mediation itself, the film-maker's discourse remains privileged. This privilege derives from the access to the means of structuration and thus cinematic cultural transformation. In other words, a difference in status and role remains (between film-maker and spectator) even where attempts are made to diminish this difference in a relocation of films' content away from autobiography and into a more public discourse. There is in this an implicit attempt to shift the enunciation from the first-person singular, 'I', to the first-person plural, 'we'. The 'we' implies an attempted co-location of film-maker and spectator within the constraints of the discourse. However, the film-maker, by adopting a first-person plural enunciation, takes on the role of the spectator's representative in the transformation of determinants through structuration of the film. If this role as representative is accepted unproblematically the spectator is again turned back towards passive consumption of the formal manoeuvres made by the film-maker in a seemingly neutral arena. Here the 'we' may become a subterfuge.

A film-maker's aim to counter the passivity of the spectator does not in itself guarantee that effect, particularly if fundamental conventions of cinema and even its basic apparatus can be shown to be predicated on this passivity. The most challenging and interesting development of film theory to emerge from France in recent years derives from Christian Metz's 'The Imaginary Signifier', and Baudry's article 'The Apparatus' (op cit.). Baudry elaborates the notion that the invention and form of the cinematic apparatus is already determined within certain ideological and psychological structures. It seems undeniable that the machinery of cinema – camera, lens, projector – and its modes of functioning and preconceptions of presentation, embody and transmit deeply rooted determinations. My major disagreement with this position as adopted by Metz is with its critical tone. This presents these basic ideological and psychological effects as immutable, not, it seems, susceptible to any transformation through the practice of cinema. Because Metz's frame of reference is almost exclusively that of the dominant commercial cinema whose forms exploit and compound the passive psychological disposition of the spectator, his analysis is drawn towards a terminology which suggests that the psychological condition of the spectator is forever fixed by the apparatus. In other respects, though with important differences, there is a close parallel between certain aspects of his analysis and concepts which have underpinned my own theory and film-making. He locates the spectator's identification with the self as more primary than that of the identification with characters portrayed in the film. This is close to my own contention that the apparent major content (a film's portrayed action) is subsidiary in its effect to more deeply embedded relations between film structure and the condition of the spectator.

Metz, however, is specific in his description of the location of this most primary identification. He says: 'The spectator identifies with himself, with himself as a pure act of perception … as a kind of transcendental subject.' Fundamental to this concept is the notion that the spectator is the 'constitutive instance … of the cinema signifier (it is I who make the film)'.

Metz recognises that the spectator's implicit, 'it is I who make the film', is a psychological reaction to support the ego in the face of an opposite condition – powerlessness to intervene. He traces the basis of this psychological disposition (with the aid of Lacan's concept of the mirror phase) to a certain stage in experience when the child could see, but not intervene in the (sexual) relationship between its parents. This classic voyeurism whereby powerlessness is accommodated through the psychological formation which equates vision with control, expressed by Metz in the epithet 'all-perceiving, all-powerful' is put forward as absolutely fundamental to the condition of cinema.

Metz's analysis is evidently valuable in defining the predominant condition of the spectator in conventional cinema. Modified, it can also assist us to grasp the determination of spectator conditions which derive from the apparatus of cinema, in particular from the basic authority relations implicit in the difference in role and status between film-maker and spectator in avant-garde practice. Though Metz refers to the social sanction of voyeurism within the cinema institution, he neither draws our attention to the particular historical and economic conditions which give the power and status to this authorisation (and thus determine its form), nor does he give any hint that the predominant psychological conditions which it engenders and rests on can be dislodged by developments in film form or changes in the cinema institution.

My practice (together with many others working in avant-garde cinema) seeks to counteract the passivity of the spectator and bring the cinematic experience into the context of their reality. It opposes an analysis which leads to an assumption that cinema is inevitably locked in voyeurism, fiction and illusion. At the same time, it confirms that the psychological determinants along the lines defined by Metz and Baudry are deeply embedded in the cinematic apparatus and its conventions even outside the dominant cinema institution.

Rather than assuming the capacity of an avant-garde cinema to produce a condition for the spectator in completely different terms, my current concerns might be described as: first, identifying (through a cinema practice) the conditions which the apparatus and available conceptions of film structure tend to produce; second, attempting to dislodge them by making them problematic rather than exploit them towards the end of aesthetic expression; and third, to raise the issue of the relationship of the cinematic work to reality. These concerns remain consistent with the attempt to define the content of the cinema primarily from the cinematic medium and its mechanisms of mediation, and consideration of the ethical and political relationship between film-maker, film and spectator.

The question then, of the choice of cinematic content, becomes primarily not what subjects are appropriate to the nature of film? but, in what arena is it possible for film to make a transformational mediation? This arena is not fixed, but develops in relationship to the forms of film and the institution of cinema. The issue of cinematic reality becomes neither simply the adequacy or truth of represented relations, nor the unconditional assertion of the physical presence of the cinematic experience, but the appropriation of the cinematic experience and mediating construction by spectators within their subsequent material realisation (their reality).

These concerns demand a review of many of the concepts already discussed, and analysis of their implications in the detail of cinematic operation.

Authority

It is necessary to consider the spectator's place in the cinematic discourse in historical and economic terms before approaching the problem of the psychological condition of the spectator. In the dominant cinema there is an unassailable difference in role, and an extreme imbalance of economic status, between the spectator and the originating source – the corporate film production machine. Even where the spectator is brought closer to the conditions and problems of production – in the avant-garde film – the prerogative of structuration of the work is not directly open to the spectator. It is assumed that structuration derives from an authority and this assumption is reinforced by the economics of production. Access to production tends to represent either the simple authorisation of finance or the committed energy of authorship (an investment of energy in production). In addition, the structuration brought about by the machinery and devices of cinema, even the formation of the photographic image itself, represents a deeply seated authority of history. This historical authority sanctions the place of both spectator and film-maker in the cinematic institution and becomes embodied in conventions of film construction, the codes of lighting, acting, montage and so on. The spectator tends, unwittingly or complicitly, to take up a posture conditioned by this implicit authority. Psychological relations are both determined and reinforced within the terms of this authority relation, and spectator and film-maker are equally subject to their effects. If the film-maker cannot circumvent the role of agent of the film's structuration, it is still possible for both the status of this authority and the definition of the spectator's role in structuration to be made problematic. In the first instance, the fact of an object and some of its conditions as a production (a produced object) made evident (or not effaced) within the work initiate a speculation on its origins and causality. In this way the source and terms of its origins become relatively more locatable and its authority begins to be specifiable rather than general. Second, the forms of structuration themselves may be defined so as not to carry the implication of inevitability and authoritative certainty. Third, the film may be structured to initiate the desire in the spectator to function more thoroughly as the constituting instance of the film, to present the possibility of extending the spectator's role in structuration of the work itself. Metz is particularly misleading in his presentation of the spectator as the constituting instance of film as though this condition was already a historical psychological fact. In the practice of dominant cinema, it is much more accurate to define film as *constituting* its subject spectator rather than the spectator constituting the film. All its devices and economic power are focused on determining the spectator's placement and psychological relationship. Indeed, in a more radical analysis, the spectating subject, rather than being seen as the ultimate agent of the film's constitution, may be viewed as only a further agency through which the film does its work of maintaining (without conflict) social and economic divisions. In this argument, the spectator is neither the constituting instance nor constituted in any full subjectivity by the film but serves merely as a partially constituted transmitting instance (of the film's cultural and social effect).

However, even in avant-garde cinema, authority relations remain through the division of roles between maker and spectator, the determination of film structure and the historical preconditions of the apparatus. Any problematisation must therefore involve a conflict between the work's authority and the demand that the spectator takes responsibility for its realisation, that is, becomes the constituting instance. This conflict might simply be located in differences of inclination between spectator and film-maker. This simple equation of author and authority (of the location of authority in the personality of the author), while now evidently inadequate, is a clear advance on the unlocatable omniscience of the authority of dominant cinema. It is one stage in the process of specifying the location and terms of a film's authority. A fundamental and more productive conflict may be located in the authority of the historical determinants acting on both film-maker and spectator. In order for a conflict to emerge in this arena, the film-maker (albeit thereby manoeuvred into the role of representative of the spectator in the historical discourse) must both recognise the condition of being subject to the historical determination and produce some form of distanciation from which it may be viewed and transformed.

These concepts of the authority relation implicit in structuration apply both to film which is based on the photographic image and abstract cinema which makes no use of photography and recording. However, it is evident that a major historical motivation for cinema is related to the desire for a method of mechanical representation. This is deeply embodied in the design and functioning of the apparatus and, if not essential to cinema, it constitutes one of its fundamental problematics.

Duration Recording

My own re-engagement recently with the problematics of photorepresentation should not be seen as a way of reopening a dialectic with the terms of dominant cinema nor as aimed at its deconstruction. I have considered it almost exclusively in terms of an extension of the readable inscriptions by which the retrospective conditions of a work might be brought to bear as a component of what is materially present when the film is screened. The theoretical arguments have been in terms of the problematics of film as *document* (*not* documentary) and *evidence*. These arguments have been developed through the recognition that traces on film, like scratches or even the material conditions of the projection, form a continuity of evidence and 'document' through their inscription in the cinematic event. Mainly through my films *White Field Duration* and *After Leonardo*, I have extended this indexical principle to the photographic process through refilming non-photographic traces. In these works, the issues of inscription, evidence and document have been directly linked to those of the experience and recording of duration. In various films and theoretical works I sought to establish and argue the primacy for the spectator of the reality of duration at the moment of a film's presentation. In my current understanding of this issue, apperception of duration cannot be completely divorced from the concept of its value (value as significance, or equally, as economic and psychological investment). Investment by the spectator in the experience of current duration (the currency of duration) carries over to a value for (evaluation of) the duration of the recorded events. The spectator's investment is matched and reinforced by the investment evident in the recording act, measured in part by its duration – its temporal magnitude. Applying the concepts of document and evidence to the issue of duration, the notion of equivalence between presentation and representation time returned as a central concept. Consequently, in recent work, I have reconsidered photography not in terms of the photographic as image but as the record of duration, stressing the cinematic aspect of photocinematic. I have been re-examining retrospective duration (as problematic) through traces of production, and through camera and projector, mirroring each others' functions within the duration of presentation.

In *Abstract Film and Beyond* and various articles, I clarified the concept of durational equivalence through comparison with the representation of time in conventional narrative film. In the representation of extensive time scales within the relatively short duration of a film's presentation, time becomes irrevocably illusionistic. Not only is the duration of the film's represented action unrelatable to the duration of its presentation, but through subversion by illusionistic continuity between shots, the shots themselves lose their durational documentality. In other words, the material duration of the film's presentation, production and represented action becomes entirely dissociated; the spectator, with no way of integrating the relations of present, retrospective record, and fiction, can only give in to the fictional duration which subsumes all others. In this way any concept of reality in the field of durational experience is undermined by the temporal compression of narrative convention. Furthermore, the conventions of editing and montage obliterate any trace of the temporal relations in the production, and reinforce the spectator's condition as passive consumer. It is possible to see some relationship between these concepts and Bazin's advocacy of long takes. For him the long take, like deep focus, permitted the reality of the pro-filmic scene and action to supersede or show through the manipulation of the film-maker's montage. Bazin compromised this challenging concept with illusionistic continuity, treating it only as a component of representational realism. I am not assuming this representational realist function. Unlike the concept of a temporal window, the long take devices I have used have not been aimed at realism in the general sense but have been concerned with defining the limits of integration between presence and record in the field of duration. Extension of a shot's duration permits a temporal space in which the spectator can reflect on the conditions and relations of production as inscribed through, for example, the form of camera action, framing, surface qualities of image and printing. The long take then has no intrinsic privilege but served (and serves) to initiate consideration of certain cinematic issues.

Arguing from a modernist position that exploration of the properties and processes of film can determine content, I have, therefore, resisted any assumption that content precedes formulation of the work. Now, through considering the photocinematic as an aspect of film's material processes, I am suggesting how the pro-filmic may be integrated with this (modernist) exploration. Recognising how conditions of authority and historical determinants of structure are built into the very production of the image by the apparatus, I also recognise that every access to the pro-filmic is mediated and cannot be separated from the processes of mediation. However, this mediation is not just a general condition but is always selectively specific (the parameters of the recording mechanism, range of light sensitivity, frame, focus, etc.) and transformational (for example reducing spatiality to a flat surface). At the same time, however much a work might stress the reality of the image over the image of reality and however much the material conditions of the production of an image are made evident, the facsimile image of photography attests to a continuum of reality extending beyond the limits of the cinematic recording. That which is specifically recorded, selected, brought within the frame and range of the parameters of recording and transformed by cinematic process asserts, through what is unavoidably *excluded* in the process, the fact of a continuum (or series of intersecting continua) beyond what is recorded. What is recorded is by definition a fragment contained within a variety of boundaries – edges – parameters. It is at these edges of empirical record (symbolised in a sense by the frame) that the cinematic discourse – the transformation of cinema's terms of mediation through practice – intersects with other discourses. These intersections are not to be seen as self-evident capacities of cinema nor as a loose plurality of codes. The capacity of film materially to relate to other discourses (at these intersections) is highly problematic.

My recent film work, *After Lumière – L'arroseur arrosé* and *Emily – Third Party Speculation*, has taken up the exploration of pro-filmic events in which actions in time and space are recorded but within the concepts of evidence and document and the problematics of temporal representation. Though the films stress the material processes of mediation, and stem from the problematics of the document encountering the issues of narrative, identification and representation have been unavoidable.

Narrative/Narration

Though the issue of narrative is most evidently brought up where representation of human action is incorporated within content, the problems attendant on narrative have much wider implications even within apparently abstract cinema. Crudely, a narrative is a story and a narration is the telling of a story. More complexly, a narrative is the representation of a series of events (occurrences in time) given a unity by some continuity of the passage of a character or characters through a set of relations presented as causal. In other words, a narrative represents a temporal causality in the field of human (or anthropomorphised) relations. Its unity is invariably determined by implied causality as it impinges on a central character or the episodic encounters of that character. Classical narrative carries its significance in the consequence of a trajectory which in turn supports a moral, ideological or psychological determinism. A more complex narrative may resist dénouement in such terms, and even resist simple linearity in the causal relations and the centralisation of a character. But the identification of the spectator, listener or reader with the characters, expressed as a concern for the outcome of their actions and encounters, is fundamental to narrative. Additional dimensions to narrative may result from the cross-section of description (the spatial and historical context) and the psychological investigation of character (what Maya Deren called vertical as opposed to horizontal developments).

I am not concerned with the more general issues of narrative, but with the particular case of narrative in cinema. At issue is not the question of whether narrative can be incorporated in a materialist cinema but how aspects of the representation of social discourse can intersect with the mediation of cinema and come within its effective arena (be 'dealt with' in cinematic terms). In the same way in which the specificity of a recording may be distinguished from a generalised representation (by stressing its specificity) the photo-cinematic record of an action (within the context of its causality) is not automatically a narrative representation. In any case, narrative is not a single phenomenon but a combination of interconnected issues like the time and status of the recorded action, the identification of the spectator with the characters and concern for the outcome of their represented actions.

These issues, raised problematically within my own film work, have led me to some refinement in terminology particularly in the locus of identification, the investment of libido in attention and its cathexis in various objects. We have already encountered the difficulty of defining the primary object of identification within cinema: whether the identification with characters and their actions; the general authority of the structuration; or the spectator's self-identification. If the narrative is broadly defined as a form of temporal re-presentation, then narration is the act of presenting it, of controlling the sequence of presentation. It is clear that much of the drama of a narrative lies not in bare events nor even in their elaboration, but in the sequence of their unfolding. (Sophisticated narration, as we know, frequently has recourse to the presentation of the narrative out of sequence – the sequence of narration is not necessarily synonymous with the sequence represented by the narrative.) The problems of cinematic structure (even in abstract and highly formal work) are bound up with the effect of temporal priority in presentation. If in one sense it is relatively simple to avoid narrative – temporal representation – it is more difficult to circumvent the condition of narration – temporal sequentiality.

Identification

Through the existentialist novel, the narrator – the source of the narration – became an element in, and often central to, the narrative. This has established a form of co-location in modern literature between fiction and autobiography. A major element of avant-garde cinema – the single person film – has echoed this shift. Even though not necessarily bodily represented in the film, the film-maker became the centre of the film text – the film became an expression of the film-maker's vision. The identification of the spectator here shifts away from identification with the represented characters (there may be none) and their actions, towards identification with the narrator structured through the autobiographical narrative. Even in the formal or structuralist film, the act and prerogative of structuration attests authorship. The special conditions of temporal structuring – its inevitable priorities of sequence – lend to its control the quality of narration. The control of significance determined in the sequential relations is narrational and thereby identification tends to be located, via concern for the structural outcome, in the originator of the narration. It may then also be argued that even in the overt narrative based on the depiction of characters, identification with the narrator is more primary and fundamental than identification with the characters.

My most recent film *Emily – Third Party Speculation* explores the problem of the relationships between the camera, a recorded action and the spectator's conceptual structuring, and focuses on the particular problems of the *movement* of identification. Theoretical work which has accompanied this development (mainly contained in the article 'Problematising the Spectator's Placement in Film') has encountered considerable difficulty in clarifying the processes and I am even far from convinced that the terminology of identification is the most appropriate. As I understand the process of identification 'with' (contrasted to identification 'of'), it involves a psychological mechanism by which we are able to treat another person's actions and experiences as though they were our own. The necessity for such a mechanism in social relationships is fairly evident and the development of these psychological mechanisms through childhood dependencies reinforced by adult and economic interdependencies can be relatively well understood. However, in daily social intercourse, the mechanisms of identification are inseparable from their attendant psychological hostilities, the (unconscious) recognition that the actions and experiences of those others with whom we must identify are not our own. Indeed, we may realise that fulfilment of their desires is often at the expense of our capacity to fulfil our own. In the social arena, and one of the major factors by which we recognise its status as reality, the condition of identification with is constantly mediated by the conflict with self-interest (or complex groupings of identifications and hostilities). In other words, if there is a movement of libidinal energy away from the ego transferred not simply to a cathexis with another object, but to the possession of that object or achievement of a goal by another person, this is attended by resistance to that transfer. Vicariousness is not synonymous with identification, but is a consequence of suppressing its component of psychological resistance.

In the narrative form, this conflict has become recuperated in the conflict between characters in the fiction but this representation elides the conflict between the spectator's structuration (desire) and the authorisation of the narration. In other words, even if a conflict of identification emerges within the represented action, there is no conflict in the more basic identification with the structuring authority within which the other conflicts are contained. The illusion which supports this suppression is the illusion of implicatedness. The primary illusion of cinema is neither the photographic illusion of a space which is not present, nor the photocinematic illusion of a time which is also not present, but the illusion that we are implicated, through presence, in the actions of another time and place. Attempts to define reality, in contradistinction to illusion, have invariably revolved around the question of physical presence and absence, leading to an assertion of the presence of the signifier (or the signifying substance).

The illusion of a space and time not physically present is counteracted by an assertion of the presence of the substance of the film image. However, the distinction between reality and illusion should not originate in the question of the physical presence or absence of signifier or signified. Materialist reality is to be found in the relationship between the action of the subject (subject, individual, person, ego) and implication in its consequence – the arena of irreversibility and the reality of realisation.

In the narrative form of cinema the non-implication of the spectator in the narrative action is hidden by the illusion of an apparent implicatedness. It is quite evident that the spectator has no capacity to intervene in the represented actions within a film. The energy invested in attention must channel through identification with the screen's protagonists who seem to have the capacity for intervention. We are implicated vicariously in the action of the narrative at one level through character identification, and at another level through our act of observation in the safety of voyeurism. The real voyeur, however, recognises certain risks of discovery, already senses social censure and is irrevocably implicated through the conflict. Though the condition of disimplication is already potentially evident in the inconsequence of voyeurism in cinema it is obscured by the ease with which our desire to remain in visible contact with the development of the action is facilitated. The predominant devices of filmic construction have been designed to match the desired extension of experience along the axis of the narrative action. As Metz says, 'not only do we see, but we seem to produce what we see'. At the very least, even if the cinematic scene is not our own product in the sense that a dream is our product, the moment-to-moment shifts of scene, through camera movement and montage seem to be chosen by us as spectators to match our desire to extend along the (pre-set) narrative line. Conflicts with our desire, inability to continue the expected line and confrontation with the fearful or repugnant become incorporated within the narrative. They are interpreted as frustrations or fearful confrontations belonging to the film's characters through whom we experience them. Frequently, those moments of frustration of our desire to see or hear the event which would carry the action forward, or particularly the confrontation with the feared object, is reinforced by the so-called point-of-view shot. This device involves a correspondence between the point of view which represents the film's spectator and that of the represented protagonist, strengthening the bond of identification rather than interrupting the narrative. Continued correspondence of the film's development with the spectator's desire through, for example, following action in camera movement or cutting into the component of the scene and action most central to this desire maintains an illusion that what is seen *responds* to the spectator's volition and is synonymous with the fictional volition of the protagonists. This apparent perceptual volition and its confusion with that of the character through the point-of-view or over-the-shoulder shot suppresses awareness of the fundamental disimplication of the spectator in the film's action. In effect, as a narrative progresses, whatever the camera placement, the shot increasingly comes to represent what is available to the sight of the character with whom we identify. Not only is the spectator given an illusion of implicatedness in the represented action through character identification, this is extended to the much more fundamental illusion of implicated volition through seeming to produce the visual and aural access to the unfolding of this action. Again, what is primarily masked by this illusion is the authority relation between the spectator and the film construct – the spectator seems to constitute the film perception while it is the film which produces the spectator as its subject.

Identification with Historical Authorisation

I have already indicated briefly how in the history of the avant-garde film, through the existentialist, one-person film, the film-maker becomes the main protagonist of the film's action. Here, in a sense, the film becomes composed entirely in the convention of the point-of-view shot. Narrator and the film's protagonist become located together. However, even if the locus of identification is shifted, the psychological conditions of its mechanism are not necessarily transformed. Extreme reductions within the film's action, for example, to sequences of empty black and white frames, do not automatically dislodge these mechanisms. Attempts, using randomisation, mathematical system and computer editing, for example, to eliminate the hierarchy of temporal priority and depersonalise the narrator by mechanising the narration (structuration) mask the relocation of the author's subjectivity in the initiation and application of the system. In addition they may tend further to embed identification into the falsely objective historical authorisation of technology. The problem of identification, like the authority relations with which it is integrated, cannot be simply circumvented.

Again, because the authority relations cannot be circumvented, the need to make them problematic within the film work becomes apparent. In my own work, a distinction between an expressive and a problematic aesthetic emerged simultaneously with the reconsideration of the problem of access to the pro-filmic through the camera. This formed the background from which the films since 1973 have developed. *White Field Duration* (1973) problematises the basic capacity of a cinematic record to transpose past reality to the present, *After Manet* (1974) the conceptual relationship of the camera to the scene in spatial terms, *Blackbird Descending (Tense Alignment)* (1976), in temporal terms and *Emily – Third Party Speculation* (1979) in terms of the movement of identification.

Identification with the Camera

In discussing identification with the camera we must be aware that its arguments derive largely from consideration of the camera in terms of a still-photographic apparatus. We must bear a number of thoughts in mind in the application to cinema. For example, the concept of a point of access to a scene must be extended into the terms of a thread of access to a temporality. Even where a camera is static within a film sequence it already has a dynamic movement along the time axis, in both its duration of recording and presentation. Consequently, the concept of spatial perspective might be extended to include a notion of a temporal perspective. Metz, following Baudry, attempts to equate an ideal transcendental self-identification of the spectator, with the ideal vanishing point in quattrocento perspective and embodied technologically in the structure of the camera and lens. He argues this vanishing point as an empty implacement centring the spectator's identification. I have a number of disagreements and difficulties with the concepts. Most fundamentally, any form of identification, however accurate its psychological description, which is placed in an ideal, transcendental location, must, by definition, involve a non-recognition of that location as historically-determined. Metz is aware of this in his psychological description but gives no indication of the possibility of its being made problematic or dislodged either in the psyche or cinematic practice. Even the basic argument that the vanishing point of perspective is intrinsically ideal can be fundamentally challenged. This vanishing point is constructed (as a convention) by an entirely definable method or mechanism. Contrary to the ideal, this represents an ultra-specific relationship between the image, its method of production and the spectator. Historically, perspective can be seen as part of the general development of the concept of individuality. By specifying the mechanism of representation it contributes to the potential distinction between the spectator and the representation. Remember, the spectator is not 'less' placed in a scene when the terms of that placement are undefined or undefinable, an issue which becomes particularly important in considering the temporal structuration in cinema. Perspective, far from *intrinsically* demanding an unconscious identification of the spectator with that point of access, initiates the possibility of a discrimination between the place of the spectator and the point of view determined by the system to the scene. Any identification then which comes about with the empty implacement is an unconscious identification with the historical authority of that system presented not as *a* mechanism of structure but as *the* true, natural (historically sanctioned) mechanism of representation.

The structure and implications of the form of identification with the camera which take place in a film depend significantly on the context. In those rare instances of cinema where a film is structured towards an awareness of the camera – its properties as a mechanism – any unspecified omniscience (of the viewpoint) is counteracted by a consequent awareness of the limits of access to the scene. In this way the viewpoint becomes traceable to a causal agency, readable in a materialist sense as an element in production and history, rather than as a generalised, inevitable, natural access. Awareness of the camera, its presence and effects within the image, must be intentionally produced and is invariably disruptive of the action. Conversely, in dominant cinema, considerable resources go into the effacement of its inscription which suggests that it is far from intrinsically transparent. Indeed, one of the cornerstones of the illusionistic codes of cinema involves the continuous denial of the presence of the material recording apparatus which in turn supports the transcendental omniscience of the point of access to the image. As the camera is not represented visibly in the scene, its inscription exists via the effects which it has on the photographed material. Consequently if the spectator is to become aware of the effects and constraints of the camera, this must be produced conceptually from the non-representational inscriptions. In this case, the spectator moves towards a conceptual identification *of* the camera, and does not simply identify through its implacement with the components of the representation.

An impetus towards such conceptualisation may derive from devices which stress the special conditions and limits of the cinematic image, differentiating them from the conditions of perception which might pertain for the spectator if the scene were encountered outside a cinematic mediation. In this way, the imaginary of the camera relation is not simply contained within the imaginary space (and diegesis) produced for the spectator by the placement in the scene (and action), but becomes an imaginary conceptual construct made possible through the specification or identification of differences. This process is, in fact, extremely complex, as certain components of the image must be identified (with?) and some spatio/temporal relations established before the unrepresented, though inscribed, relations of the camera can be conceptually produced. In addition to which, identification of the camera is not a single, but multiple identification, it cannot be simply determined in the fact of its presence, nor any one of its specific limitations, like framing, focus, focal length, spatio/temporal relation to the recorded scene. Its identification is also implicitly related to the identification of the agency of its manipulation and the historical conventions of that manipulation currently in play.

Devices which denaturalise the camera implacement, counteract its unconscious reading as representing a (disembodied) human eye and draw attention to the fact and conditions of its mediation initiate a *speculation* in the space between what is recorded (seen and heard) and what is not directly evidenced. Certain interruptions in the flow of desire for identification into the scene and into its continuing action, by specifying and making evident the conditions of spatial access (or other mediations of the camera), make it possible to *differentiate the point of view from the action* and thus *the camera implacement from the position of the spectator*. Speculation in the arena of what can be known, through the recorded inscription (image and sound) and what can be deduced or guessed at, begins to problematise various other intersections at the fringe of inscription of the image. The differentiation of the spectator from the scene initiates speculation within the arena of the symbolic production of (and belonging to) the spectator. Delineating the intersection of discourses occurs simultaneously with the speculative symbolic production by the spectator and becomes the basis of a relationship of appropriation in contrast to passive consumption. As the spectator has no capacity to intervene in the arena of a film's fictive action, nor in its documentary action, nor even further in its material structuration, the region of appropriation must be defined within the conceptual and symbolic operation of the spectator. Consequently, any illusions of implicatedness and presence which tend to derive from the various levels of identification need to be counteracted if the objective is to give to spectators their own symbolic realm. At the same time the lure which maintains attention, a basic apprehension, the various structures of libidinal movement and the economics of this investment must be taken into account.

Reflexiveness and the Ego

Some criticism of the concept of the speculative/reflexive spectator has emerged along the lines that this reinforces the coherence of the spectator's ego which is an illusory unity. However, this must be seen in the context of the alternatives of practice. If the spectator subject is to encounter the inadequacies of unification and stability of the ego, in a way which may be psychologically integratable, as in psychoanalysis, this must be produced (paradoxically) in the arena of a self-identification in its encounter with implicated consequentiality. On the one hand, structural incoherence in film does not of itself confront the spectator with fundamental difficulties of ego coherence. On the other hand, the twenty-two conventional practices of cinema which do not differentiate the spectator ego from the film produce an unconscious and restricted coherence along the axis of the narrative identification. Here the continuous dissociation of spatial and temporal access through camera movement and editing, by disrupting any possible self-produced coherence of viewpoint by the spectator, makes the spectator unavoidably subject to the narrative and narrational coherence of the film.

Spectator Economy/Production Economy

In order to understand the mechanisms of this disruption, it is necessary to consider the relationship between the economics of producing a cinematic sequence and the psychological (motivational) economics of perception. In daily life, perceptual changes for the subject are deeply intricated with the expenditure in energy needed to bring them about. This expenditure operates at all levels from the muscular adjustments in the eye to larger expenditure of motivational energy in bodily movement – acts initiate consequences even in the arena of perception.

In addition, the energies invested in the complexities of motivation are derived from the deep psychological history of a subject's implicated and consequential encounters. In film production, economic investment is made in achieving a viewpoint and continuity of spatio/temporal experience, outside of the constraints acting on lived experience. A fundamental example which forms a major foundation of cinematic practice is the montage (editing together) of two distinct spatial viewpoints as if continuous in time. The economics of this production (implementing the relocation of camera, lighting and re-enactments of performers between takes, then editing and all the complex preplanning of one in terms of the demands of the other) are incompatible with the economics of perception of the spectator when confronted with the result. Instantaneous shifts in spatial viewpoint and time would be impossible for the spectator outside of the conditions of film and any equivalent shift would involve an expenditure of energy and occupy time. The interim time is suppressed both in the conditions of production (the time of camera relocation, etc.) and in perception. At issue here is not the capacity of film to produce experience outside and beyond the economics of daily perception, but that by *exploiting* such a capacity the dialectics and conflicts of its (economic) difference are made impenetrable. The possible dialectical conflict which is implicit in the spatial dislocation of shot construction in action montage (and similarly spatial and temporal dislocations in the larger-scale movements of a film action) is suppressed by the maintenance of the narrational continuity. Through the suppression of this dialectic, the spectator's ego has no alternative but to abandon the attempt to produce a spatio/temporal (psychological) economic coherence outside the film's diegesis – a construction which would 'belong' to the spectator. The special and limited ego coherence which is produced in and by the narrational coherence of the film is not compatible with the attempt to promote some (coherent) differentiation of the spectator ego within the dialectics of a perceptual economy. It is consequently evident that a project which seeks to define the arena in which the spectator may appropriate the film experience (a speculative/reflexive, conceptually symbolic operation) must extend the dialectical encounter with viewpoint as discussed in the terms of camera identification to the various economics (financial and psychological) of the film splice.

Splice as Time Frame

Though elided by continuity, and even by the temporal proximity of instantaneous juxtaposition, the splice always inscribes a fissure of discontinuity. It functions as a frame to duration in a similar way in which the picture edge functions as a frame to space. Each case constitutes a fringe and intersection with a continuum to which, as a fragment (incompleteness), it attests. The frame of the picture – particularly the photographic picture – always retains its arbitrariness as the cut-off point of perception. Even if suppressed, by for example 'unifying' composition, there is an implicit awareness that the initial event of the image continues beyond the frame. Though the conventions of narrative cinema hide the awareness, the film sequence is similarly 'framed' but here it is a framing of time. In any film sequence there is a period before and after 'shoot-ing', and within the conventions of montage there is a further framing through the discarding (editing out) of the moments before and after the 'intended' action. Both picture frame and particularly the time frame of each shot is suppressed in cinema by the continuity of the montage. Indeed the replacement of an absence (loss of the before and after of the shot) at the moment of the splice is exchanged for a new and illusory continuity in the narrative.

Conclusion

So, I might conclude, inadequately as in all conclusions: film's content is not tauto-logically confined by its material manipulations, nor by the documental empiricism of its recorded inscriptions but its extension remains critical and problematic at the edge of its material inscriptions. This edge, which may be defined in some instances literally by the frame or the splice for example, or which may be represented in their function as metaphor for all the limits of inclusion/exclusion which the cinematic mediation currently encounters or might encounter, is the edge at which the invisible becomes visible, the inaudible, audible and in general all those non-visible, non-audible relations impinge in the causality of the visible and audible inscription. Exploration of this critical edge (critical edges) within the aspiration of a material-ist practice is bound up with the definition of the terms in which the spectator may establish an implicated, consequential relationship with the exploration of an issue with repercussions both in the structure of films and the institutions within which they are produced and presented.

References

Baudry, J.-L., 'The Apparatus', *Communications* no. 23, 1975, translated in *Camera Obscura* no. 1, 1976.

Bazin, André, 'The Ontology of the Photographic Image', in *What is Cinema?* vol. 1 (Berkeley: University of California Press, 1967).

Deren, Maya, 'Poetry and the Film Symposium', *Film Culture* no. 29, Summer 1963; reprinted in P. Adams Sitney (ed.), *'Film Culture': A Reader* (London: Secker and Warburg, 1971).

Heath, Stephen, 'Repetition Time', *Wide Angle* vol. 2 no. 3, 1978.

Le Grice, Malcolm, *Abstract Film and Beyond* (London: Studio Vista; Cambridge, MA: MIT Press, 1977).

—, 'Problematising the Spectator's Placement in Film', in this volume.

Metz, Christian, 'The Imaginary Signifier', *Screen* vol. 16 no. 2, Summer 1975.

Wollen, Peter, 'The Two Avant-Gardes', *Studio International*, November/December 1975, reprinted in *Edinburgh 76 Magazine*, 1976.

15

Cinemology [1982]

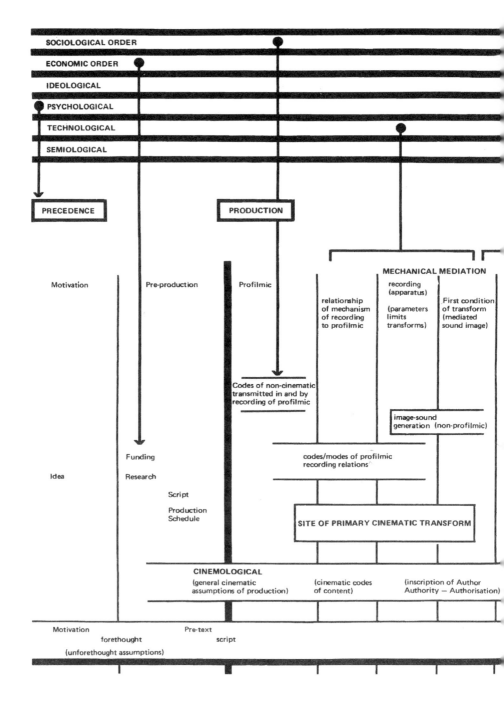

Note: this diagram is reproduced in facsimile from the original source.

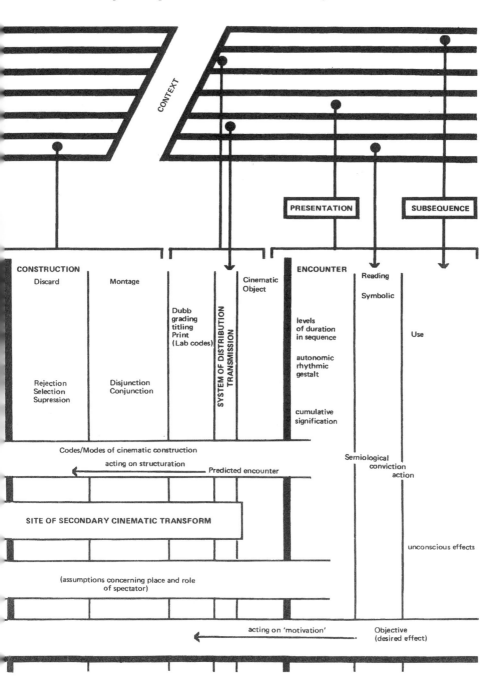

V

DIGITAL THEORY

16

Outline for a Theory of the Development of Television [1970]

The way in which television has developed is largely due to accident and the result of a multitude of barely definable social pressures. Though design has gone piecemeal into this development, it is plain that the total conception cannot be seen as designed in any real sense.

It may be thought inevitable that this evolutionary process occurred, bearing in mind the period in which TV began. However, we now largely have the capacity to predict what our technology is capable of and of determining which of many possible developments are to be fed the necessary resources. We must now see that the present way in which TV is used only represents one among a number of potential concepts; also that we are in a position to define practicable alternatives and relate these to the conditions of human society we wish them to serve.

So – any theory of the development of TV should have expression in technological, economic, psychological and sociological form and if possible a mathematical form, seen as a development from communication theory. The problem of the development of TV should not be seen in isolation from the development of our whole system of information/communication media.

Before beginning any analysis it must be clear that this is not in itself a coherent theory but an attempt to indicate the terms in which such a theory should operate.

First I would like to define the various kinds of function within the general field of information/communication media.

1. *Information media* – being defined as neutral systems through which relatively stable data may be obtained on request. They must comprise the following aspects:
   a) information store
   b) method of organisation and access (index and retrieval)
   A library is a primitive and inefficient form of information medium.
2. *Data processing media* – being defined as any system which automatically manipulates specific data according to a determined program. For example, all occupational machinery.

3. *Communication media* – being defined as systems whereby two sources of data are connected in such a way that both the output and intake are equivalent in form and amplitude. In other words this exists as a system of reciprocal feedback between two elements (people) where there is little imbalance between the amplitude (use of line time/air space) and form of coding between the two elements. A two-way process, like the telephone, is an example of a communications medium.

   The more such a system moves into imbalance and limits feedback to a lower amplitude and lower efficiency coding (that is the more it tends to become a one-way system) the more it can properly be described as a propaganda medium.

4. *Propaganda media* – being defined as systems whereby 'messages' are transmitted at an amplitude greater than the amplitude available to feedback. This constitutes most of what we misleadingly call communication media such as radio-television and the press. I think that however programs or content are balanced, the nature of the system makes it unavoidable that such media become propaganda media. The ultimate function (or if you like, effect) of such media is to condition the responses and data-context (area of awareness and information) of the receiver. Any system which operates as an 'inflexible environment' on the individual ultimately subsumes the individual's behaviour within its terms. This inevitably inhibits the motivation towards change.

The Present Relation of TV to Individual Choice

TV looked at from a sociological and psychological point of view presents us with a problem of very great complexity. In an article of this length all that can reasonably be done is to indicate some of the more pertinent questions which need to be asked.

1. Does TV as a largely centralised transmission medium function as a social co-ordination tool? If so, how? What are the political implications?
2. Does TV engender basically passive responses to authority and is it used as a social placebo?
3. Can we define 'rights of the individual' in respect to his choice of information field?
4. Can we give a psychological description of the individual's need to exercise effective choice?

Of course these questions are loaded and implicitly indicate much of my point of view. I would like briefly to look at the question of choice for the TV user, and assume that in general the individual should demand the maximum possible control over the information, sensations etc. to which he is subject (this is of course seen dialectically and also needs greater qualification in respect of news).

TV has, or can call on, a mass of data stored in televisual form. The proportion of material in transmission to material in store is infinitesimal. What is equally ridiculous is that for any one receiver the amount of really useful (pertinent) data available per week at a convenient time is very small. It always seems to be assumed that the only method of increasing choice for the TV user is to increase the number of channels. This is a dead-end approach: it can never go far enough. It is linked to the error of relating TV production to TV transmission which leads to competitive duplication of low-quality entertainment material on every channel rather than an expansion of real variety. These preconceptions grow from the accident of TV being developed as a branch of radio (broadcasting) rather than, say, the telephone system or, for that matter, the whole field of audiovisual storage not being incorporated into the library conception at an early stage.

Possible Development for TV

In the long term the only method which can reconcile the maximising of user choice to efficient (line time/cost) transmission is through the design of a feedback system, where what is received is in response to what is requested, i.e. where there is little redundant transmission.

Without going into detail concerning the design of such a system, its broad outlines are conceived as follows:

1. Information store – the development of efficient forms of data store for audio-visual interface.
2. This store would be linked by access lines to each individual user, who would receive only requested material.
3. On the air, transmission would be reserved only for relay of immediate news material where the time-lag between an event and its presentation needs to be short.
4. Off-peak, i.e. night transmission of material – to be copied from one store into another.
5. A necessary off-shoot of this type of structure would be the need to develop adequate indexing systems with audiovisual presentation so that the full potential of the store could be grasped by the user. The very limited cross-reference indexing of present libraries is not a useful model or starting point.

Practical and Political Problems

It is evident that such a system involving local storage and complex 'on-line' networks, computer indexed and controlled, would be costly. It would involve complete reorientation of priorities and a special form of co-ordinated development. The main resistance to such development would come from the following:

1. Ignorance of any alternative to the present structure of television.
2. Unwillingness to alter present financial priorities in order to make such a conception realisable.
3. Inability to co-ordinate the development of the whole system of information/communication media.
4. Unconscious political pressure to maintain control of social attitudes through centralised transmission.
5. Conscious right-wing political pressure to maintain the existing social structure (or reinstate a more reactionary one).
6. Unwillingness of the film and TV unions to allow a restructuring of the industry through the separation of the functions of production and transmission.
7. Real lack of research into the technological problems and cost of development of a system as outlined, for comparison with existing research and development projects in this media field (for example general, colour transmission etc.).

I think that our new systems of information/communication media (electronic media) constitute the basis of a new 'literacy' which is at present in a stage comparable to the period in which the Bible was read from the pulpit by the only literate group in the community. I also see no reason why the case for a general articulateness in this medium will be any easier to establish than for general literacy, as the power held by the articulate few is very great.

In the development of our media it should be taken for granted that we rationally relate what is possible to what is desirable.

17

Computer Film as Film Art [1974]

Surprisingly large numbers of people who have either worked as independent film artists, or who have developed in that area of liaison between art and technology which has evolved steadily during the last twenty years, have recently found themselves concerned in making computer films.

On the following pages I have considered their work in its relationship to the field of computer art in general, to the computer film in all its existing aspects, and to the history of independent film art and abstract film.

Aesthetic Criteria in Computer Art

I want to attempt to discover if there are any aesthetic criteria which are special to, and grow out of, the use of the computer as an artistic tool, or as part of the artist's process. It would be dangerous and unhelpful at this early stage to try to define some kind of categorical aesthetic for computer art, but it could be valuable to indicate how such a basis for criteria could be established, and try to define some preliminary principles.

One must be wary of taking the 'negative' factors of certain present limitations, like the costs of computer time, and the sensuous poverty of interface equipment, and building an aesthetic around these. One should seek some common and more permanent ('positive') factors inherent in the functioning of computers, and see how these are related to the actual structure, image, sound, etc. of the output. What special capacities can the computer offer the artist? The need to produce a program as a means to achieving a work of art imposes one very significant process on the artist, that of some kind of analysis of the component factors of his image (or output), plus an analysis of the kind of principles by which these components are brought together. This situation is particularly true where an artist attempts to use a computer to create work similar in conception to that already produced without a computer. Or, where a person attempts to use a computer to produce work 'like' that already produced by another artist; in a sense, as a test of the accuracy of the analysis of that artist's aesthetic – for example, the Michael Noll *Mondrian*. This kind of work can be thought of as largely 'imitative' of non-computer art, and serves the valuable discipline of analysis. But there are a number of by-products of such work, chiefly the discovery that the output can be continuously modified without altering the basis principles of the program. It is this capacity to produce multiple output with perpetual variety which has been for the artist the most seductive aspect of working with computers. Taking this into account, we should try to define the most common general principles by which such variety is achieved.

The three most important methods are the use of systems of incrementation, permutation and random number generation. What is interesting about all these techniques is that they are widely used in computer work in general, and are highly suited to the basic programming methods. Before continuing with the discussion of this aspect of computer art, it is important to note that the developments of more interactive, real-time computer, and near-computer, art have not made such wide use of these basic techniques, but have rather been concerned with the use, modification, transformation and translation of current events in the environment into new input to that environment in an interactive feedback loop. It would be possible to discuss basic and recurrent principles which are emerging from this kind of 'interactive' art but we will limit this treatment only to considerations which may have some bearing on the problems of computer film.

Returning to the questions of 'product-orientated' computer art, we must begin to discuss the validity of the kinds of use that computers have been put to. There is little doubt that unless the underlying principles of a program are interesting, and the output from it is able to make a significant contribution to the field of art, no degree of continuous variety produced by the techniques described can make that work valid. However, what is also evident is that these 'variety' techniques have an 'appropriateness' to the computer which can provide one sort of justification for the artist's making use of it. The interesting questions arise when we ask if there are any similar cases of 'appropriateness', not so much in the field of output modification, as in the field of more fundamental algorithms of the program. This question can only begin to be answered with a more fundamental examination of what kinds of problems computers are most suited to deal with, and seeing this in relation to the needs and aims of artists. Without completely sidestepping this problem, it seems premature to deal with it in any but a preliminary and undetailed way.

Computers are ideally suited to dealing with complex relationships of data precisely and very rapidly, and they are being developed towards highly efficient indexing and retrieval capability. Although the second of these functions will ultimately be of great significance to computer artists, in the immediate future they will find themselves restricted to more limited data, and have little useful call on larger data banks. Another computer development of some significance is the more limited, computerised control of machinery to carry out processes previously dealt with at a time-consuming, manual level. Aspects of this general development will certainly affect the film computer artist, as well as the musician. Indeed, in the field of music, the computerised studio of Peter Zinovief in London goes a long way to providing this for music, and its structure could provide a useful model for the design of a computerised visual studio for the future.

We could go on from this to see two possible, justifiable reasons for an artist to make use of computers: the first, to explore aspects of art which would not be possible without computers, and the second to produce work more easily, which could nevertheless be made without the use of a computer. Of these two possibilities the former is the most challenging, and necessarily involves the artist at the level of program and even hardware development, and also implies that the events which take place within the program become an integral aspect of the meaning of the product, work. In its most extreme sense it also implies that aspects of the output must remain 'unpredictable' for if this were not so, the artist would simply be making use of the 'mechanical' production capacity of the computer, which would not be playing its role of expanding the range in which the artist can make conceptions.

The basic thesis is that computer art is of no real significance to artists unless it is significant art, and the area in which it is most likely to be significant as art is where it makes a positive use of the computer to expand conception, sensitivity and experience.

That very little computer art can 'live' with such extreme criteria is mainly because most computer art now is primarily engaged in a struggle with the less interesting and peripheral limitations previously mentioned.

Computer Film Art

As with computers in general, the bias of computer-film hardware and software development has been towards science, technology and business. In many ways it is even misleading to talk of the development of computer film hardware at all. Until recently the possibility of making movie film on a computer has barely been 'designed' for at all. Films have mostly been made either by setting up a cine camera before a visual display tube, or by using a microfilm plotter, designed around the output of individual frames of static microfilm to produce consecutive animated frames. Many shortcomings of the film equipment available to artists can be put down to the relatively early stages of the technology and its slow development, but other limitations come about because the only point at which an artist has been consulted about the design is in the choice of shape and colour for the box and buttons. Between the computer-controlled film 'process' camera, or animation rostrum, and the microfilm plotter lies a whole range of possible computer-film output machinery which has hardly begun to be thought about in a coherent way by film artists and computer technologists. Much thought is at present going into the design of the display processor so that it can operate in a more suitable way for visual output, and the whole analogue and mechanical aspects of the display tube and camera are under development. The direction which such developments take (as well as the ever-present, and unavoidable economic factors) depends on the formulation of what kinds of output are to be needed, and it is important that the needs of the film artist are taken into account at an early stage.

At present it is very difficult for the film artist to achieve acceptable control over the output image at a sensuous level unless the film produced by the computer is used by the film-maker as raw material in further processing, using optical printing and colour filters. Most of the films made by artists on computers have been modified to a large extent in this way. Of the two most common existing computer film methods, the camera in front of a visual display system such as the PDP11, and the microfilm plotter like the SC 4020, the former has distinct advantages in flexibility of camera positioning, focus, and other forms of 'hand' intervention, plus the possibility of seeing and manipulating the images to be used on the computer screen and, even if slowed down below their projection rate, seeing some of the intended animation. This means that (which is most important for the artist) the whole process can be reasonably organic and plastic with a fairly rapid feedback. But the microfilm plotter, although allowing greater precision, is very inflexible from the artist's point of view and feedback is slow (being off-line), with no real visual output other than the photographic. (There is no recirculation through the data to keep it on the tube face.) In addition to this, most such machines have their cameras mounted and with lenses so as not to permit the whole film frame to be accommodated within the plotting area. This is because the plotting raster is square, and to fit all of this into the rectangular film frame a margin must be left on either side. This may be economical in terms of information storage, but for the film artist it gives a clumsy aspect to the image, unless an unnecessary and costly optical copy is made from the original film. Even if we discount the needs of the artist as a factor in such mundane technical considerations, we must allow that the same 'appearance' factors will apply if computer animation is to have any role as, for instance, a means of producing teaching films, where the costs involved in further processing can represent a major aspect of the budget.

These are examples of the sort of criticism which can be levelled at the existing machinery from the film artist's point of view and they largely result from designing with insufficient consideration for the film-making problem.

The next problem is of a different kind, and is simply to do with the present stage of development in technology. This is the colour factor. It is likely that the next generation of film plotters will be designed around a colour tube. It is by no means clear if the basis for this will be the calligraphic type of tube, or the television-type scan tube. However, from the artist's point of view it is not so important which type of colour output is used as long as the design of the camera relationship, display processor, capabilities and software are developed with the needs of film production in mind.

While the film artist waits for direct colour capability in the film output to become available, it seems likely that he will have to reprint (through colour filters) most of the work which he does.

We have examined some of the problems faced by film-makers brought about by the design of the hardware. We must now look at some of the problems in the software.

The calligraphic tube is most suited to the production of individual points, or of vectors from point to point. It is not well suited to the 'filling-in' of regions of tone, for if these are made by close-spaced lines, or dots, the information needed is prohibitive. The Beflix method of using the hardware character matrix, incorporated in the tube, in order to produce areas of tone, has been an important innovation, but it has to be admitted that the definition is too crude and strongly imposes its zig-zag character on all the output. However, both the linear mode and the Beflix-type approach offer a large number of possibilities for exploration. One of the major problems for the design of software for film is the comparatively large quantities of information needed to program a system not adequately designed at its output stage for film, or even visual work. It is difficult to see how the software can develop significantly until more suitable kinds of local storage in the display processor and a better choice of analogue and machine control capacity are incorporated in the hardware. In the interim, it would be valuable to work on programming methods which could combine some aspects of linear and tonal output in the same image, and, accepting the frequent need for some superimpositional reprinting, to establish a special-purpose film printer alongside the plotter and to consider the software in terms of outputting aspects of the final image on one length of film, and other aspects on other lengths of film, for later reprinting.

In the short period of computer-film production what kinds of films have been made?

We could roughly classify the films produced by computers as follows:

1. Films produced chiefly in the development of software by experimental programmers.
2. Attempts to make visual equivalents for complex phenomena in physical science and mathematics. For example A. M. Noll's *4-Dimensional Hypercube* and *Forces Acting on a Steel Bar* by G. A. Michael at the Lawrence Radiation Laboratory and *Galaxy Simulations* by R. Hockney at Reading. Films like these are of particular interest because in many ways they could not be visualised or produced at all without the aid of a computer, which gives them an 'appropriateness' not always shared by the films in the next category. And as Professor Hockney has pointed out, in some cases the amount of data which is to be output by the computer makes animated graphics the only method of presenting it in assimilable form to the human mind.

3. Explanatory or descriptive films, such as E. E. Zajac's *Two-Gyro Gravity-Gradi-ant Attitude Control System*, which often attempt to emulate the hand-animation teaching film but without the understanding of problems of film structure, and the visual 'attractiveness' available to hand-animation. Some of the best films of this kind are those produced at Boeing which mix some hand-animation techniques with output from the conventional pen-and-paper graph plotter; and while the limitations of the hardware remain as they are, this approach could serve as a useful model for the application of computer-film graphics to the teaching film in the immediate future. A more recent teaching film project by the Senses Bureau directed by Bob Weis (under Professor Kent Wilson in San Diego) called *A Protein Primer* not only has a new indirect approach to teaching but also uses the techniques of colouring the black and white material, developed by the film artists in the field, and is the most accomplished computer teaching film so far.

4. The production of graphs in time. This development grows directly out of the single- frame, microfilm function, and in most cases, the products are more acceptable seen as a series of still microfilm images placed side-by-side, than as an animated film, because what is usually needed is the possibility of comparison across time rather than a sensation of the change, although a sensuous awareness of the comparative rates of change is often valuable and interesting.

5. Films produced explicitly as works of film art, like those by John Whitney, which will be discussed at greater length later. For the moment we could simply observe that so far the films produced in this category often have a close relationship to those in the first two categories and the fact that they have been produced at all probably comes from an awareness that they can contribute to the impetus for the development of software.

Historical Background to Computer Film Art

It seems a little curious to be considering the background history of something that has barely begun to exist. But it could help to clarify some of the possible directions which computer film could take. For this reason we must look at the historical situation of films with more than a superficial resemblance to the present computer films. However, let us begin with films which have the most evident link with the present computer films.

It is impossible to be certain when the first totally abstract film was made but one of the earliest was Viking Eggeling's *Horizontal Vertical Orchestra* (1921) of which no copy now seems to exist, but his second film completed in 1924, *Diagonal Symphony*, is in many respects eminently suitable to have been made by a computer. It is largely linear and composed of simple abstract elements which are put together in a gradual formation of a single complex abstract unit. Not only is the image one which could be output on present computers, but, more importantly, the kinds of relationships and animated developments could have been analysed and programmed. This possibility would certainly have appealed to Eggeling and would have assisted his deliberate search for a conscious and describable language of visual form and movement. The title of this film together with his expressed aims indicate a surprising similarity to some of the intentions expressed by John Whitney about his computer work. Unfortunately Viking Eggeling died in 1925 and the search for a precise language of motion graphics was not taken up again until after 1940.

Another early abstract film which must be seen as having a bearing on computer film is *Anaemic Cinema* (1926) by Marcel Duchamp. This is a film which uses revolving spirals and texts in order to isolate certain perceptual problems, and while there is no doubt that this particular film would still be more simply achieved employing the original techniques, if it were to be seen as part of a larger exploration or examination of perceptual behaviour in time, the capacity of the computer to produce numerous alternatives with small basic variations would be a distinct advantage. Of other abstract film-makers from this period, Walter Ruttman and Oskar Fischinger, Fischinger must be seen as a more important influence in later work. Fischinger made a series of abstract film studies from 1924 onwards. While these were often concerned with geometric forms, one major distinction beween his work and that begun by Eggeling is that it is difficult to conceive that any approach could be made to defining a series of algorithms for the processes involved in his work, or that such an attempt would have been of any great interest to him. He may well have welcomed any kind of machinery which would make his manual work less demanding, and this potential of computer animation may have interested him, but not the discipline of the analytical aspect of programmed art. However, Fischinger is important in another way. He is one of the many European artists who moved to the US in the 1930s and formed a link between the early avant-garde movements in Europe and the resurgence in the US in the post-war period. There is no doubt that Fischinger was very influential in stimulating the interest in abstract film which has provided the background, not only to strictly computer film, but also to the wider surrounding area of films using a variety of technological aids like the oscilloscope films of Mary Ellen Bute and Ted Nemeth and the early experiments of the Whitney brothers and the later lightbox work of Jordan Belson.

Two other Europeans of the period Alexandre Alexieff and Claire Parker have made a large number of films since 1932 using the 'pin-screen' technique which they invented. The similarity between this technique and Beflix programming is plain, and during a later period in Canada they certainly had some influence on both the Whitneys and Norman McLaren.

While the relationship between the earlier abstract film-makers and later computer and technological films is obviously valid, it is also simple, predictable, and to some extent a product of using the present limitations of the computer output image as a filter screen through which to observe the historical background. If we accept that the future relationship between computers and film-making could extend to incorporate the manipulation of banks of live film sequences, or that the analogue aspects of the interface will become more flexible, then some other films and film-makers may appear relevant to the computer film. If one begins from the notion of programmability then there are some examples of films which do not have abstract images, but whose structure of image relationship or editing rhythm could be translated into program form. Many of the possibilities for this kind of film structure stem from the work of Dziga Vertov. His dissolution of narrative, and 'psycho-narrative' continuity in favour of thematic and associative continuity, in turn allowed continuity of live photographic material to be conditioned by abstract factors of motion, tonality, texture, rhythm etc. It is not purely coincidental that Vertov primarily worked editing newsreel material, and that the most likely early function for computer-aided editing of live action material will be in continuous televisual newscasting. However, though Vertov makes programmable live action a possibility, none of the films which he made could be described as programmable.

One or two of the films by the Viennese film-maker, Kurt Kren, however, certainly could be programmed, in particular his film *T.V.* which uses a single sequence of film cut into five short pieces and reprinted many times. These short pieces are presented in various orders according to a mathematical formula. Again making use of repeated sequences of live action, there are sections in some of my own films, particularly *Castle II*, which could be compiled in their present and alternative structures from a program. There are two other important examples of films of a different kind, which could potentially be produced from a program, the first by another Viennese, Peter Kubelka, called *Arnulf Rainer* and the second by the American, Tony Conrad, called *Flicker*. Both these films explore the simple situation of an alternating, completely black and completely white screen.

Both of these films would be equally 'programmable' as they are controlled by mathematical 'scores'. Whereas Kubelka explores the formal aspects of the film in time, the Conrad, like *Anaemic Cinema*, is concerned with exploring perception, in this case stroboscopic rates. What can be seen as having an enlightening relationship to computer film should not be too conditioned by the present limitations of the art.

Recent Developments in Computer Film Art

In post-war America interest in abstract film developed towards an interest in expanding film image technology of which strictly *computer* film-making is one aspect. Again we must look at computer film in the wider context to try and define what kinds of hardware and software development would be desirable from the film artist's viewpoint.

The earliest attempts to expand film machinery so that it could, in a sense, produce its own images were made in about 1942 and began as a collaboration between John and James Whitney. For two or three years they produced a series of film exercises, exploring a variety of techniques using an optical printer, cut-out cards, pantographs and filters. Their experiments included an electronic equivalent to Norman McLaren's hand-painted soundtracks. This involved a complex series of pendula connected to a single wire (a 'wiffle tree'), which carried the sum of all their respective oscillations to vary the slit size of an optical soundtrack printer. Another example of the continuity of direction which abstract film-makers have taken is provided by Oskar Fischinger who also experimented with directly constructed optical soundtracks in the 1930s and there is no doubt that the computer film could continue these experiments, but plotting a soundtrack directly on to film by a microfilm plotter is still not possible, due to the limited design.

In the 1950s, many experiments were made using the oscilloscope as the basis for producing film images. Mary Ellen Bute and her husband Lewis Jacobs, referred to earlier, made a number of films exploring this kind of technique. Norman McLaren made a three-dimensional film using oscilloscope patterns for the Festival of Britain in 1951. The film *Eneri* by Hy Hirsch used oscilloscope patterns with multiple colour superimpositions around 1955. Many of these experiments were interesting and decorative and satisfied the need for an 'electronic' image for a while, but although the image itself was a product of a machine, the changes had to be brought about by hand-manipulation.

During the same period, John Whitney continued his own experiments in the mechanical production of film images and sequences, including a stylus system working into a back-lit oil bath producing films like *Celery Stalks at Midnight* and some oscilloscope experiments, but his most significant step during 1957–8 was to link a war surplus analogue computer device to his very flexible animation table. This allowed the production of very complex spiral and concentric circular development to be made easily and mechanically from relatively simple, original drawn material. Although John Whitney did not make any single complete film with this equipment, the film *Catalogue*, completed in 1961, after another analogue computer unit had been added to his system, contains much of the most successful material produced during this period. It is also interesting that many of the products of this machinery were used commercially for film and television titling sequences through John Whitney's company, Motion Graphics.

His brother James Whitney, who had worked with him up to this point, continued his film work independently from about 1950, making *Yantra*, which was not completed until 1960. Although this is frequently described as a 'computer' film, it was in fact produced entirely by hand using the kind of animation technique developed by the brothers for the earlier *Exercises*. His next film, *Lapis*, however, was produced between 1963 and 1966 using a system similar to John Whitney's and including an analogue computer device. Both these mandala-like films are exceptionally beautiful.

The production methods of all the films made by both brothers in this period are very complex and varied. They certainly represent a movement towards the mechanical production of film images, and the desire to have modifications of the image mechanically controlled and programmable. Having said this, it is evident from viewing the films that a great deal of manual intervention in the machinery and subsequent reprinting and selection took place, and none of the films could really be described as wholly computer films. This does not alter their importance as works of film art, and furthermore they indicate, *Lapis* in particular, that at the present moment, if computer films are to be sensuously satisfying, the hybrid product may be preferable to a 'pure' computer film. At least, the lack of access to, or dissatisfaction with, existing computer film equipment can create some extraordinary and resourceful invention. This is particularly true of the first computer-aided film made by an artist in Europe.

Marc Adrian's film *Random* (1962, Vienna) was made by the extremely unlikely method of placing a camera with no lens directly against the face of an X-ray receiver tube linked to an IBM 1620–21 where the signal direction in the tube is reversed to extinguish the luminous cells on the screen, and the computer, instead of analysing patterns of X-rays from a patient, was used to program the signals to the receiver tube. Adrian's two later computer films, *Text I* and *Text II*, were more conventionally made in Berlin on a luminous, lineprinter type terminal, and are based on his earlier poem programs.

John Whitney and Stan Vanderbeek

Only since 1966 have film artists been able to use general purpose digital computers for film production. The two film-makers who have produced most work by this method are John Whitney and Stan Vanderbeek, and it is not surprising that theirs is the most significant work as yet available in this field. Both film-makers have a background of technical experiment in film. Much of the preparatory work of John Whitney has been described. Stan Vanderbeek was never involved in the 'abstract' film school which developed on the West Coast of America and provided the major context in which the Whitneys worked. He was more aware of the New York underground film developments and all his experiments were with figurative imagery. He has made many 'montage' films, mixing live action and still photographs of political and personal material and has experimented with transferring TV techniques onto film. The most evident characteristic of his work is its visual poetry of transformations. He has made about ten computer films, *Poem Field* one to eight and *Collideoscope* all made with Ken Knowlton at Bell, based on the Beflix program, and a new film, *Ad Infinitum*.

The main preoccupation in his computer films has been flow of words into each other, with the word become the field and vice versa, although his latest film *Ad Infinitum* was made by filming directly from an interactive visual display and is a linear, calligraphic film which relates much more to the flexible organic forms of his earlier hand-animation films. Unlike John Whitney he seems to have no special 'commitment' to computer films, nor any coherent plan or long-term aim for his work with them. His computer work is just one more aspect of an exploration of himself, through the exploration of a medium. Like Whitney he is well aware of, and uses, reprinting with colour filters in order to make his computer image more sensuously complex.

All John Whitney's recent work, excepting his latest film *Matrix*, produced since 1966 on an IBM grant, explores the possibilities available in a polar co-ordinate program developed for him by Dr Jack Citron. The images, although built up from dots, tend towards the linear mode which is common from the calligraphic terminal, and in spite of the relatively rapid pace of the animation, there seems to be a movement towards a greater austerity, the work being held within a set of fairly well-defined intentions. This tendency is continued in *Matrix*.

One feels that he will now accept the computer film as his central and permanent medium. He does not use the Beflix method and works on the more flexible set-up of a camera in front of a standard visual display. He is seeking to establish a language, or a coherent 'musical' form of visual structures. His present work is reminiscent of that of mathematical abstract sculptors like Naum Gabo, and in many ways accepts a similar aesthetic extended into time.

Until *Matrix*, which needs to be considered separately, it has been possible to criticise the work of John Whitney, on the grounds that many of his aesthetic concepts have been familiar, and that the formal structures did not pose any strikingly new problems. This has come about for a number of complex reasons, the most important being the general retardation of film as an abstract medium, compared with the other arts, and Whitney's own determination to deal with the formation of some kind of background abstract 'language'. Another reason is that Whitney has recognised the need for technical innovations, before the problem could be tackled, and has spent most of his creative time since 1940 making machinery rather than films. Much of his work is contained in experimental sequences, and he has only three complete digital films so far, plus the film *Aspen Talk*, which compiles some of the experimental work which preceded the making of his first digital film *Permutations* (1968). *Permutations* relies heavily on his ability to edit and reprint with colour the short sequences of film from the computer. Consequently, the structure of the film as a whole is not affected by the computer to any great extent. His next film, *One, Two, Three*, produced for the IBM Pavilion at Expo 70, Osaka, Japan, is much simpler, composed of white lines on black, and explores the development of a set of linear centre-oriented figures, with no editing or reprinting. Whereas in *Permutations* the structure of the film as a whole is complex, but determined by familiar, subjective, notions, in *One, Two, Three*, the problem is not dealt with at all. The austerity of this film continues into *Matrix*.

Matrix is in many ways the most advanced computer film produced by an artist to date. Unlike all the other work it does not use the computer simply as a convenient producer of abstract sequences of film for later manipulation. Whitney has talked of his work in terms of defining a language of motion graphics, and described configuration as being like words, and sequences as sentences. In *Matrix* we see the development of these elements towards an articulate whole structure, which grows out of the program. There is still some later manipulation of the material, and though it is coloured by the same methods as in his other films, this is done with a great deal of restraint. What is important in this film is the way in which all the major developments and transitions are an integral part of the program. It begins to explore the area where the capacities of the computer can be used to expand our notions of film structure.

With the present difficulties of computer film production, it is surprising how many of the films which have been made by artists stand as works of art in their own right, and not just as curiosities. Although only *Matrix* begins to satisfy the more rigorous criteria suggested earlier, it is important to consider the work of film-maker artists other than Stan Vanderbeek and John Whitney, at present experimenting in this area. In almost every case, what makes the work of the creative film-makers more accomplished than that by scientists and programmers is not, surprisingly, their visual and technical control, but in particular their editing, pacing, and colouring of the material. But this is also the source of the main weakness in their work; it is understandable that they should want to maintain the fullest possible sensual qualities and with the present state of the machinery and software to which they have access, so much time and energy must go into dealing with these limitations, that few are ready to take on the higher level programming problems. The conceptual and formal level of their work is very primitive. In some ways this makes certain of the films made by mathematicians and scientists more interesting than the artists' films, particularly those by A. M. Noll, G. A. Michael and R. Hockney mentioned earlier.

Other Recent Developments

Of the other film-maker artists currently working in this area, the most important to consider are; two of the sons of John Whitney, John Jnr and Michael, John Stehura, Lillian Schwartz and Marc Adrian. It is predictable that the films of the Whitney sons are highly developed, complex and technically accomplished.

John Whitney Jnr has produced some material on the digital computer, but his main concern is with the development of the analogue system begun by his father, and his three complete films have all been producing using it. The first film, *Byjina Flores* (1964), explored some possibilities of analogue-controlled split-scan techniques, but artistically does not match his second film, an untitled three-screen film completed in 1967, and shown during the Canadian Expo 67. This is an exciting film which explores fast-changing geometric forms in symmetrical configurations. It shows again that the specially designed analogue system can have immediate advantages in ease of control. The possibilities, and commercial potential of this system, are further displayed in his most recent film *Terminal Self* (1971). In this film John Whitney Jnr has begun to explore the use of a photograph of a girl as the basis for the transformations brought about by the analogue system. At the semantic level the symbolism of this film is naive, but the visual effects of interweaving veils of colour brought about by the system in a precise way are very impressive. His intention to develop the machinery further to incorporate the possibility of dealing with moving sequences at the input end, and using a digital unit in the control section could make it into a versatile and commercial piece of equipment.

The direction which Michael Whitney will take is uncertain; he has done some general work on the development of a computer language suitable for film application, and has made a digital film *Binary Bit Patterns* (1969) which utilises a 'game of life' program to create a symmetrical pattern of small dots and crosses, like a Persian carpet design. The centre orientation of this film echoes a preoccupation with the mandala image and the interest in Eastern meditative philosophy which is seen in the work of the whole family.

Others

John Stehura has been concerned with the problems of developing computer language systems of general use to film animation. He began to study programming at UCLA in 1961, and started work on the film *Cybernetic 5.3* in 1965, completing it in 1969. Throughout this period he produced many isolated sequences of film, as he developed the more general program. These sequences, together with some live-action material, subjected to various forms of colour filtering and reprinting, are all displayed in a spectacular, exuberant, loosely structured firework display. In spite of his command of programming his film shows in a more extreme way the discrepancy between the production of animated graphic sequences by a computer and the possibilities of using the computer to structure the general sequential output.

Lillian Schwartz is a film-maker who has very rapidly begun to do some important and interesting computer film work. Since 1969, she has completed five films, all of which contain large amounts of computer-generated material. Her first two films *Mathoms* and *Pixillation* interrelate sections of Beflix output with other film material, like microscope film. These two films began her liaison with Ken Knowlton, with whom she continues to work. Her next two films *Olympiad* and *U.F.O.s* use a development from the Beflix program, EXPLOR, designed as a crystal growth program. *Olympiad* is a decorative presentation of film of a running athlete cunningly built and animated as a special case of crystal growth; this film is brightly coloured and well produced with an easy flow, which will be of great interest to animators within the film industry. Even though the program which produces the figure is inflexible and special-purpose, it indicates the capacity to produce attractive, figurative animation on the current digital equipment. Although both the colour and the superimpositions are somewhat superficial in this film, in *U.F.O.s* she begins to examine colour perception, and the formation of Gestalts in a perceptual situation at a time threshold. Judging by a preview of the material from which her latest film *Enigma* has been made, it continues to explore the perceptual problems indicated by *U.F.O.s.*

The work of Marc Adrian is difficult to compare with that of the American abstract film-makers. His film *Random* has been mentioned already, but, though this film is of interest at a technical level, his two later 'poem' films are probably the most important and coherent 'computer films' produced yet by a film artist in Europe. *Text 1* uses a largely random process for the placing and duration of the words and syllables, and *Text 2* is based on a completely permutative program. In a special way these two films come near to the use of a computer program to determine the whole structure of a film rather than as a method for producing sequences for later organisation.

Most computer film work done by other film artists can only be considered as at an early stage of development, or as isolated computer films. The following work should be mentioned: *Humming Bird* by Charles Csuri and James Shaffer, *Linesthetic* by Lloyd Sumner, *Genesis II* by Richard Childs, *'69* by Denis Irving, *La Raison avant la passion* by Joyce Wieland, and my own films *Your Lips* and *Reign of the Vampire*.

It is too early to indicate with confidence any general directions which computer film art might take. It is clear that the 'purist' abstract direction of John Whitney is well founded and suited to the present state of the technology. There also seems to be an indication of a desire to relate computer film-making to figurative animation, or to live-action film. Some indication has already been made about the potential of the computer to enter into the film process at the editing level, at present a relationship is only realised to the extent of incorporating computer-generated material with live action film. However, some impetus is there, and it is interesting to consider how this might be affected by extension of the most recent and spectacular technical developments in the medium, as indicated by the films *City Scape* (1968) by Peter Kamnitzer and *Hancock Airport* (1971) produced at General Electric. Both of these films are made from a TV type display, on which near-photographic images in colour are reconstructed and animated, digitally, in real-time, and in an interactive mode using a 'joy-stick'. It is unlikely that film artists will be given access to such costly systems, although the proportion of the films so far produced on computers which have been made by experimental film-makers is surprising. It is possible that the somewhat primitive film medium will be superceded quite quickly by videotape systems, or even digital image reconstruction. Certainly, interactive systems will become more common, and given these kinds of developments the 'single state' work which a film is may become archaic.

In the interim, as much thought as possible should be given to the design of 'hybrid' systems, which would have their own characteristic aesthetic, and to exploring the possibilities of applying the computer to film-making in areas other than the output of a graphic image.

There has been much mutual benefit from the amount of computer film time the industry has made available to experimental film-makers, but in future they should be consulted at the earliest stages of designing any kind of visual display, film or videotape system. The quality and method by which visual and graphic information is displayed is of great significance to the effectiveness of that information, and not a neutral factor to be thought of as only of special concern to the artist.

18

The Implication of Digital Systems for Experimental Film Theory [1974]

This paper is based on one first delivered in Vienna in October 1990 for the symposium 'Im Off der Geschichte' organised by the Gesellschaft für Filmtheorie. It is intended to be used as the basis of a presentation including three computer-generated works (image and sound programmed by Malcolm Le Grice) which were incorporated in a video programme *Sketches for a Sensual Philosophy*, first shown on Channel Four on 3 July 1990, and an audiotape of Conlon Nancarrow's *Study No. 21 CANON X*.

The computer pieces are:

Digital Still Life (completed and recorded to video in 1989). This work explores the sequencing and digital re-treatment of a series of 'frame-grabbed' video images. The program which controls the image sequence uses the same 'mathematical' structures to determine the musical form and structure. The origins of this work draw on concepts of visual representation determined by artists like Seurat, Cézanne and the Fauvist work of Matisse. In the video form it includes two short live-action sequences edited into the computer-generated material.

Arbitrary Logic (originally titled *Osnabruck* completed 1988). The work is an interactive computer, sound and image performance piece which draws heavily on the tradition of the 'light organ' which may be considered to have its origins as far back as the sixteenth century through experiments made by Giuseppe Archimboldi[1] and which informed aspects of the work of both Oskar Fischinger and Walter Ruttmann through the theory of Bernhard Diebold.

Heads I Win – Tales You Lose (which exists as both a continuous computer installation or as recorded to video in 1989). This piece is based on the computerised fragmentation and re-combination of a series of drawings made by myself over a period of five years. It explores a 'nested' series of permutative cycles in the selection and re-combination of the images. The sound mixes music generated by the program with keyboard (hand) performance.

Study No. 21 CANON X Conlon Nancarrow (intentionally undated by the composer). This is a recording of a (mechanical) PLAYER piano piece composed by punching holes directly into the paper rolls which control the piano mechanism.

It explores two crossing sequences of notes, one of which decreases in pitch and tempo while the other increases. The piece would be impossible to play by hand.

The aim of this paper is to explore some general theoretical issues raised by the potentialities offered as a result of digital (computer) technologies and their use in cinema.

Theoretical Context

The primary theoretical context for this paper is that which has become known as 'materialist' or 'structural materialist film'. The most dedicated and consistent exposition of this theory has been made by Peter Gidal in various publications including the book, *Materialist Film*.[2] It might reasonably be said that my own contribution to this theoretical development, through writings and film work, has been more pluralistic and less 'strict' than Gidal's but, is none the less equally committed to the same fundamental principles.

The key features of the theoretical position which I have come to hold may be briefly summarised as follows:

- The attempt to structure cinema works so as to promote the spectator as an 'active' rather than 'passive' participant in the construction of the meaning of the work;
- The attempt to counteract cathartic identification by problematising illusion, metaphor and narrative;
- The attempt to stress the material conditions of production and viewing of works both as a creative basis of practice and as a strategy for the counteraction of narrative identification.

It is in relationship to the last of these that the attitude towards technology needs to be clarified. Consistent with a fundamental 'tenet' of twentieth-century art, evident in the plastic arts and music but rarely in mainstream film, is the concept that there can be no convenient separation between the material 'means' of a work and its meaning – that meanings derive from the working of the material. This is a concept similar to that of semiologists, that there can be no separation between the production of a thought and the operations of language.

In other words, ideas do not pre-exist the form of their expression but derive from the interplay between motive and various forms of conception and modes of expression/production.

In this respect, the technologies of art production (or communication media) may be seen to function like language. Embodied in their 'design' for certain purposes (or unconscious emergence) is a tendency to predetermine the forms of their products.

This predetermination is like the predetermination of language, and, like language, may be seen to have unexplored potentialities as well as constraints (habits of usage).

Jean-Louis Baudry in his essay 'Cinéma: effets idéologiques produits par l'appareil de base'[3] established the terms of a dialogue by which the basic effects of the cinematic apparatus (as technology) may be related to their psycho-ideological constructs in the field of semiology.

The technologies of cinematic production are thus not 'neutral' in relationship to the ideas produced and promoted through them. The technologies already embody (cultural) intellect, motive, ideology and consequently all artefacts produced through these technologies have the characteristics of 'dialogue' with this embodied 'intellect'. For the artist, this dialogue takes place in the space between the technical limits, the habits of application, and the attempt to break those constraints in the exploration of potentialities. Therefore it has become fundamental to my theory and practice in cinema to treat the technological base as integral to the construction of meaning. However, the technological base of cinema is not static. It has been and continues to be the site of considerable development, investment and ingenuity which includes the incorporation of a wide range of new and electronic technologies.

Cinematographic Technologies

With the proviso that the model outlined below should not be interpreted as implying 'progress equals better', I offer an analysis of three distinct and developmental stages of technology facilitating the construction of cinematic recording, and presentation or representation.

1. Photochemical/Mechanical

The application of photographic technology and nineteenth-century mechanics, characterised by the rapid sequential recording of a stream of whole photographic images – film.

2. Analogue Electronic

The application of continuous magnetic recording technology involving a rotating scan (where the images themselves are represented as a linear sequence rather than simultaneously recorded) and sequentially reproduced through cathode ray tube presentation – video.

3. Digital Electronic

The application of computer and microprocessor technologies where images are recorded as discrete items of data (or data subject to defined algorithms) and their sequence is a matter of specific address within the context of Random Access Memory. Current systems are only partially developed with respect to the elimination of analogue and mechanical components.

Technological Differences

It might be seen as a consistent feature of technological development in general that it progressively seeks to incorporate the functions of earlier technologies with greater efficiency and flexibility.

Again with a caution about the relationship between 'improvement' and technological progress, while the different technological bases clearly bring with them different opportunities for their use, these may also be seen as not merely different but hierarchic (at least potentially so).

The main basis for claiming a hierarchical relationship between the digital/electronic capability over the photomechanical and analogue electronic forms of cinematography is the contention that: the digital/electronic can 'contain' the conditions of the other two but cannot be contained by them – it is a more general system. It represents an intrinsically more efficient system allowing greater capacity for flexibility in storage and retrieval at lower cost in energy input. The factors on which this claim may be supported also represent, in some cases, the areas of difference from which the expansion in artistic form may be initiated.

Key factors in the use of electronic and subsequently digital technologies are:

Economic

a. The use of non-precious (iron) rather than precious (silver) materials in the storage medium.
b. The use of low voltage current. Low energy – high information.

Technological

c. The reduction or elimination of rotational (wheel) technology, reducing moving parts in favour of high speed electronic signal transfer and solid state storage.
d. Through Random Access Memory (RAM) the establishment of non-linear access. Sequentiality is replaced by non-linear code addressing the potential to massively extend the flexibility of data recovery and combination.
e. Higher order of recoverable abstraction of image data allowing more fundamental levels of manipulation.

Experimental Cinema Practice Based on Digital Systems

However fascinating the most general implications of digital systems for cinematography or their application to aid conventional film or video production might be, the objective of this paper is theoretical speculation concerning experimental, artistic issues. As such, a number of factors concerning the role and concept of theory need to be borne in mind.

While it may reflect or import elements of scientific theory, theory for the practising artist is not strictly scientific in method. Its place in relationship to practice is, if prioritised, secondary rather than primary. The practical work is not simply equivalent to the experiment which proves or disproves the theory. While it might seek 'generality', underpinning practice with some analytic understanding (frequently post-hoc serving more as a critical rationalisation than a theory), its most consistently valuable function has been in stimulating, generating and critically guiding the development of a practice.

At the same time, the practice itself may be an aspect of the theoretical speculation so that the theoretical embodiment is not simply separable from the practical works. A good example of such a relationship between theory and practice in music is provided by the development of Note-row by Schoenberg (following Hauer) which attempted to establish a logic for composition following the dissolution of classical harmony.

The theoretical expression outside the work took the form simply of a formula or method of composition. However, the development, traced through the works, shows how adoption of the 'method' emerged from the 'theoretical' discourse within musical history itself and was a consequent stage in the resistance to classical scale structure initiated by the whole-tone composition by Debussy.

Evidence of its generality, whether articulated or not within the theory (embodied outside the works), is the parallel between the equalisation of musical values in the Note-row system and the similar effect and consequence of Cubism in the visual arts. That the theoretical examples of Note-row and Cubism, both with their atomisation of units and equality of value in each auditory or visual element, might be seen as philosophically consistent with the potentialities of digital systems would need more extensive argument. The issue serves here to indicate:

- something of the difference between theory in the art and science;
- the interrelationship between artistic theory and practice;
- the aspect of theoretical speculation embodied in the historical discourse of art practice itself (whether externally articulated or not).

As an artist seeking to proceed through some interchange between theoretical speculation and the practice of art as a historical discourse (rather than a merely idiosyncratic expression), I am concerned to identify those aspects of digital technology which provide the opportunity for innovation in artistic form. These are divided into the factors related to:

- the cinematic image;
- sound;
- sequentiality and temporality;
- authorship.

Digitalisation of the Cinematic Image

Every element which makes up the image must be specifically defined either as a specific stored element or as the outcome of a constituting algorithm/formula. Every image is subject of necessity to analysis and synthesis (either specifically by the user, by the capacities built into the system hardware/software or by dialogue between the two). The image is consequently open to manipulation at a range of levels allowing:

- the exploration of various 'hypotheses' of image reconstruction based on the range of parameters defined;
- the translation of non-visible phenomena into visual form;
- the more fundamental synthesis of image based either on abstract principles or analysis of 'natural' phenomena allowing the projection of virtual 'realities'. This capacity, exercised in the arena of the recorded image, undermines the documental veracity long assumed to be implicit in the mechanically recorded image. A new range of fundamental artistic (and philosophical) problems are initiated as a result of this capacity.

Digitalisation of Sound

The opportunities afforded by digitalisation in the field of sound are better established in the practice of music than are their equivalent in the visual arts. The capacity to record and reproduce sound digitally allows the same range of manipulation and intervention open to the image and it is similarly possible to synthesise sound from abstract or basic principles. The history of music offers a strong context of experiment using mechanical and programmed systems as the basis of composition.

Movement, Sequence and Temporality

The problematic of movement and its representation, the implication of sequential order and the concepts of temporality are fundamental to the context of cinema and its theory. Prior to digitalisation, all systems of image recording tied the elements of that recording (the separate images) strictly to their sequence of recording through the design of the technology and the recording medium. Any deviation in the presentation sequence involved an uneconomic exchange with the technology. On the other hand, it is a fundamental theoretical feature of digital systems and Random Access Memory that the storage of the recorded data is independent of its recording sequence. (This is a theoretical property and depends technically on the progressive replacement of linear recording media by solid state systems). In other words (again in theory), as a consequence of the concept of RAM, presentation of recorded material which adopts the same sequential order as that of the recording has no higher priority than any other basis of sequential presentation.

Not only does this open sequentiality more thoroughly to experimentation, but the philosophical implications for our concept of memory or its 'modelling' in artistic terms and the relationship between time in representation and reality become accessible in a new way through digital applications in cinema.

Authorship

In other work, I have identified two main issues in the debate concerning authorship in cinema.[4] On the one hand, this is centred on the degree of control which can be exercised by the artist in the context of the historical constraints on meaning embodied in the cinematic production institution, the language and the technology. On the other hand, this focuses on the relationship between the artist, the work and the spectator, in the context of the spectator's 'construction' and appropriation of the work and on the devices available to the artist to maximise the role of the spectator. For both aspects of this debate, digital technologies have substantial implications. These can be taken up in relationship to: the intelligent machine, program, permutation, system and interactivity.

The Intelligent Machine

All machines embody the application of intellect to the fulfilment of a need or desire. Following the arguments of Baudry, it is evident that cultural/social/psychological factors influence the emergence and design of the sophisticated machinery of communication and representation. All production with such machines becomes (consciously or not) a dialogue with the historical constraints on thought and expression intrinsic to that technology.

Digital (computer) technology is the most sophisticated form of the embodiment of intellect (and all the attendant aspects of cultural determination) in mechanical form yet devised. This is not a neo-romantic notion about machine or artificial intelligence, it is no more than a recognition that digital hardware and software is the consequence of the investment of intellect and that this and its specific characteristics (its ideology) is transmitted as a set of constraints on its users. Experience of working with computers makes the characteristic of 'intelligent' dialogue increasingly evident and to a level not comparable with any other technology.

The greater the complexity of the (intelligent) machine, the more simply it can achieve sophisticated product, the more difficult it is to differentiate the intellect of the machine from its user. It is consequently more difficult to trace the responsibility or 'centre of authorship' for any product. Authorship becomes submerged in the cultural artefact produced in dialogue with the intelligent machine. This problem is not different in kind to that faced in relationship to work in other media but its terms are more complex and less well theorised. The crucial issue in relationship to the theory of materialist film is not that of the assertion of authorship (in the subjective sense) but that of the capacity to trace the interaction between the 'author' and the cultural determinants of the language and technology through the artefact.

Program Permutation System

In narrative cinema much of the determination of significance rests on the singularity of resolution. The sequential structure is culminative within codes of dramaturgy. The implicit fatalism of narrative determination rests on the implicit singularity of resolution. There is, by now, in music, literature and certain aspects of experimental cinema, a history of strategic resistance to this fatalistic tendency in form. Many of these strategies have involved the capacity to specify the structural determinants of a work, making use of system and repetition. This strategy puts the author's subjectivity into a more definable relationship with the work, allowing the spectator to respond to the work independently of the author. The structures in such work frequently imply (or signify) the possibility of alternative structures which the material might take, thereby undermining the fatalistic determination of spectator response in favour of the speculation on alternatives. The responsibility for signification and hierarchies of meaning is thereby somewhat shifted from author to spectators.

Through digital technologies and particularly the control of image sequence by program, the exercise of alternative structures becomes economically feasible in a way out of the range of traditional film and video technology. The flexibility in structure, the exploration of system and permutation dislodges signification from singular resolution.

Interactivity

The technologies of film and video have been based on a clear demarcation between the stages of production (recording) and structuring of the material into a work, as have the stages between the construction of the work as a whole and the presentation to an audience. Cinematic works reach the audience conclusively finished. Digital technologies intrinsically erode these sharp demarcations. The raw material for a work remains independent from any single resolution, and the capacity to restructure (within the limits of storage, parameters or the program and particular hardware system) remains open throughout. Thus the distinction between producer and spectator has the increasing potential to become blurred and to make the spectator more directly a user who can actively participate in the construction of meaning from the work.

Such developments within the technology are by no means absolute (nor fully developed) and the shift to participation through interactive systems does not automatically shift authorship closer to the user. However, they represent a clear tendency in practice and an even clearer potential in theory. The issues carry far-reaching implications for the assumed relationship existing between artist and the user/spectator.

Conclusions

The application of digital systems to cinematography does more than assist film and video production. It raises fundamental theoretical issues which challenge assumptions concerning documental veracity, narrative structure, and the relationship between author and user.

Many of its particular capacities lend themselves particularly well to further exploration in areas which have been initiated in experimental film and video, particularly those related to image transformation, sound-image relationships and sequential structure.

As with any other aspect of art, technical experiment of itself has little validity. Art practice remains a matter of significance in the area of meaning as a cultural activity. Thus work with sophisticated technology carries no guarantee of relevance or quality. By the same token, major work can be produced by simple and primitive means.

It is important that experimental work with digital systems can be related to a context of art practice able to provide a theoretical and critical language concerned with meaning and philosophy and which is not dominated by technical theory.

Notes

1. Scheugl and Schmidt, *Eine Subgeschichte des Filmes* (Frankfurt: Suhrkamp, 1974).
2. Peter Gidal, *Materialist Film* (London: Routledge, 1989).
3. *Cinéthetique* nos. 7–8, 1970, translation Alan Williams, *Film Quarterly* vol. 27 no. 2, 1974.
4. See essays, 'Towards Temporal Economy' and 'Problematising the Spectator's Placement in Film', both in this volume.

19

Kismet, Protagony and the Zap Splat Factor [1993]

Some Theoretical Concepts for Interactive Cinema

Recent technological developments have brought us to the point where all the elements of cinematic art – high resolution, colour and high-fidelity sound – are available to digital interactive systems. This raises fundamental theoretical and practical questions about how the history and practices of cinema may relate to the use of new computer-based technologies.

Interactivity in the plastic arts is not new, since the mid-1960s at least, artists have produced electronically and digitally controlled feedback projects where the actions of the spectators have altered the work in some form or another. It is, however, only recently that there has been a realistic convergence between the recorded cinematic sequence, aspects of virtual reality synthesis and sophisticated interactive possibilities. There is a developing practice in this field, some aimed at education and training, but also some quite clearly artistic.

It is the aim of this paper to take up some of the theoretical issues which must arise if we are to bring cinema and interactivity together in the context of the creative arts and in the search for artistic forms *appropriate* to the resulting new opportunities.

Cinema and television art has been overwhelmingly dominated by the form of linear narrative. The presentational structure of the cinematic media (film and video tape) has intrinsic characteristics which reinforce this linearity and a concept of a consequent and singular resolution. One major aspect of this presentational linearity is the reel of film or tape itself with the images held in a locked sequence to be seen 'from beginning to end'. It is an economic issue (both financial and that of psychological investment) the extent to which this linearity of presentation can be broken or interrupted by the viewer. The economics of making and presenting a film establish a major difference between the *active* production of the work and its *passive* viewing in cinema or during TV transmission.

Though only limited, home videotaping is already a form of interactivity putting greater opportunity for selection in the hands of the domestic viewer. This extension of choice is most evident in expanding the range of which films or programmes to watch and when, but from the film structural point of view the important matter is the capacity this offers viewers to reorder the artistic experience to suit themselves.

Though in this example, the choices may seem trivial, the opportunity for the viewer to fast forward sections of little interest, repeat sections of particular interest and, in a more sophisticated sense, study the cinematic construction in detail, puts the viewer in a significantly different psychological position with regard to the work. In most instances, this type of changed relationship with the spectator is not envisaged at all in the initial form of the works presented. Even the limited form of interactivity is contrary to their structure which remains that of the classical narrative cinema constructed around the passive viewer.

Kismet

The predominance of the narrative form in our culture makes it difficult to establish any critical distance allowing narrative to be seen as one *particular* form of representation rather than a 'natural' and inevitable system.

As Renaissance perspective is a mode of spatial representation among other modes (maps, diagrams, isometric projections or Cubist space for example), so linear narrative is one method by which events in time and their causal relationships may be represented. In this sense narrative form is a representational *model*; it is a tool by which human-beings grasp and structure their understanding of the world. While being appropriate in certain circumstances it also has shortcomings; it is well suited to representing certain forms of temporal linkage but incapable of modelling others. Its form imposes a philosophical bias (an ideology) on its subject and because of its predominance we are blind to the limits of its 'truth' and level of generality as a representational system.

A fundamental characteristic of the narrative form in cinema is the inevitability of its fictional resolution. The outcome of the plot is predetermined and the plot carries its primary significance in the relationship of action to the ultimate resolution. The form of a narrative text itself, in the predetermination of its resolution, is intrinsically fatalistic in form. The viewers' subjective relationship to this form is in this respect always fatalistic. The end (as represented in the text) is already determined, it is known. Viewers 'know' it is known when they start watching the film and the events of the film only have their rationale in their contribution to the ultimate consequence.

So even in films where the *intended* representation is of a non-fatalistic world, the representation is in conflict with the intrinsic form of linear narrative and its experience by the viewer. Certain attempts have been made within classical cinema to break both the linearity and tyranny of the singular consequentiality of the narrative form. There are examples of attempts at ambiguity in resolution, alternated resolutions, parallel action, branching 'detours' in the plot or multiple viewpoint in the representation of the fiction (through the different represented characters) but none of these substantially question the structure of linear causal representation.

Protagony

As well as looking at the structure of linear narrative, it is crucial to analyse the characteristic form by which the viewer is 'involved' in the traditional cinematic experience. The viewer watches, as if through a window, an action between a group of protagonists. Normally, one or two of these protagonists are central and become the focus of a psychological identification by the viewer. The viewer becomes engaged in the action of the narrative by an imaginary leap into the position of one or other of these depicted characters. The viewer experiences the desires, frustrations, pleasures and satisfaction of these characters in the unfolding of a plot by 'living through' the represented action as if they were in the place of the character in the action being depicted. However much the viewers may become psychologically engaged they can never be truly protagonists and any experience they may have of being a protagonist through identification is illusory.

To be a protagonist there must be a perceivable relationship between action and effect. In other words, an action on the part of the viewer must be able to change the course of events which follow from that action. The characters within a narrative are represented as taking part in the complex relationship between action and consequence. When they perform an action the plot takes its course as a result of that action (within the limits of the represented power and scale of the action – King Kong flattening a New York sky-scraper is of a different order to Philip Marlowe lighting a cigarette). However, in the cinematic convention this representation of protagonism is already itself a fiction, an illusion (not the same in sports or news coverage in the conventions of live TV).

The characters – moving photographs of actors – are not creating the consequences they seem to be. They are playing those actions to a set of consequences predetermined within the script. They are enacting their protagonism. For the viewer then this, added to their identification with the actor, becomes a double illusion of protagonism. For the viewer, protagonism is twice removed in the determination of the plot – the only protagonism in this sense is in the authorship of the text.

Thus, in the context of digital technologies and the opportunities for artistic approaches to interactivity, I have identified two major issues implicit in the dominant culture of narrative cinema, the *linear consequential structure* and the *condition of the viewer in relationship to the work*.

In the search for alternative approaches, matching artistic structure to the new technological possibilities, I offer two potentially fruitful sources: the cinematic grammar developed by the experimental cinema (the avant-garde), which has resisted, transformed or created alternatives to linear narrative; and perhaps more surprisingly, the computer game.

The first of these offers an approach to different models of connectivity, temporal structuring and concepts of the relationship between the cinematic sequences (as data) and their relationships (as program).

The second offers a model in which the viewer becomes a user and protagonist in a psychologically motivated field.

Only the radically experimental cinema has seriously questioned the inexorable linearity of narrative seeking instead to model a more 'multidimensional' connectivity within the form of cinema – what Maya Deren described as the 'vertical' rather than 'horizontal' exploration in cinema. Fundamental to this enterprise has been recognition of the inadequacy of the narrative form to represent a philosophical and ideological structure seen by experimental film-makers to be appropriate to their perception experience. This perception has involved many forms of both abstract and representational linkage not susceptible to the structures of linear causality and determinate consequence which is the mainstay of narrative form.

Capricorn the Ram

The following characteristics of digital (computer-based) systems are formally or philosophically crucial (not just technologically innovative):

- Random Access Memory (RAM);
- Programmability or permutation;
- The process of analysis – synthesis from fundamental principles;
- Interactivity.

In computer technology, the separation of data from their programmed combination or interaction is fundamental. As a consequence the relationship and connections between instances of data is not fixed. The instances of data retain *potential*, they may be combined and recombined according to a variety of principles and permutations.

In the cinematic context it remains problematic what might be considered an instance of data – this is not determinate, it depends on the level at which the analysis (or classified digitalisation takes place). It can range from the individual pixel of the image, a fragment of digital sound, a single picture, a shot sequence or, most radically, an analytical set of principles on which three-dimensional motion audio-graphics might be synthesised. Additionally, it is a matter of creative ingenuity to define the program structure by which these levels or instances of data may be combined. In the artistic context, whatever principle of the program or sequence of connectivity between the data is created, it carries with it the implication of signification and a relationship (as model) between the artistic construct and the world on which it reflects (or into which it is placed as an intervention). Its structures have and promote philosophical and ideological positions, they become part of the vocabulary or grammar by which we grasp and understand the world.

The flexibility of the relations between data in programmable sequence offered by computers is a consequence of technology offering random access to whatever is defined as data. At its most radical, this random access is wholly non-linear. Though both the storage and retrieval processes are sequential as is the user's inevitable access, the structure of access is not governed by the priority established in initial storage but is only subject to the chosen hierarchy of combination. At this radical level, the concept of random access, when applied to the audio/visual arena, substantially undermines the linearity of narrative sequence.

In practice, in the developing technology of high information storage, where the data is defined as cinematic sequences (shots), aspects of the access remain partially linear (through the rotation of storage disks). At a theoretical level, the main technological distinctions to be made involve a range in the storage medium from linear tape (or film) to rapid cross-access disks to fully solid state storage. At the level of theory with regard to artistic structure, the concept (and exercise) of random access places the instances of data into a structure which may be considered as a matrix (three- or multidimensional grid) no longer confining presentational sequence nor connective principle to the conventions of narrative causality. Narrative structure becomes a subset of temporal structuring.

In the experimental cinema with references as far back as Dziga Vertov's *Man With a Movie Camera* (1928), and more recently, the work of Kurt Kren, Maya Deren, Stan Brakhage and many others, may be read as aspiring to a form of temporal connectivity better represented as a matrix than as a single linear causality. This experimental approach in cinema, through specific exploration of devices like repetition, partial repetition, review and reworking, permutation and system, prefigures many of the structural principles inherent in the technology of Random Access Memory. What is more important in the artistic context is that they represent the development of philosophical constructs which constitute more appropriate 'models' for contemporary experience than do those offered by the singular and fatalistic structure of classical narrative.

Zap Splat

It would be difficult to interpret the development of the computer game as led by artistic or philosophical principles. It has been a spontaneous popular development directly from the potentialities of the computer. None the less, in certain aspects of the search for forms of audiovisual (cinematic) art, it has initiated – unconsciously – crucial and fundamental differences and opportunities. Though interactivity has had some 'serious' applications in the development of educational and simulative training systems, like rock music, the computer game has captured a major popular

field of psychological investment and desire. The major characteristics on which this
seems to rest are:

- the exercise of interactivity in a field of high motivation;
- the establishment of the user as an engaged protagonist;
- an adequate degree of representational simulation into which the user may project;
- the possibility of failing to reach a satisfactory resolution.

For the current exploration let us compare the condition of the user of the computer game with the viewer of a conventional narrative.

The factor of interactivity of itself demands a change of vocabulary. Viewers are
now 'players'. Their interactive relationship offers a level and range of control in a
data field and program offering sufficient variety to veer their experience very
strongly towards that of being an active participant and away from that of passive
viewer. The actions and, in some instances, sophisticated strategic or tactical
decisions of the players have strong and perceptible effects in the audio/visual field
into which they project themselves and in the direction of the outcome of the 'play'.
This evident responsiveness of the game to immediate and longer-term actions *impli-
cates* the player in the action. Though some games like 'Street Fighter' have the user
controlling the actions of a visually represented character (a figure visible within the
game), in many instances, like the classic 'Space Invaders' or more sophisticated
simulations like 'Grand Prix' or 'Gunship' (a helicopter war simulation), the protagonist is significantly not represented in the visual field.

Thus, one aspect of the identification process fundamental to classical narrative
cinema is not at work. Though this is often different in experimental cinema where
in many instances there is no visually represented protagonist. In these cases, the film
traces the film-maker as 'protagonist' and the viewer's identification is with the film-
maker. In the computer game, the interaction experienced by the user/player is one
of direct intervention in the scene. The unrepresented player is traced (traces him or
herself) through the effects brought about within the game. Clearly the motivation
of the player can only be maintained if there is a sufficiently desirable goal to be
sought or the results of the interim interaction are sufficiently satisfying. Or, perhaps
more crucially, if the interaction is sufficiently frustrating, promising later satisfaction
through the development of greater skill or intelligence. The creator of a game must
have a grasp of the motivational objectives of the potential player/user, but must also
devise sufficient complexity in the program to offer a range of both interim and ultimate outcomes. This requires programming a high degree of intended redundancy
(or superfluity) – a range of options either failures, successes or different routes –
which may or may not be used during the interaction.

This principle of redundancy must also be a major factor in the development of satisfactory artistic uses of such systems. The economical creation of this redundancy would seem to rest heavily on the complexity of the initial analysis of data (and algorithms) for synthesis in the interaction.

For example: in a pilot or driving game, if based on a large number of single pictorial screens and picture units (sprites), it may produce its variety through the various combinations of elements, but would soon be exhaustible in relationship to the user's actions. On the other hand, the same game structure based on a three-dimensional mapping of the space and objects, though initially more difficult to achieve, retains a much greater potential of variety in the interaction. In these cases, the user can genuinely explore options which may not have been expected or intended by the programmer (like driving the racing car against the traffic, going the wrong way round the track). In developing artistic applications this principle of redundancy or superfluity is equally crucial, as is an understanding of how its economy is dependent on the quality and depth of the structural analysis at the basis of the program. In seeking appropriate structures for the application of interactivity to cinema, the structural principles underlying the satisfactory programs will need to take on the issues of psychological linkages between sequences and a complex understanding of dramatic and abstract relationships beyond the range of linear narrative.

It may reasonably be argued that the examples which can be drawn upon from popular computer games all involve relatively trivial forms of psychological objectives or dramatic structure. However, it would not be wise to underestimate the enormous lure which is represented by the desire to master the skills needed to resolve a game, the intrigue represented by the unknown and inaccessible possibilities yet to be unlocked in playing it and the enormous gain for the user in being implicated in the plot. Clearly computer games, like 'Dungeon', have imported much of the fundamental range of dramaturgy from narrative cinema and theatre, incorporating danger, threat and suspense, though many games also draw heavily on competitive sport with its own inherent psychological forms and symbolism.

In most computer games, the visual simulation does not come close to the level of photographic representation of cinema but the enhanced dramatic experience which is available to the user/player as a result of the interactive element and their implication in the way in which the game develops is evidently a more than adequate compensation for the lack of 'realism' in the visual illusion.

Conclusions

Interactivity replaces the concept of the passive viewer by the active participant.

The experience of being a protagonist, while still operating in a symbolic field, is more direct in interactive systems than in the traditional forms of identification which operate in cinema.

An interactive cinema needs to offer a fundamental range of choices to the user in the interaction with the work. This cannot be confined to a few alternative linear routes, endings or character viewpoints in an otherwise linear narrative structure.

The experimental cinema offers some models for a greater complexity of sequence linkage being based on the concept of a cinematic 'data' matrix. With the opportunity of computer programs determining structure, this matrix can be subject to genuinely multidimensional conjunction in response to interaction.

The computer game represents a significant field of interactive practice with many aspects of potential value to the development of an interactive cinema.

Parallels should be sought between the kind of structural analysis which produces economic 'redundancy' in three-dimensional simulations (for example) and psychological or dramatic structures as the basis of synthesis from fundamental (artistic) principles.

20

The Chronos Project [1995]

Chronos – the Titan who came to rule the universe, is time – not the clock-tyrant measuring every quartz-accurate second as commodity, but the one-way flowing medium in which events come into being, mature and decay. It is the separator of moments, and the reminder of mortality. We sense it indirectly through the rhythm of our bodies, the rotation of sun and moon, and the ever-quickening cycle of the seasons. The passage of Chronos is cursed by the unrelenting process of ageing but celebrated through music, dance and song.

We deny and at the same time confirm Chronos through memory – we resist it through making images, but these also fade, shatter and decay. The fear of loss and the desire to hold and make permanent are latent in every image, every representation. In ecstasy, presence, sensual experience, colour, pitch, tone, Chronos seems to be ignored or at least forgotten but returns in the trace, representation and symbol.

I have just completed a production (an Arts Council/Channel Four commission) entitled *Chronos Fragmented*. It is a one-hour programme intended for a normal 'linear' transmission. However, this is just one outcome of a much broader project which already has alternative versions and remains 'open-ended'. And it is related to developing technologies like CD-ROM.

In the same way in which the project has no prospect of a completion, it is also impossible to define a clear origin to the work.

Questions of Art and Technology

The most important issues remain the aesthetic, philosophical and theoretical questions which the work raises. These are difficult to approach directly, especially for the artist who has made the work. Choosing to start from questions of technology is due partly to the simpler approach to some of the artistic issues which this offers. But it is also because the artistic choices and opportunities in this project are fundamentally tied in with technological matters. I have always contended that form (or language), content and technology are inseparable.

Two major technological shifts in my work are crucial to the development of the Chronos project.

One is the increasing involvement with computers applied at a variety of levels, from the merely technical control of editing to the synthesis of image and sound and the selection of sequences in the editing process. Although I made a computer-generated film and some other computer art pieces in the late 1960s, the first serious work I did of this kind was incorporated as three of the sections in *Sketches for a Sensual Philosophy*, all of which involved writing programs to generate or manipulate picture and sound directly on the computer (an Atari ST in 'real time', subsequently recorded on to video for the programme.

The second technological shift is the availability of acceptably high-image resolution from light, portable video. In 1988 I bought one of the first Video-8 cameras. Although as a film-maker I have shot most of my own film, I had never enjoyed the weight and wait involved in film production. What Video-8, and later Hi-8, achieved for me was a less intrusive and more spontaneous way of recording images: the tapes were cheap, lasted 90 minutes, could be reused; the camera was small, light and recorded good quality sound as well as vision. It came in a soft bag I could slip over my shoulder and carry with me even if I had no particular purpose in mind. When shooting, I was unobtrusive – like any home-video-maker – attracting no particular attention. In addition to all these virtues, I liked the image on the screen. It was sharp, had good contrast, strongly coloured and bright. Even before Hi-8, I used Video-8 material on *Sketches for a Sensual Philosophy* without encountering any problems with transmission engineers.

I found I did not hanker after the big-screen film look. On the contrary, video and the TV screen provided me with the lower-key, less pressured context that I wanted. They satisfied the need I felt, and continue to feel, to bring the making of work closer to lived life. This was not a desire to make myself overtly the primary subject of the work – in a sense this is unavoidable, however existentialist or abstract the starting point – but it was an attempt to close the gap between life experience and the subject of the work and, in particular, to re-enliven my investment in the shot image. I remain fully aware that the immediacy and convenience offered by video is no more 'natural' or neutrally unmediated than working with film: the choice is symbolic as well as technical, bringing its own established discourses and interpretative codes.

Though this technology created some new conditions for me, it did not involve a completely new departure from my previous work in film, particularly in the area of image manipulation. It replaced laborious photochemical processes with electronic and digital methods and represented a continuity with one major aspect of experimental film history – that which stresses individual authorship through the act of 'writing' with the camera.

For my own practice and psyche, working with Video–8 answered my needs at the level of recording or collecting (sequences, images, sounds) but it did not in any direct way answer other questions concerning the next level of selection, order, synthesis, symbol, metaphor – the structures taken on in making this into a work in public discourse. I resist the diary interpretation which places the 'life' rather than the constructed, symbolic work at the centre of interpretation. So there are at least two issues: one is the raw material, the video sequences on tape, their meanings and interpretation; the other is the structuring and transformation of this material through juxtaposition and reworking. The first issue spins theoretically around understanding how meanings enter and are inscribed in the recorded material, the second depends on what structures for connection or models for experience we can bring to bear on the ordering of the material.

The Material

The raw material – some sixty hours of video images, growing in both directions (forward as I shoot new material and backwards as I incorporate earlier film images) – is not a 'diary'. It ranges from near 'home movie' to almost camera-edited short video poems. In between is a range of sequences recorded on impulse or according to some very tentative idea of a theme to which it might relate.

Almost everything has been recorded with an attitude of 'low-key' intervention in the pro-filmic – a reluctance to intervene and an awareness that what seems 'charged' at the moment of shooting may not seem so in the subsequently screened image, and vice versa.

Though the material has been deliberately shot to resist any overriding preconception, it is none the less motivated and organised within causal chains, some personal and some derived from circumstances of which I am an 'agent'. This motivation or causality is inscribed in the material as latent meaning which may be more or less dominant.

This inscription of meaning can be located in:

- the signification of the events themselves occurring before the camera;
- why I am where I find myself at the time of recording;
- the details of the act of recording as traced through the choices made like framing, centring, camera movement or when to start and stop recording;
- the technology and its inbuilt technological/language discourse lens structures, colour biases, auto aperture, recording level limiters, etc.

In addition to the meanings inscribed in the individual sequences, certain sets of sequences are themselves already determined within themes or have other kinds of coherence (geographical – all shot within a short time; similar subjects – shot intermittently over a period of time; psychological coherence and so on) even if these are not consciously predetermined.

The Structure

There is an evident parallel between the problem of structure I faced and that implicit in the concepts of Dziga Vertov. His Kino Eye theory similarly assumed a structuring process aimed at 'making sense' of material which had been recorded beyond the confines of a narrative or documentary script.

On montage Vertov said: 'Kino Eye, flinging itself into the heart of the apparent disorder of life, strives to find in life itself the answers to the questions it asks; to find amongst a mass of possibilities the correct, the "necessary fact to solve the theme".' And Vertov again: 'Montage – when I decide upon the order in which the filmed material will be presented (to choose from amongst the thousands of possible combinations the one that seems most appropriate, bearing in mind the nature of the filmed material itself or the demands of the chosen theme).' However, for the Chronos project there were some distinct differences from the assumptions made by Vertov. Coming from a background of formal/structural experiment, I could no longer assume a singular form of resolution to thematic notions, nor their full consistency with the 'nature' of the filmed material. This view emerged out of the anti- or non-narrative concepts which have accompanied my filmic exploration of repetition, improvised variations on visual themes, the notions of 'verticality' proposed by Maya Deren and the awareness of programmable, permutational or multiple solutions to structural problems. It also emerged from the actual possibility of exploring complex multi-connectiveness or multiple variation implicit in the use of computer technology.

For my project I sought, and continue to seek, structural models which have a high degree of flexibility and correspond more adequately to the fluidity and uncertainty of the way in which the mind works on remembered or learned experience. I have thought of these structures in terms of a 'memory model' where I at the risk of over-simplification, the shot sequences represent perception and structure, and juxtaposition the act of memory.

From my experience it seems clear that in memory, images from one source are linked with others in a continuing variety; they are used, reused and constantly transformed in the process. In other words, meanings are not locked into the initial form of the memory, but develop through re-juxtaposition. This is an active rather than nostalgic (or factual) notion of memory.

The new computer technology applied to video makes it possible both to develop structures for single 'linear' works and more radically, to produce works which remain open in their form of presentation, either through permutational options or interactive responses with the user.

The most challenging concept relevant to cinematic structure to emerge from computer technology is Random Access Memory (RAM). Conceptually, RAM represents a system of information storage where the sequence in which information is retrieved may be entirely different from the sequence in which it has been recorded, with no additional cost in time or energy. In all print, film or tape systems, the retrieval sequence is linear – shot one must be passed to get to shot two. In a RAM-based system, the location addresses of any data are equidistant – location one is as close to location one hundred as it is to location two. Of course, various constraints create gaps between concept and technological realisation. On the other hand, what is taken to constitute a unit of the data (a pixel, a frame, a sequence) is a matter of choice (and technological capacity).

For the Chronos project these conceptual gaps are of no great consequence. What is of importance is the concept of RAM as a model for memory and a structuring principle for the video source material, together with sufficient technical opportunity to exercise this in an artistic work. The philosophical and artistic implications influencing the structure of the work are more important than the actual technology employed (which has to date been hybrid). But I take the concept of RAM as a reference point because it offers me a more appropriate basis for following my artistic intention than other available models.

The Work

I am faced with a very large source of recorded material, in all of which I have a strong personal interest. It is intrinsically confused and confusing (it would be of no interest if it were not). While I am trying to make artistic (creative) sense of this material, I do not believe in the hyper-significance of the single artistic solution, but seek levels of symbolic generality beyond the idiosyncratic and randomly made connection. I adopt the concept of RAM to explore flexible and multiple interconnections between the material, but RAM needs a program (or programs) on which to base connections. This has led me to concepts of clusters and themes, where both take different forms in different conditions.

In fact, my approach has been to catalogue all the video material as a database of shots where each shot has a description line. For example, here are the first three shots from reel 31 section 1, showing the time code start and end and the description line, including an 'image preference value' (the highest value given to any shot is 15):

31 – 1 shot # 1 snow children 16:04:13:08–16:04:31:10 children play snow mountain cold grey winter windy pan zoomin 2;

31 – 1 shot # 2 play snow 16:04:37:03–16:05:57:20 oliver sera play snow hill whirl gesture jiggle wind cold children 4;

31 – 1 shot # 3 car 16:06:13:07–16:06:21:17 car snow hand wheel driving vcu 5.

The description line is subjective rather than schematic, but includes abstract factors like colour and movement. It was not necessary to pre-define categories for description, as a 'lexicon' of terms used was derived automatically from the database. This is a short section of the lexicon derived from reel 31 section 1:

snow children play mountain cold grey winter windy pan zoomin oliver sera hill whirl gesture jiggle wind car hand wheel driving vcu drive window landscape passes road lights trees trackleft clouds sky blue white mist panright valley tiltdown autumn waterfall splash noise power beehives basket spiral craft zoomout stilt orchard cu leaves tree sun branches trunk bark moss sway green trunks tractor

This made it possible for the computer to sort the material by word, either on a simple basis or using Boolean logic ('and', 'or', 'not-and', 'and-or' etc.), and to convert these sorts into edited video sequences by compiling Edit Decision Lists. (The process, thanks to the number of procedures that could be invented for selection, could be endless. It could also be generated by so-called Artificial Intelligence programs or 'expert systems'.)

Again, as my concern remains entirely artistic and not technological, wherever I have felt it appropriate (which is frequently), I have short-circuited the procedures in favour of building on them subjectively. They have, none the less, provided a number of connections and starting points which I would not have arrived at otherwise. Most importantly, because the computer selections were based on subjective description and a preference value for the shots (also subjective) these selections reflect various potential coherences, and the clusters resulting from the process have thematic tendencies. Thus themes have mostly been emergent not imposed, related to the connections which may be said to have been intrinsic to or latent in the material.

Different kinds of theme or cluster which have emerged from the process:

- themes that emerge from the strong and particular content of the material itself. These include some of the material shot in China and Croatia, for example, though material in this category finds itself in constructions which followed another theme;
- following through an idea where the material was shot 'as a piece'. In some cases almost edited in camera. Examples of this are 'TV Song' (an interaction between video of watching and birds singing on the aerial); 'Weir' (a water cascade transformed through shutter speed variations, freezes and superimpositions); 'Warsaw Window' (shots of events during the day and at night below an old hotel window);
- sequences which lent themselves, through their image or sound qualities, to computer or electronic manipulation in a way that relates to the material itself, such as the gestures and costumes of the Peking Opera material shot off Chinese TV;

- themes working outwards from the evocative basis of the original image subjectively described in poetic terms;
- general but open themes drawing on material across the whole sequence 'bank'. Examples are earth, air, fire and water, seasons, childhood, age and death, East and West.

Review

It is difficult and unwise for artists to be their own interpretative critics, therefore some of the more interesting questions about the meaning of the continuing work and the completed aspect of this project are beyond the scope of these notes. I have tried to discuss the process in relation to some general theoretical concerns about meaning and structure. It seems clear to me that one major part of my motivation in this work has been related to the problem of how general significance can be constructed from the very particular building blocks of one's own daily, lived experience. In one sense these video-recorded building blocks are highly idiosyncratic. They are special, particular and arbitrary, and can represent the general only through inference (for example, the inference of economic causality), or through juxtaposition which transforms the experience into metaphor. None the less, this is the only way through which individuals can approach any understanding of their place in history or society. And, it seems to me, the only way in which any reliable sympathy with the experience of others can be constructed. It is that which makes up the individual life – the direct place of our knowledge, experience and crucially felt reality.

It is also untidy. The intersections between the personal and the historical are unpredictable: when filming a sunrise in Corfu, a refugee from strife-torn Albania, swimming on a tractor inner tube, became a small speck traced in the magnetic fields of my videotape. I can control the camera, more or less, but little of what takes place in the real world in front of it.

All the material which makes up the Chronos project is at base idiosyncratic. In its raw state it traces, in recorded fragments, my momentary impulses and reactions to events in the world encountered by my camera. These events have been minimally structured as symbolic at the time of shooting. But all carry intent, meanings and potential links with other sequences which remain as 'layers' of latent interpretation, provided the form does not close off these 'responses to image' through over-determination.

One approach to the potential layers of meaning (and here 'layering' is a concept, not a 'reality') is through the treatment and reworking of the material. By editing, montage, juxtaposition, superimposition, matte (key) and visual image transformation, the idiosyncratic image eases its way towards communicative generality – becomes symbol, metaphor, allegory.

In this sense, one single sequence – the electromagnetic trace on videotape – may contribute to a range of themes. The meaning in the image is always latent – it becomes fixed temporarily as it contributes to a theme, as (so it seems) does a transient particular human memory held in an electrochemical bond in the cells of the brain.

The structural aim of the work lies in retaining a trace of the movement from the idiosyncratic towards the allegorical. This is to hold on to the concept (reading) of the material as raw and latent – available for new juxtapositions and new transformations – or perhaps remaining insignificant and trivial. Not all the themes opened up have matured and survived in *Chronos Fragmented*, but I hope the form in this work implies the possibility of other connections, explorations and variations available both to me as the maker and to the viewers.

In keeping with the concept of non-linearity, the sequences and themes of the current version have been thought of as simultaneous rather than sequential. In other words, the form of editing and the episodic structure seek to imply that themes not currently available to view might be continuing 'underneath' (as in the unconscious memory) and could be made available by traversing the current visible material. In a non-linear interactive form like CD-ROM, this movement through layers of simultaneous development could be made actual, preserving other versions and variations.

The project continues.

21

Colour Abstraction – Painting – Film – Video – Digital Media [1995]

Isolating colour as an issue in art is inseparable from the historical development of abstraction. The abstract form of visual, time-based art – film, video or digitally produced – is aesthetically continuous with the tradition of abstraction in painting which began with Impressionism.

Subjectivity and Sensibility

Why write about art? Art objects work within their own 'discourses' needing no translation in order to achieve their meaning. It is particularly difficult for artists to write about art – we are unavoidably subjective, drawing on our idiosyncratic experience as practitioners.

In addition, writing is often given a higher status in the hierarchy of knowledge than it deserves. To counteract this, theoretical writing should not be considered as a meta-text but an exploration of a *parallel* discourse. As such, it can have points of convergence with the art work itself, even clarify some general concepts but, more hopefully, provide a stimulus to further creative speculation; it should never be taken as an explanation replacing the continued living uncertainties of artistic experience.

As a student I did some scientific study – about wavelength – the visible spectrum and its place in the broader band of electromagnetic radiation – about the electrochemical perceptual mechanisms of the eye – and was taught about colour wheels, harmonies and contrasts, mixing pigments, organising pallets, the effect of tonality (luminance) on colour perception. But, like other artists, I mainly developed a sensibility to colour through looking at other painters' work and through practice.

Sensibility is not the same as knowledge – it develops from the trained ability to work from the eye to the hand ultimately without the intervention of words – to make decisions directly in the discourse of art making itself, manipulating its components – colour, shape, texture, rhythm of line and so on. This sensibility, which is a refined ability of the eye to discriminate, match and combine elements, builds up through practice. It costs a great deal in discipline, time and effort, but, in a process which is so gradual, it becomes an invisible part of the way you work and is subsequently difficult to analyse.

What is Colour?

Scientifically the visible spectrum of light is a short segment of the continuum of electromagnetic radiation which goes from radio waves through heat and infrared at the lower end then, above visible light, at the upper end ultraviolet, X-rays and gamma radiation. Thus in the rainbow, red shades in from infrared at the 'warm end', passes through the oranges, yellows, greens to blues and violets shading off to ultraviolet at the 'cool-end'. Perceptually, the eye is dependent on a photo-chemical process capable of responding to the continuum of wavelengths and firing-off the resultant stimulation electrochemically through the optic nerve to the visual cortex.

However to say that colour *is* the measurable wavelength in the spectrum of elec-tromagnetic radiation is of little artistic or philosophical interest. At the level of human perception, and more importantly, in terms of the place of colour in our psychological, social, semiotic or artistic schemes, it is the complex discrimination and use of colour which matters.

In these terms colour is better defined as the *experience* we have in our dis-crimination between sensations of different wavelengths of light. This discrimination is measurably consistent. Provided we do not lie, we individually always report seeing blue if exposed to the section of the spectrum known as blue. What is more, this seems consistent with the discriminations reported by others. We all agree, more or less, on the matching of colour perceptions. Two people shown the same blue would almost certainly both be able to match this with a simi-lar blue as well as agreeing its blueness verbally. The dispute between life partners, decorating their kitchens or choosing a shirt, on whether a particular hue of blue-green is indeed a bluish green or a greenish blue may be a problem for the marriage counsellor. But, such disputes on the boundaries of giving name to our discrimi-nation confirm rather than deny the general consistency of our perceptions of colour.

However, this consistency of matching cannot prove that we share the same *sub-jective* experience of a colour.

We may always recognise a colour consistently: I may be confident that when I see blue, you also see what we both call blue but I cannot know what that quality of blueness is for you. For all I know, what I 'see' when I say I see blue may be the experience you have when you see red. In other words, we cannot assume the same experience of colour between individuals, but we can assume a broad biological consistency in perception, matching and naming.

The links between consistency in colour recognition and the meanings of colour in a cultural sense are much more problematic and of course more crucial.

Here we are obliged to treat colour, like language, as being within a human dis-course. Colour is a property of the perceived world and is part of the mix of properties by which we identify or recognise objects, but it is also abstractable from it as the basis or fundamental component of an artistic or communication system. We must at least start from the assumption that the meanings of our psychological responses to colour derive both from our experiences of the natural world and from the place given to colour in a variety of human communicating systems. It is not unreasonable, for example, to assume a correspondence between redness and heat, the fire or cooking ring develops psychological responses including warmth and comfort but also fear and danger. Though we must beware that even apparently fundamental consistencies are subject to change in different cultural and social conditions – redness and heat are becoming increasingly dissociated through our technologies.

A child of the new millennium may never see a fire and experience cooking only with invisible microwave; its primary experience of red may derive from holding an ice-cold, bright-red can of Coke – where then is the basis of psychological consistencies in colour associations? So, while colour responses may continue to retain common associative links, even archetypal psychological meanings through our experience of colour relationships in the natural world, it is probably more productive to approach the relationship between colour and meaning mainly in the cultural arena, where colour has become abstracted as a distinct component of a discourse. This is particularly the case in the history of painting, in some cases in cinema and more recently in the electronic arts of video or digital systems.

The Medium

By the time light hits the retina and is electrochemically transmitted to the visual cortex, it makes no great physical difference if that light has come reflected from the pigment of a painting or has been emitted from the video screen. But in the interplay between the bland physical properties of colour and its place in a cultural discourse, there is a fundamental link between meaning and medium – in colour as elsewhere there is a continuum between medium, technology and semiotic system. This is significantly affected by the historical context of the medium, its place in society and culture and the kinds of meanings it tends to take on in the prevailing context. From the point of view of the artist, the physical properties of the medium or its technologies are also fundamental in what kind of images or experiences can be produced by that medium. As well as similarities there are clear differences in the kinds of experience which can be produced by placing pigments side by side on a permanent surface, as in painting, and manipulating high intensity coloured light in temporal sequence on a film or video screen.

Technically it is possible to define four distinct systems for colour presentation broadly, though not strictly, corresponding to the media of painting, film, video and digital art:

- pigment systems where light falls on a surface, some wavelengths are absorbed and others reflected back to the eye;
- photochemical cinematic systems where coloured light is recorded through lay-ered filter emulsions and reproduced either by an equivalent photochemical copy or by colour dye application systems like Technicolor for projection by light again being filtered through the image onto a screen;
- electro-analogue systems where colour is recorded on magnetic tape as a contin-uously changing signal, coding luminance and chrominance for later presentation via a cathode ray tube which separates the signal into three component red-, green- and blue-filtered intensities;
- electro-digital systems where recorded images are analysed into discrete pixels given intensity values for three component colours (red, green and blue) then re-synthesised from the digital information for presentation in a variety of output technologies.

In moving from a bland technological description of media to consider the more important artistic implications there remain two interconnected issues – the special artistic opportunities offered by the medium and the constraints on meaning con-ditioned by the predominant social and cultural context in which it is used.

Simply, while film, video and particularly digital art offer the possibility of increas-ingly flexible manipulation of colour as well as other aspects of image, the predominant history of cinema and television as both photographically perspectival and narratively dramatic inhibits the development of a discourse based on the abstraction of aesthetic components.

The Historical Context of Colour Abstraction
Painting
The history of pictorial art and particularly western pictorial art has given priority to the object and its location in space. This is epitomised by the development of Renaissance perspective, a philosophical and social construct as well as an aesthetic system.[1] In this system, colour is subsumed as an integral property of an object having symbolic value only through agreed iconographic codes related to costume and so on. It is well understood in general how Impressionism first dislodged colour from the object, simultaneously allowing it to become a separable – abstracted – element in its own right and implicitly contributing to the dissolution of the fixed spectator in perspective. In the movements within post-Impressionism and particu-larly in the work of Henri Matisse and the Fauves, though still applied within an object-based representation, colour became almost the predominant means of artis-tic expression. In his 'Notes of a Painter', Matisse said:

The chief aim of color should be to serve expression as well as possible. I put down my colors without a preconceived plan. If at the first steps and perhaps without my being conscious of it one tone has particularly pleased me, more often than not when the picture is finished I will notice that I have respected this tone while I have progressively altered and transformed the others. I discover the quality of colors in a purely instinctive way.[2]

This wonderfully honest and subjective note reveals how colour was becoming central to an artistic discourse seen as the basis of symbolic expression, however imprecise or subjective the interpretation of colour meanings might be.

With a progressively greater degree of abstraction, dissolving the pictorial conventions which attached visual shapes to the representation of objects in a form determined by perspective, some artists, notably Wassily Kandinsky, tried to find and describe a new basis of pictorial logic. This included attempts to analyse some consistency in human response to colour. In his seminal *Concerning the Spiritual in Art*, he says:

The eye is strongly attracted by light, clear colors, and still more strongly by colors that are warm as well as clear; vermilion stimulates like a flame, which has always fascinated human beings. Keen lemon-yellow hurts the eye as does a prolonged and shrill bugle note the ear, and one turns away for relief to blue or green.[3]

Though Kandinsky always questions single associative meanings for colour in contrast to deeper, more direct psychological effects, he goes on in the essay to suggest processes by which colour, separated from its subservience to the representation of objects, may create its meaning through association with other object properties or sensations like '. . . bright yellow looks sour, because it recalls the taste of a lemon . . .' or 'Many colors have been described as rough or prickly, others as soft or velvety . . .'. He draws further associative analogies between color and temperature or smell, and expressing a concept which remains fundamental to the concept of colour in time-based art, with sound, on which he says: 'The sound of colours is so definite that it would be hard to find anyone who would express bright yellow with bass notes, or dark lake with the treble.'[4]

Clearly in the historical development of painting, whatever approach might be taken to the question of meaning in colour, since the initial steps of abstraction, the assumption that colour acts as an independent vehicle for visual expression has become commonplace, a part of the mainstream discourse in the medium. This has not been the case in film.

Film

The attempts made between about 1912 and 1930, by visual artists from the Futurists, Bruno Corra and Arnaldo Ginna, through Walter Ruttmann, Viking Eggeling, Oskar Fischinger and Fernand Léger, to establish an abstract concept of cinema, have been documented by myself and other authors. Whatever the achievement of these artists, this work neither became incorporated into the mainstream of cinema, nor does it feature strongly in the central histories of pictorial art. The reasons for this are both cultural and technical.

While the invention of photography may have contributed to freeing painting from perspective-based pictorial representation, the fundamental principles of camera design by becoming the basis of cinematography has had the opposite effect for the development of cinema. All the technological developments in film, from the camera, through the film printing processes and the structure of colour response in film emulsions, have taken place broadly in the interests of producing images which maintain a perspectival simulation of the world, coupled with a film form based on narrative dramaturgy. So, at the same time as painting was establishing a twentieth-century aesthetic, embodying a philosophic separation between objects and their properties through abstraction, the new medium of cinema was reinforcing an earlier assumption of coherence of the object, its secure place in space and more fundamentally its place in the form of omnipresent narrative. The abstraction of colour, which was fundamental to the development of abstraction in pictorial space, in conventional cinematic representation was again structured to form a coherent integral property of the object.

Those artists who challenged this perception in cinema did so against the odds of the technology and increasingly against the odds of the way in which cinema functioned and was financed in society. Even after the availability of less expensive 16mm film, which assisted a renewal of abstract experimentation in film after 1945, the technology remained difficult to control artistically. Many of the successful experimental film artists found themselves having to work at levels of the technology which only technicians in the industry normally touched – working directly on the film material, like Lye – innovating printing and camera systems like Fischinger – spitting on the lens like Brakhage – or developing and printing the material in unconventional ways like myself and others at the London Film-makers' Co-operative. Without these approaches, the basic abstraction of colour from the object and its position in space could not be achieved – film could not begin from a post-representational position.

My own experience in making *Berlin Horse* is a good example of the technical process necessary to be able to work with film with the equivalent plasticity expected by painters. This film began as Kodachrome 8mm film, where the horse was brown, the grass was green, the sky was blue and the face of the man Kodak flesh tone. I refilmed this in various ways on black and white 16mm, then produced both a positive and negative printing copy. Using the negative and positive materials in an old Debrie step-contact printer, I manually pulled coloured filters through the printing machine colouring the black and white image in its negative and positive areas with a wide range of pure spectrum colours onto colour film stock. The results of this were then reworked through various superimpositions and the film structured to retain some trace of this progressing improvisation. The concept was simple, the process convoluted, haphazard and invented as I went along.

Artistically, the note made by Matisse, 'more often than not when the picture is finished I will notice that I have respected this tone while I have progressively altered and transformed the others. I discover the quality of colors in a purely instinctive way', would apply very well to my approach in this film. There is nothing artistically exceptional in this process but it becomes exceptional in the context of cinema, its language assumptions and methods of production. It is a Fauvist film and at the time I even argued the need for film to re-create or reinterpret the aesthetic manoeuvres of modern painting before it could 'move on': I argued that film was an artistically retarded medium.

However, if there is one single fundamental difference between painting and cinema it is the matter of time. Film 'unfolds', its present image is transient, becomes a trace in memory while new perceptions appear. The abstraction of colour is here placed in a temporal rather than simply proximate relationship and is subject to other abstractions belonging to the structural articulation of time.

A consistent thread in the conceptual approach to abstraction in film has been the attempt to establish an analogy with music. This has been both the attempt to apply musical compositional concepts to film structure and to seek a parallel between colours and musical notes.

In pre-cinema there are numerous examples, like those of Louis-Bertrand Castel, Bainbridge Bishop or Wallace Rimington, of attempts to make colour-organs.

One of the earliest theoretical works on abstract cinema, Bruno Corra's 1912 article was significantly titled 'Abstract Cinema – Chromatic Music'. In this he describes three film experiments made with Arnaldo Ginna (now lost):

> To hand I have three chromatic themes sketched on strips of celluloid. The first is the simplest one could imagine. It has two colours only, complementaries, red and green. To begin with the whole screen is green, then in the centre a small red six-pointed star appears. This rotates on itself vibrating like tentacles ... until it fills the whole screen.[5]

In 1921 the art critic Bernard Diebold, also developing a musical analogy, in his article on Walter Ruttmann's abstract film – *Opus 1*, 'A New Art – the Eyemusic of Film',[6] drew parallels between musical concepts and their potential application to abstract cinema. Oskar Fischinger, who knew Diebold well, clearly shared and developed the idea that music could provide the basis of a time form for abstract cinema replacing narrative as a structuring principle – a different kind of dramaturgy applied from another time-based art.

In retrospect, importing the images of abstract painting, the swirling circles and anthropomorphic forms found in Fischinger or Ruttmann, look brave but 'wrong' – the principles of abstraction when applied in film should probably not result in paintings in motion.

In some of the works of Paul Sharits, particularly *Ray Gun Virus* (1966), where he relies only on interchanging full-frame saturated colour, the issues of response to colour relationships in time at the perceptual level are isolated as both the content and the basis of the experience. This cinematic equivalent to the colour experiments of Joseph Albers also explores the relationship between colour perception and our capacity to form structural concepts of colour sequence across time. That this is an intentional issue in the work is brought out by Sharits's decision in 1973 to display the complete film as a static work under plexiglass where it is titled *Frozen Film Frames*.

Although the structural basis of the colour sequences in this film is mathematically systematic rather than musical, and Sharits makes no claim of a relationship between colour and musical notes, the work does contribute to the artistic tradition of 'chromatic music'. This is so, not only because of its complete reliance on chromatic experience in time, but because its mathematical structures parallel the system-music explorations begun by Conlon Nancarrow with his piano-roll, hand-punched musical systems, and continued by composers like Philip Glass.

Video

It is no longer easy to separate purely analogue video from digital media. Almost all video effects generators now incorporate a digital frame store as a final stage and much of the manipulation of image takes place at a digital rather than analogue level. There are though, some examples of artistic experiment which manipulate the analogue video image abstractly and where colour abstraction deriving from the characteristics of video and the cathode ray tube is integral to the work. The best example of this direction are the experiments of Nam June Paik made in 1963 and 1964, made in collaboration with video engineer Shuya Abe and the Uchida Radio Research Institute in Tokyo. Gene Youngblood describes this work:

> There are approximately four million individual phosphor trace-points on the face of a 21 inch television screen at any given moment. Paik's canvas is the electromagnetic field that controls the distribution of these trace-points in horizontal and vertical polar

coordinates at 525 lines per second. By interfering, warping, and otherwise controlling the cathode's magnetic field, he controls the four million glowing traces. 'It creates the possibility of electronic drawing' he [Paik] says. 'It's better than drawing on a CRT with a light pen because it's multicolored and provides interaction with the air programme.'[7]

If there is aesthetic value in applying the concepts of abstraction to time-based media, and the abstraction of colour remains fundamental to this direction, then video and certainly its current hybridisation with digital systems provides a more flexible technology for this than film. Film allows the direct colouring of the film base by hand, the selective adding of colour to a whole frame or scene with filters, the reversal of colours to their negative values and further degrees of more selective re-colouring through 'mattes' used in printing as in *Berlin Horse* where the black and white negatives acted as colour mattes. All these abstracting devices of film, with the exception of hand-colouring, are available to video with much greater ease and with more immediacy as the effects can be seen by the artist at once.

In addition, video offers its own 'media-specific' opportunities, working directly with image scan reversals, distortions and colour selective superimposures through 'keying' (broadly equivalent to film's 'matte' process). The immediacy of video has been particularly attractive to the visual artist, because there is an element of plasticity in the development of an image which more closely corresponds to the conditions of painting, and which is largely denied in film production.

Like film, the discourse of video as an artistic activity has its dominant cultural equivalent – television. Also like film, the abstract art of video has not transformed broadcast television, though it has had more impact and incorporation than abstract film enjoyed in cinema. The distance between the abstract language of the video artist and the makers of television programmes is much less great than between the experimental film-maker and the cinema industry producers. In the areas of advertising, music-television and arts broadcasting, even if the artistic intention remains different, there is some continuity of visual language and the basis of a more popular sensibility, however unconscious, towards abstract concepts.

The development of abstract time-based art has also had a greater impetus in video than was enjoyed in film by its incorporation into the art gallery context. The greater ease of presentation, the lesser dependence on strict scheduling and the much smaller dependence on difficult blackout conditions have encouraged curators to present video while they have largely resisted film.

These two factors of institutional context, though not directly affecting the art works themselves, have indirectly created better conditions in which the abstract visual tradition in time-based art could be extended and developed through video than through film.

Digital Media

Though the development of computer or digital art is still new, it is already not a single phenomenon. The artistic opportunities offered by digital processors and computers extend beyond the construction of images on screens to include environmental control and feedback systems, user-interactive systems and a variety of cross- or inter-media concepts.

One characteristic of digital technology is its capacity to incorporate other forms and to be linked in a hybrid way with them. Thus current practice in video, and even film production, increasingly includes digital elements, or production control systems. For this essay, fortunately, I am not concerned with all the possibilities of digital systems in art but only with those which contribute to abstraction and colour in time-based forms.

As with video, from the artist's point of view, digital methods of manipulating images and images in time take the flexibility and plasticity offered by video over film a stage further. They offer much greater and more precise control of the transformation of colour and a range of other features of the image than does video. This is based on a fundamental technological property of digital systems that all the information, whether visual, auditory or textual, is analysed into digital code.

In the visual field, this means that each component of the image, normally assumed to be a 'pixel' or single point of the image, is stored as numerical data giving precise value to its intensity (luminance) and colour (chrominance). As a consequence, by rewriting these values through a computer program, their properties and locations may be manipulated as desired within the limits of the program to select and restructure the data.

Of course, the possibility is not the art – the words of the popular song 'it ain't what you do – it's the way that you do it' remain true – perhaps even more so in the field of computer art where much of the potential for creative manipulation is the product of sophisticated commercial software packages, not directly the product of the artist. If in abstract film, the history of cinema provides the predominant framework of the discourse and in video it is television, in the digital media, this discourse is built into the 'intelligent' technology and its complex, sophisticated software. The 'language' may be much less separable from the medium, much less under the fundamental control of the artist in this area than in more artisanal technologies.

With this 'health warning', in certain respects, digital technology offers the most appropriate basis yet of developing many of the concepts which have been partially explored in abstract film and video, for example, those related to colour and image transformation.

In my computer piece *Digital Still Life* (incorporated in my video/TV work *Sketches for a Sensual Philosophy*, 1989), like in *Berlin Horse*, representational images, in this case recorded on video not film, have been transformed, mainly in respect of their colour values. However, in the digital work, I wrote a program which achieved this transformation across a much broader base for discriminating regions of the image than was possible in the essentially two-component 'matte' of *Berlin Horse*. The program also exploited a much greater variety of possible colour combinations and superimpositional strategies based on computer logical combinations ('and', 'or', 'nand', 'nor' etc.). However the process remained fundamentally within the model that a work begins with the image of objects in space, certain properties, like colour, are then abstracted from it, transformed, returned, or not, to the pictorial representation of the object. This remains a post-Impressionist concept – still Fauvist at base though a development from it through other aesthetic principles related to time, rhythm, dramaturgy and particularly music.

My technological descriptions so far have assumed that digital abstraction is based on the transformation of recorded images. It is perhaps in the continued development of the recurrent, more radically abstract theme of 'chromatic music' that the digital media could make their most significant contribution. Again some fundamental properties of digital systems make this possible.

Digital systems, because the data is transformed to code which bears no resemblance to its source, require an initial stage of analysis before storage of the data (recording) and synthesis before its representation. We have seen how, in image transformation, the synthesis may involve different principles to those assumed in the initial analysis. More radically, the synthesis of image is possible in digital systems without a preceding analysis. That much of the effort directed towards image synthesis to date has been devoted to reconstructing a Renaissance perspective-based universe, so-called 'virtual reality', is a social, and cultural matter – it is not intrinsic to the potentialities of digital synthesis.

In addition to the capacity for synthesis without analysis is a capacity for translatability of data. As the data held in the computer memory is numerical, it does not matter to the computer how those numbers are used in an output device. Numbers representing the colour values of pixels in an image may be as easily output in a form which made sounds as in a form which made pictures. Computer data is easily translated as well as transformed (though not necessarily making any sense in the process).

In another of my computer pieces *Arbitrary Logic* (also included in *Sketches for a Sensual Philosophy*), I exploit this capacity of the computer to use the same set of numbers generated by a computer program to control output both as colour fields on a screen and sound through a MIDI (Musical Instrument Digital Interface) synthesiser. This work overtly takes up and develops the early light-organ and 'chromatic music' concepts in a medium where its principles can be more easily realised.

Colour and Music

As the title of my work *Arbitrary Logic* implies, one of the quests of this long-term artistic project, to find a *precise* translation between colours and musical pitches or timbres, is being questioned if not entirely dismissed. That lower pitched notes do seem more appropriately identified with darker tones of purple or blue, or higher pitches with oranges and yellows, may be no more than already-conditioned social assumptions.

Another assumption of the quest is that, even if pitches do not have direct colour correspondences, there is an equivalence between the concept of musical and colour harmony.

Classical musical harmony is primarily based in physics (initially identified by Pythagoras), having its origins in the physical properties of vibrating materials where the fundamental intervals such as octave, fifth and third sound as sub-vibrations above the primary vibration from which is derived the system for combining notes in chords and defining the predominant scales. It is clear that a concept of colour harmony could not possibly be based on the same system of intrinsic sub-harmonics. However, colour perceptual psychology, the empirical work of Joseph Albers and the evidence of our own experience all confirm certain consistencies in colour relationships based, instead, on the electrochemical mechanisms of the retina where a colour stimulus produces an 'opposite' colour in what is known as 'afterimage', and that these 'afterimage' residues interact with adjacent or subsequent colours.

If we need some logic on which to support our subjective experience of colour harmony, though not the same as music, this perceptual consistency would be sufficient. Additionally, we know that in music, conventions have emerged both exceeding and contradicting the constraints of classical harmony despite their physical causes, so a concept of music is not dependent on a universal concept of harmony.

Though clearly different in kind to music, colour, when separated from its utilitarian functions of assisting the identification of objects, is, like musical sound, capable of:

- eliciting emotional response;
- creating complex experiences of 'harmony' and 'dissonance', both in combination on a static surface and in temporal sequence; and
- forming the basis on which we can articulate time structures analogous to musical composition.

Colour – Music – Meaning

The question of the meaning of colour in general or of colours in particular is different when colour is subsumed as a property of the object world. The red of an apple in the real world helps us to identify if it is an apple, if it is ready to eat and so on. The red of an apple in a painting of an apple helps us to read it as an apple and may contribute to the symbolic interpretation of the apple in an iconographic system. The red field in a painting which may have been initially derived from an apple, when isolated and presented in an independent context, may continue to elicit a response associated with apple, but may also not elicit that association at all. Or, that apple association may be one of a number of composite associations which are elicited in an individual by a particular hue of red. The more separated and pure the hue, the less specific its fixed associative or 'retrospective' representational meaning becomes.

The first stage in the abstraction of a quality from an object-whole is to de-specify meaning, shifting the attention to the phenomenological experience of the quality abstracted. In the second stage, when colour has become abstracted, by losing its specific object association but retaining an emotiveness in unspecific association, it is able to provide us with one of those strong phenomenological stimuli, like musical sound, capable of opening a new imaginative space. And like sound, when it is separated from the utilitarian purpose to become music, *it becomes available*, as the basis for structured abstract experience. This more general similarity rather than any one-to-one correspondence is colour's main analogy with music. Music and colour share the capacity to create the situation where experience is able to precede interpretation. We return, if momentarily, to the pre-verbal, regressive and ecstatic – we suspend interpretation in favour of the experience itself.

By removing the experience from representational meaning, then creating a complex experience in its own aesthetic terms, colour and music are able to transform existing meanings and create new ones which did not previously exist. The new meanings produced, being based on the physical, psychological experience of the work, *belong* to the viewer. They are made in and by the viewer from their own experience, not closed by a representational function. The meanings emerge and collect around the work both individually for the viewer and socially as the work takes its place in the cultural discourse. The development of meaning becomes a dynamic process, hopefully, as with this essay, it is not finished when the artist completes the work.

Notes

1. For further debate on the concept of the ideological implications of perspective, see J.-L. Baudry, 'Cinema: effets idéologiques produits par l'appareil de base', *Cinéthetique* nos. 7–8, 1970, and Malcolm Le Grice 'Problematising the Spectator's Placement in Film', in this volume.

2. 'Notes d'un peintre', in *La Grande Revue*, Paris, 25 December 1908, pp. 731–45, translated by A. H. Barr in *Matisse: His Art and His Public* (New York: Museum of Modern Art, 1951).

3. *Uber das Geistige in der Kunst* (Munich: R. Piper, 1912; English translation, New York: Wittenborn, Scultze, 1947).

4. Ibid.

5. See *Il pastore, il gregge e la zampogna* (Beltrami: Libreria, 1912).

6. *Frankfurter Zeitung*, 2 April 1921.

7. Gene Youngblood, *Expanded Cinema* (New York: E. P. Dutton, 1970), p. 303.

22

Mapping in Multi-Space – Expanded Cinema to Virtuality [1996]

With all the problems of subjectivity it entails, this is a view of a historical development from an artist who was deeply involved in the practice and theory while it took place. I have taken the opportunity to review some of the ideas from a contemporary perspective with particular attention to concepts related to digital media and communications.

Breaking Art Boundaries

In the 1960s many artists actively questioned the containing boundaries of their art. This involved both a re-examination of the physical constraints of the medium and a 'philosophical' re-view of the contextual discourses in which their work had its meaning or impact.

Jasper Johns or Robert Rauschenberg extended the physicality of their paintings into the three-dimensional space before the canvas. Sculptors like Anthony Caro painted their surfaces in ways which created a represented space acting with or against the material space occupied by the work. Painters incorporated elements of sculpture – sculptors worked with the aesthetics of painting. John Cage created works where silence or the accidental sounds of the environment became incorporated into the music, making the boundaries between the experience of art or life problematic in the work. Claes Oldenburg among others imported elements of theatrical performance into the sculptural domain through the 'happening'.

Many artists saw the fascination of creative approaches to new technologies – electronics, video or the computer – areas with no previous artistic history. The seminal Nine Evenings of Art and Technology in the US in 1966, a collaboration between a number of visual artists and research technologists mainly from Bell Laboratories, even saw austere abstract painters like Frank Stella flirting with electronics. The video experiments of Nam June Paik and computer explorations by John and James Whitney or Marc Adrian are also examples of artists extending aesthetic concepts into fields not initially conceived to serve the visual arts.

The concept of Expanded Cinema was part of this general move by artists to break old artistic boundaries, explore cross-media fusions, experiment with new technologies but, most importantly, to challenge the constraints of existing art discourses.

There are different understandings of the concept of Expanded Cinema. Gene Youngblood largely, if not exclusively, understands Expanded Cinema in the exploration of new effects, techniques and technologies in the broad field of experiment with image and sound. The artists who are his main points of reference – the Whitney brothers, Jordan Belson or Nam June Paik, tend to be those who extend the tradition of experimental film through the development of new visual devices based on innovative technologies – computer generation of image, novel forms of optical printing and video-electronics. Though Youngblood incorporates the performance work of Carolee Schneemann as 'inter-media', he does not establish any critique around the interplay of discourses deriving from the mixing of media. A concern for the effects of 'inter-media' on meaning was of much greater significance in Europe than in the US, Youngblood's unashamed centre of attention.

Technological innovation also played its part in European Expanded Cinema, but the interplay between aesthetic experience and a conceptual discourse, in the work of Valie Export, Peter Weibel, William Raban, Annabel Nicolson and myself for example, was more important than the creation of new visual effects. Those European artists exploring new technologies, like Marc Adrian in his work with computers, also tended to stress the conceptual over novel, visual effect.

Experimental Film

In the same way in which Expanded Cinema is closely linked to the broad extension of the media boundaries in art, it is also a direct development from what was known variously as experimental, underground, structural or avant-garde film. This international subculture has its roots in film experiments by artists like Léger, Man Ray or Moholy-Nagy and Futurists like Arnaldo Ginna and Bruno Corra as early as 1914.

Though the development of experimental film was slowed by the economic and political disruption between the world wars, there was a substantial resurgence in the US in the 1950s and 1960s, linked there, as elsewhere, to the growing availability of low-cost 16mm film. This was echoed in Europe with the earliest work being done in Austria by artists like Peter Kubelka and in other countries a little later, notably Germany (Birgit and Wilhelm Hein) and Britain (Peter Gidal and Le Grice).

There are few examples of artists in the post-war experimental film movement whose ambition was to work within the forms of the dominant narrative cinema. The overwhelming majority either came to film from the visual arts – painting and sculpture – or saw their work as an extension from that tradition. Indeed, many, like Peter Gidal, developed strong theoretical positions in clear opposition to the mainstream narrative cinema and used a critical language which was derived more from the history of modern (modernist) art than from film. A dominant concept which emerged is embodied in the notion 'Film as Film' ('Film als Film' used as the title for an exhibition tracing this history curated by Birgit Hein and Wulf Herzogenrath in 1977).

Fundamental to the concept of 'Film as Film' is an equivalence to the modernist view that the meaning and aesthetic base of a work derives from its material rather than from an illusionist representation. Stressing the primacy of the work as material, as process, and constructing the aesthetic experience from the characteristics of the medium, is not to eliminate meaning, or the symbolic, but to shift it to an arena where the art work becomes a component in the developing world rather than a passive reflection on it. Meaning is formed in and by the work as it moves dynamically from the acts of making into its passage through the world.

Thus meaning is at the same time more direct – closer to a condition of effect – and less circumscribed than in representational forms. As was seen from the paintings of Rauschenberg or Johns, once the primacy of the work as material (and importantly as material process) is established, then representational elements can be reincorporated without revision to an illusionistic (retrospective) symbology. In simple illustration, the silk-screened images of photographs or other works of art which are applied in a Rauschenberg or Andy Warhol sit on the surface of the canvas – their reference is to the image as a picture in its cultural reading not through the image to illusory objects in an illusory space behind the canvas (and by implication having their existence in another, non-present time).

The conflict for the experimental film artist working in the 1950s and 1960s was between the desire to use film as a 'physical' medium and the transparency of the image as illusion in the predominant cinematic forms and discourse. The discourse of dominant cinema was fundamentally pre-modernist. The spectator went through the picture and plane of the screen to live in the illusion of its represented time – a time existing in the illusory space behind the screen. The 'behind' of cinema's perspective supported the parallel 'perspective' of narrative structure placing the action in a mythic past.

The concept of 'Film as Film', which was never a programme or manifesto, but a critical recognition of a broad movement which had already taken place, was based on a consistent tendency among experimental artists to establish a modernist standpoint (or starting-point) in the field of cinema.

In the main, Expanded Cinema in the European context is continuous with the development of 'Film as Film' and represents some of the more radical strategies by which its concepts became established in film 'language', became embodied in the form.

While Jean-Luc Godard, unable to escape the illusionist language of cinema, could only symbolise the modernist possibility of breaking cinematic illusion by the narrative representation of a man who destroys the screen while trying to enter the action (I think in *Le Petit Soldat* or *Les Carabiniers*), artists like Valie Export established the screen as a reality on which, or in front of which, the action of the work took place. The language or discourse of cinema is fundamentally altered – philosophically and in the social/cultural arena – by emerging forms which first establish the screen as surface then reverse the symbolic space from behind to before the screen. Even more fundamentally, the relationship of the spectator to the work is transformed when the time of the action is reversed from being the 'once-upon-a-time' of the mythic past to the critical arena of the present. This becomes the time in which the spectators individually live – it is their time, their present based on a material experience of the presentation event. The conditions for this, like establishing the screen as surface, must be achieved in the *form* of the work not, as in Godard, re-invested in the narrative, if the work is to change the experiential relationship with the spectator away from that of the passive, surreptitious viewer.

A number of film artists explored what were crucial strategies in establishing a basic reorientation of the cinematic experience and the place which becomes available for the spectator. These frequently revolved around the problematics of locating 'the real' in cinema around the material conditions of film as a medium.

These problematic explorations were applied variously to:

- The film base (celluloid, actually acetate) and its characteristics like sprockets and scratches. *Roh Film* (1968) by the Heins is an example;
- The screen as 'actual' surface established through empty fields of colour or simply light and its absence as in *Arnulf Rainer* (1960) by Peter Kubelka;
- The perceptual phenomena as neuro-optical reality through the exploitation of autonomic thresholds as in the rapid colour frame changes of, for example, *Ray Gun Virus* (1966) by Paul Sharits;
- The photographic image as self-representation through repetition, transformations in colour or simply changes in grain and contrast as in *Shower Proof* (1969) by Fred Drummond;
- The photographic, cinematic image as problematic illusion through juxtaposition of the representation and the enacted real as in William Raban's *2 Minutes 45 Seconds* (1972);
- The sculptural space of the projection event itself through multi-projection onto various surfaces or attention to the projector light beam itself as in *Line Describing a Cone* (1973) by Anthony McCall;
- The time of the projection as a concrete (sculptural) dimension of the work as in my own *White Field Duration* (1973).

This list of devices is not exhaustive. There are others less easily codified, as the symbolic touching of the unseen 'real' in Valie Export's *Tapp und Tass Film* (1968) where the context of cinema is stretched almost to breaking and is there only through the declaration of 'Film' in the title. In other works like Annabel Nicolson's *Reel Time* (1973) performance – where a film loop is projected as it is gradually perforated by being stitched on a sewing machine in the real space – many of the characteristic devices are brought together in single works.

In an article I published in 1972, 'Real TIME/SPACE', I concentrated on the way in which establishing the actual space and time in which the audience encountered the work as being 'real' was necessary in order to place the spectator at the centre of the construction of meaning. However, in that earlier essay, the relationship of the real to the symbolic was over-simplified – a problem, fortunately, more of the theory than of the works to which it applied. In a context where the symbolic arena of a work is brought closer to the active presence (present) of the spectator then the interplay between the real and the symbolic is both fluid and complex.

In my six-projector film *After Leonardo* (1974), an old, crumpled, black and white detail reproduction of the *Mona Lisa* is attached, during the projection, to a blank white screen. On the other screens are various filmed images of the same reproduction shot at different distances and also images, a further refilming of the film from the screen. One interpretation of the juxtaposition of a real object (albeit a reproduction of a cultural icon) alongside its cinematic representation is that it highlights the reality of the cinematic in the context of an object we assume to be part of the real physical universe. By 'reflection' it reinforces a reading of the cinematic as similarly composed of physical substance and the product of material processes.

However, another interpretation, contingent on the first, comes from the 'reflection back' of the symbolic representation on the real. For while the 'real' object serves to point up the realness of the representation, the representation in turn undermines the security and stability of the real. The real loses its secure unity through incorporation into the symbolic. The spectator unavoidably has to reread and therefore be aware of the symbolic transformation in the arena of the real. The real is seen to be equally mediated as experience by language and context. What is assumed to be real is no longer a stable point of reference against which the insecure symbol or representation can be measured.

A similar process was already at work in Valie Export's projection and mirror play, *Split Screen-Solipsimus* (1968) and had also been explored by Jasper Johns in a painting like *Fools House* (1962), which contains both a real broom suspended from the canvas and a trace of the mark of the swinging broom in an arc-shaped streak of paint.[1]

Further variations on the problematic relationship between the assumed real and the representational symbolic are developed in Export's *Auf+Ab+An+Zu* (1968) and *Das magische Auge* (1969), but here there is the further complexity of symbolic transformation or translation. In the first case this is through an attempt by the spectator actually to draw the outline of a moving and obscured film representation and in the second, the transformation of light signals into sound.

In all these works, and others could be cited, the most important philosophical/aesthetic concepts revolve around the changed relationship between the audience, the work and the artist.

The audience, or individual spectators, are being dislodged from the condition of passive consumers fundamental to the previous discourse of cinema – through:

- a confrontation of the cinematic as a physical experience in the context of their real world;
- an extending uncertainty about the stability of symbolic systems brought about by works where the symbolic meaning is in flux; and
- the demonstration that the assumed real world is subject to similar instability of interpretation.

In order to achieve this, Expanded Cinema (certainly in the European context) built on a tradition of experimental film which had incorporated artistic tenets of modernism directly into the medium and operation of cinema. It also treated the cinematic and its 'inter-media' explorations – like exploration of the quasi-sculptural and the quasi-theatrical – as a collision of discourses carrying cultural implications for meaning and form.

Expanded Cinema – New Technologies

Both the appeal and the problem for a concept of Expanded Cinema based on the exploration of new technologies is its lack of a historical artistic discourse. Of course, the 'freedom' this lack of context or constraint offers is questionable, however, certain technological developments do open up artistic forms and therefore artistic meanings which could not be achieved in other media.

Youngblood, like myself, sees the main origin for the experimental drive of Expanded Cinema in the underground or experimental film. He recognises the radical influence of an artist like Stan Brakhage who made very few innovations in the technology of cinema but instead took existing technology and used it in innovative ways. For the Youngblood history, the first largely technological focus, under the rubric 'New tools generate new images' (p. 97, *Expanded Cinema*), is on the film 'optical' printing technology and its development particularly with film-makers like Pat O'Neill or Jordan Belson. The second technological focus is on computer film mainly through the work of John and James Whitney and the third is with video or television through Nam June Paik.

My concern here is not with any artistic evaluation of particular works exploring expansion in cinema through new technologies, but with understanding how technological innovation and artistic meanings relate.

Broadly, the development of film printing techniques by Pat O'Neill, for example, is more or less continuous with developments which were explored (in another form) by Méliès or Vertov. They involve various methods of selective superimposition or image matting and transformation of tonal, colour, horizontal or vertical orientation, blow-up, reduction, image freezing and so on, through ingenious uses of the film printing technology. In terms of the discourse of meaning, the points of reference by which the images produced can be interpreted is already available in the history of both narrative and experimental cinema. Vertov particularly exploited the cinematic equivalent of 'collage' through the simultaneous combination of different film sequences adding to the more established concepts of sequential montage. It involved shifting the reading of the cinematic image towards that of a-temporal symbol rather than consequential narrative, or if narrative, towards simultaneity, dream or parallel action.

However, the further such transformations are taken the more abstract they tend to become. Multiple superimpositions and distortions in photographic shape or colour tend to remove the recognisability of the source objects, or, as in works by Pat O'Neill, place the images 'on' the screen surface through devices of extreme flattening of colour fields. In certain sequences by Belson, for example, the experience is shifted towards the abstract qualities of colour and movement rather than object symbolism even though these experiences in Belson's work are ultimately locked into a more conventional narrative interpretation by the context of the other images of the films.

Again, viewing this development as a discourse – the evolution of a language – the references are already there in the cinema experiments of Walter Ruttmann or Oskar Fischinger for example. Fischinger had a direct influence in the US when he left Germany for California in the 1930s. The terms in which this discourse developed have already been extensively debated (David Curtis, *Experimental Cinema*, Malcolm Le Grice, *Abstract Film and Beyond*, various essays by William Moritz for example).[2] It is a history in which various aesthetic principles from abstract painting, or more challengingly from music, have been incorporated into film.

The initial problems of a relationship between cinematic abstraction and technological innovation are best examined through the work of John and James Whitney. Though their earliest work, the *Five Film Exercises* (1943–5), was produced through a hybrid between film copying and analogue computer technology, artistically, like others in their historical context, the Whitneys made films which extended the tradition of abstract cinema. Like the work of Oskar Fischinger, their form extends the tradition of abstract painting through the dynamic addition of the dimension of time and sound. But it also becomes increasingly discontinuous with that discourse the more the potentialities of the radically new technology are explored in their own terms. The Whitney brothers (the technical invention being mainly the responsibility of John) evolved a very complex machine which was ostensibly designed to create film images. Though this was programmable and rightly seen as originating computer film, it was a hybrid of animation rostrum and ex-military gun-directing, analogue computers. The characteristics of the machine both constrained the kind of images it could produce and was open to exploration of products not preconceived in its initial design.

Both the constraint and opportunities of this machine become traced in the images/sequences produced. These images are its 'semiology' – they imprint the meaning of the machine in the work. A work like *Lapis* (completed in 1966) carries the implicit characteristic of the machine to a greater extent than the earlier *Five Film Exercises*.

We might understand this aesthetic development as being an example of the way in which a new technology extends the creative range of an art form – in this case abstract cinema – the exploration of a new technology creating new images. However, I have argued elsewhere that all machines – and particularly machines with complex capabilities – embody the intelligence and social motives which have produced them – their invention is discursive building on or evolving from previous machines. A symbolic object produced with a complex technology carries so much of an imprint of that technology – is so much an extension of its capabilities – that the 'language' of the technology is inseparable from the other constituents of the symbolic language at work in the discourse.

In other words, in a Whitney film the framework of interpretation requires a 'reading' (not necessarily conscious) of the combined discourses of cinema, abstract painting, and the technology used in the production of the image. This reading of the technology is not a reading of the 'way the work was made' as has often been assumed. The reading of the technological semiology is in the full range of its 'meaning' in the context of the social, psychological, cultural and so on. These meanings are transmitted through the work integrated into the form of the symbol and symbolic system – image and grammar.

Because the Whitney brothers invented their own technology to serve their purposes as film artists, the gap between their art discourse and that of the technology was relatively small. The capabilities of the machine were designed and evolved towards their artistic ends. More recently in computer-related art, and to a lesser extent, in the early work of the seminal video artist, Nam June Paik, the art discourse is linked to technologies more clearly devised for other purposes.

Paik's work is rightly seen at the origin of what has become 'video art', but initially, he and others spoke of it as 'experimental television'. This is not simply a semantic nicety, it can be enlightening in understanding the relationship between art and technology. Paik's work in the early 1960s was concerned with television. As well as 'abstract' experiments with one of the components of television, the cathode ray tube receiving device, he was also working with broadcast material transformed in image and context within gallery installations.

While in this installation work, the fundamental arena could not be the artistic control of transmission – not an option available to him at that time – the social and political power of television as a centralised transmission medium was both lure and content in the work. A gesture of power over the images from another discourse was achieved by their incorporation and transformation within the context of a discourse – gallery art – in which the artist is seen as the author. This incorporation is gestural as the incorporated image remains politically beyond the scope of the artist's social power. On the other hand, experimenting abstractly with the cathode ray tube and videotape recording, brought into the art discourse those discrete aspects of the technology which could be realistically colonised. Additionally, the particular audio-visual characteristics of video, despite significant differences as an electronic rather than photomechanical medium, remained continuous with those of experimental cinema. The symbolic discourse of art could again achieve an integration with that coming from the technology, but at the expense of abandoning a discourse with the broadcast aspect of the technology.

Recent work by Van Gogh Television using 3-Sat and in a less radical way by *10 vor 11* on RTL and various TV works by artists for Channel Four in Britain have revived consideration of an art discourse with television rather than video.

Digital Technologies

By far the greatest challenge for linking art and technology and for the theoretical assumptions of Expanded Cinema comes from digital (computer) technology particularly when this is linked to communications as in the internet.

Except in a few cases where digital systems have been produced for specific art works, most recent approaches to computer art have made use of general computing equipment. This equipment is the result of developments which initially envisaged no cultural, or media application. Consequently its basic discourse initially had little in common with the symbolic systems of art, even those of mass communications or entertainment.

That this technology increasingly intrigues artists probably derives in part from an awareness of its fundamental difference from other 'mechanical media' systems. Though evolved from machines – the earliest computer was a mechanical device of interconnecting gears – a computer is a machine like no other. In its electronic miniaturisation and logic-based circuitry it is intrinsically non-mechanical – should ideally have no moving parts. Though current systems continue to have rotation (wheel-based) devices like disk drives, digital technologies are intrinsically solid state. The characteristics of digital systems not only open up new artistic approaches but challenge many fundamental artistic and philosophical concepts.

Solid state electronic systems (machines) achieve all their connections, do all their work, by electronic pulses; even if hierarchic, they are fundamentally non-linear. Whatever is conceived as the unit of data, its storage and retrieval is substantially freed from a predetermined sequence derived from the physically linear conditions of a mechanical medium (both film and video are locked into the mechanics of the linear sequence of the recording medium). Through the Random Access Memory (RAM) structure of the computer, the sequence of retrieval does not have to match the sequence of storage and all address locations are effectively equidistant.

In addition to this non-linearity, they offer:

- complex operations and transmissions at very high speed (approaching the speed of light transformation into equal valued digital pulses;
- multifunctionality through re-programming rather than hardware modification.

Its generality of function and digitalisation makes it a technology which is highly incorporative of other media or symbolic systems, has a high potential for translatability based on the complete abstraction of information in digital form, links easily and directly to other electronic communications systems and can model multivariable (multidimensional) conditions with ease and speed. It is fundamentally flexible with regard to both input and output devices.

Media Specificity and Digital Systems

If we assume that the notions of Expanded Cinema or the concepts underlying the history of 'Film as Film' remain valid, how do they relate to the opportunities offered by digital media? The greatest difficulty posed by digital media is to the idea of basing an artistic language on the 'material' conditions of a medium – the notions of media specificity.

Digital technology is too incorporative through the abstraction of symbols, images or sounds into a common digital form and through the flexibility of its output devices to support an idea of media specificity based on any one state of the technology. This is exacerbated by the very rapid and constant development of the technology. Thus, if considered as a medium, not only are its physical characteristics unstable, the potential composite discourses to which it contributes are already too broad to allow any single concept of digital art.

With any one work we can still see the interplay between the constraints and opportunities offered by the technology. But, this is only to say that any media specificity is the interplay between artistic intention and the current available technology.

Though a modernist principle of integration between the 'medium' (or technology) and the symbolic discourse – between means and meaning – may survive for the artistic success of a particular work, it is difficult to sustain a concept of a general discourse based on media specificity in the face of the 'inclusive' characteristics of digital technology.

However, with regard to the context of experimental film or video, it is apparent that some of the more prominent current technological developments in digital media are driven by a desire to produce a time-based auditory and visual capacity which is more or less continuous with the forms and language developed from the history of cinema. And there is a growing theoretical debate on the ways in which non-linearity, programmability and interactivity relate to the assumptions of both narrative and experimental cinema.[3]

Like the way video art developed from only aspects of the televisual technology, the quasi-cinematic developments from computer or digital technology are specific rather than paradigmatic, though some of the theoretical issues being raised may have more general application.

One application of digital technology to art and particularly to film and video is significant in its effect but not theoretically challenging – this is the use of computer technology to assist a wide range of production processes, like video editing. However, if we are to look more broadly at the interface between art practice, digital and communications technologies, can we identify any more general theoretical issues or concepts?

Media Modelling

What are the implications if digital technology is capable of incorporating or modelling other media? While the physical properties of a medium like painting were determined by an evolution in history, their incorporation into digital technology is a matter of analysis of their constituents. We might define these constituents as a set of parameters which are combined in any work.

We might define the physical characteristics of painting as follows: a two-dimensional flat surface on which are mapped regions of colour with tonal intensity and texture. Each of these characteristics could be codified into numerical data related to these identifiable parameters for storage in digital form. An existing painting could, again for example, be analysed, digitally stored and represented on any type of screen. But also, given an appropriate output technology, it could be actually reproduced in a facsimile at any desired level of verisimilitude at any location to which the data could be transmitted.

At this level of modelling the physical properties, any medium is theoretically susceptible, only the range and type of parameters would be different – the real constraints being data storage space, computing capacity and appropriate output devices (sophisticated robotics could even allow the modelling of 'live' theatre – if in doubt go to Disneyland). It is also evident that between one medium and another, certain of the characteristics might be the same while others might vary. Thus the analysis of the parameters of a range of media open up the possibility of the synthesis of media with any chosen combination of parameters.

We are accustomed to the concept of modelling space according to the mapping of points in the three dimensions of length, breadth and depth. For a computer, these values simply need to be given consistent places in the digital code for their coherent storage. The form of their reproduction (output) is a matter of choice. This could be within a convention, like perspective which is representational – but it could equally well be given an output form which translates this data into other equally coherent terms – spatial parameters being expressed as musical sounds or colours for example. Conversely, three defined parameters of a musical sound (its pitch, volume and timbre) could be expressed as a particular location in a perspective representation of 'real' three-dimensional space. For the computer, the mapping of dimensions is not confined to three. The number or type of the parameters in any system can be, if not infinite, very large and any single combination of specific value for these can be considered as a point in multi-dimensional space.

At the conceptual level, this multidimensional space is virtual, the form in which it becomes real through output is a matter of choice and the constraints of available output technology. It is also a matter of choice, habit or social constraint whether the output is made in a conventional form of representation – perspective or narrative for example – or whether a different concept of translation is used.

Neither is the parametric analysis and synthesis theoretically confined to the 'physical' properties of material objects. Any definable range of phenomena including definable characteristics of human psychology or social relationships can be given values and mapped into a virtual, multidimensional space. Nor is it necessary to confine any synthesis to the representation of a previously analysed, external reality. It can be entirely synthetic, produced from parameters which combine any conceivable set of properties, so enabling the possibility of modelling virtual worlds as well as the representation of existing conditions. For, it is another general characteristic of digital systems that, while for representing (modelling) an external phenomenon, the constituents must be analysed, the synthetic process can be equally well applied to parametric relationships which are entirely invented.

Permutation and Interactivity

Though it is possible to make works with digital media which, like traditional art works, are singular, a computer program is intrinsically constructed for a multiplicity of outcomes based on changing values applied in the program. Following Walter

Benjamin's argument on the undermining effect of mechanical reproduction on the special value of the unique art object, the programmable digital system, by producing works which are at the same time multiple and singular through 'permutation', further undermines the reliance of artistic creativity on the unique work and the art-commodity system of which it is part. The multiplicity is no longer reproductive of a single original but represents singular permutative possibilities deriving from a program.

Where the opportunity for multiplicity of outcome is also linked to interactivity, then many of the relationships of status between artist, work and user (audience) are significantly shifted. This shift in status and responsibility is not simple and is certainly not a complete reversal of power relationships in the art experience because the artist remains at the centre of producing the framework, style and symbolic field in which the interactivity takes place. This shift in locating 'authorship' is further complicated by the extent to which the artist relies on 'corporate' software for the realisation of the interactive structures used.[4]

None the less, interactive and permutative work does seem to offer a continuity with one of the major motives for Expanded Cinema as it was understood in the European context – the attempt to give the spectator the framework for more direct involvement in the symbolic construction of the work. In the Expanded Cinema of Export, Weibel, Nicolson and Le Grice, the role and position of the spectator was a very central concern in the form. Though spectators were often brought into and could affect the 'performance', Annabel Nicolson's *Light Readings* or Valie Export's *Auf+Ab+An+Zu* are examples, mostly the involvement remained symbolic. Interactive digital work, exploiting the multiplicity of outcome, sequence of encounter or selection of components, brings the spectator into the work as an actual protagonist, increasingly sharing in aspects of the construction of the work.

Interactivity and Communications Technology

There is much hype concerning the internet, but this link between an international communications network and digital processing technology is rightly recognised as having the potential for exceptional social and cultural change. Its scale, power and accessibility have a fascination for the creative artist. At the same time, as with other aspects of digital technology, it has not been devised for the purposes of art. It is another 'general' rather than 'specific' technology whose potential therefore inevitably exceeds any of the preconceptions which have contributed to its development.

While a communication system, the internet can be exploited for remote access to works of art. At a media festival in Zagreb in March 1995, at a time when travel and electronic links with Sarajevo were impossible, I called up an Exhibition of Pop Art by Bosnian artists through the University of Westminster's world wide web site via London. But again, the most challenging artistic opportunities are not in the use of the internet merely for reproduction and transmission, but in the arena where its structure demands new concepts.

In one respect, the remote linking of computers as data and program servers turns the internet into a massive international computer and database. It combines this with many of the characteristics of a two-way communication system. The user-centred structure – accessing material on the user's not the producer's demand – the continued updating or re-configuration of blocks of data (art works?) by producers and users – takes further the tendency for the dissolution of coherent, unitary works as the product of an individual artist.

Perhaps the best illustration of this potential is evident in the internet 'form' called the 'MUD' – the Multi-User Domain. A Multi-User Domain is an imaginary space constructed for and by a group of people accessing a set of computer memory locations in which each of them is represented in some form. On the internet, the domain's occupants (users) may be physically on opposite sides of the world but their symbolic representation, through the modifications they are making in the computer encounter, is contained in the instantaneous, electronic traces made in the computer. The computer in which these traces are being made would normally be a single computer server but could as well be in a group of remotely linked servers. For the users, the interaction is a dramatic encounter between themselves as a character and other characters currently occupying the imaginary space which provides the context for the encounters.

In this system there are three distinct spatial considerations. The first is the remote actual location of the interacting users. The second is the actual but microscopic trace of electronic (digital) data on transmission lines and in the computer, which, by their speed and simultaneity, deny the physical remoteness of the users. The third is the virtual (imaginary) space which the users conceive themselves as occupying in the encounter. This virtual space certainly does not correspond to the remote locations they occupy in fact. For the user it is an imaginary, virtual, psychological space in which they project their encounter. However, it is also the product of another virtual space which is the conceptual space of the interactions of data in the computer. None of these spaces have any direct representational or conceptual correspondence.

While the virtual imaginary space which user and program jointly define may conform to representational models – rooms in a house, a landscape, and to interactive representations like narrative – there is no reason why other virtual relations should not be constructed to symbolise or transform encounters. Neither does the construction of such interactive encounter spaces remain the responsibility of an individual. The broad framework for establishing a multi-user environment could begin as the work of an individual 'artist' with its forms of interaction proscribed, but the interaction allows for modification and development where the authorship, even for the system, becomes dispersed.

Virtuality and the Real

The juxtaposition of representation and the real in certain Expanded Cinema works made illusory representation and the spectator's encounter with the actuality of the work a central aesthetic problem.

The interactive encounter in computer works and particularly remotely through the internet demand a further review of this issue.

In retrospect, the conflict between a representation as 'illusion' and the 'real' object which it represents or the evident physicality of the representing medium could now be seen as one strategy for initiating a philosophical/aesthetic discourse in the experience of the work. This includes awareness that the insecurity of the symbolic representation is transferred to the 'real'. The real is itself seen to be mediated through the symbolic. The real is itself 'in language'.

Some works of Expanded Cinema made it evident that if the concept of 'the real' is to retain any currency it cannot be based on the unproblematic tactile physicality of objects – their evident presence. In these terms, the electronic transformations within the computer are as real, even if invisible and untouchable, as any broom stuck on a Jasper Johns painting. Both are simultaneously real and symbolic. The only concept of the real which would seem able to survive this condition of mediation through the symbolic is one defined in terms of the dynamic, living condition. This is the condition in which consequence follows crucially on action. What defines the real here is the consequential encounter and its irreversibility.

The Expanded Cinema, following the tradition of 'Film as Film', opposed the reality of the medium to the dominant cinematic illusions of space and time 'behind' the screen. It reversed the location of the symbolic arena through strategies which stressed the material substance of the work by making the cinematic processes visible. In digital work, both strategies for stressing the material and the visibility of process are largely denied by the intrinsic invisibility of the processes and the virtuality of their presentation. It is unfortunate that the predominant use of the concept of the virtual has been applied to the representation of perspective spaces in interactive computer systems – so-called 'virtual reality'. This application of computer processes to modelling and synthesis is only one particular approach to the interpretation of the virtual 'space' both within the computer operation and the imaginary arena of its experience by the user.

In this sense, virtuality is an intrinsic property of the analysis, synthesis and transformations taking place through digitalisation – the virtual is not synonymous with illusion. Only when the synthesis is used to produce an illusion where the representation is confusable with an experience of the real does the philosophical opposition remain. The virtual in either sense of the imaginary constructs of the user or the synthetic models constructed in the computer program are already both symbolic – it is the form of the encounter, its location in the arena of consequence, which remains the crucial consideration.

Digital Expanded Cinema?

It can only remain a question whether the opportunities and problematics of working with digital technologies have any continuity with the discourses which were initiated in Expanded Cinema. The gradual incorporation of new technological approaches to the experimental cinema project clearly continues, particularly through the exploration of interactivity as in work like Grahame Weinbren's *Sonata* (1993). The active interplay between artist, work and user, shifting the work closer to the users' life experience, does seem consistent with one major aspect of the form of Expanded Cinema (again mainly in the European context). Some of the problematics uncovered in this history, concerning the spectator as participant and the art work as an encounter in the real, could be applicable to digital art and the internet.

It is possible that digital technology and the internet offer the convergence between the Expanded Cinema of new technologies and the more conceptual approaches characterised by the European developments.

It is of course also possible that the concept of Expanded Cinema has no further use in a context where the intersection of discourses defies continuity with any single historical medium of expression.

Notes

1. Reproduced as plate 98 of the 1977 Whitney Museum Exhibition Catalogue of Johns's work.
2. See David Curtis, *Experimental Cinema* (London: Studio Vista, 1971), Malcolm Le Grice, *Abstract Film and Beyond* (London: Studio Vista; Cambridge, MA: MIT, 1977), as well as essays by William Moritz including 'Musique Chromatique – Cinéma Integral', in *Poétique de la couleur* (Paris: Louvre, 1995), pp. 9–13, and 'Non-objective Film: The Second Generation', in *Film as Film* (London: Arts Council of Great Britain/Hayward Gallery, 1979), pp. 59–71.
3. See, for example, *Millennium Film Journal* no. 28, Spring 1995 (articles by Andrew Cameron, Grahame Weinbren, Richard Wright and Malcolm Le Grice).
4. See 'The Implication of Digital Systems for Experimental Film Theory' in this volume.

23

A Non-Linear Tradition – Experimental Film and Digital Cinema [1997]

Because digital applications in the field of cinema are beginning to have significant commercial potential, two features – interactivity and non-linearity – are becoming widely debated. If there is to be a recognisably new 'digital cinema', these two concepts will probably be inseparable in its realisation.

It is difficult to find many examples from the history of the arts which might be seen as prefiguring interactivity – direct involvement of the user in modifying the art object itself is genuinely new territory.

Non-linearity, on the other hand, has precursors. Cinematic structures which break with the assumptions of single-track, single-resolution narrative can be seen to have strong roots in a number of directions explored in experimental film and video during its eighty-year history.

The current fashionability of the term 'non-linear' creates some problem of definition. We hear much of non-linear editing systems – called non-linear because shots or sequences can be easily accessed from a computer hard drive and easily assembled and reassembled in a different order from the one in which they were stored. But normally, the principles on which they are combined in the finished product conform to linear narrative concepts. The technology allows non-linearity – the concepts remain linear.

Given the current hype and imprecision it is unwise to assume that concepts of non-linearity are unproblematic. Here are a few questions which just scratch the surface of the issues:

Is linearity synonymous with narrative? Are there forms of sequential structure which are linear but not narrative? Can concepts of dramaturgy be applied to linear structures which are non-narrative? Given that, for the viewer, the sequence in which any time-based work is experienced is inevitably 'linear', how are non-linear concepts and experiences embodied in a work?

Starting from the experimental cinema, with the risk of over-simplification, there have been two broad directions or features of its history which can be related to the current notions of non-linearity:

- the first direction is abstraction – in the sense of non-representational imagery;
- the second is the break with narrative form – including work which incorporates photographic representation.

Abstraction and Anti-Narrative

In the strictly non-representational form of cinema, 'abstract cinema', the model for the experience and the aesthetic framework was derived from painting and music.

Though I prefer to define 'abstraction' as the process of separation of the component features and qualities from the 'whole' of an object and as such it is not synonymous with non-representation, in cinema, as in the other arts, the manipulation of non-representational elements like colour and shape have become the widely understood connotation. Given this popular connotation of 'abstract cinema', the attempts made by experimental film- and video-makers to break with the constraints of narrative – the second major feature – may be seen as a more general characteristic in its history.

This resistance to narrative and the search for alternatives is already evident in theoretical writing in the 1920s by, for example, Fernand Léger or Dziga Vertov and has been expressed not just as 'non-narrative' but polemically as 'anti-narrative' in the more recent and crucial writings of Peter Gidal.[1] While the resistance to narrative form is confirmed in theoretical work on experimental film, it is most evident in the search for alternative cinematic structures in works themselves. This fundamental search for cinematic forms which do not conform to a linear narrative structure and resolution is the main characteristic which differentiates experimental film from mainstream cinema and is ultimately its major claim to radical intervention at all levels – aesthetic, ideological and political.

So 'abstract cinema', based on colour, shape, movement and rhythm and without representational imagery, as in the films of Walter Ruttmann, Oskar Fischinger, John Whitney or Harry Smith, is an aspect of the non-narrative enterprise but the majority of non- or anti-narrative works are based on or include photographically representational imagery: non-narrative is not synonymous with non-representation.

Narrative and Ideology

What is it in narrative that the experimental cinema has reacted against?

In the same way in which physical space can be represented in two dimensions by a set of conventions – most predominantly the perspective system developed in the fourteenth century, events in time are represented by conventions, most predominantly narrative. As perspective represents an apparent coherence in spatial relationships so narrative is a method by which events – real or imaginary – are given coherence through the representation of sequential connections. Like perspective, the form of coherence constructed by narrative is only one particular method by which temporal events and their 'causal' relationships may be represented (mod-elled). But, the adequacy or otherwise of the resulting 'unity' produced by the narrative form – its 'truth factor' – is, like the particular spatial coherence of per-spective, the result of an interplay between the subject (in its various meanings) and the conventions of linkage or representation. However ubiquitous, narrative remains a particular method of representation and, like perspective, it is not a neu-tral or natural system, its effect is to 'place' its spectator/listener both psychologically and ideologically.

Because these narrative conventions have become dominant cultural norms this process of placement is largely unconscious. Its invisibility allows the dominance of a convention to become integral to the fusion between social order and culture. Constrained within a predominant convention not only the listener but the narrator as well remain unconscious of its function. The particular conditions of the place-ment – its ideological and psychological effects – its detailed techniques and devices (grammar) – only become evident through resistance, the creation of other models and the search for other conventions.

This is a matter of theory but primarily, to become effective in the cultural dis-course, it requires the establishment of new forms in practice – working in and transforming experience, concepts and meanings.

Ideologically we can interpret the innovations of Cubism and the development of non-narrative forms in cinema as a process of dislodging the fusion between social (state or economic) power and dominant conventions of representation. At the same time the process creates new conventions by which we can understand and experi-ence our world.

Looking more closely at the structure of cinematic narrative the issue of linearity begins to be clarified. The classical narrative is constructed through the represen-tation of characters who interact with each other through a series of incidents depicted in a social or natural environment. The story or plot is a schema made up of the events in the 'causal' sequence in which they are represented to have taken place. The narration itself is more complex than the plot in that it may reorder the disclosure of these events, through representing recollection, premonition or separ-ate exclusive viewpoints – flashback, jump-cut, parallel action – and may incorporate the represented subjectivity of the narrator or even reference the subjectivity of the reader. Both plot and narration may conform to structures of dramaturgy – the con-trolled psychological effect of phasing the release of information to create intrigue, suspense, apprehension and pleasure in resolution.

Underlying the formal structures of narrative are the complex processes of the identification between the audience/viewer and the represented characters – acting vicariously for and on behalf of the viewer in the 'play' – and the psychological/ideo-logical effect of the story resolving the moral dilemmas of the subject in society through its narrative resolution. The issues of linearity or non-linearity are not fully defined in this description of narrative process.

For the viewer of a film, the experience inevitably takes place in linear sequence. This is, incidentally, equally true of the viewing of a painting or the interaction with a CD-ROM. This (apparent?) continuity of consciousness in time is – excepting the fantasies of time travel – a condition of our personal subjective singularity and the irreversibility of time.

In a sense, all our perceptions and consciousness take place in a 'timeline' but it is evident that from these discrete temporal elements – our perceptions – we are able to construct concepts which are not themselves fundamentally temporal. For example, from our temporal perceptions we can model spatial relationships, or link temporal events to construct a hierarchy which is not itself linearly causal – as in the psychological associations of memory.

So, in the history of experimental as in conventional narrative cinema, the inevitability of 'perceptual' linearity must be accepted, both in the condition of the viewer and particularly in the predetermined sequence of presentation of the work (even if, as with some presentations by the quintessential underground film-maker, Jack Smith, the reels of a particular film might be shown in different orders at different screenings).

The problem then of narrative is not the linearity of presentation or perception but the ideology hidden beneath the unproblematic 'linearity' – the particular causal chain of representation – made invisible and validated in dominant culture. This linearity of causal sequence is by definition authoritarian. Even if the content is transgressive or anarchic, the form locks the audience into a consequence which unifies the subject impotently with and within the narrative. It is the linear coherence of the narrative and its conclusion which represses the subject (viewer) by implicitly suppressing the complexity of the viewer's own construction of meaning. Transmitted as a culturally validated convention, narrative subsequently becomes a model by which experience is interpreted, becomes a filter for the life experience outside the cinematic.

Towards the Non-Linear

Historically, experimental film has grappled with these issues bit by bit through developments of the cinematic language within the discourses of art and cinema. At the risk of constructing my own repressive historical narrative, we might note some key stages and fundamental concepts in the process.

Chronologically, the earliest challenge to narrative cinema came from the direction of abstract film, almost certainly beginning with the work of Futurists Bruno Corra and Arnaldo Ginna between 1910 and 1914 (well documented but now lost or destroyed) and carried on in the early 1920s by Walter Ruttmann, Viking Eggeling, Hans Richter and Oskar Fischinger.[2]

From this axis, innovations are largely imported from the developing ideas in con-temporary painting and based visually on manipulation of shape, line, tone or colour. Brought into the temporal arena of cinema, this import forced formal solutions involving shape transformation, movement into and across the screen and the rhythm both of the changes within the frame and the 'beat' created by montage. Though the images of 'abstract cinema' are essentially non-representational (they may have residual anthropomorphic or object references), they are not outside meaning or interpretation either in the images or the logic of their transformation. Indeed, abstract transformations can even parallel the identification and conse-quence of narrative.

However, the solutions found for the temporal structure in abstract films have been most predominantly analogous to musical structure. This was both an intrin-sic parallel which emerged from the practice of 'abstract cinema' and a theoretical quest mainly deriving from Wassily Kandinsky who sought a broader philosophical and formal basis for a 'language' of abstraction.

Viking Eggeling's abstract film *Diagonal Symphony* relates directly to a theoretical enterprise, following Kandinsky, where he sought a 'Generalbass der Malerei'. This represented a systematic attempt by Eggeling to establish a language of visual form and fundamental rules of transition equivalent to those which had guided the devel-opment of western music.[3] In fact, the work itself is more mathematical than musical in character and prefigures the development of computer film through its 'pro-grammability'. It is probably the first hint of one of the later widely used experimental film strategies where an arithmetic system becomes the basis of a non-narrative but temporal structure.

'Abstract cinema' remains a major and radical challenge to the hegemony of nar-rative at the level of initiating new structural principles. At its most radical, it demands a priority for physical experience over interpretation, creating an extreme point of reference both for dominant and experimental cinema.

The more general experimental or avant-garde cinema which is based on repre-sentational (photocinematic) imagery is not as simply differentiated from narrative form. Common to both experimental and dominant cinema, images which derive from the interaction between a camera and the world inevitably establish the con-ditions where the viewer becomes 'implicated' in the scene through the camera and the decisions of the cinematographer. Irrespective of the subject before the camera, this basic identification into the cinematic scene (spectacle) is filtered or mediated through the camera as 'viewpoint/trajectory'. The camera and cinematographer unavoidably act as the representative of the viewer, establishing the psychological and symbolic traces through which the viewer must pass and out of which meanings are formed by juxtaposition. This process of identification – the collusion of the viewer in becoming subject to another viewpoint, another authority and power –

extends from the act of the camera to the represented objects (people, things or landscapes).

Strategies of resistance to this fundamental identification have become incorporated into the traditions of experimental cinema. Many of these have been based on affirming the separate identity of the image – as a pattern of light and colour on a screen – from its object reference. Transforming or manipulating the image itself – *Adebar* by Peter Kubelka or my own *Berlin Horse* for example – shifts the experience of the viewer away from a passage through the image to its denotation towards an experience of the image construction and transformation itself. Other strategies, as in Michael Snow's *Back and Forth*, have foregrounded the operation and movement of the camera so that it no longer remains invisible, its condition as mediator is made evident and problematic in the meaning of the work.

In addition to the basic condition of identification through representation shared by experimental and narrative cinema, the juxtaposition of cinematic sequences inevitably creates, for both, assumptions of causal (or 'motivated') linkage. These linkages, if conforming to dominant convention also confirm established meanings within the juxtaposition – as in action montage – if they do not conform directly to established forms they demand interpretation.

It is in establishing a new basis for the creation and interpretation of linkages in the montage of cinematic sequences that experimental cinema is most radically challenging. Experimental cinema has explored a range of approaches to the connection of sequences including mathematical systems, randomness, musical analogy, unconstrained subjectivity, creating conditions of montage, all of which counteract and create alternatives to narrative structure. As with the strategies which work on the image itself, those which work on montage may be initially expressed in terms of resistance, but through the developing practice of experimental cinema, have established a range of new formal models. Many of the works which make up this history employ a combination of strategies working on both the image and the montage.

Though we might see Méliès as the primitive originator, outside 'abstract cinema', the first intentionally non-narrative but clearly representational work emerged from Dadaism and Surrealism. The crucial reference points are well known – René Claire's *Entr'acte*, the Buñuel/Dali collaboration on *Un Chien andalou* and *L'Age d'or* and Germaine Dulac's *The Seashell and the Clergyman*.

It is not coincidental that the emergence and codification of psychoanalysis was a crucial influence on the development of Surrealism from the anarchic, nihilistic drive of Dada. Both movements for which, despite manifestos, there is no hard dividing moment, were vehemently anti-bourgeois. They recognised the constraints on thought and behaviour which came, not just from censorship of the subjects of art, but from the fundamental constraint in the structure of language and conventions.

Psychoanalysis itself questions the way in which linearity in the narrative is capable of representing the underlying causal structures. Its reference to dreams and free association are both instances where the dominant forms of causal representation are loosened or dissolved to permit cross-references between layers of memory in turn to create different connective hierarchies. In many ways, the constructions of experience implicit in psychoanalysis represent another parallel to the dissolution by Cubism of the single spatial viewpoint of perspective and the dissolution by experimental cinema of the single linear resolution to social interactions of narrative.

Experimental cinema, in resisting the cultural unification of narrative, has also resisted the establishment of a single new unifying form. In this its references remain provisional rather than dogmatic and the psychoanalytic model is no exception. The resistance to linear causality and predetermined consequence by definition precludes the acceptance of a new unifying form. This is not a matter of fashion and novelty, as has often been interpreted in the art world, leading to the cynicism of the post-modern, but a reflection of a fundamental shift in philosophical assumptions of the knowable. Knowledge and experience have become irreversibly problematic while the attempt to give form to experience remains the unavoidable basis of artistic practice.

Within experimental cinema, the development of a form of non-linear 'provisionality' which took on the issue of subjective content is best seen in the work of Maya Deren. Her *Meshes of the Afternoon* has many of the normal components of a narrative work – there are distinct characters in a staged enactment, which is filmed through conventional camera set-ups employing long, medium, close-up and point-of-view shots. There are also sections of montage which describe or represent moments of coherent action. However, in major aspects of its form, the interpretation of the meaning of the sequential montage is significantly shifted from narrative through the device of repetition and development or variation in the repetition. Each repetition of a simple and basic action sequence introduces new variations of detail requiring reinterpretation. The work describes a spiral passage – the linear perceptual passage of the viewer – through a symbolic experience where each spiral collects (allows a review) of the material from that place in the spiral on the previous circuit. Again however, the continued spiral does not lead towards a new definitive interpretation but only serves to increase the complexity of interpretation available to the previous as well as to the present experience. The form acts, a little like psychoanalysis, to initiate a reinterpretation of the covert matrix of interconnected symbolic memories as represented in the film. But it also acts to set up a formal relationship of the viewer to the work where the meanings must be made and reviewed by the viewer independently of the film's maker as it becomes increasingly apparent that any resolution is unreliable – subject to change – problematic – provisional.

In this film, as in many experimental cinema works, the inevitable linearity of the presentation is not subservient to the representation of a linear coherence of consequence. Instead it initiates a construction (comprehension) of the images where their relationships are non-linear. The connective linearity of the work models a relationship of the 'content' which is non-consequential – thus speculative, descriptive terms like 'spiral', 'matrix', 'psycho-associative' or Deren's own description of the exploration of 'verticality' as opposed to the common 'horizontal' trajectory of conventional narrative. Deren's film is an exemplar in experimental cinema of the development of non-linearity as an aesthetic experience, and, through the participation of the viewer in the self-construction of meaning – forced by the form, not simply available to the critical cineaste – it is also a key point in cinema of a symbolic interactivity.

Digital Cinema

The computer, which is fundamentally based on what is called Random Access Memory – which has little to do with randomness in the sense of the generation of random numbers, but is the designation of the non-sequentiality of memory addressing – intrinsically opens up the condition of non-linearity. Non-linearity is a factor of Random Access Memory – unlike in linear media, film, audiotape, video – though the computer remains (temporarily?) tied to partially-sequential devices like CD-ROM, its basic structure of storing and controlling data is sequential only in as far as the sequentiality is specified. However, the non-linear potential and its application does not ensure that its products are constructed around the philosophical, ethical, ideological and psychological issues of non-linearity in human discourses.

The tradition of experimental cinema and video has already developed the basis for exploring these artistic concerns, not as a response to the new technology but as a consequence of artistic reflection on the human condition and the search for contemporary expressive models. Indeed, the forms developed in this artistic tradition are more suited to the intrinsic opportunities offered by computer technology for a non-linear and interactive cinema than are those derived from the narrative film.

Notes

1. Peter Gidal, *Materialist Film* (London and New York: Routledge, 1989).
2. See David Curtis, *Experimental Cinema* (London: Studio Vista, 1971) and Malcolm Le Grice, *Abstract Film and Beyond* (London: Studio Vista; Cambridge, MA: MIT, 1977).
3. Louise O'Konor, *Viking Eggeling* (Stockholm: Almqvist & Wiksell, 1971).

24

Art in the Land of Hydra-Media [1998]

Almost by habit now I begin an article with a health warning. The reader should know that I am firstly a film, video and digital artist. My theoretical work is almost completely based on the issues I have encountered in analysing my work and understanding its relationship to other artists, culture, technology and society.

Much of my recent writing has been based on getting a clearer understanding of the way in which the new electronic and digital technologies are having an effect on possible forms of cinema. Though technological innovations are crucial, my concern is not with technology itself but with the changes in form, language, concept and meaning in cinema which result from it. Neither am I concerned with charting or predicting the way new technologies can be incorporated into old cinematic ideas by, for example, making more 'realistic' dinosaurs for more *Jurassic Park*s. My interest remains clearly that of the experimental artist and my issues derive directly from the tradition of experimental cinema. Indeed, much of my earliest film and written work took up a position which was overtly opposed to the forms and social function of conventional narrative cinema. Though more recent writing admits a greater complexity in the issues of narrative as a cinematic form, if anything, my opposition to 'Hollywood', particularly as it fills and influences our daily diet of television psychodrama, has increased. I have no great interest in fuelling innovation which makes the genre of the international Hollywood 'psychotic' more believable by better special effects.

With that attitude 'off my chest', I should like to trace a historical continuity looking at cinema as a medium which has become diversified as a combination of media through electronic and digital technologies.

My own earliest film work dating from the late 1960s, like that of Birgit and Wilhelm Hein in Germany, Peter Gidal in England, Kurt Kren and Peter Kubelka in Austria, Andy Warhol and Tony Conrad in the US and Michael Snow in Canada (the list could be greatly extended), brought a modernist aesthetic firmly into cinema. This happened in the context of an explosion of artistic experiment with form and media we can now see as characteristic of that decade. It took as its origins implicit assumptions about the artist, the medium, the spectator and the work, which had become fundamental in painting, sculpture, music and even major parts of literature and theatre, but had never had any serious impact in mainstream cinema.

Of course the history I am paraphrasing was much more complicated, it did not begin in the 1960s; it built on a prehistory of experimental cinema – even if unconsciously – and prefigured some characteristics which have since become known as post-modernist. An abstract cinema, now well-documented, can be reasonably traced back to the 1912 experiments titled 'chromatic music' by Italian Futurists, Arnaldo Ginna and Bruno Corra – a direction taken up again in the 1920s by Viking Eggeling, Walter Ruttmann, Hans Richter and Oskar Fischinger, and the photographically representational but equally 'abstract' films of Fernand Léger or Dziga Vertov.

Parallel to this abstract development in cinema was an equally radical movement coming from the influence of psychoanalysis, Dada and Surrealism including the well-known works resulting from the collaboration between Louis Buñuel and Salvador Dali, and the films of Germaine Dulac or Man Ray. However, this early experimental work in cinema remained largely unknown or sporadic; it was almost completely invisible to the mainstream cinema but neither was it part of collections in the art museums. Experimental cinema only took on the scale of a movement, with a large number of artists developing a range of ideas, after World War II – a movement which became possible through the accessibility of 16mm film and improved international communications. Bridging this first period of experimental film with the cross-media experiments of the 1960s is the seminal work of Maya Deren, Stan Brakhage, and the pioneers of computer film, John and James Whitney.

For my own part, in 1965, initially unaware of this American underground cinema or the early abstract films or contemporary experiments with film in Europe, I came to film like many other artists of the period from painting and the visual arts. Typically for a child of my generation in Europe (unlike in the US), I grew up without any exposure to television but with regular – often twice-weekly – visits to the popular cinema: as a painting student in London in the early 1960s I was also up to date with the films of Truffaut, Godard, Bergman, Fellini, Antonioni and Resnais. But when I decided to make films, with the possible exception of *La Jetée* by Chris Marker and *L'Année dernière à Marienbad* by Alain Resnais, even the celebrated new cinema from France and Italy seemed to belong to an entirely different era to the work in the other arts which mattered to me.

The influences on my early experiments with film were almost all from outside cinema – the paintings of Willem de Kooning, Arschille Gorky, Jasper Johns or Robert Rauschenberg – the music of Dizzy Gillespie, Ornette Coleman or John Cage – the theatre of Samuel Beckett. Even the most advanced forms of film I saw in the cinema seemed constructed along the lines of the nineteenth-century novel and certainly had no sense of the improvisation, spontaneity or presence which had become fundamental in the other contemporary arts. The cinema looked and felt to me 'out of date'.

In all the work which stimulated me the artists had become 'visible' protagonists manipulating the medium of their particular art as if in the existentialist 'first person'. The spectator had similarly been repositioned by this change to be much closer to the work as real substance, much less placed as the observer of a representational spectacle and more of an active participant confronted by the work. While painting since Cubism had abandoned illusionistic representation and perspective – the depiction of characters in a scene from a fixed viewpoint – in favour of material and surface, film was still making pictures. It was telling fatalistic stories as if from the viewpoint of an omnipresent God. I began to understand the coherent line of the narrative as a device to fix the spectator. I saw this unbroken narrative continuity as an extension into time of the fixed viewpoint of traditional perspective, continuing the illusionistic aesthetics which had been overturned by modernism in the other arts. Along with modern art in general, I had long abandoned the coherent, passive fixity of the spectator which I still found in cinema together with its philosophical implication of omniscience. For me the form and content of cinema belonged to another age, it remained untouched by Nietzsche, Marx, Sartre, the relativity of Einstein, the uncertainty of Kafka, the improvisation of Charlie Parker or the immediacy of Little Richard. Not only did I reject the forms of cinema, but the stories films told were not relevant to me. Unlike my experience of modern painting or music, in the cinema I resented my loss of identity and lack of choice as the spectator – I came from the cinema feeling drained rather than exhilarated by the catharsis. So when I made film it was as a primitive, reinventing cinema, attempting to relate myself to the medium as I had to painting and with concepts of time and temporal structure which drew more from jazz than the narrative traditions of literature. I wanted to treat film as an art medium.

What did it mean to be working with film as a medium? When Marshall McLuhan dropped 'the medium is the message' bombshell I rejected his utopian view that the new media technologies would, of themselves, bring a unifying democracy to the world – this seemed politically naive in the European context. However, his concept, while obviously flawed, also seemed radically correct – or at least, for an artist experimenting outside mainstream cinema as well as challenging a conservative art institution, it provided a much needed theoretical support. It seemed to apply a theoretical idea to all media which had long been fundamental to modernist art – namely that the conditions of the medium were more fundamental to communication or effect than the surface codes. As a painter in the modernist tradition, I had come to understand the medium to be defined largely in terms of its materials – the canvas, its surface and perimeter (frame), the pigment, its colour, luminous intensity, texture or thickness. I also understood the 'language' to be built out of or on top of these materials, as surface combined with colour or line defined shape. These forms, which were of themselves a direct sensory experience, did not originate as language but became icons or symbols in the process of making the work. With the action painting of Jackson Pollock, this iconography also radically became a trace of the process itself. The manipulation of the materials of painting was the source of new form, new experience, new language, new meanings. Language was now problematic, not fixed, and was in continual development through innovation in form. At the same time, the artist strived continually for innovation outward from the intrinsic materials of the medium – a philosophy described, not invented, by Clement Greenberg which applied equally as an artistic attitude in jazz or contemporary theatre. This striving for innovation came into inevitable conflict with another modernist orthodoxy, the specificity of a medium. The concept of specificity sought to define the intrinsic differences for example between painting and sculpture and later, in experimental cinema, the differences between video and film. Indeed video has struggled for two decades to define itself as an autonomous art form based on the specificity of the medium. The notion of media specificity tries to define the range of idea, concept or form which can be handled in a particular medium – to define those properties which are intrinsic to the medium. However, the art experiments of the 1960s, by stretching the creative language outwards from the material base of the medium, challenged and broke the 'intrinsic' boundaries. This challenged the very concept that a medium has stable and intrinsic properties. The challenging of media boundaries is one of the origins of post-modernism and initiated questions which have become crucial in the arena of electronic and digital art.

I shared in this process of challenging boundaries. In the 1960s I made paintings where the canvas surface was physically cut and twisted joining two surfaces in space stretching painting into the realms of sculpture. I also made paintings which attached themselves through strings to objects in the space in which they were exhibited (the Arts Laboratory, Drury Lane, London, October 1968), incorporating these temporarily into the work. These attachments extended to become microphones which recorded and replayed sounds from the exhibition space, or flashing lights which randomly changed the illumination of painting and space. What began as painting had also expanded into the realm of musical performance (a group of performances with the radical improvisation group AMM and Cornelius Cardew at the Kingley Street Gallery, London, 1969). Though my own work after 1966 came to be centred around film, it included experiments with early video and the digital computer. In a two-week, non-stop exhibition, 'Drama in a Wide Media Environment' (the Arts Laboratory, Drury Lane, London, August 1968 – see *Interfunktionen 4*, January 1970 for documentation), I presented two 'live' video installations incorporating the audience and also mixed video and off-air TV images with improvised performances in collaboration with theatre director Tom Osbourne. My earliest experiments with computer art used primitive 'mainframes' – a performance work with actors 'Typo Drama' in an exhibition of computer art 'Event One' (Royal College of Art, London, April 1969) and *Your Lips*, a computer-generated animation produced using the largest computer in England in 1969 and the only one with a direct visual output, the Atlas at the Atomic Energy establishment at Harwell.

Of course I was far from alone in the 1960s in experimenting with new media or of tracing a course where the stretching of the boundaries of one medium led to the importation of aspects of others. While the cross-media, or multimedia experiments of the 1960s, like the Nine Evenings of Theatre and Technology, in New York in 1966 – and the earlier Happenings movement – challenged media specificity, all this work still began from exploration of the potentialities of the raw material of the medium or technology rather than any existing language – language continued to be built outwards from the materials.

Like many other artists of the time I brought attitudes and assumptions from contemporary art and 'applied' them to the new media. This expressed itself in my films in a variety of ways. First the films were improvised in a process of making with no division between a plan or script and the construction of the work. The film thinking was done directly in the making of the work, in the physical process of collecting sequences and montage often using found footage (*Castle 1 – The Light Bulb Film*, 1966, and *Castle 2*, 1968), for example. The structures evolved from the process in a direct parallel to contemporary jazz or other freeform music. Images, whether shot by me or found, were treated as raw material. Like in an assemblage painting by Robert Rauschenberg, these moving-image sequences could be combined, repeated and recombined as my subjective and improvised instinct directed.

Parallel to the experience of painting, handling the film material directly drew my attention to the material substance and properties of film – its transparent but scratchable base, the emulsion on its surface and its transport mechanism of sprockets for example (*Little Dog For Roger*, 1967, and *White Field Duration*, 1973). What Hollywood tried desperately to hide – the material basis of the medium – in order to retain an illusion that the spectator was inside the scene of the narrative, I, the Heins, Landow, Conrad and others tried to stress. This attention to the material simultaneously disrupted illusion and established a new basis on which artistic experiment in the medium could be built. What, at the time, because of its effect on the audience, I frequently expressed as a Brechtian alienation principle and saw as political as well as artistic in implication. This attention to film substance, as in the Heins' *Roh Film* of 1968, introduced to cinema the concept that it was a medium in the sense understood by modern art. Further developments of this material(ist) approach involved taking direct control of film printing and developing (*Yes No Maybe Maybe Not*, 1966, or *Berlin Horse*, 1970, for example) opening up the manipulation and transformation of film image to the artist.

Approaching cinema as a medium in the physical sense, but with an attitude which challenged boundaries, also led to a break with the 'intrinsics' of the apparent material limits of film – what has been called Expanded Cinema. My early interest in multiprojection – many of my films between 1967 until the mid-1970s were designed for up to six projectors and screens – also involved a variety of approaches to live performance with the film projection. This treated the projection event as a theatrical 'confrontation' extending the (Brechtian) active role for the spectator in resolving the conflicting interplay between image and material – for example my shadow and other film performance work like *Horror Film 1* (1971), a concept also explored by Austrian, Valie Export, in *Splitscreen Solipsismus* which used an interplay between a projection and a mirror. Expanded Cinema, mainly in its European aspect, also explored the conceptual and historical conditions of cinema, as for example in my *Principles of Cinematography* (1972), or challenged the boundaries of both film and sculpture by treating the light beam as an object as in Anthony McCall's *Line Describing a Cone*.

Even though extreme philosophical difference from the traditions of mainstream cinema made the development of a modernist approach to film difficult – and it remains firmly outside the mainstream of cinema – the physical, mechanical basis of the technology did allow a relatively coherent transposition of concepts of medium from the other arts. The material film surface could reasonably be understood as equivalent to the surface of a painting; manipulation of image qualities in printing or painted directly onto the film could be seen as equivalent to the construction of the painterly image. This material-based approach to the language could also go beyond painterly equivalence and be applied to more specifically cinematic properties and processes. This included, within Expanded Cinema, the treatment of the projection process and situation as material. It also included a very wide range of experiment with the mechanism of the camera, like Michael Snow's *La Région Centrale* and exploration of numerical and other systems of editing as in work by Kurt Kren or Takahiko Iimura.

Experimental and expanded cinema of the 1960s and 1970s gave rise to works which confirmed but also challenged aspects of modernism. If Expanded Cinema, multiprojection or installation, challenged the concept of media specificity in cinema, the development of electronic and digital media – video, but particularly the computer – challenges the more fundamental concept of medium as material as a result of the form of the technology itself.

While cinema, based on the optics, wheels and cogs, the physical base of acetate film and chemistry can be treated as physical substance and manipulated in a way continuous with the 'tactile' traditions of art, the computer has no graspable substance – or what graspable substance it has, the boxes in which the components are housed and the micro-chips themselves, have a completely arbitrary relationship between their visual form and their function. Where we can see, however small, the picture on a film strip, and grasp the relationship between projected image, camera shutter, mechanics, physics and chemistry, the 'image' in the computer is no more than an invisible sequence of electronic impulses combining together at the speed of light. Though obeying the laws of physics, the physicality of the computer function is beyond reach – its operations are too minute and fast to link directly to our sensory system without translation to a form of representation with which we are already familiar. In this, video as a medium, is no more than an interim stage, a hybrid between the mechanics of film and the electronics of digital media.

The attempt to delineate video as a specific medium of art, based on its intrinsic properties, has always been difficult to sustain. Certain of its properties – its materials – like the form of the video monitor, were always doomed to transience. Other aspects, like the linear form of the tape, merely continued the mechanics of film into the electronic age. Video extended cinematic possibilities through instantaneous image, and much of the most successful video work, like that of Dan Graham, explored the instant representation and transformation of physical space through this property of video. Exploring electronic manipulation or synthesis – like the work of the Vesulkas – created novel forms of image transformation, and achieved more simply some forms of montage, colouration or solarisation which film and photography had already worked with. The recent work of Nam June Paik shows how the technology of video has become archaic, even nostalgic – which is not to negate art works made by Paik or any other video artist as the aim of art is not simply to support current technology. In its televisual aspect, the combination of the properties of video production – cameras and tape – with the electronics of 'radio-wave' broadcasting, satellite and cable transmission, defies a concept of medium as it is already a mix of media technologies. With the further complication of digital forms of production, storage, presentation and transmission, the interface between video, television and the internet not only represents a combination of media technologies, but also of institutions, political and financial interests.

I became interested in both the theoretical implications for media resulting from the application of computers and the possibility of extending my own artistic work in this area in the late 1960s. In January 1970, I published 'Outline for a Theory of the Development of Television' (in the first number of *Cinemantics* – which also contained articles by Umberto Eco, Peter Gidal and an interview with Jean-Marie Straub by Andi Engel) where I schematically outlined the potential links between information technology (computers) and televisual technology in the context of politics and user choice – a kind of utopian blueprint for the internet. I produced a performance work, *Typo Drama*, where the text and instruction for the actors was generated by a computer program written in collaboration with programmer, and music artist, Alan Sutcliffe. This was performed at the computer art exhibition

'Event One' in London in April 1969. In the same year, and with knowledge of the work of both John and James Whitney and the computer film experiments of Stan Vanderbeek, I began work on a computer-generated abstract film *Your Lips* completed and shown in various versions in 1970 but finally, re-coloured and superimposed, making up one component of *Threshold* (1972). Even though I negotiated access to Britain's largest computer, there were no facilities for real-time output of digital images available in the UK in this period and the work, which took me over nine months to program (I learned Fortran 4 in order to complete it), was produced on a sequential 'graph-plotter' with a computer-controlled 16mm camera mounted above the cathode ray tube. The difficulties of producing computer work with any complexity at that time led me to put this interest on the back burner until the arrival of the first generation of personal computers at reasonable cost in the early 1980s. Though I wrote a complex sound program with simple graphics for the Sinclair Spectrum using machine code (instructions written in a series of numbers to be read directly by the computer's central processing unit), all the exhibited computer work I did during the 1980s was programed by me in Fast Basic on the Atari (initially the 1040). This resulted in three works which were transferred to video and incorporated with six other mixed film and video works in *Sketches for a Sensual Philosophy* (completed in 1988 and first transmitted on Channel Four in the UK in 1990). This period of work also resulted in a program for a live computer music performance (untitled) which I did with Keith Rowe at the London Film-makers' Co-operative in December 1989. I recently used a different approach to combining a computer program with video in manipulating a database of sequences from an extensive video diary (more than sixty hours shot over ten years) in the early editing of *Chronos Fragmented* (1995, transmitted on Channel Four in 1996).

During the production of these works, I also began theoretical work which attempted to define the characteristics of the computer as an art medium (in the modernist tradition) and to see this in the context of experimental film. As with all my theory, while it runs parallel to the artistic work, one feeding the other, it is not directly connected. The general concepts which I have attempted to define in various published articles can be illustrated in part by the computer 'videos', but the concepts have a more general application and the creative works are not seen as a paradigm (which I might have claimed for some earlier film work).

The characteristics I have defined as being predominant (if not intrinsic) in computer-based work are:

- the unavoidable analysis of all input to the most abstract imaginable form, that of digital pulses, destroying any trace of similarity between the initial form of the input and its representation in the computer;

- the unavoidable synthesis of this stored data into a form of analogue or language for output if it is to be used by human beings;
- the requirement of a program specifying the form, interaction, manipulation and transformation of the data – the computer is not a single-purpose machine but changes its purpose relative to the program;
- the fundamental non-linearity of the information storage system normally expressed as Random Access Memory (random here meaning arbitrary access rather than randomised in the sense of chance operations); and
- the potential for interactivity allowing (or expecting) the user to influence, by input, the particular form in which a program emerges.

These characteristics are not strictly material properties of a medium in the way understood by modernist art and could conceivably change substantially through developments in technology (the digital may even be superseded by a form of genetic analogue computer – then we shall need to think again). However, they do represent characteristics which currently come into play in any digital work and have both practical and philosophical consequences affecting their use in art.

Each of the characteristics offers creative possibilities (as well as constraints). For example, in my work *Digital Still Life*, three video sequences are the source of sixty-four still, frame-grabbed images. Digitised at relatively low resolution in sixteen shades of grey in order to fit the limited memory of an Atari (4 Megabytes), a program I wrote could reorder these images in real-time and at will, according to sequences generated by various formulae – thus separating their presentation from their initial movement-based sequence. This exploited the opportunity offered both by programmability and the capacities of non-linear Random Access Memory where the image storage locations are all equidistant or, in other words, equally adjacent to each other. Each is only the distance of a few electrons at the speed of light accessed so quickly that I needed to build waiting routines into the program to accommodate our perceptual rates. The complete abstraction of the imagery as a series of numerical values made of ones and noughts, on or off pulses of electricity, meant that any set of values could also be selectively transformed for their output. What was stored to represent black and white gradations, was, through the program, progressively transformed to areas of colour, again according to the formulae of the program. The condition of digital abstraction, where all data fundamentally loses its identity, allows the possibility of selective transformation into output which is different but in the same category – the colour transformations in *Digital Still Life* remain within the designated shape allowing the pictorial identity to be retained even though transformed. The opportunity is equally simply available to transform the pictorial aspect beyond recognition, or to use the basic numerical data for complete translation into another form, like for example sound. Nor would such translation necessarily be without structure. For example, the numerical values used to store a picture, because of the pictorial gradations of colour, tone and shape, have a coherence, an interior logic which can remain recognisable as a structure even if translated into another form – again for example, darker values becoming low notes, lighter values high notes and so on. In *Digital Still Life*, the numerical values controlling the order in which the stills are shown are used to control the pitch of the main 'melody' and the colour values, determined in the program as three interacting values of red, green and blue, also control the main notes forming the harmonic progression in the sound. Other values used in the image control volume and timbre and all are conditioned by a set of formulae which determine the rhythm and sub-cycles within the structure. Variations of this form of translatability between image and sound are used as a starting-point in both *Arbitrary Logic* and *Heads I Win – Tails You Lose*. In the latter work, the co-ordinates defining the position of frame-image fragments (digitised drawings of punks) on the screen are (as I recall without re-analysing the code of my own program) used to define the main pitch variations and other harmonics and rhythm features are related to the size of picture fragments. This work also includes an input of 'hand-played' music from a piano keyboard being fed to the program via the computer's MIDI port (Musical Instrument Digital Interface port used by musicians for all modern performance synthesisers).

Arbitrary Logic, which was the first completed work in this group (finished in 1986 and shown at the 7th Internationaler Experimentalfilm Workshop, Osnabruck, in May 1987), though existing as a video, it was (and remains) an interactive work. My interest in linking sound and colour in this series began with this work (acknowledging the long history in abstract film and the early concept of the light-organ in this respect). In *Arbitrary Logic* both the visual and sound elements are entirely synthesised. There is no initially-recorded data and the program is constructed entirely from formulae which generate the initial (rectangular) forms, the colour sequences by values of red, green and blue, and the selection of instrumental timbres. The program controls a basic, and consistent system of changes in value which is modified and interrupted by the movement of the mouse. Different movements and conditions of the buttons change the instrument voices, pitches, volumes and speeds as well as controlling an incursion of random values. These mouse movements also control a system by which the visual vertical stripes are copied to other sections of the screen and combined (superimposed) according to the system of computer logical operators (and, or, nand, nor etc.).

The application of digital systems in the more recent *Chronos Fragmented* is both less consistent and more complicated. The Chronos Project is a continuing work which is based on a video 'diary'. I used computers at various levels in the work from simple digital manipulation of some images, through use of a non-linear editing system in the production. At the more conceptual level, I developed a database approach to the subjective organisation of the video sequences using a simple word-based sorting program I wrote to suit the material and to generate some initial edits. The aesthetic approach I used applied a concept of non-linear connections fundamental to Random Access Memory as a 'model' for the memory structure in the project. In this respect the TV version of the work (approximately one hour long) expresses this concept rather than applies it strictly as the production system. As the diary continues to develop, I continue to reinvestigate and rework the material. Future technology may allow the raw material to be stored in digital form and the development of relationships within it to be subject to both computer program and an interactive approach – though it is not essential to the project which can continue with any level of video and computer technology.

My concern in all these works has not been with the technology for its own sake but with exploring the potential in the technology for new meanings which are a continuation of the philosophical stance implicit in my other work – the concepts and experience are more important than the technology.

My aesthetic position continues to be based on the integral relationship between medium, technology and meaning and continues to understand language as being built on the material processes of the medium. However, in the context of digital production technologies combined with remote electronic transmission, the concept of media specificity as the basis of language cannot survive. Nor can we see any simple relationship between the material basis of a medium and the construction of the symbolic language. The fully electronic media, which are rapidly abandoning the last residue of mechanics – only surviving for the moment in the rotating magnetic disk drive – may have definable properties and characteristics but not a single set of intrinsic forms. Its properties are – in theory at least – a matter of selective combination – we can put together our media from a recipe of components as Fluxus proposed some thirty years ago. One important general characteristic of digital electronic media (a thought not available to Fluxus) is its capacity to incorporate other media and language systems while not being incorporated by them – digital media achieve a greater degree of generality. Indeed it is possibly a principle of media advance that a genuinely new medium can incorporate (and reproduce) the conditions of earlier media in a way which is not reversible. In this process, the digital can record, contain or reproduce in output most aspects of text-based, audio or visual media. Faced with this level of incorporation, the artist may abandon media coherence acting as a post-modernist, eclectic agent at the mercy of the prevailing context, or select a combination of media properties within which to develop a specific, if not intrinsic, basis of language.

In truth the options are not exclusive and the latter represents a continuity of discourse rather than a cold selection of components. What we learn about the properties of a medium from the new conditions of digital technologies has probably been the case with all media.

A medium, like the language it supports, is structured as a set of constraints to which we subscribe (often without choice). There has never been any intrinsic delineation of a medium in material terms. Its definition might first be a convenience and then later a cultural institution which maintains the boundaries. Surface, paint and brushes serve as the basis for making visual forms. It becomes a discourse of painting as unwritten agreements are made regarding the frame, canvas, or arrangements for commission, sale or exhibition, and within this discourse consistencies of language develop with use and allow meanings to derive from differences. However, the limits of a medium can always be redefined theoretically, and, considering a definition of the constituent properties – flatness, scale, transformation in time, projection – almost any range of combinations is feasible within the constraint of economics and technology. But here is the catch – it is the power of economics, politics and the technology which determines our options and certainly determines where the crucial edge of our discourse lies. For the media based in advanced technology, this economic, historical constraint is crucial. Here the discourse becomes unavoidably entangled with the historical condition as it is transmitted to us in and by the technology. Any technology, as with simple tools which preceded it, embodies the historical intelligence which has led to its design or evolution. As well as this intelligence, which offers economical solutions to once difficult tasks, technology also embodies the ideology, and desires, from which it has emerged. Exercising the function built into a technology reproduces the ideology as the cost of the gain in 'efficiency'.

The evolution of technology beyond the simple tool, starting with the machines of the eighteenth and nineteenth century, first impinged on the arts through photography, then phonography and cinematography. The camera for example reproduces one particular form of visual representation. It is a machine which economically produces a coherent image of the world according to the principles of perspective. These principles are built into and determine its construction, but simultaneously transmit all the ideological implications through its product. Differences of representation within or against this constraint become the basis of the discourse. Aspects of a discourse may be challenged more radically, as Man Ray did in photography with his 'Rayograms'. Such challenges demand a reconsideration of the terms of the language or assumptions made about a medium.

While the modernist approach to cinema has produced work clearly different from the mainstream it is as a discourse with the constraints of both technology and history that it has had its radical effect and from which it has produced new meanings. These works were not simply different, but their radical intention sought to place them as paradigms in the cinematic discourse. The arts which began in cinematography, and moved through video and television are now at the threshold of complete incorporation into the digital. Neither the range nor limits of the digital media can be adequately defined – they are not only eclectic in content but continuously hybrid and in constant technological development. In a medium where the technological boundaries cannot be defined, and where the discourse is already equally hybrid, it is difficult to see how innovations can establish their position as radical paradigms, unless they buy into existing institutions, like the art world, providing a stable context. Outside this, artists can continue to experiment, innovate and challenge but with no security that they have found a crucial centre to the discourse – the heads of the hydra-media will continue to grow.

References

Greenberg, Clement, *Art and Culture* (Boston: Beacon Press, 1961).

McLuhan, Marshall, *Understanding Media: The Extension of Man* (New York: McGraw-Hill, 1964).

25

Digital Cinema and Experimental Film – Continuities and Discontinuities [1999]

The arts using computers are too recent to have established any orthodox history or theory of their own. The technology itself is in rapid development and digital and electronic systems allow hybrid links between various technologies which has not reached, and may never reach, any stability. It is tempting to see this as supporting a theoretical approach where digital art is outside historical constraint and interpretation.

Digital media link together computers, various audiovisual display and recording systems and remote multi-user networks, like the internet, all with the capacity for interactivity which is built into the computer interface. Almost by definition the computer is an eclectic medium. It seems able to incorporate or interface with almost all previous media – the written word, pictures, music and even the time flow of images and sound which makes up cinema and video and communication forms like the telephone, or TV. Though it does not as readily incorporate the physical, spatial forms of sculpture, performance or drama, it has a growing presence in these art forms through interactive systems applied in three-dimensional construction and the arena of performance.

In other words, it is difficult to define digital media as a single form – a medium – with its own distinct characteristics. Definition of the intrinsic characteristics of a medium has been a major component of the modernist enterprise. As long as a medium had a relatively limited set of physical characteristics which could be seen as having a direct link with those features at the base of its aesthetic form – the flatness of the canvas or colour in painting – the physical basis of harmonics in music – the modernist argument could demonstrate a continuity between the special characteristics of a medium, its aesthetic components and its 'language'. Modernist art, with its aesthetic language rooted in the physical properties of the medium, simultaneously allowed a phenomenological relationship between the work and the spectator. This put at the core of modern art a condition of 'presence' – an encounter with the physical, specific to the art object, its medium, its location in space and historical time. It was an experience constructed between the spectator and the art work as a component of the physical world. The perception of the phenomenolog-

ical world in the art work might be transformed through the aesthetic experience –
the interplay of colour, or sound for example – into a symbolic or semiotic experience, but it remained, and in the modernist work, stressed, the physical continuity
between medium and meaning.

While the information technology arts remained fundamentally mechanical, as in
photography, film and phonography, these mechanics also permitted a modernist
approach to those media – they allowed a parallel concept of continuity between the
physical encounter with the medium, its characteristic aesthetics and its symbolic
language. Thus experimental film could develop as an extension from modernism.

The modernist approach lost theoretical credibility to the concepts of post-modernism for a number of reasons. One was a confusion by both artists and critics of
the phenomenological concepts of art with notions of a pure essence of medium.
Here the material constraints and possibilities of a medium which were in fact being
constantly modulated within a historical context became interpreted instead as an
idealist and immutable condition residing in the medium. At the same time, the
'avant-garde', which did understand the materialist approach to the medium as
being within a developing historical discourse, fell foul of post-modernist argument
for its progressive view of history. This progressiveness, being broadly attached to
Marxism, became increasingly difficult to sustain as the communist world failed to
establish either viable political or economic systems.

However, perhaps the greatest difficulties facing a modernist view have come
from mixed-media art, recent use of electronic or digital technologies by artists and
the more general cultural effect of telecommunications, and the mass media.

Mixed-media arts combine not only the physical characteristics of different media
but also their historical discourses as language. Digital arts extend this process
through increasing the range of potential media but add the discourses which relate
to the computer itself both inside and outside art. The combination of different
media makes it increasingly difficult to distinguish the limiting boundaries of the
medium from which to draw its 'intrinsic' characteristics. Digital systems, by incorporating other media, extend this difficulty but add to it the fundamental
non-tactility or non-visibility of its electronic data and processes. Digital and electronic media seem to defy finding a physical basis for the aesthetic unless this is
added through the output technology.

Mass media, particularly television, have progressively created a cultural schism
between the representation and the physical object. Instantaneous transmission of
images and sounds across space have created a cultural habit reading the electronic
representation as if it were present. Our discourse with the real has become a discourse with the represented image, a presence of the image not in conflict with its
lack of physical proximity. In addition, the recorded documentation, photo, audio
and cinematic, has begun to bring the historically remote into the same condition

of presence as the physically remote. In other words, telecommunications and mass media have produced a near simultaneity of representation across space and time which we may treat as the real world. This is maintained provided we do not create a conflict between image and physical presence. The image represents presence and mass culture has become wholly semiotic linking equally space, historical time, fiction and fact.

Post-modernism, by embracing cultural simultaneity in an ultimate eclecticism of image across time and space, has responded to a major social and cultural change brought about by technology. It has rightly recognised the difficulty of sustaining the concept of the specificity of the medium in the electronic multimedia or mixed-media context. However, by abandoning the attempt to maintain a continuity between physicality, the medium of representation and the condition of the represented, it has left the spectator with no resistance to the image, no measuring conflict between the reality of the image, the illusion of the image or the distinction between different forms of presence. For the artist, abandoning awareness of the continuity between medium and meaning only makes it more difficult to recognise the constraints on the creation of meaning which exist in the digital domain just as they do in any other area of art practice.

These constraints derive from at least three areas:

- the media or technology itself;
- the artistic languages or discourses which are available to it;
- the prevailing social or cultural context.

In approaching an understanding of digital media, their potentialities, constraints and artistic languages, some aspects of the modernist approach can be usefully revised.

It is clear that the physical aspects of the computer would not provide a sensible basis from which to seek intrinsic characteristics of the medium. These are either insignificant, like the boxes in which the components are contained, or electronically of such small scale that they are outside our perception. There will be physical aspects as the digital becomes structured into art works, but the form of these will depend on the chosen output medium for any particular work. Instead, with any technological art, it is the processes rather than the material which provide the most fruitful source for consistent or intrinsic properties. This is particularly true with digital media where both input and output forms are flexible and varied.

Fundamental Characteristics of Digital Systems

This is an attempt to define the main intrinsic characteristics or basic concepts of digital media. They reside in the systems and are fundamental to equipment using digital electronics.

Digitisation

The most fundamental characteristic of the form of data used in the computer is its ultimate abstraction as discrete electrical pulses. These have only two possible states which can be described as – 'on' or 'off', 'yes' or 'no', 'one' or 'zero'. Any element of information which resides in a computer as data or as instruction for processing data takes this form. Thus the data in a computer does not resemble its source in any sense, it is sheer codification. Without an agreed system for interpreting the coded data, the data for one type of information looks exactly like the data for any other type of information. It is difficult to imagine a greater degree of abstraction than digital information and it is from this form of the data that many of the other characteristics derive. Though the pixels, the component 'dots' from which computer images are constructed, are not strictly synonymous with the digital data, they may be considered as a symbol for the process of digitisation in the visual arena.

Analysis

It is impossible for data to have a coherent form or relationship to the information it represents without analysis. The analytical processes employed must be built into the software or the hardware system before even the simplest operation can be performed. Again taking the pixel as an example, the analytic process for this must contain a number of elements, each given a value in a coding system which is consistent. First it must define its co-ordinate position in the whole picture, next it must define its luminous intensity, then its colour values normally within a range of intensities of three basic colours usually defined as red, green and blue. This principle of analysis of the components of information and how they are to be codified applies at every level of computer operation including those complex programs capable of ordering higher levels of distinguishing text, sound and image.

Synthesis

In the same way in which the storage and handling of data must be related to an analysis of what is to constitute the various aspects of the data, its output must undergo a reverse process of synthesis. The data must be retrieved, recombined and in some way output so that the information which became data as it was stored is returned to our visual or other domain of the senses in a form retaining its intended coherence. However, the concept of synthesis is more complex than that of the mirror to analysis. While the synthesis may be put to the service of the reproduction of information brought to and stored in the computer, this is not the only possible application of the synthetic process. It is possible for the synthetic process to generate both the data and its form of presentation. This synthesis without stored data may be aimed at a recognisable representation derived from a fundamental analysis of the component features of the world being modelled, or it might be more limited and based on the generation of an imaginary or aesthetic environment with no intended resemblance to the 'real' world, or more accurately, with no resemblance to the predominant systems of representing the real world.

When a computer is used, the various levels of analytical or synthetic process must take place even if the artist does not take responsibility for defining or implementing them. It is a serious question for digital art where fundamental authorship resides when the artist does not take responsibility for the form of analysis underlying the aesthetic processes within the output work.

Translation or Transformation

As any data stored in a computer is in digital form and bears no intrinsic resemblance to its initial source, the way in which it may be recombined for output is subject to transformation as well as synthesis. This transformation may take any level of linked coherence from minor transformation of the colour bias in a photographic image, to major revision of colour and positional structures. It may be taken to greater extremes of translation, using data stored for one representational purpose to be output in a completely different form. For example, the data stored as a picture may be output as sound. The computer has no opinion on the way in which data is used – it is as happy for the ones and zeros of a photograph to be sent to the loudspeaker as to the screen. Of course, a greater discrimination in which components of the data would be suitable for which translation can result in a greater or lesser coherence in the translated output. For example, the probable smooth transitions light and dark in an image translated into volume or pitch differences at output might retain a coherence which approaches aspects of musical form. This concept of transformation or translation is not simply an available option. In some respects it is one of the components of any synthetic relationship to data if the computer is to be used to process rather than simply reproduce data.

Program or Programmability

Beyond the basic concept of digitisation and its consequent features of analysis, synthesis and transformation the next crucial feature of the computer is its programmability. It is a third stage technology following the simple tool then the machine. Its main distinction from the first two stages of technology is that it is an information machine without a single purpose. It is an intelligent system needing instruction on what work it is to perform and how it is to interface with other machines. The instructions are its programs. For art also it represents a kind of third stage following the direct media of the hand and body – painting – music – sculpture – dance, then the media of mechanical reproduction – the printing press – photography – film – the phonograph. A major characteristic of the program is that its outputs change depending on the data or procedures selected. The program is a

set of instructions to manipulate data in a particular way which can include responding to new input of data or new input of the way in which it may be manipulated.
As a consequence, the resulting works will follow a consistent pattern formed by the
program but each particular version of the work may have differences. These differences are a component of the work and may be based on a range of factors or
strategies within the program. Though the range of possible strategies are developing with the development of computer art, some of these may be defined. The first
retain a single program combining data but permutate combinations in some way,
or respond to new data being input as the work progresses. Another explores input
to make modifications to aspects of the program itself through looping, partial looping or branching structures. Within each of these there may be varying algorithms
or mathematical formulae which produce different results depending on the data
used and various uses of randomisation of values producing unpredictable variety
within certain defined limits. In all these cases, the resulting work goes beyond the
singularity of the hand-made object or the multiple but identical copy of the mechanical reproduction.

Arbitrary Access (Random Access)

A major characteristic of digital systems is the fundamentally non-linear way in which
information (data) is stored and retrieved. Codified data or information in the form
of blocks of consistent code, when it is put into the computer is assigned a location,
a position in memory – an address. This address, which may be expressed as a number, defines the starting-point for the block of data to be store or retrieved. However,
as the time taken to relocate from one address to another is electronically equal, whatever address number is chosen, all address locations are conceptually equidistant. The
computer does not walk past house numbers 2, 3, 4, and 5 to get from 1 to 6 – number 1 is as close to number 1000 as it is to 2. Thus the storage and retrieval of
information is not confined to simple arithmetic sequence and proximity. Though large
storage systems retain aspects of linearity through rotating disks, the memory chips of
a computer are conceptually best understood as a three- or even multidimensional
matrix. Combining this multidimensional storage structure with speeds of access
which are so fast as to be almost negligible creates a condition for information storage and retrieval quite unlike those which have existed with the physical structures of
books or pictures or the linear mechanical systems of film, video or audiotape. This
form of storage is known as Random Access Memory. The use of the term 'random'
here is confusing as it has little to do with randomisation or chance. The term 'arbitrary' in its classical sense of 'chosen' expresses this concept better. Whatever terms
are used to describe this, if seen as an intrinsic property of digital media it has radical
implications for art, structures of aesthetic expression and representation. The principles on which data, information or fragments of the represented world may be

combined are only limited by the systems which can be defined for creating links, and these systems are clearly not confined to simple linearity.

Interactivity

Though the computer need not always involve interactivity in the execution of a program, it is fundamentally structured to respond to input as well as output. As with arbitrary (or random) access structures in memory, the implications for artistic practice of incorporating performance feedback by the artist or, more radically, the action of the spectator in the sequential development of a work creates significant new possibilities for art practice. It also creates significant new issues for the understanding of the relationship between the work and the spectator and for the concept of authorship which may also be seen as intrinsic to digital media.

Digital Media – Artistic Language and Discourse

In general, this outline of digital media using a modernist approach demonstrates that it is possible to define characteristics which stem from or belong to the medium. However, it also demonstrates the way in which computers represent some significant discontinuities with many of the assumptions which have led art practice in both the 'hand-made' and mechanical periods. But, it is not only the medium, mechanics or technology which produce the determinants of the art work. The major historical continuity for art is best understood through its 'languages' or discourses. The concept of discourse is probably more appropriate, as the evolving relationship between symbolic and formal systems in art of the twentieth century have reduced the stability normally associated with the concept of language. Art discourses establish meaning within particular works through the development of symbolic and formal relationships by reference to previous work within a medium and its cultural institutions.

Artistic work which has taken up the possibilities offered by the computer have their continuity both of meaning and form with a variety of established art practices or discourses. We can see at least two aspects to this continuity. One is the incorporation into computer art of forms drawn from existing practice, the other, more radically, sees a development of formal ideas in previous work which prefigures some of the concepts intrinsic to digital art. Though both aspects of this continuity could be demonstrated in a range of art practices, this essay briefly maps some of the points of reference in experimental film which have begun to prepare us for aesthetic notions related to the capacities of digital art.

Experimental Cinema – Proto-Digital

There are four areas or directions of experimental film which develop concepts now seen as integral to digital media – Abstract Film, Transformed Image Film, Non-Narrative Film (structuralist and surrealist cinema) and Expanded Cinema.

Abstract Film

In the field of experimental cinema, abstract film was historically first with its origins in the Futurist experiments of Bruno Corra and Arnaldo Ginna around 1914. Like abstract art in general, abstract film involved the 'analytic' abstraction of visual qualities from their representational function and their 'synthesis' in a new language often described as visual or chromatic music. This direction of cinema not only provided the basis of cinematic ideas – it discourse – from which the computer film itself emerged through the pioneers John and James Whitney in the 1950's and 1960's, but it prefigured the possibility of programmability through the key work *Diagonal Symphony* (completed between 1921 and 1925) by Viking Eggeling. Viking Eggeling's work is crucial in this history. *Diagonal Symphony* is an animated abstract film based closely on Eggeling's theoretical attempt to describe a new logical basis for abstract form and its development either in time, or laterally in horizontal 'scroll' shaped drawings. Though he based his concepts on seeking a parallel between abstract art and music with particular reference to Johann Sebastian Bach, both the drawings and the film correspond most closely to the mathematics of topology. Eggeling explores the development of simple shapes, first stated as themes, then taken through addition, subtraction and combination of component features. The work is not mechanistic – it follows no single logic and the changes are the result of subjective artistic decision but it would be easily programmable. Its position as a key work prefiguring the digital is not based on its surface similarity to programmable abstract film but is held in the similarity of its concept and aesthetic philosophy with the process of analysis, synthesis and the attempt to make formal principles explicit.

Transformed Image Film

There are many examples from the history of experimental film of the attempt to transform the photographic image through technical devices. The photographic experiments of Man Ray, using solarisation and negative devices, are among the earliest attempts to use defined technical procedures to transform the photographic image. This approach reached its most coherent point in work by film-makers who had direct access to film printing equipment and could selectively matte and recolour sections of the film image. Examples can be found in many works by Pat O'Neill beginning with *By the Sea* (1963) or my own *Berlin Horse* (1970). The key film exploring the transformation of image qualities in a representational context is Len Lye's *Trade Tattoo* (1937). This film, which pioneered the use of the three colour separation Gaspar Colour system, immediately exploited the opportunities inherent in a technical process based on the abstraction of image components for a resynthesis which manipulated the components. This dissociation of the recorded information from its original representational identity and its recombination according to other principles – a form of transformation or translation – creates in *Trade*

Tatoo an original aesthetic experience. But it also embodies in the meaning of the work a philosophical concept that information subject to abstraction as component 'data' becomes a new form of 'raw material' available for 'retrieval' in ways which construct a new experiential model of the world.

Non-Narrative Film

Perhaps the most significant principle of experimental cinema which unifies both abstract and representational work is the search for structures which do not conform to linear narrative constraints. In this respect, non-linear concepts which relate to the intrinsic feature of Random Access Memory in computers can be seen to have had their origins in many works. In particular, Germain Dulac's *La Coquille et le Clergyman* (1927) or the surrealist cinema of Buñuel and Dali – *Un Chien andalou* (1928) or *L'Age d'or* (1930), by attempting to embody a concept of psychological association or dream in the structure of cinema, used montage to establish links which did not describe causal action or a narrative line. Also from the early history of experimental film, but developing from a very different trajectory, is the thematic associative montage of Dziga Vertov's *Man With a Movie Camera* (1928). However, what serves best as a key work here is Maya Deren's *Meshes of the Afternoon* (1943), not only because of the film but also because Deren herself established a significant theoretical idea in a symposium in 1953 which reinforces the non-linear interpretation of the work. The film explores a complex form of a repeated, dreamlike, symbolic event. At each repetition, small changes expand the spectator's imaginary construction of the symbolic space rather like a spiral through a matrix of action images. The spectator's passage through the film requires each previous 'version' of the action to be reviewed by the next – not replacing it by a more definitive version but deepening the experiential references in a cumulative transformation. The inevitable linearity of the film is used to explore a symbolic space which is not resolved as a causal narrative. In the 1953 symposium, 'Poetry and the Film' (Maya Deren, Arthur Miller, Dylan Thomas, Parker Tyler and chair Willard Mass from *Film Culture* no. 29, Summer 1963). Deren, in developing an equivalence between poetry and the poetic film, introduces a concept of 'verticality', an exploration at right angles to the 'horizontal' development of the narrative. She says, referring to Shakespeare,

> you have the drama moving forward on a 'horizontal' plane of development, of one circumstance – one action – leading to another, and this delineates the character. Every once in a while, however, he arrives at a point of action where he wants to illuminate the meaning of *this* moment of drama, and, at that moment, he builds a pyramid or investigates it 'vertically' . . .

Then applied to film she says:

the short films, to my mind (and they are short because it is difficult to maintain such intensity for a long period of time), are comparable to lyric poems, and they are completely a 'vertical', or what I would call a poetic construct, and they are complete as such.

This search by Maya Deren for both a cinematic form and a theoretical framework for an alternative to the narrative trajectory – a non-linearity – represents a guide to the development of cinematic models which relate directly to the intrinsic non-linearity of the computer.

Expanded Cinema

There are two conflicting definitions of Expanded Cinema, one which derives from Gene Youngblood (*Expanded Cinema*) and one which had currency in Europe from 1967 through to 1980 (see Le Grice, 'Mapping in Multi-Space – From Expanded Cinema to Virtuality' in *White Cube Black Box*, EA Generali publication, 1996). The European interpretation (which is being used here) was largely characterised by a concern to bring the cinematic experience consciously into the space of the spectator through performed action and installation. Film structures were developed to initiate a positive reflexive role for the spectator, a concern also debated in theory by film-makers at the time. There are few works, if any, where the spectator could be said to interact directly with the development of a film and there is no single key work prefiguring interactivity. However, there are a number of cases where aspects of the work change through the visible action of the artist, the specific location or some form of involvement of the audience during the presentation which point a direction seeking to change the relationship between the artist and the audience towards an interactive concept. In *Auf+Ab+An+Zu* by Valie Export (1968) a member of the audience is invited to draw the outline of a moving film image onto the screen. In my own *Horror Film* (1971), the shadow cast by the performer onto an overlapping colour field screen delineates the screen size and shape at various points in the space between the screen and three projectors. In 1972, two works explored the space and time of projection and audience interaction with it in different ways. Anthony McCall's *Line Describing a Cone* invited the audience to move physically into the projection space as a line of light from a filmed dot expanded to become a cone of light of a filmed circle. In *2 Minutes 45 Seconds*, by William Raban, a blank screen is filmed and the film projected and refilmed over successive performances, progressively recording as receding layers the sound and image of artist or audience intervention at each presentation.

Digital Media – Continuous and Discontinuous

Many of the possibilities offered by computers and their links with other digital or analogue systems represent new directions not envisaged in previous art. However, the concepts embodied in the computer as a technology have emerged together in parallel with other contemporary philosophical, conceptual or aesthetic developments. Various forms of continuity can be demonstrated as stemming from the technology itself or the discourses belonging to the art forms which have become incorporated into the digital arts. In addition, the general development of philosophical or cultural ideas provides a context where the underlying forms or meanings produced in art have a conceptual continuity in the broader field of knowledge and social interaction. It is only through understanding the determinants of art practice and the historical continuities that the genuinely new and particular can emerge.

Index

Notes: italicised entries refer to titles; p = passim, throughout; (c) = computer game; (e) = exhibition or conference; (m) = magazines and journals; (n) = newsreel; (w) = written materials